Praise for Jay Feldman's

MANUFACTURING
HYSTERIA

"A readable and interesting history of an important period that explains, in part, how we got to this sad juncture."
—*New York Journal of Books*

"A richly researched, engrossing book." —*Death and Taxes* magazine

"Expansive. . . . Remarkably detailed and researched. . . . *Manufacturing Hysteria* proves particularly adept at identifying and explaining the dangerous ground on which national and political solidarity stand during times of perceived crisis and threat. Feldman's historical lens, in the final analysis, has its focus firmly on the present."
—*The Post and Courier*

"A chilling tale about what lies ahead if aggressive political discourse continues to divide and conquer the American people." —*The Daily*

"What Feldman makes clear is that . . . American ideals—which it is clear he treasures—are so frequently undercut by American actions. . . . Fascinating."
—*Sacramento News & Review*

"Jay Feldman's highly readable account of the long, sad story of civil liberties in America is as close to entertaining as such a history can be. He reminds us that the protections of the Bill of Rights are always available to us except when we have dire need of them."
—Nicholas von Hoffman, author of
Radical: A Portrait of Saul Alinsky

"An exhaustive look at how the United States government officially and unofficially, legally and illegally, monitored and controlled the populace. *Manufacturing Hysteria* is an excellent reminder to readers to exercise vigilance in preserving civil liberties."
—*San Francisco Book Review*

JAY FELDMAN

MANUFACTURING HYSTERIA

Jay Feldman is also the author of the critically acclaimed *When the Mississippi Ran Backwards*. He is a widely published freelance writer whose articles have appeared in *Smithsonian*, *Newsweek*, *Sports Illustrated*, *Gourmet*, *The New York Times*, and many other national, regional, and local publications. He has written for television and the stage, and is the author of the novel *Suitcase Sefton and the American Dream*.

www.jfeldman.com

MANUFACTURING
HYSTERIA

MANUFACTURING
HYSTERIA

A History of Scapegoating, Surveillance, and Secrecy in Modern America

JAY FELDMAN

Anchor Books
A Division of Random House, Inc.
New York

FIRST ANCHOR BOOKS EDITION, NOVEMBER 2012

Copyright © 2011 by Jay Feldman

All rights reserved. Published in the United States by Anchor Books, a division of
Random House, Inc., New York, and in Canada by Random House of Canada
Limited, Toronto. Originally published in hardcover in the United States by
Pantheon Books, a division of Random House, Inc., New York, in 2011.

Anchor Books and colophon are registered trademarks of Random House, Inc.

The Library of Congress has cataloged the Pantheon edition as follows:
Feldman, Jay.
Manufacturing hysteria : scapegoating, surveillance, and secrecy in modern America /
Jay Feldman.
p. cm.
Includes bibliographical references and index.
1. Civil rights—United States—History. 2. Dissenters—United States—History.
3. Marginality, Social—United States—History. 4. Hysteria (Social psychology)
I. Title.
JC599.U5F415 2011
323.4'90973—dc22
2010039998

Anchor ISBN: 978-0-307-38823-0

Author photograph © Ian Martin
Book design by Virginia Tan

www.anchorbooks.com

Printed in the United States of America
10   9   8   7   6   5   4   3   2   1

To the memory of Howard Zinn

Democracy can come undone. It's not something that's necessarily going to last forever once it's established.

—Sean Wilentz,
Newsweek, October 31, 2005

Contents

Prologue: Against the Wall

On the night of April 4, 1918, nearly a year to the day after the United States entered World War I, a harrowing spectacle was unfolding on the streets of Collinsville, Illinois, a small market center and coal-mining community of four thousand, located twelve miles across the river from St. Louis. Trailed by a roused and swelling crowd, a forlorn, barefoot figure wrapped in an American flag hobbled along in the cold night air. An occasional catcall rang out in the dark, and the threat of festive violence loomed heavily. The man at the head of the discordant parade stumbled frequently as the march made its way up the main street of Collinsville toward city hall.

The unfortunate leading this unsettling procession was Robert Paul Prager, a thirty-year-old German immigrant and, by some accounts, a radical Socialist.[1] Born in Dresden, Prager had immigrated to the United States in 1905, at the age of seventeen. He bounced around the Midwest for several years, working as a baker, serving fourteen months for theft in 1913–14, and eventually finding his way, in 1915, to the St. Louis area, with its sizable, well-established German-American population. He worked for a time in a coal mine in Gillespie, about forty miles northeast of St. Louis, then headed to Collinsville in the fall of 1917, where he took a job in Lorenzo Bruno's bakery.

According to Mrs. Bruno, Prager was extremely intelligent and an outstanding worker, but "a certain peculiarity in his makeup . . . made him quarrelsome with people who did not agree with his ideas on ways of doing things."[2] Despite his ready inclination to apologize once his temper had cooled, Prager's argumentativeness led to his being fired early in 1918.

Turning to the only other work he knew, Prager got a job on the night shift at the No. 2 mine owned by the Donk Brothers Coal and

Coke Company in Maryville, four miles from Collinsville. The leadership of United Mine Workers of America Local 1802 accepted him conditionally until his application for UMWA membership could be reviewed.

It was here that things started to go seriously wrong for Prager. Looking to improve his lot, he thought to become a mine manager. In late March, he approached the mine examiner John Lobenad and, informing Lobenad of his desire to advance, questioned him about a manager's responsibilities. One of the areas he asked about was mine explosions, and exactly how an explosion could cause the greatest damage. Lobenad's suspicions were aroused, and when rumors—utterly unsubstantiated—suddenly began circulating about a supply of blasting powder vanishing from the mine, some of the six hundred miners at Donk No. 2, including the Local 1802 president, Joe Fornero, concluded that Prager was a German agent bent on sabotage.

In the hypercharged winter and spring of 1918, the mere suspicion of harboring pro-German sentiments, let alone actively working for Germany, was enough to invite the attention of federal, state, and local law-enforcement agencies, as well as a myriad of quasilegal vigilante organizations. Since entering the war, the federal government had whipped the American public into a froth with a calculated program of propaganda issued by the Committee on Public Information.

Headed by the newspaperman George Creel, the CPI utilized every available medium to sell the war to an initially skeptical citizenry. The committee's job, as Creel wrote, was "to drive home to the people the causes behind this war, the great fundamental necessities that compelled a peace-loving nation to take up arms to protect free institutions and preserve our liberties," and "to weld the people of the United States into one white-hot mass instinct with fraternity, devotion, courage, and deathless determination."[3] As the *New York World*'s editor Frank Cobb later wrote, "Government conscripted public opinion as they conscripted men and money and materials."[4]

Creel and his associates—including some three thousand historians recruited for pamphlet writing—did their job only too well, cultivating a hatred for everything associated with Germans and Germany. The press enthusiastically took up the chant. As one New York newspaper would put it, "Scrutinized historically, and presented baldly, the German cannot be but recognized as a distinctly separate and pathological human species. He is not human in the sense that other men are human."[5] Promoting anti-Germanism and love of country, the CPI infected the American public with a virulent strain of patriotism tinged with a streak of potent xenophobia. All dissenting voices on the war were, by implication, disloyal and therefore pro-German: pacifists, Wobblies, Socialists, anarchists, Mennonites, Irish-Americans, and above all, German aliens and German-Americans were some, but not all, of the tainted and suspect.

Throughout the country, scores of Germans came under attack. On December 22, 1917, Charles H. Feige, who had been taking photographs near the border in El Paso, tried to cross into Mexico and was shot and killed by a soldier, who assumed he was a spy.[6] Six days later, an Evangelical Lutheran pastor, the Reverend W. A. Starck, and another man barely escaped being hanged in the public square of Audubon, Iowa, before deputy sheriffs intervened.[7]

On January 5, 1918, one Maximilian Von Hoegen was beaten, suffered a broken nose, and was forced to kiss the American flag in Hartford, Connecticut. The following week, Philadelphia police rescued a man named Paul Beilfuss from a lynch mob.[8]

By the spring of 1918, the nation was in a patriotic frenzy. Reports of German spy networks and espionage filled the newspapers, with wildly exaggerated numbers of German agents supposedly operating in the country. On March 1, citing the Department of Justice as his source, the international president of the Rotary Club informed a Chicago audience that at least 110,000 German agents were operating in the United States.[9] The number was never confirmed.

The next day, a Denver "squad of loyal Americans" tied Fred Sietz, by a rope around his neck, to a truck and paraded him through the streets.[10] They delivered Sietz, who had refused to kiss the flag, to the office of *The Denver Post*, where he collapsed and was rushed to the hospital in serious condition.

On March 3, the senator and future president Warren G. Harding, speaking at a large patriotic meeting sponsored by the Maryland Council of Defense, offered his opinion that the only place for Germany's "miserable spies . . . is against the wall."[11]

The violence escalated into the first week of April. On the second, in La Salle, Illinois, 150 miles from Collinsville, Dr. J. C. Bienneman was dunked in a canal, made to kiss the flag, and ordered to leave town. The same day, Rudolph Schwopke was tarred and feathered in Emerson, Nebraska, for allegedly refusing to contribute to the Red Cross.

Two days later, a group of men waiting to be called for the draft shaved the head of seventy-two-year-old H. C. Capers in Sulphur, Oklahoma.[12]

Such was the climate in which Robert Prager's fellow miners deduced that he was a German agent intent on blowing up the Maryville mine, and union officials denied his application for membership. On April 3, a group of miners seized Prager and, employing the ritual widely practiced on anyone suspected of disloyalty, compelled him to kiss the flag. They accused him of being a German spy, led him to the outskirts of town, and harshly warned him not to come back. The Local 1802 president, Fornero, and another union official, Moses Johnson, escorted Prager back to Collinsville, where they asked the police to place him in protective custody; without charges being filed against him, however, the police declined. The union leaders then took Prager to his rooming house and asked him to meet them the following day at the sheriff's office in Edwardsville, the county seat.

Instead, Prager composed a one-page document titled "Proclamation to Members of Local Union No. 1802" and, ignoring the miners' admonition, returned the next day to Maryville, where he posted a dozen carbon copies of his handbill around town. "I have been a union man at all times and never once a scab," wrote Prager, "and for this reason, I appeal to you . . . In regards to my loyalty, I will state that I am heart and soul for the good old U.S.A. . . . and also declared my intention of U.S. citizenship, my second papers are due to be issued soon if I am granted. I am branded by your President [Fornero] . . . a German spy which he cannot prove."[13]

In fact, if Fornero and the others had taken the trouble to investigate, they would have discovered that Prager's loyalty could hardly be questioned. In the previous year, he had registered, as required, both for the newly established draft and as an "alien enemy" (any noncitizen from a country at war with the United States), and had even volunteered for the Navy but been turned down on account of his glass eye. Moreover, he had indeed, as he noted in his flyer, applied for citizenship and was awaiting his second papers.

Prager's "proclamation" had the opposite effect from what he intended. The miners who had turned against him were further infuriated by his attack on the well-liked Fornero.

That evening, a group of miners left a Collinsville bar shortly after nine and walked to Prager's rooming house, where they ordered him to leave town immediately. He agreed, but then the crowd demanded that he come out into the street.

"All right, brothers," Prager said, "I'll go if you don't hurt me."[14] One of the men promised not to harm him.

Once he was outside, Prager's shoes, socks, and outer clothing were forcibly removed. He was wrapped in the Stars and Stripes and instructed to start walking and singing "The Star-Spangled Banner."

When the crowd got near the center of town, Collinsville's mayor, Dr. John H. Siegel, was just leaving a Liberty Loan meeting at the Opera House. He saw the approaching parade, but made no attempt to intervene, reckoning that "the crowd was orderly and there was no disturbance."[15] Siegel crossed the street and let himself into his medical office, from which point he kept an eye on events.

The crowd now numbered several hundred. The Collinsville police officer Fred Frost, patrolling the downtown area, grew apprehensive about the direction in which things were moving, so he waded into the crowd, wrested the terrified Prager away from his captors, and shepherded him into city hall.

In the meantime, the Collinsville bars were ordered closed in hopes of cutting down on the likelihood of violence. At each watering hole, the officer charged with making the rounds explained that a German spy had been arrested and was being held at city hall, so the patrons naturally made for downtown, further increasing the size of the throng. Among the new recruits was Joseph Riegel, an Army veteran and a former miner, who joined up with a small group on its way to the scene. A saloon worker named Wesley Beaver produced an American flag, and "the crowd fell in behind it."[16]

Watching the growing assembly, Mayor Siegel could tell that "things were taking such a turn as to become menacing."[17] Leaving his medical office, he climbed the steps of city hall and tried to calm the crowd. He pleaded with them to disband, telling them that Prager had been taken away and promising that he would be handed over to the federal authorities. But the mob refused to disperse. Joseph Riegel, who later admitted to being drunk, assumed the mantle of leader and pushed his way to the front. He waved his discharge papers, claiming them as proof of loyalty, and demanded to make a search of the jail. The mayor agreed to admit Riegel alone, but when the doors were opened, the crowd surged forward and swarmed into the building.

The police had removed Prager from his cell and hidden him in the basement of the building. It took Riegel and Beaver some time, but they eventually found him and marched him back out into the street, where his terrible ordeal resumed.

Turning south on the St. Louis road, the parade proceeded toward the outskirts of Collinsville, with Prager all the while being forced to kiss the flag and sing patriotic songs. Without warning, the latent violence suddenly erupted as somebody punched Prager, knocking him to the ground. A couple of men helped him to his feet, and the march continued.

By the time they reached the city limits, the crowd had thinned considerably, and the police, who had been following at a safe distance, turned back, their jurisdiction ended. When they reached the crest of a hill about half a mile outside of town, fewer than fifty men were left. They stopped under a good-sized hackberry tree and decided upon a coat of tar and feathers, but no supplies could be found. However, when somebody discovered a towing rope in one of the vehicles that had accompanied the march, Prager's fate was sealed.

A noose was fashioned, and the rope was looped over a large branch of the hackberry. The noose was slipped over Prager's head and tightened around his neck. The remaining crowd members fired questions at him, demanding to know the details of his alleged bomb plot, including why he stole the explosives and who his accomplices were. Exhausted from his tribulation, Prager shook his head and fell silent.

Riegel then pulled on the rope in an attempt to hoist Prager up, but he lacked the strength. "Come on, fellows, we're all in on this," he said to the others, "let's not have any slackers here."[18] Several others took hold of the rope, including some boys as young as twelve years old, and Prager was lifted off the ground.[19] The lynch mob had forgotten to tie his hands, however, and he grabbed the rope to prevent himself from choking.

They let him back down, and Prager asked permission to compose a farewell note to his parents. Someone furnished a pencil and paper, and he was led to one of the automobiles. "Dear Parents," he wrote. "Today, April 4, 1918, I must die. Please pray for me, my beloved parents. This is the last letter or testimony from me. Your loving son and brother, Robt. Paul."[20] Prager handed the letter over, then asked to pray. Kneeling, he begged forgiveness for his sins and declared himself innocent of disloyalty. When he finished, he walked calmly back to the tree.

Someone tied Prager's hands with a handkerchief, and the noose was once again placed around his neck. The crowd again harangued him with questions, telling him they would kill him if he didn't make a complete confession, but Prager said nothing.

"Well, if he won't come in with anything, string him up," called one of the mob.

Before they could, Prager said, "All right, boys! Go ahead and kill me, but wrap me in the flag when you bury me."[21]

Once more, they raised his body off the ground. This time, they were successful.

Less than two months later, eleven defendants—six of whom had apparently left the mob before the lynching—were tried for Prager's murder. One reporter later called the trial "a farcical patriotic orgy."[22] The jury deliberated for forty-five minutes before acquitting all the defendants.

Robert Paul Prager was a sacrificial lamb, a casualty of wartime madness. His lynching was an extreme case, but it was not an aberration. In the months leading up to America's entry into the war and during the year and a half that the nation was an active participant, attacks on German aliens and German-Americans were all too commonplace.

But Germans were not the only group that felt the wrath of Americans' superpatriotic fury—all dissenters were stigmatized, as the federal government fanned the flames of suspicion and fear, creating an environment in which opposition to the war, for whatever reason, was synonymous with disloyalty and even sedition. Creating fear and then exploiting that fear, the government used the "threat" of these groups to justify a larger crackdown on civil liberties and a suppression of dissent. Both legal and illegal tools were employed, including legislation, surveillance, intimidation, and secrecy.

Since World War I, this pattern has played out repeatedly in the United States in periods of real or exaggerated crisis. Democratic and Republican administrations alike have scapegoated "dangerous" minorities—be they ethnic, racial, political, religious, or sexual—citing them as the excuse for using a variety of lawful and unlawful methods to stifle opposition and curb civil liberties. It is most often carried out in the name of national security, but in at least one case the justification was economic. Nativism, certainly, had been a force in American life since the early nineteenth century, but it was during World War I that the government established the precedent of manipulating nativist fears as a way of clamping down on civil liberties and curtailing dissent.

Seen in this context, the persecution of dissenters during World War I; the red scare and Palmer raids of 1919–20; the Mexican deportations and repatriations of the 1930s; the internment of Japanese-, German-, and Italian-Americans during World War II; the witch hunts of the Cold War years; and the COINTELPRO operations of the 1950s and the Vietnam era were not isolated threats to democracy but related, recurring manifestations of a profoundly antidemocratic streak that lurks just below the surface in American society. President Harry S. Truman, whose Cold War loyalty program for federal employees was itself just such a manifestation, observed—with no apparent irony—that there have always been those who "have seized upon crises to incite emotional and irrational fears. Racial, religious, and class animosities are stirred up. Charges and accusations are directed against many innocent people in the name of false 'patriotism' and hatred of things 'foreign.' "[23]

From this perspective, the recent excesses of the George W. Bush administration in attempting to put a stranglehold on civil liberties after 9/11 were not an anomaly; although the Bush government went far beyond what many people thought possible, those extremes were a difference of degree, not kind. It has been happening in one form or another for nearly a century.

This book is an account of that history. It is not necessarily a pleasant story, but it is a crucial one, for the themes that run through it return again and again in our national life. And while it is a cautionary tale, it is hopefully neither a reductionist account nor one governed by conspiracy theory.

As we emerge from the shadow of one of the most repressive administrations this country has ever known, it serves us well to look back and reflect on these issues in the hope that we can begin to move forward without endlessly repeating our mistakes, for though the election of Barack Obama in 2008 may have relieved the all-out assault of the Bush years, the surveillance apparatus is still in place, and President Obama has demonstrated little if any inclination to dismantle it.

In an 1852 speech to the Massachusetts Anti-Slavery Society, the great abolitionist Wendell Phillips declared, "Eternal vigilance is the price of liberty."[24] More than a century and a half later, his admonition has lost none of its relevance. Now, as ever, vigilance is required if liberty is to survive.

MANUFACTURING
HYSTERIA

CHAPTER I

The Fine Gold of Untainted Americanism

The drumbeat started right after the sinking of the British luxury liner *Lusitania*. When the passenger ship was torpedoed by a German U-boat off the coast of Ireland on May 7, 1915, and 128 American citizens were among the 1,198 killed, the cry for "preparedness" quickly arose.

Preparedness meant two things. In the more conventional sense of the term, it required that the nation arm itself in preparation for the eventuality of being drawn into the war that had raged across Europe for the past year. Before the *Lusitania*, the idea of a military buildup was supported only by the most vociferous and belligerent proponents of American intervention and international adventurism, the most prominent of whom was the former president Theodore Roosevelt. When the passenger ship went down, however, there was a decided shift, as public officials and an outraged press loudly condemned German aggression.

President Woodrow Wilson also now adopted the preparedness stance, and despite his continuing public insistence that the United States would maintain its neutrality, he grew increasingly resigned to the inevitability of participating in the war.* In late July, Wilson directed his cabinet to develop a plan for rearmament.

---

*Wilson's shift away from his previous insistence on neutrality and peace was undoubtedly influenced in part by political realities. The preparedness movement was dominated by Republicans—bankers, industrialists, and munitions manufacturers—which left the Democrats open to charges of being weak on national defense.

On a subtler level, preparedness also entailed gearing up the propaganda machinery to mobilize public opinion—which lagged far behind the official point of view—in support of the mounting likelihood of American involvement.* A major part of this effort included instilling in the populace a crisis mentality with regard to the dangers on the home front—it was much easier, certainly, to create alarm about an allegedly immediate threat to internal security than it was to demonstrate the peril the United States faced from another nation an ocean away. Wilson gave the engine a jump start in October, when he told the Daughters of the American Revolution, "I am not deceived as to the balance of opinion among the foreign-born citizens of the United States, but I am in a hurry for an opportunity to have a line-up and let the men who are thinking first of other countries stand on one side and all those that are for America first, last, and all the time on the other side."[1]

In early November, Wilson proposed a program of "reasonable" military preparedness, which would include a newly created reserve force of 400,000 men and a significant increase in shipbuilding. On December 7, he used the occasion of his third annual message to Congress to sell his rearmament plan, arguing that preparedness would allow the United States to maintain its "providentially assigned" neutrality.[2] His remarks were received coolly, eliciting only mild applause from the assembled legislators.

At the end of his talk, however, Wilson brought his listeners to their feet when he launched an all-out attack on the menace posed by the nation's "disloyal" immigrants:

> I am sorry to say that the gravest threats against our national peace and safety have been uttered within our own borders. There are citizens of the United States, I blush to admit, born under other flags . . . who have poured the poison of disloyalty into the very arteries of our national life; who have . . . sought to destroy our industries . . . and to debase our politics to the uses of foreign intrigue . . . [W]e should promptly make use of

---

*As Arthur Link wrote in *Woodrow Wilson and the Progressive Era, 1910–1917*, "Americans were shocked and horrified" at the sinking of the *Lusitania*, but "except for a small group of ardent nationalists headed by Theodore Roosevelt, few Americans wanted to go to war to avenge the wrong" (p. 164).

processes of law by which we may be purged of their corrupt distempers . . . [W]e are without adequate federal laws to deal with it. I urge you to enact such laws at the earliest possible moment . . . Such creatures of passion, disloyalty, and anarchy must be crushed out . . . and the hand of our power should close over them at once.[3]

These words were the opening salvo on the domestic battleground and would set the tone for the next five years. "WILD APPLAUSE GREETS THE PRESIDENT'S DENUNCIATION OF DIS-LOYAL CITIZENS," read *The New York Times* headline the following day. Based on the lawmakers' reaction, the *Times* article predicted that there would be "no difficulty" enacting federal legislation aimed at prosecuting "plotters against the peace and well-being of the nation," noting that both Republicans and Democrats joined in their approval of Wilson's condemnation of "certain hyphenates."

"Hyphenates"—as in German-Americans—were the first scapegoats of the World War I domestic conflict, recipients of the latest wave of nativist anger directed against immigrants, a theme that had surfaced repeatedly in American life throughout the nineteenth century, most notably against Irish Catholics. The implication of the term "hyphenates," or "hyphenated Americans," as it was sometimes expressed, was that immigrants' and second-generation Americans' retention of their ethnic identities was a sign of divided loyalties. As George Creel lamented the month after Wilson's speech to Congress, "The melting-pot has not been melting."[4]

The German-American community took deep umbrage at the implication behind Wilson's call for new legislation, and the German-language press forcefully expressed its indignation. "No one could have objected," wrote the *Cincinnati Volksblatt*, "if the President had asked Congress for a law to check lawlessness . . . He might have said, 'I demand a law against incendiaries, against violators of the neutrality laws,' but he had no right to say, 'I demand a law against German-Americans.' "[5]

With a combined immigrant and second-generation population of more than eight million, German hyphenates were by far the largest ethnic minority in the country. Although, as with most immigrant groups, they retained a significant part of their native culture and even in many instances strong emotional ties to their homeland, Germans on the whole had fulfilled the American dream, becoming assimilated to a great extent and achieving success in such varied fields as business, farming, civil service, and the skilled trades. The leaders of the German-American community were self-assured and outspoken, and ever since the war in Europe had broken out, they had not hesitated to voice their sympathy for the fatherland, especially as America was not yet involved in the fighting.

At the same time, the British War Propaganda Bureau had skillfully and successfully worked American public opinion, and U.S. "neutrality" leaned heavily toward the Allies, as U.S. arms manufacturers sold vast quantities of munitions to Britain and France on credit. American bankers also granted huge loans to the Allies, including the house of Morgan's $50 million advance to the French. Pointing out the hypocrisy of this situation, the maverick Republican senator Robert La Follette of Wisconsin, a staunch peace advocate, asked, "How . . . can we maintain a semblance of real neutrality while we are supplying the Allies with munitions of war and the money to prosecute war?"[6]

German-American leaders asked the same question, demanding an end to America's arms shipments to the Allies and calling for an embargo on the export of munitions. Preparedness advocates denounced this stance as an attempt to influence U.S. foreign policy in favor of Germany while themselves endeavoring to sway foreign policy in support of the Allies.

When representatives of all the major German-American organizations met in Washington on January 30, 1915, to press for an embargo on arms exports, they were harshly taken to task in a *New York Times* editorial. "The meeting of so-called German-American societies held in Washington Saturday evening," said the *Times*, "professed to 're-establish genuine American neutrality and to uphold it, free from commercial, financial, and political subservience to foreign Powers.' Never since the foundation of the Republic has any body of men assembled here who were more completely subservient to a foreign Power and to foreign influence, and none ever proclaimed the un-American spirit more openly."[7]

The hyphenate problem was the hot-button issue of the day, and perhaps the only thing about which Wilson and Roosevelt agreed. And though they both, together with the press and many German-

American leaders, tried to distinguish between the overwhelming majority of "loyal" German-Americans and what Roosevelt often referred to as the "professional German-Americans," the fine differences were largely lost on the public.[8] Indeed, the implication that only a small minority of Germans were disloyal produced an edgy wariness in the general population, which was now faced with discerning exactly who the treacherous Germans were.

After the *Lusitania* incident, many German-American leaders rushed to express support for Wilson and the United States. On May 15, the German-American Alliance's president, Henry Kersting, said, "The manner in which the so-called German-American citizens" had supported the president proved that "there is no such thing as a German-American or any other hyphenated American."[9] The following day, Rudolf Bernerd, president of an organization representing more than twenty thousand leading German-Americans whose fathers were German war veterans, vowed that should war be declared, every single German-American would fight for the United States. Several months later, twenty-four New York business and professional men, most of them of German extraction, called on "American citizens of foreign birth or parentage to come forward and declare themselves for the United States."[10] None of these statements made much of a dent in public opinion.

The mistrust only got worse when it came to light that German agents in the United States, operating as the German Information Service, had spent more than $25 million on propaganda efforts that included supporting pro-German lecturers, furnishing material to over one thousand foreign-language publications, sponsoring the showing of movies depicting German valor, attempting to control the editorial policy of an influential German-American publication, secretly purchasing New York's *Evening Mail*, and financing the arms embargo efforts. Although these tactics were legal, they were excoriated in the press, which labeled them, among other things, "double-faced treachery" and "unscrupulous and colossal machination."[11]

Even more damaging was the revelation of German attempts at espionage and sabotage. A network of German agents had initiated a variety of activities aimed at disrupting U.S. munitions production and arms shipments to the Allies. In addition to the fomenting of strikes and walkouts in defense-related industries, there were attacks on railroads, bridges, munitions factories, shipyards, warehouses, military installations, and cargo ships; the two most notorious were the July 1916 Black Tom explosion in New York harbor and the bombing of the Canadian Car and Foundry Company of New Jersey in January 1917. Although German agents were responsible for the overwhelming majority of these incidents (the kaiser's military and naval attachés were banished from the country as a result), and no significant degree of involvement by German-Americans was ever conclusively established, the propaganda and espionage/sabotage efforts nevertheless brought the entire German-American population under increasing suspicion.

On May 13, 1916, a Citizens' Preparedness Parade with more than 135,000 marchers was held on New York City's Fifth Avenue, which was lined with American flags and patriotic signs. According to *The New York Times*, the procession of "rich persons and poor . . . in every walk of life" took eleven hours to pass the reviewing stand, and the "only disturbing incidents of the day" came from anti-preparedness organizations like the Women's Peace Party and the Church of the Social Revolution, which distributed leaflets and displayed pacifist banners.[12]

By this time, a significant and outspoken opposition to the preparedness movement had arisen, and it was by no means limited to hyphenates. Certainly, German-Americans were prominent among the dissenters; they were joined by many Irish-Americans, who objected to U.S. support of Britain. But also to be found among the resistance were pacifists, with their principled opposition to war; Socialists, anarchists, Wobblies, and other left-wing radicals, who saw the European conflict as a capitalist war; and many farmers, members of mainstream labor organizations, and others, who could perceive no benefit to America's becoming embroiled in such far-distant hostilities.

The anti-preparedness forces were bolstered by numerous influential progressives, many of whom were pacifists and had been previously allied with Wilson in his determination to keep the United States neutral, but were now dismayed over his commitment to rearmament and to what President Dwight D. Eisenhower would more than forty years later label the military-industrial complex.* On the floor of the Senate,

---

*Wilson himself foresaw that such an alliance portended the loss of much of the Progressive Era's gains. "Every reform we have won will be lost if we go into this war," he told Secretary of the Navy Josephus Daniels. "War means autocracy. The people we

La Follette declared that "the commercial, industrial, and imperialistic schemes of the great financial masters of this country" were behind preparedness efforts.[13] *The New York Evening Post* and *Nation* editor Oswald Garrison Villard wrote to Wilson, expressing his "most profound regret" that the president had "decided to go on the side of the large armament people . . . The new departure seems . . . anti-moral, anti-social, and anti-democratic, and the burdens rest primarily on the already overtaxed and overgoverned masses . . . You are sowing the seeds of militarism, raising up a military and naval caste."[14]

All of these groups and individuals believed that rearmament would inevitably prove more likely to push the nation closer to war rather than to preserve America's "providentially assigned" neutrality, which Wilson had asserted to Congress in December 1915. For their opposition to preparedness, opponents of rearmament were vilified and lumped, by preparedness advocates and the press, into the same "disloyal" camp as hyphenates, thereby interweaving three threads: anti-hyphenate sentiment, the preparedness movement, and antiradical attitudes.

Throughout the spring of 1916, Wilson continued to lay a foundation of intolerance and suspicion, as he repeatedly introduced the themes of hyphenates and disloyalty into his speeches. In May, he posed a hypothetical question to a Charlotte, North Carolina, audience: "What kind of fire of pure passion are you going to keep burning under the [melting] pot in order that the mixture that comes out may be purged of its dross and may be the fine gold of untainted Americanism?"[15] In a June Flag Day address, he again stated his belief in the loyalty of the majority of those "whose lineage is directly derived from the nations now at war." Nonetheless, he warned, "There is disloyalty active in the United States, and it must absolutely be crushed." He ended with a challenge to his listeners: "Are you going yourselves, individually and collectively, to see to it that no man is tolerated who does not do honor to that flag?"[16]

Roosevelt also hammered away. "I stand for straight Americanism

---

have unhorsed will inevitably come into control of the country for we shall be dependent upon the steel, ore and financial magnates. They will run the nation" (Baker, *Woodrow Wilson: Life and Letters*, vol. 6, p. 506 n. 2).

unconditioned and unqualified," he thundered in a May speech in St. Louis, "and I stand against every form of hyphenated Americanism . . . [U]nless the immigrant becomes in good faith an American and nothing else, then he is out of place in this country and the sooner he leaves it the better."[17]

The admonitions of Wilson and Roosevelt kept the twin threats of ethnicity and dissent on the front burner, as the preparedness engine steamrollered along, steadily gaining momentum. In the months following the huge New York City parade, similar demonstrations were held in large cities throughout the country.[18] Wilson himself, decked out in a straw boater and carrying a large American flag, marched at the head of the Washington preparedness parade.

In his September speech accepting the Democratic renomination for the presidency, Wilson once again equated hyphenates with infidelity. The party platform, which Wilson was instrumental in drafting, denounced every organization seeking "the advancement of the interest of a foreign power" or tending "to divide our people into antagonistic groups and thus to destroy that complete agreement and solidarity . . . so essential to the perpetuity of free institutions."[19]

Wilson's 1916 campaign slogan, "He Kept Us Out of War," contained an implicit vow to stay that course, his escalating espousal of preparedness notwithstanding. Believing in Wilson's sincerity, officials of the American Union Against Militarism, which represented the pacifist wing of the anti-preparedness movement, campaigned for his reelection. Only Villard was not taken in; he withheld his public support, believing that Wilson had "not a principle on earth he would not bargain away."[20] Still, Villard refrained from publicly renouncing Wilson, convinced that he was a lesser evil than his Republican opponent, the Supreme Court justice Charles Evans Hughes, who campaigned on a platform of increased preparedness. (Roosevelt, who had received the Progressive Party nomination, withdrew from the race and campaigned for Hughes.)

In the end, Wilson's promise to keep the United States out of the war played a pivotal role in the race, as voters handed him a slim majority and a second term in office. Those who supported him on the basis of that promise would all too soon have a bitter pill to swallow.

On January 31, 1917, less than three months after the election, U.S.-German affairs approached the boiling point when Germany announced its resumption of unrestricted submarine warfare in the Atlantic. In restarting the attacks on merchant ships, which had been suspended following the outcry over the sinking of the *Lusitania*, the German high command was attempting to isolate Britain by cutting off all commerce to the islands, and thus forcing the British to surrender before the United States could enter the war and become a significant factor in the outcome. In response, Wilson broke off diplomatic relations with Germany on February 3, the same day the American merchant ship *Housatonic* was torpedoed and sunk near Sicily.

As international events simmered, the domestic front also heated up. On February 14, in a harbinger of things to come, Congress passed the Threats Against the President Act, which called for a $1,000 fine and up to five years' imprisonment for "knowingly and willfully" making written or spoken threats against the president.[21] The law, while understandably intended as a protection for the chief executive, was also a first step toward the criminalization of expression. In short order, a Texan was convicted for saying, "I wish Wilson was in hell, and if I had the power I would put him there";[22] the court's instructions to the jury stated that "neither hostility to the President nor an intention to execute the threat, constituted essential elements of the crime. The knowing and willful utterance of such a threat was held to be sufficient."[23] The law was a portent of legislation restricting civil liberties and limiting dissent that would be enacted once the United States entered the war.

A major step in that direction was taken on March 1, when the infamous Zimmermann telegram was published in American newspapers. Dated January 19, the encoded cable was sent by the German foreign secretary to Germany's ambassador in Mexico for transmission to the Mexican government. It proposed that if Germany's renewed policy of unrestricted submarine warfare drew America into the war, Mexico— bolstered by German financial support—should in turn attack the United States. As a reward, Mexico would receive back the parts of Texas, New Mexico, and Arizona that the United States had annexed during the Mexican-American War. The telegram further suggested that Mexico should act as an intermediary between Germany and Japan in the interest of drawing Japan into the conflict on Germany's side and participating in the attack on the United States. American intelligence intercepted and decoded this dispatch, and its publication in the U.S. press raised a firestorm of public opinion.

While many Americans regarded the notion of Mexico and Japan invading the United States as an absurdity, they also took the Zimmermann telegram as a definitive statement of German hostility, in the face of which America's entrance into the war now seemed inescapable. Antagonism toward Germany and Germans climbed another notch, prompting the Council of National Defense to issue a statement calling "upon all citizens" to treat aliens with "neither suspicion nor aggressiveness . . . [but] with unchanged manner and with unchanged mind."[24]

Pacifist groups, a small but vocal minority, worked desperately to restrain the rising war fever. In response to the publication of the Zimmermann telegram, the Emergency Peace Federation, headquartered in New York City, distributed a million copies of a leaflet urging Americans not to be swept along by the tide. "Patriotism is love of country," read the flyer. "Love your country enough to keep it out of war. What we dread is a stampede. 'Remember the Maine' made one war. Don't let the newspapers make another."[25]

A month and a half after the *Housatonic* went down, the sinking of three more American merchant ships during a twenty-four-hour period in the middle of March brought matters to a head. On March 21, the day after his cabinet had unanimously expressed its approval for war with Germany, Wilson called a special session of Congress for April 2 to hear his request for a declaration of war.

The country was polarized. The antimilitarists swung into high gear as the mood of the "patriots" simultaneously took an ugly turn toward anybody opposed to America's entry. For their increasingly outspoken opposition to the headlong rush, pacifists were now branded, along with hyphenates, as disloyal by preparedness advocates. With war clearly looming on the horizon, tensions between "patriots" and pacifists broke loose at a March 23 Carnegie Hall meeting to celebrate the overthrow of Russia's tsar, Nicholas II. When New York City's mayor John Purroy Mitchel told the crowd, "It is now inevitable . . . that the United States is to be projected into this world war," he was greeted by a chorus of "No! No!"[26]

Mitchel retorted, "And I say to you in the galleries that tonight we are divided into only two classes—Americans and traitors! . . . You are for America or you are against her."

That night a prowar demonstration was held at Madison Square Garden, and the following evening pacifists called their own rally at the same location. More than twelve thousand people packed the auditorium, and another three thousand were turned away for lack of space.

One of the main speakers was the former Stanford University president David Starr Jordan, who was on an eleventh-hour whirlwind speaking tour of eastern cities in support of finding a peaceful solution to the crisis. In the next week, Jordan spoke in Boston, New Haven, Philadelphia, and Princeton, where Princeton University president John G. Hibben refused permission for a peace rally, forcing the sponsors to meet at a church.

On the evening of Sunday, April 1, the day before Wilson was scheduled to seek a declaration of war from Congress, Jordan was slated to speak at Baltimore's Academy of Music. He had barely begun addressing an audience of five thousand about the need for peace when a loud commotion arose outside the hall. The manager of the building hurried onto the stage to inform the meeting's organizers that an angry crowd of over a thousand had gathered outside, "howling, hissing and shaking their fists," and that the thirty police officers assigned to maintain order could not control the throng.[27] He urgently advised them to end the meeting.

Suddenly a group that included businessmen, students, and professors from local colleges and universities, led by a man carrying the American flag, broke through the police barrier, entered the hall, rushed up the aisle, and climbed onstage. Confronting the chairman of the meeting "with profane and foul epithets," the standard-bearer thrust the flag forward and demanded, "What do you say to this?"[28] The gathering was on the verge of erupting into a melee when one of the pacifists jumped onto a chair and began singing "The Star-Spangled Banner"; the entire assembly took up the song, and the belligerents were forced to remove their hats and join in. The national anthem was followed by "America" and "Columbia, the Gem of the Ocean" as members of the audience filed out the side doors. By this time, police reinforcements from all over the city had arrived. Swinging their clubs, the officers waded into the counterdemonstrators and carted off over twenty people, at least one of whom had to be hospitalized.

Jordan was able to leave the building safely, but for the next several hours the patriotic horde prowled the streets of Baltimore, singing, "We'll hang Dave Jordan to a sour apple tree," to the tune of "The Battle Hymn of the Republic." They stopped in at all the hotels, trying to find Jordan, who was spending the night at a friend's house.

The following morning, Jordan went to Washington and tried in vain to meet with Wilson as thousands of people poured into the "flag draped" capital to demonstrate support for either peace or war.[29] Two special trains of prowar supporters—or "anti-pacifists," as *The New York Times* called them—came from New York, and others arrived on their own, but they were outnumbered by representatives of the peace camp, "the most eager" of whom, according to the *Times*, "spoke with a pronounced German accent." Police refused to allow parades or demonstrations of any kind and prevented about fifteen hundred antiwar partisans from holding a rally on the steps of the Capitol building.

That evening, Wilson addressed a joint meeting of Congress that also included the justices of the Supreme Court and members of the diplomatic corps. When the president was introduced, he received "such a reception as Congress had never given him before in any of his visits to it."[30] Except for a small handful, including senators La Follette, James Vardaman of Mississippi, and George Norris of Nebraska and the House majority leader, Claude Kitchin of North Carolina, the assembled legislators each wore or carried a small American flag. They cheered Wilson for a full two minutes before allowing him to begin his speech, which history would remember for its keynote line, "The world must be made safe for democracy."

Wilson started by reviewing a list of German crimes and American attempts to avoid war, which his audience listened to without interruption. When, in turning to recent events, he said, "We will not choose the path of submission," the chief justice of the Supreme Court, Edward Douglass White, "with an expression of joy and thankfulness on his face, dropped the big soft hat he had been holding, raised his hands high in the air, and brought them together with a heartfelt bang; and House, Senate, and galleries followed him with a roar like a storm. It was a cheer so deep and so intense and so much from the heart that it sounded like a prayer."

White led another outburst when Wilson urged Congress to "declare the course of the Imperial German Government to be in effect nothing less than war," at which the chief justice, rising from his seat, "compressed his lips together as if he were trying to keep tears back, and again raised his hands as high as he could and brought his mighty palms together as if he were trying to split them." At this display, the entire audience—minus the small group of dissenters—joined White and rose to deliver a standing ovation.

Listeners also applauded Wilson's proposals to strengthen the Navy, expand the Army to half a million men, and institute a military draft. The final round of applause came when he touched upon the issue of German-Americans. Most of them, he affirmed, were "true and loyal Americans"; however, he warned, "if there should be disloyalty, it will be dealt with with a firm hand of stern repression."

At the end of Wilson's talk, "the great scene which had been enacted at his entrance was repeated." As he left the chamber, senators and representatives, Democrats and Republicans alike, diplomats, Supreme Court justices, and people in the galleries stood and waved their flags, as those who had worn, rather than carried their banners, "tore them from their lapels or their sleeves and waved with the rest, and they all cheered wildly."

All but a few, that is. La Follette, who had pointedly and defiantly chewed gum throughout the president's address, "stood motionless with his arms folded tight and high on his chest, so that nobody could have any excuse for mistaking his attitude."

La Follette was by this time one of the most maligned men in the country, a result of his unwavering opposition to the preparedness movement and the war momentum. He was condemned as a traitor and likened to Benedict Arnold and Judas Iscariot. *The Cincinnati Times-Star* said, "In a democracy majorities must rule. The vast majority of senators are patriotic Americans. They should use their power to deprive La Follette and his little group of perverts the opportunity of continuing to drag our flag in the dust and to make this great American Republic ridiculous and without honor in the eyes of the world."[31] In Roosevelt's opinion, the Wisconsin senator had "shown himself to be an unhung traitor, and if the war should come, he ought to be hung."[32]

As expected, La Follette delivered a solemn speech against the war resolution, which had been introduced in both houses immediately following Wilson's April 2 address. In a four-hour talk during the Senate debate on April 4, he rebuked "the irresponsible and war-crazed press" for its "doctrine of 'standing back of the president,' without inquiring whether the president is right or wrong," and accused Wilson of guaranteeing "to make this fair, free, and happy land of ours the same shambles and bottomless pit of horror that we see in Europe today."[33] He dared Wilson and the bill's supporters to let the people vote on whether or not there should be a declaration of war. And, in possibly the most provocative of his remarks, he ridiculed the idea that the United States had ever been neutral in the conflict. "From early in the war [we] threw our neutrality to the winds . . . I say Germany has been

patient with us." At the end of his speech, wrote Amos Pinchot, La
Follette "stood in silence, tears running down his face."[34]

La Follette was not the only one to speak forcefully against American involvement. Echoing his Wisconsin colleague, James Vardaman
stated that if the people, "the plain, honest people, the masses," were
consulted, the resolution would be defeated.[35] George Norris, whose
talk was greeted by shouts of "Treason!" declared that entering the war
"would benefit only the class of people . . . who have already made
millions of dollars, and who will make many hundreds of millions
more . . . We are going into war upon the command of gold. . . . [W]e
are about to put the dollar sign on the American flag."[36]

House opponents argued no less ardently. When called upon to
cast her vote, Jeannette Rankin of Montana, the first woman elected to
Congress and only four days into her term, said, "I want to stand by my
country, but I cannot vote for war. I vote no."[37] Isaac Sherwood of
Ohio, who had fought in the Civil War and been forever after haunted
by the carnage he witnessed, stated, "As I love my country, I feel it is
my sacred duty to keep the stalwart young men of today out of a barbarous war 3,500 miles away, in which we have no vital interest."[38] But
perhaps the most telling comment was made by Majority Leader
Kitchin, who lamented, "For my vote I shall be not only criticized but
denounced from one end of the country to the other. The whole yelp-
ing pack of defamers and revilers in the nation will at once be set upon
my heels."[39]

According to one historian of the period, the opponents of the war
possessed "the greater abundance [of] the virtues of consistency, clar-
ity of purpose, and prophetic accuracy," but they were hopelessly outnumbered.[40] The Senate adopted the war resolution by a vote of 82–6,
the House by 373–50, and Wilson signed it on April 6. The "patriots"
had their war.

CHAPTER 2

A Democracy Gone Mad

On the afternoon of July 1, three months after the United States entered the war, eight thousand Socialists and trade unionists gathered outside Socialist Party headquarters on Boston's Park Square for a peace parade. The march was scheduled to start at 2:45, but even as prospective participants were assembling, the hint of trouble was already in the air.

A group of onlooking uniformed servicemen took umbrage at some of the placards they saw. "Who Stole Panama, Who Crushes Haiti?— American Democracy," read one. "If This Is a Popular War, Why Conscription?" asked another. "A Six-Hour Day in Socialist Russia. Why Not Here?" demanded a third.[1] But the sign that was most offensive to the men in uniform was the one that claimed, "The United States Government Has Ordered 200,000 Coffins for Our Boys."

Determined to do something about the affront, the soldiers and sailors left the square and walked a few blocks to Boston Common, where they rounded up all the uniformed men they could find. At an officer's command, they marched in double-rank formation back to Park Square, where they planted themselves directly in the line of the parade and announced that the protest would not happen. Hoping to avoid a repeat of a riot that had taken place five weeks earlier at a Chicago peace demonstration, police intervened, and the servicemen withdrew.[2] A noncommissioned officer "congratulated them . . . and advised them to disperse without further disturbance," but the enlisted men had other ideas.

Meanwhile, the marchers—including women, "many of whom carried babies"—had set out, fronted by an American flag and a huge red banner borne by a dozen men, with the gilt inscription "Workers of the World, Unite, You Have Nothing to Lose but Your Chains, and the World to Gain." When the march reached the military recruiting tents on Tremont Street, the soldiers and sailors, whose ranks were steadily increasing, advanced and met the parade head-on. They pulled down the red banner with its revolutionary slogan and tore it to shreds, but the police once again stepped in to prevent events from escalating out of control.

The march resumed. After a few blocks, the "patriots," now numbering three hundred servicemen and a thousand civilians, barged in from a side street and marched in formation through the length of the parade, "effectively ripping it apart and destroying all semblance" of its order. The American flag at the head of the procession was seized, and patriots snatched away the red flags with white circles, symbolizing peace, that many of the marchers carried. Fistfights broke out everywhere. One of the attackers was clubbed over the head by a police officer just as he grabbed a protester's flag, but a Justice Department agent stepped in and whispered something to the patrolman, and the man was released. Boston's finest tried to restore order, but "the willingness of the uniformed men and their followers to pitch into any who denied their demands was so evident few cared to encounter them," and the police soon gave up trying to restrain them.

With their parade destroyed, the marchers "flowed onto the Common like a flood," gathering with their remaining signs on the baseball field, where the melee resumed. The planned speakers, who included the president of the Pennsylvania State Federation of Labor, tried to make themselves heard, but the affair was beyond the point of rescue. The crowd ran about, "not unlike cattle," rushing from one fight to another, as the rest of the protesters' signs, banners, and flags were confiscated and trampled underfoot. Many of the usual Sunday visitors to the Common, who had unsuspectingly turned out to enjoy the sunshine, were buffeted about like driftwood in rough surf, suffering minor bruises and torn clothing. To avert worse trouble, the Boston police superintendent, Michael Crowley, revoked the marchers' meeting permit that had been granted by the mayor's office.

At about 4:00 p.m., the servicemen got the idea "to do a systematic job," and they fell into formation and marched to Socialist Party headquarters at 14 Park Square. A crowd rushed up the two flights of stairs to the office, broke down the doors, and poured in. When a marine bugler appeared in one of the windows and played the opening notes of "The Star-Spangled Banner," the crowd in the street below took up the national anthem. After they finished, "the work of destruction began." The office telephone was torn out; records, publications, furniture, and a suitcase containing clothing and personal effects were thrown out the windows onto the square, where they were fed into a bonfire. Servicemen draped the American flag that had been seized from the head of the parade over the Park Square statue of Abraham Lincoln.

Their work at the office accomplished, one of the soldiers cried out, "Come on, we'll go back to the Common and bust up that meeting." A group of servicemen and civilians formed up and began a parade of their own, waving the tattered and defaced banners they had taken from the protesters. Superintendent Crowley ordered his men not to interfere with the new march lest an even greater disaster ensue. The rest of the crowd surged back to the Common, exhorted by "dozens of leaders, each with a different idea of how to proclaim the triumph of patriotism." More flags were planted on more statues. The throng swelled to about twenty thousand.

Adding a bizarre, surrealistic touch to the bedlam was the customary Sunday concert on Parkman Bandstand, which started up and continued, even as the contiguous pandemonium raged. Soon the men in military uniforms had taken over the management of the concert, instructing the orchestra on which songs to play and commanding the assembled listeners on when to doff their hats, as an ad hoc vigilance committee made sure they complied.

The mayhem had been in progress for almost three hours when a Justice Department agent telephoned the Navy Reserve office at Commonwealth Pier to request troops. Just before six o'clock, a squadron of thirty armed reservists arrived, creating the discomfiting prospect of reserve men acting against uniformed soldiers and sailors. In full view of the crowd, the three ensigns in charge "unlimbered their revolvers and made sure that the cartridge chambers were stocked." Followed by a large crowd, the reservists cut through the Common to Park Square, where a second sacking of Socialist Party headquarters was under way. The order to fix bayonets was given.

As the reservists were locking their bayonets into place, a reporter asked one of the ensigns about who had ordered them to the scene and if they were enforcing martial law. He was told to "get out." The ensign then ordered someone, anyone, to arrest the reporter, after which a uniformed man punched the journalist in the face, breaking his glasses. To prevent worse, a small group ushered the writer out of the area.

Working with the Boston police and federal Secret Service agents, the reservists methodically cleared Park Square and restored an air of order to the Common before withdrawing. By the end of the afternoon, ten people had been arrested.

One Boston newspaper called the assault on the march "a deep disgrace to Boston and a sorry stain to the American uniform . . . in a year when the nation has been urged to give its blood to 'make the world safe for democracy.' "

Among the protest signs that were demolished in the fray was one that read, "First War Victims—Freedom of Assembly, Freedom of Speech."

The repression began immediately after Congress declared war, as the Wilson administration unleashed an all-out assault on dissent with a three-pronged attack of legislation, propaganda, and surveillance.

When the American people reelected Woodrow Wilson in 1916, they voted to stay out of the war. It is questionable, however, whether Wilson ever felt bound by his campaign slogan, "He Kept Us Out of War," with its implied promise of continued neutrality, as his veiled intentions were revealed in a letter to a friend two days after his war message to Congress. "It was necessary for me," Wilson wrote, "by very slow stages indeed and with the most genuine purpose to avoid war to lead the country on to a single way of thinking."[3]

Now that war had arrived, the Wilson administration went to work to stifle opposition and to make certain that the entire country adhered to that "single way of thinking." On the very day that the United States entered the war, Wilson issued a proclamation, based on the Alien Enemies Act of 1798 (one of the Alien and Sedition Acts), categorizing "all natives, citizens, denizens, or subjects of Germany, being males of fourteen years and upwards, who shall be within the United States and not actually naturalized," as "alien enemies."[4] The proclamation contained twelve regulations "for the public safety," forbidding alien enemies to, among other things, possess firearms or other munitions, use aircraft or wireless devices, criticize in writing the U.S. government, and reside or remain in any area designated by the president as "restricted." Violation of any of the twelve regulations meant "summary arrest." Ten days after the United States declared war, Congress passed an updated version of the Alien Enemies Act.

Even before war was declared, "elaborate preparations" had been made for the detention of German aliens deemed dangerous.[5] Since August 1914, the Department of Justice had been compiling the names of Germans and German sympathizers, and on March 30, Assistant Attorney General Charles Warren (who framed Wilson's April 6 proclamation on alien enemies) wrote to Attorney General Thomas W. Gregory to recommend a swift and repressive course of action, despite having no indication of illegal activity. "There are many dangerous leaders and plotters in New York and elsewhere," wrote Warren, "of whom we have no absolute evidence, at present, of having committed a Federal crime but yet who would be very dangerous if left at large. It seems to me the height of folly to wait until these German aliens commit crimes before we arrest them. I believe that the wise policy is to avert trouble and not try and remedy it after it has happened."[6]

On the heels of the declaration of war, sixty-three German aliens— now "enemy aliens"—were arrested. This was just the beginning of the crackdown, and German-Americans were not the only ones who would come under attack as the government used the alleged threat from hyphenates to institute a wide-ranging curtailment of civil liberties and the expression of dissent. In turn, the public carried on these tactics as a popular extension of official policy.

As early as December 1915, in Wilson's third annual message to Congress, in which he attacked immigrants who "poured the poison of disloyalty into the very arteries of our national life," the president had appealed for stronger laws to deal with "disloyal" behavior.[7] The day after his speech, Wilson's cabinet instructed Gregory to develop such legislation, and in June 1916 the attorney general's proposals, aimed at addressing "the new conditions of warfare by propaganda," were presented to both House and Senate committees for consideration.[8] The proposed legislation was aimed at restricting freedom of speech and the press as well as punishing sabotage, but Congress adjourned before any bill could be considered.

During a special session of Congress in early February 1917, Senator Lee Overman and Representative Edwin Webb, both of North Carolina, introduced bills in their respective bodies based on Gregory's recommendations. The Senate version passed on February 20. At the House Judiciary Committee hearings, Norman Thomas, then a young New York minister, testified on behalf of the American Union Against Militarism, a stronghold of pacifist principles and activism. Despite guarantees from the bill's supporters that it would never be brought to bear against "loyal" Americans, Thomas expressed his disquiet, arguing, "It certainly could be used to muzzle such conscientious objectors as the Quakers and other good souls, although treason would be the last thing to enter their minds."[9] Thomas's concerns were not without basis—from Wilson on down, the definition of "disloyal" had never been spelled out.

Though the House adjourned on March 4 before the Overman-Webb bill could be brought to a vote, the special congressional session did bring forth the Threats Against the President Act, which presaged the coming trend.[10] When Congress reconvened on April 2 to hear Wilson's war message, the Overman-Webb bill, now known as the Espionage Act, was placed at the top of the legislative agenda.

Just how quickly the wheels were rolling may be evidenced by an April 17 letter from the AUAM to Wilson, expressing alarm over the snowballing infringements on civil liberties, even before any restrictive laws had been passed.* The letter, signed by such notables as Jane Addams, Herbert S. Bigelow, Samuel Gompers, Morris Hillquit, George Foster Peabody, Amos Pinchot, and Rabbi Stephen Wise, communicated trepidation that

> the administration of such laws . . . may easily lend itself to the suppression of free speech, free assemblage, popular discussion and criticism . . . Even by this time, we have seen evidence of

---

*One unknown security measure was Wilson's secret April 7 executive order regarding federal employees, which authorized heads of civil service departments to dismiss any employee who, "by reason of his conduct, sympathies, or utterances, or because of other reasons growing out of the war," appeared to be a security risk. (The complete text of Wilson's order can be found in Paul Van Riper, *History of the United States Civil Service*, p. 266.) By the beginning of July, *The New York Times* reported, "Suspected individuals have been subjected to strict surveillance and discharges from public service among this class have been frequent" (July 6, 1917).

the breaking down of immortal rights and privileges. Halls have been refused for public discussion; meetings have been broken up; speakers have been arrested and censorship exercised, not to prevent the transmission of information to enemy countries, but to prevent the free discussion by American citizens of our own problems and policies. As we go on, the inevitable psychology of war will manifest itself with increasing danger, not only to individuals, but to our cherished institutions.[11]

The letter urged Wilson to "make an impressive statement" that would remind people "of the peculiar obligation devolving upon all Americans in this war to uphold in every way our constitutional rights and privileges," but no such statement was forthcoming from the White House.

What emerged instead was the Committee on Public Information, the official state organ of propaganda, created by Wilson on April 14 and headed by George Creel. The CPI, with its daily publication, the *Official Bulletin*, and a torrent of other pamphlets, films, signs, and additional media output, was instrumental in creating the climate of paranoia and war hysteria, feeding the notion, as one historian has written, "that spies and saboteurs lurked behind every bush."[12]

According to John Lord O'Brian, director of the Justice Department's Emergency War Division, "No other one cause contributed so much to the oppression of innocent men as the systematic and indiscriminate agitation against what was claimed to be an all-pervasive system of German espionage." Writing after the war, O'Brian cited "the large number of false stories of enemy activities within the United States, put forth through the medium of press dispatches, pamphlets of patriotic societies and occasionally speeches on the floor of Congress."[13]

The efforts of the CPI were coupled with the emergence of a rash of patriotic vigilance organizations with names like the All-Allied Anti-German League, the American Anti-Anarchy Association, the Anti–Yellow Dog League, the Boy Spies of America, the Sedition Slammers, and the Terrible Threateners. By August 1917, Gregory reported having several hundred thousand private citizens engaged in spying on their neighbors. (This despite Gregory's opinion, expressed in a July cabinet meeting, that all the "talk of spies" was little more than "hysteria."[14])

Two of the most powerful of these groups were the National Security League, originally formed at the beginning of the European war to advocate for preparedness and universal military training, and its offshoot the American Defense Society, which had declared itself upon formation to be "the announced enemy of those peace organizations who urge disarmament."[15] The former was funded by men like Cornelius Vanderbilt, J. P. Morgan, John D. Rockefeller, and Simon Guggenheim; the latter had Theodore Roosevelt as its honorary president. According to Creel, these two groups "were chiefly responsible for the development of a mob spirit in many sections."[16]

But the largest, and probably most influential, of the vigilance organizations was the American Protective League.[17] The APL was created in late March 1917, when the Justice Department accepted the offer of the Chicago businessman Albert Briggs to form a volunteer organization that would act as an arm of the department and investigate foreign agents and "persons unfriendly to this Government."[18] On May 12, the Justice Department announced that the APL would gather intelligence but would supposedly have no authority to make arrests "except after consultation with the Federal authorities."[19] In the first three months, the APL enlisted almost 100,000 bankers, businessmen, industrialists, and professionals in six hundred locales; by the end of the war the membership would grow to 250,000.

From its Washington office, the APL used Justice Department letterhead, giving it the appearance of a legitimate arm of the government. Reinforcing this impression was the badge members bought for one dollar that originally said "Secret Service Division" but was later changed to read "Auxiliary of the U.S. Department of Justice" after the Treasury Department complained that the first wording might cause confusion with its own Secret Service.

Despite its semiofficial status, the APL was in fact a vigilante manifestation of what O'Brian would later call the wartime "spy mania," a domestic surveillance organization that functioned as a quasilegal, quasigovernmental adjunct to the Justice Department.[20] One writer has characterized the APL as a "government-sponsored lynch-mob which proudly took the law into its own hands in summary and brutal fashion."[21]

APL members were responsible for countless illegal arrests and detentions, and in his book about the organization, Emerson Hough boasted that the APL had illegally opened mail, tapped phones, and broken into homes and offices "thousands of times [but] never been detected."[22] Hough claimed that the league brought three million cases of disloyalty to judgment. As preposterous as that figure appears, it is not beyond credibility that in its patriotic zeal the APL actually conducted "investigations" of and maintained files on that many citizens—a year after the founding of the organization, Gregory said that vigilance groups enabled the government to keep tabs on hundreds of thousands of individuals: "We have representatives at all meetings of any importance. We use large numbers of men, and some women, who understand and speak the German language. Gatherings of Germans are given special attention."[23]

The vigilance organizations were merely one component of the new surveillance state that was taking hold. People were also actively encouraged to spy on their neighbors. "Complaints of even the most informal or confidential nature are always welcome," Gregory told U.S. district attorneys. "Citizens should feel free to bring their information or suspicions to the attention of the nearest representative of the Department of Justice."[24] As a result, a thousand letters or more poured into the department every day, the overwhelming majority of which, not surprisingly, were of no importance.

The government also instituted a practice of factory surveillance called the Plant Protection Section in companies with defense contracts, which may have amounted to as many as 37,000 firms.[25] Ordinary workers, without their knowledge or consent, were kept under observation by their fellow employees. PPS members infiltrated unions, filing reports on organizing efforts, strike tactics, and leaders' activities, and often causing dissension in the ranks. They opened mail, broke into homes, and employed a variety of other illegal tactics in gathering information on "suspects."

Spying on civilians thus became the order of the day. At the end of April, First Assistant Postmaster J. C. Koons sent a directive to local postmasters, instructing them to "keep on the lookout" for "anything which might be important."[26]

The Bureau of Investigation (precursor to the Federal Bureau of Investigation), which had grown from a hundred agents in 1914 to three hundred in 1916, continued its rapid expansion during the war. The Military Intelligence Division mushroomed to three hundred uni-

formed officers and a thousand civilian employees. Both the BI and the
MID were heavily involved in spying on civilians. The Justice Department conducted investigations of sixty thousand enemy aliens in the
course of the war.[27] By 1918, Gregory would boast that "never in its
history has this country been so thoroughly policed as at the present
time."[28]

The press also picked up the call for surveillance. The *Literary
Digest* invited readers "to clip and send us any editorial utterances they
encounter which seem to them seditious or treasonable." *The New York
Times* proclaimed, "It is the duty of every good citizen to communicate
to the proper authorities any evidence of sedition that comes to his
notice. He may be mistaken, but nobody will be injured in that case"—
a strikingly ingenuous assertion that would prove mistaken many times
over.[29] In Iowa, the editor of *The Des Moines Capital* wrote, "In the
present crisis, what is the duty of every citizen? It is his duty to join a
patriotic society. It is his duty to support President Wilson and the
patriotic men who are struggling against all opposition in congress. *It
is his duty to find out what his neighbor thinks* . . . It is every patriot's duty
to find out what the school teachers are intending to do in regard to
patriotism."[30] Freedom of thought now joined freedom of speech and
freedom of assembly on the list of endangered liberties.

While Congress was debating the Espionage Act, there was another
piece of business that needed attention. In his war message, Wilson
had proposed a military draft, and on May 18 the Selective Service Act
was passed and signed into law. The fifth of June was designated as the
date when men between twenty-one and thirty years of age were to
register; failure to do so would bring a year in jail. Ironically, many
immigrants from Europe, particularly Germans, who had fled to avoid
conscription were now facing the same situation in their adopted
country. "Thou shalt not Prussianize America!" challenged a broadside
titled "No Conscription, No Involuntary Servitude, No Slavery."[31]
Pacifists, Socialists, anarchists, and Wobblies all swore resistance to the
draft.

On the night the draft law was signed, there was "a wild
anti-conscription demonstration" in Harlem, sponsored by the
No-Conscription League.[32] The speakers included Emma Goldman,
who has been accurately characterized as "the central figure of Ameri-

can anarchism" in early-twentieth-century America.[33] "Red Emma," as the press called her, was born in Lithuania, then part of Russia, and immigrated to the United States in 1885 at age sixteen. To the cornerstone anarchist belief that the perfection of humanity would render government unnecessary, Goldman brought a feminist consciousness, advocating issues like gender equality and birth control. Despite not being a native speaker, she was thoroughly fluent in English and an eloquent, charismatic orator.

The government and the American public had plausibly been on edge with regard to anarchists since the May 1886 Haymarket riot, in which anarchists were accused of throwing a bomb that killed a police officer at an open-air labor meeting in Chicago's Haymarket Square. In the ensuing melee, seven other policemen and four workers were killed, and dozens more policemen were injured. Eight anarchists were tried for conspiracy to commit murder, and despite a conspicuous lack of evidence all were convicted. Seven were sentenced to hang, the eighth to serve fifteen years. One of the condemned men committed suicide in prison, and four others were executed in November 1887; the remaining two first had their sentences reduced to life imprisonment by one governor of Illinois and later received pardons from another.

Fears of anarchists in general and Goldman in particular were exacerbated by the September 1901 assassination of President William McKinley by Leon Czolgosz, a self-styled anarchist with a history of mental illness, who claimed to have been influenced by Goldman. Goldman was arrested as being the mastermind behind the assassination but was released after two weeks in custody for lack of evidence. Her editorial "The Tragedy at Buffalo," published in *Free Society* the month after the killing, was not so much a defense of Czolgosz as a condemnation of "the economic and political conditions of this country," but it nevertheless reinforced her image as a treacherous foe of American society.[34]

Goldman had undeniably been a thorn in the side of the government for decades, but despite her fiery and unwavering radicalism she had largely managed, except for two short prison terms, to escape attempts to prosecute her before the war. In the months leading up to America's entry, however, Goldman's incendiary rhetoric brought her under increasing scrutiny. Giving no quarter, she wrote in her publication *Mother Earth* in March 1917:

President Wilson and other officials of the administration assure us that they want peace. If that claim had even one grain of truth, the government would have long ago . . . put a stop to the export of munitions and food stuffs . . .

Washington is capable of nice phrases, but . . . it has never made a single determined step for peace . . .

[W]ar in this country is at present only a possibility, and already the Germans and the Austrians are being deprived of employment, ostracized and spied upon, persecuted and hounded . . .

These millions of Germans and Austrians . . . are now to be treated like enemy aliens, just because Wall Street feels itself checked in its unlimited use of the seas for plunder, robbery and theft . . .

Then there is the systematic, barbarous persecution of radical and revolutionary elements throughout the land . . .

The workers must learn that they have nothing to expect from their masters. The latter, in America, as well as in Europe, hesitate not a moment to send hundred thousands of the people to their death if their interests demand it . . .

I for one will speak against war so long as my voice will last, now and during war. A thousand times rather would I die calling to the people of America to refuse to be obedient, to refuse military service, to refuse to murder their brothers, than I should ever give my voice in justification of war, except the one war of all the people against their despots and exploiters—the Social Revolution.[35]

In the face of America's growing war fever, such strident, outspoken opposition understandably alarmed the government. As the U.S. attorney Francis Caffey said, "Emma Goldman is a woman of great ability and of personal magnetism, and her persuasive powers are such as to make her an exceedingly dangerous woman."[36]

At the May 18 anti-conscription meeting in Harlem, Goldman railed against the draft and promised that the rally would be just the first of many to come. In advising young men to refuse conscription, she would finally provide the government with a justification to take her out of circulation. No arrests were made, but police stenographers recorded the speakers' every word, in order to later determine whether action would be taken.

As Goldman promised, there were more protests in New York and other locations around the country. "GOVERNMENT MOVES SWIFTLY TO CHECK WIDESPREAD EFFORT TO COMBAT CONSCRIPTION LAW," read a May 29 *New York Times* headline, as more than two dozen men and women were arrested in Texas, Virginia, Detroit, Chicago, and Seattle. Attorney General Gregory was quoted as saying, "These arrests should be accepted by the country generally as a warning against interfering with the enforcement of the provisions of the new army law."

On June 5, the day all men of draft age were required to register, there were incidents—including demonstrations, arrests, and beatings—all over the country. In Butte, Montana, a parade of six hundred men and women was "pounced upon by patriotic citizens, reinforced by the police"; troops with fixed bayonets broke up the ensuing riot, and the city was placed under martial law as soldiers patrolled the streets.[37] National Guardsmen were called out in a Michigan mining town to prevent an anti-conscription demonstration from taking place. Members of the Navajo nation in northwestern Arizona drove a government agent off their reservation when he tried to register them, and Utes in Colorado similarly refused to sign up, spending the day instead performing traditional dances, while the governor of the Santo Domingo Pueblo in New Mexico was arrested along with two other prominent members of the pueblo for conspiring to prevent more than twenty Santo Domingo residents from registering.

In a June 10 editorial, *The New York Times* equated draft resistance with disloyalty, specifically laying the blame at the feet of those old bogeymen, the hyphenates, and keeping alive the conflation of dissent and anti-Americanism. "The Selective Draft act," said the *Times*, "gives a long and sorely needed means of disciplining a certain insolent foreign element."

At a June 11 meeting in New York where Emma Goldman spoke, U.S. agents detained thirty men who could not produce registration cards. "We would have been entirely justified in arresting every man who attended this meeting," said the U.S. marshal Thomas D. McCarthy, "and they can be thankful that we did not. The United States is at war, and the people who attend and applaud anti-American utterances are not good Americans. I have informed this Goldman woman that we will not permit her to organize such meetings. If she does she will be arrested if I have to do it myself. This goes for all of her kind, too."[38]

McCarthy did not wait for Goldman to organize another meeting. On June 15, he led a raiding party of two dozen men on anarchist headquarters in uptown Manhattan. Refusing to produce a search warrant, McCarthy and his agents confiscated a "wagon load of anarchist records and propaganda," including an extensive card file and the ten-thousand-name subscription lists of *Mother Earth* and another anarchist publication, *The Blast.* They arrested Goldman and her colleague Alexander Berkman—according to *The New York Times*, "the two most notorious anarchists in the United States"—who had for weeks "been conducting a campaign against all the aspirations and activities of this Government," during which time they had "almost preached sedition."[39]*

Within weeks, the two anarchists were convicted, and each was sentenced to two years and a $10,000 fine. "It took a world war to put Goldman and Berkman where they should have been years ago," crowed *The Wall Street Journal.*[40]

Meanwhile, the Espionage Act had been making its way through Congress. Title I, section 4 of the original bill gave the president the power during wartime to prohibit the publishing of "any information relating to the national defense which, in his judgment, is of such character that it is or might be useful to the enemy."[41] Despite the qualifier that this provision did not "limit or restrict any discussion, comment, or criticism of the acts or policies of the Government or its representatives," a furor ensued as Congress and the press correctly interpreted this section of the bill to be a thinly disguised attempt to gag the press. Alarm bells went off everywhere.

The American Newspaper Publishers Association sent a letter to Vice President Thomas R. Marshall requesting that the provision be eliminated, claiming that it "strikes at the fundamental rights of the people, not only assailing their freedom of speech, but also seeking to deprive them of the means of forming intelligent opinion . . . The censorship proposed is believed to be a violation of the Constitution of the

---

*Berkman had previously served a fourteen-year sentence for the attempted assassination of the Homestead Steel manager Henry C. Frick, whom Berkman held responsible for Pinkerton detectives' having fired upon striking workers at the Homestead plant in 1892. After his release from prison, Berkman renounced violence.

United States, which prohibits Congress from abridging the freedom of speech or of the press . . . In war especially the press should be free, vigilant, and unfettered."[42]

Papers across the country reacted strongly. The *Los Angeles Times* accused the administration of "establishing a Caesarism, a Kaiserism, at home in the very era in which it is seeking to dispossess a Caesarism abroad," while *The New York Times* said, "Let the attempt to suppress freedom of speech, in whatever guise it appears, be defeated unanimously."[43]*

Despite Wilson's insistence that it was "imperative that powers of this sort should be granted," anti-press-censorship sentiment prevailed, and the provision was struck from the legislation.[44]

Another troubling stipulation of the bill provided that any publication in violation of "any of the provisions of this act" or "of a treasonable or anarchistic character" could be banned from the mail by the postmaster general. Calling the provision "a menace to all," Representative Meyer London of New York, the only Socialist in Congress, condemned its inherent potential for stifling dissent.[45] Senator Charles S. Thomas of Colorado agreed, labeling it "a far greater evil than the evil which is sought to be prevented."[46]

Representative Dick T. Morgan of Oklahoma, on the other hand, argued that "in time of war, in time of danger, in time of great national peril, it is necessary sometimes that individual citizens shall be willing to surrender some of the privileges which they have for the sake of the greater good." He also expressed the opinion—which would be proved many times over to be mistaken—that "a man who is a true and loyal citizen, whose intentions toward this Nation are right and proper, need not fear that he will be convicted and sent to prison unjustly and unfairly."[47] (In fact, not one spy or saboteur would be convicted under the Espionage Act during World War I—the law would instead be directed against individuals who opposed the war on the basis of philosophical, political, or religious beliefs.)

Noting that the mailability provision gave broadly repressive powers to the postmaster general, London argued fervently against it:

*Six days later, the same *New York Times* would thunder against Emma Goldman's right to speak out against the draft.

There is nothing more oppressive in the world than a democracy gone mad, than a democracy which has surrendered its rights to an individual . . .

I want to lift my voice on behalf of free speech and the free word, both written and spoken. If there are any treasonable thoughts in the minds of the American people, I want them expressed; if there is any discontent with the war, I want to hear it. Is it or is it not treasonable to plead for international peace? . . . to demand a revocation of the war resolution? . . . to oppose the sending of an army abroad? . . .

I heard some people here attack certain utterances as treasonable which were nothing more than a protest against the war . . .

Let men speak freely. Do not drive them into the cellar of conspiracy. Do not turn people into hypocrites and cowards. Let us not, while we talk of fighting for liberty abroad, sacrifice and crush our liberties here.

. . . I am entirely willing to vote for every measure that will guard the military and naval secrets of the country. Further than that I will not yield. I will not surrender any of the liberties of the humblest citizen of the United States.[48]

London's impassioned plea may have had an effect, for the bill's final version removed the phrase "treasonable or anarchistic character" and substituted "any matter advocating or urging treason, insurrection, or forcible resistance to any law of the United States."[49] It was a Pyrrhic victory, however, as every fear that London and others expressed would soon be realized.

In the Senate, William Borah was one of only six to vote against the Espionage Act. In a letter to a friend, he wrote that "a more autocratic, more Prussian measure could not be found in Germany. It has all the ear marks of a dictatorship. It suppresses free speech and does it all in the name of war and patriotism."[50]

On June 15, the same day that Emma Goldman and Alexander Berkman were arrested in New York, the Espionage Act became law. In addition to the powers granted the postmaster general, the statute made it illegal during wartime for any person to make any statement intended to interfere with military or naval operations, including recruitment and enlistment. The punishment for violating the act was up to ten years in prison and/or up to a $10,000 fine. The passage of the Espionage Act was a crucial step in the marginalization of dissident minorities, narrowing the avenues of opposition and making protest against the war increasingly dangerous.

CHAPTER 3

The Heel of the Government

On April 7, the day after Congress declared war, 176 representatives of the Socialist Party of America had assembled at an emergency convention in St. Louis. At the time, Socialists were a significant minority force in American politics, particularly at the state and local levels. Party membership had peaked at nearly 120,000 in 1912, the year Eugene V. Debs received 900,000 votes—6 percent of the total cast—for president of the United States. By 1917, membership had declined to about 80,000, but Socialists still held many offices, and the Socialist Party publication *Appeal to Reason* enjoyed a weekly circulation of over half a million.

With their view of the war in Europe as a capitalist plot, Socialists had played a prominent role in the anti-preparedness movement. In March 1917, with war looking ever more likely, the party called the St. Louis meeting to decide the question of what stance it would take in the event that the United States became involved in the conflict—a fait accompli by the time the convention opened.

The position adopted by the delegates caused many prominent Socialists to resign from the party, but it was nevertheless approved by the national membership. It stated, in part, "Modern wars as a rule have been caused by the commercial and financial rivalry and intrigues of the capitalist interests in the different countries . . . War brings wealth and power to the ruling classes and suffering, death, and demoralization to the workers . . . We, therefore, call upon the workers of all countries to refuse to support their governments in their wars. The wars of the contending national groups of capitalists are not the concern of the workers." The statement further asserted: "The American people did not and do not want this war. They have not been consulted about the war and have had no part in declaring war. They have been plunged into this war by the trickery and treachery of the ruling class of this country through its representatives in the national administration and National Congress, its demagogic agitators, its subsidized press, and other servile instruments of public expression." In conclusion, the delegates vowed to maintain "continuous, active, and public opposition to the war."[1]

They might just as well have painted targets on their backs. When the Espionage Act went into effect, the Socialists were fish in a barrel, and the government wasted no time in starting to pick them off. Leading the target practice was Postmaster General A. S. Burleson.

A Texas native, Burleson was a small-minded autocrat with what one biographer described as "a calculated pomposity that provoked Woodrow Wilson to call him 'the Cardinal.' "[2] In the course of his tenure as postmaster general, Burleson saw to it that white and black postal workers were segregated, and throughout the South he routinely demoted and fired large numbers of African-Americans.

In applying the non-mailability provision of the Espionage Act, he would make a mockery of Wilson's assurances that no part of the law would "be used as a shield against criticism" or to deny people "their indisputable right to criticize their own public officials."[3] Burleson's heavy-handed tactics in banning from the mail virtually all publications critical of the war and the administration would lead Upton Sinclair to write, in a letter to Wilson, "Your Postmaster-General reveals himself a person of such pitiful and childish ignorance . . . it is simply a calamity that in this crisis he should be the person to decide what may or may not be uttered by our radical press . . . It is hard to draw the line, Mr. President, as to the amount of ignorance permitted to a government official; but Mr. Burleson is assuredly on the wrong side of any line that could be drawn by anyone."[4]

As soon as the Espionage Act became law, the postmaster general rolled up his sleeves and got down to serious business. The day after Wilson signed the new legislation, Burleson sent a secret directive to local postmasters across the country, instructing them to "keep a close watch on unsealed matters, newspapers, etc.," looking for anything "calculated to . . . cause insubordination, disloyalty, mutiny, or refusal of duty in the military or naval service, or to obstruct the recruiting, draft or enlistment services . . . or otherwise embarrass or hamper the Government in conducting the war."[5] Local postmasters were instructed to forward any suspect material to Washington. By including material that might "embarrass" the government, Burleson clearly exceeded his authority, imputing to the Espionage Act stipulations that its language nowhere expressed or even implied.

On July 6, Burleson banned Chicago's *American Socialist* from the mail for advertising a leaflet called "The Price We Pay," which the newspaper had published as an article two months earlier. The piece claimed that America's entry into the war "was determined by the certainty that if the allies do not win, J. P. Morgan's loans to the allies will be repudiated, and those American investors who bit on his promises would be hooked."[6]

By the following week, a dozen more Socialist publications had been denied mailing, including Chicago's *International Socialist Review*, Detroit's *Michigan Socialist*, St. Louis's *Social Revolution* and *St. Louis Labor*, Philadelphia's *People's Press*, Cleveland's *Socialist News*, New York's *Four Lights*, and Girard, Kansas's *Appeal to Reason*. Yet Burleson would steadfastly maintain that he was not targeting Socialist publications, disingenuously asserting that a publication was non-mailable only if it contained "treasonable or seditious matter," then adding, "The trouble is most socialist papers do contain this matter."[7]

Burleson also went after Max Eastman's monthly, *The Masses*, an attractive and dynamic journal in both its style and its content, with a distinguished list of contributors that included luminaries like Sherwood Anderson, Elizabeth Gurley Flynn, John Reed, Bertrand Russell, Carl Sandburg, Louis Untermeyer, and Mary Heaton Vorse. As one admirer saw it, *The Masses* was an elegant publication, "with bright-colored covers and oversize pages filled with bold drawings and lively satire, political criticism and intellectual commentary."[8] Another referred to it as a repository of "almost everything . . . alive and irreverent in American culture."[9]

The government viewed *The Masses* quite differently. The attorney general's report described it as "not an official Socialist paper," although "the group of men editing it may be said to belong to the literary, as distinguished from the political, type of Socialist agitators." The magazine's content was characterized as "glorifying those who objected to war and resisted military service, and picturing the war as a base conspiracy of the capitalists, and all who participate in the war as nothing better than abject victims of this conspiracy."[10]

In the June 1917 issue, Eastman had written of America's involvement in the European conflict, "It is not a war for democracy. It did not originate in a dispute about democracy, and it is unlikely to terminate in a democratic settlement. . . . [M]en have already been sent to jail since April 6th upon the theory that it is treason to tell an unpleasant truth about one's country." The article also advised readers of *The Masses* to resist the "war-fever and the patriotic delirium" and save their strength for the "struggle of human liberty against oppression."

The August issue of *The Masses* contained a number of cartoons and articles critical of the war and the draft, as well as a poem praising Emma Goldman and Alexander Berkman. Burleson declared it nonmailable, and when Eastman repeatedly asked post office officials to identify those passages that were causing the publication to be banned, they refused, citing simply the "general tenor" of the issue.[11] "I spent the whole winter," Eastman told an emergency meeting of publishers in New York, "trying to think up the worst possible consequences of our going to war . . . but I never succeeded in thinking up anything half so bad as this."[12]

On July 12, Eastman, Amos Pinchot, and John Reed wrote to Wilson, listing a dozen publications that had been effectively suppressed and asking him whether he thought that "free criticism, right or wrong, of the policy of the government ought to be denied at this time . . . Is it not of the utmost importance in a democracy that the opposition to the government have a free voice? Can it be necessary, even in war time, for the majority of a republic to throttle the voice of a sincere minority?"[13]

Forwarding the letter to Burleson, Wilson sought the postmaster general's advice. "These are very sincere men," the president wrote, "and I should like to please them."[14] Burleson's answer was that the listed publications had not been suppressed; rather, particular issues of them had simply not been approved for mailing. He further assured the president that the post office had no intention of stifling criticism of the government.

Eastman sought a restraining order against the mailing ban, and in a courageously independent decision Judge Learned Hand of the Southern District of New York granted a temporary injunction, thereby declining to make the Espionage Act a vehicle for suppression of all dissent against the war.[15]

The same day Hand signed the injunction, however, Burleson

appealed to a circuit court judge in Vermont, who, using a rare and long-discarded practice, issued an order staying Hand's order until a hearing on Burleson's appeal could be held. As Eastman later wrote, the judge "decided to hold up our August issue until its value was lost in order to find out whether it should be held up or not."[16]

Then, adding insult to injury, Burleson rescinded the publication's second-class mailing status on the grounds that because it had missed mailing one issue, it was no longer a periodical. As Upton Sinclair protested to Wilson, this Kafkaesque decree was "as if a policeman were to knock a man down, and then, because he cried out in pain, arrest him for making a public disturbance."[17] Nevertheless, it was a tactic that Burleson employed against all the banned publications.

In the course of Burleson's assault on the dissident press, Wilson made only the feeblest attempts to control him. Wilson's biographer Ray Stannard Baker recounts an exchange in which the president told the postmaster general, "Now Burleson, these are well-intentioned people. Let them blow off steam."[18]

According to Baker, Burleson replied, "I am willing to let them blow off steam, providing they don't violate the Espionage Act. If you don't want the Espionage Act enforced I can resign."

"Well, go ahead and do your duty," Wilson acquiesced.

On another occasion, Wilson urged Burleson to "act with the utmost caution and liberality in all our censorship," and in one case he advised the postmaster general that "there is a margin of judgment here and I think that doubt ought always to be resolved in favor of the utmost freedom of speech."[19]

Burleson brushed off all of these directives, and Wilson rolled over, never pursuing the issue to any meaningful degree. "I am willing to trust your judgment after I have once called your attention to a sugges-tion," he told the postmaster general, essentially giving him free rein.[20] In public, he defended Burleson's actions as "very just and concilia-tory," telling those who expressed concerns that they had misinter-preted the postmaster general's intent.[21]*

When the circuit court of appeals reversed Judge Hand's ruling in

---

*Whatever Wilson's reservations or misgivings may have been about Burleson's assault on the dissident press, the campaign extended executive branch power, which was a priority item on Wilson's own agenda and therefore almost certainly not dis-agreeable to him.

the *Masses* case in early November, it delivered a devastating blow for repression. Emboldened by the decision, Burleson stepped up his campaign against left-wing publications. The aftermath of the decision against *The Masses* ravaged not only the Socialist press but the Socialist movement nationwide, particularly in rural areas, where subscribers were dependent on their newspapers for information and thus lost the drift of the mainstream Socialist current.

The more militant Industrial Workers of the World suffered even rougher treatment than the Socialists, from whose bosom they had sprung a dozen years earlier. The Socialist movement at least had some leaders who were looked upon by the ruling class as respectable. Principals like Allan Benson, Charles Edward Russell, Upton Sinclair, John Spargo, and Rose Pastor Stokes had been quick to endorse the war and repudiate the April 7 St. Louis declaration. The Wobblies, on the other hand, hardly retained a claim on respectability in 1917.

With an ideology that the IWW historian Melvyn Dubofsky called "a peculiar amalgam of Marxism and Darwinism, anarchism and syndicalism—all overlaid with a singularly American patina," the Wobblies were situated on the extreme left wing of the labor movement.[22] Formed in 1905 in Chicago, at a convention that included many prominent Socialists, anarchists, and radical trade unionists, the IWW was founded as a reaction against Samuel Gompers's American Federation of Labor, after the latter group repudiated socialism and aligned itself with capital. As the only labor group to organize migrant workers, the Wobblies attracted many immigrants but also counted many U.S. citizens as members.

The IWW gained worldwide attention in 1914–15, when the Wobbly organizer Joe Hill was convicted, upon the flimsiest of evidence, of a Utah murder and subsequently executed, despite the blatant holes in the prosecution's case and an outpouring of support from around the globe.

While the IWW supported the AFL's fight for an eight-hour day and higher wages, the Wobblies' long-term goal was to take over industry and abolish the wage system altogether. Whereas the mainstream union movement was committed to working with employers in order to secure better pay and working conditions, the preamble to the

IWW charter bluntly stated, "The working class and the employing class have nothing in common . . . It is the historic mission of the working class to do away with capitalism."[23] The IWW slogans "One Big Union" and "An Injury to One Is an Injury to All" were a repudiation of traditional trade unionism in favor of a worldwide syndicalist affiliation of workers, "with an uncompromising attitude of hostility toward organized capital."[24] It was this animosity to the employing class and the expressed intent to take over industry that so alarmed business interests and eventually led to the government crackdown on the IWW.

Focusing on the bottom rung of the labor force—the unskilled and the migrant workers whom organized labor ignored—the Wobblies were considered an unadulterated threat to the American way of life. This was hardly surprising, given published statements like, "Of all the idiotic and perverted ideas accepted by the workers . . . patriotism is the worst,"[25] and pronouncements from the IWW leader William D. "Big Bill" Haywood like, "It is better to be a traitor to your country than to your class."[26]

Though membership would never reach beyond 100,000, the union's strident militancy alarmed big business from the outset, and the federal government, in its alliance with capital, had been gunning for the Wobblies since early 1912, when the union's growing strength and influence were amply demonstrated by its management of the successful Lawrence, Massachusetts, textile strike.

In September 1912, the Republican National Committee proposed "vigorous action" against the Wobblies in California as a way of delivering the state to President William Howard Taft in the upcoming presidential election. The RNC argued, "Regardless of the political aspect of the situation . . . the Government should use all its power . . . to stamp out the revolutionary methods of this anarchistic organization."[27]

At the same time, a group of five hundred powerful Southern California Republicans sent a delegate to Taft with documents that supposedly showed a conspiracy of ten thousand anarchists and Wobblies, headed by Emma Goldman, poised "to introduce a new form of government, or non-government," in California. Taft agreed that California was a hotbed of subversion and recommended to Attorney General George W. Wickersham, "We ought to take decided action . . . [I]t is our business to go in and show the strong hand of the government."[28]

After an investigation of the evidence, however, the attorney general's office found no cause to move against the Wobblies.

By 1913, it had become clear that the Wobblies, with their belief in direct action—strikes, propaganda, boycotts—stood in opposition to the Socialist program of political action, and when Big Bill Haywood was removed from the Socialist Party's National Executive Committee in 1913, the two organizations went their separate ways. Over the next several years, the union continued to make gains in the wheat fields of the Midwest, the mines of the Southwest, and the timber industry of the Northwest, even as it attracted further scrutiny.

When war fever gripped the country, the Wobblies took an intractable stance against American involvement. "Let the capitalists fight wars for their interests!" proclaimed an editorial in Seattle's *Industrial Worker*. "The working-class are fighting for theirs, and arrayed against us, we find the very interests that are now asking us to fight for them. Capitalists of America, we will fight against you, not for you!"[29] Many IWW leaders viewed American involvement as an opportunity to make inroads against the bosses. "Why should we, on our part, sacrifice working class interests, for the sake of a few noisy and impotent parades or antiwar demonstrations?" wrote one prominent Wobbly in February. "Let us rather get on the job of organizing the working class to take over the industries, war or no war, and stop all future capitalist aggression that leads to war and other forms of barbarism."[30]

Such talk unnerved the big-business community. In a confidential May 1917 report to the Council of National Defense, James A. B. Scherer, president of the college that would later become the California Institute of Technology, stated that the IWW "recognizes no law, no obligations, no ethical control . . . It should be exterminated as we would exterminate a nest of vermin—swiftly, secretly, and completely, since otherwise it will more and more infest the body politic and ultimately reach the very heart of government."[31]

By the summer of 1917, the IWW had become, according to the National Civil Liberties Bureau, "the most bitterly attacked and most deliberately misrepresented of all labor organizations."[32] In little more than a decade of existence, the Wobblies had been assigned a place among the most feared and despised bogeymen in America. As the investigative reporter Robert W. Bruère wrote in his 1918 chronicle, *Following the Trail of the I.W.W.*, "Very few people had any accurate knowledge of the tenets or tactics of the I.W.W. The three letters had come to stand in the popular mind as a symbol of something bordering on black magic; they were repeated over and over again by the press . . . and were always accompanied with suggestions of impending violence."[33] In no small part because of the revolutionary rhetoric of their publications, the Wobblies had acquired an undeserved reputation as property-destroying anarchists, "cut-throat, pro-German . . . desperadoes who burn harvest-fields, drive iron spikes into fine timber and ruin the mill-saws, devise bomb plots, who obstructed the war and sabotaged the manufacture of munitions—veritable supermen, with a superhuman power for evil, omnipresent and almost omnipotent."[34]

In addition to their own published statements, another dynamic contributed to the unfair demonization of the IWW. All too often, the more radical of the Wobblies—that is, those advocating violent measures—turned out to be company or government infiltrators who were trying to incite some form of illegal activity. In an August 20, 1917, letter to Attorney General Thomas Gregory, the U.S. attorney for Massachusetts attributed "a good share of the virulent socialism and IWW-ism to private detective agencies . . . These agencies are the meanest, lowest, parasitic pests now present in the community." He went on to explain that the agencies would place one of their men in a factory job, making it impossible to tell whether the radicalism of any given labor group was genuine or "one of these pseudo, artificial creations of the trouble-making detective agency."[35]

With business interests exerting increasing pressure on the government to shut the Wobblies down, U.S. involvement in World War I provided the government with a golden opportunity. In early summer, IWW-instigated strikes broke out both in the copper mines of Arizona and Montana and in the forests of Washington and Idaho.

The mining and timber industries were both vital to the war effort, and the strikers were viewed by many as putting their own interests above those of the nation. In reaction, a wave of hysteria swept through the press as newspapers throughout the country condemned a supposed nationwide IWW conspiracy to hamper essential war production. In fact, as opposed as the Wobblies were to the war, there was no evidence to indicate any coordinated national effort on their part—of the 521 labor disputes that occurred between April and October

1917, the IWW was involved in only the aforementioned locales—much less in any plot to interfere with the war effort.[36] The strikes, as later investigations would clearly show, were about higher wages, shorter hours, overtime pay, union recognition, better working conditions, and in the case of the northwestern lumberjacks—whose camps were unimaginably squalid—better living conditions.

The mining strikes started in Butte, Montana. The immediate cause was a fire in the North Butte Mining Company's Speculator mine that killed 164 miners on June 8. Three days later, between ten thousand and twelve thousand miners walked out. Mine owners refused to negotiate their demands for a six-hour day, a $6 daily wage, better working conditions, union recognition, and an end to the practice of "rustling cards," a de facto system of blackballing used by the owners to weed out potential "troublemakers," that is, union members and political undesirables.

In assessing the Montana mining troubles, Wade R. Parks, a Montana county attorney, suggested that the underlying problem was the owners' intransigence. He told Gregory, "I think that if the employing class of the West would meet the I.W.W.'s and other . . . employees of theirs half way on a common ground that there would be no general discontent."[37] But in the opinion of John D. Ryan, chairman of the Council of National Defense's Cooperative Committee on Copper (a negotiating group for management) and an official of Anaconda, the nation's largest mining company, the trouble stemmed not from depressed wages, extended hours, or inhumane working conditions but from the sinister motives of Wobblies and German agents.

The strike quickly spread to Arizona, whose four mining districts produced 28 percent of the nation's copper. By the first week of July, twenty-five thousand men were off the job, effectively shutting down the state's copper mines. The owners were obdurate. "Wrapping themselves in the American flag," as the IWW historian Dubofsky has written, "the employers declared total war in defense of the status quo."[38]

Predictably, the press took the side of the owners and attacked the Wobblies. "Break the I.W.W. Now," demanded a headline in *The Independent*. The *Wall Street Journal* likened the Wobblies to venomous snakes, saying, "Copperheads . . . are in the copper mines and lumber camps and threaten to invade other fields. Instead of waiting to see if their bite is poisonous, the heel of the Government should stamp them at once." *The New York Times* was convinced that "if the whole gang could be deported from the United States, the United States would be greatly improved."[39]

Without a shred of evidence, the IWW was widely accused of being in the service of the kaiser and being backed by German money. Senator Charles Thomas of Colorado charged that "a conspiracy directed by German agents to work through the Industrial Workers of the World is crippling . . . industries in the West."[40] Bill Haywood angrily denied such rumors, stating, "I want to deny emphatically that German money, German influence, or war-time motives are behind the Western copper strikes . . . It is not German influence, but simply an effort to get living wages and just working conditions for our miners that is behind the strikes."[41]

While the copper strikes were in full swing, workers in the timber industry of Washington and Idaho were also walking out, shutting down 75 percent of the industry, in what has been called "the most spectacular and widespread lumber strike ever to occur in the United States."[42] Again, with no real evidence, employers and the press made wild and hysterical accusations of violence on the part of Wobblies, as mine owners and lumbermen alike demanded that the federal government send in troops to quell the work stoppages.

Many contemporary reports by government agents, however, mentioned the peaceful nature of the strikes. A War Department observer reported "no violence or disorder" in the Bisbee, Arizona, copper strike;[43] and in reference to the Butte situation, the U.S. attorney and future senator Burton K. Wheeler told Gregory, "The strike is being conducted . . . in a manner heretofore unheard of in mining regions. No violence or disorder is observed or been reported."[44] A Justice Department report found no "disorder or disturbance or undue activity whatsoever on the part of the I.W.W." in Missoula.[45]

Frightened by exaggerated reports in the press, local citizens in many communities beset with labor unrest decided to take matters into their own hands. In Jerome, Arizona, mine owners and other businessmen formed the Jerome Loyalty League and had sixty-seven Wobblies rounded up on July 10. They were loaded into cattle cars and shipped into California, where they were met at the border by armed citizens, who forced the cattle cars back across the state line. The following day, most of the men were apprehended by Home Guards in Kingman, Arizona, and released after promising to leave the area.

The tactic spread. On July 12, police in Lincoln, Nebraska, met a freight train with fifty Wobblies fresh from the Kansas harvest fields and prevented them from getting off the train. The same day, in nearby Fairbury, thirty Wobblies were put on a freight train and banished from the town.

Nothing, however, compared to the roundup that took place in Bisbee, where the IWW-affiliated Metal Mine Workers' Industrial Union had been conducting a peaceful strike since June 27. At the beginning of the strike, the former Rough Rider and Cochise County sheriff Harry Wheeler telegraphed Arizona's governor, Thomas Campbell, to say, "The I.W.W. strike here is most serious and I anticipate great property loss and bloodshed. Majority strikers seem foreign. The whole thing appears pro-German and anti-American. I earnestly request you use your influence to have United States troops sent here to take charge of the situation."[46] Campbell, in turn, requested federal troops, and the secretary of war sent a high-ranking Army officer to investigate. On June 30 and July 2, the officer reported that there was no need or reason to send soldiers, an assessment that was confirmed by others.

Frustrated by the government's response, the Citizens' Protective League, made up of businessmen, and the Workmen's Loyalty League, composed of non-striking miners, met in secret on the night of July 11 and planned a mass deportation to be carried out under Wheeler's direction.* They agreed to censor interstate telephone and telegraph lines in order to prevent news of the deportation from getting out and intentionally neglected to inform their own legal advisers, the Arizona U.S. attorney, or other state and county law officers of their plan.

At dawn on July 12, Wheeler and his deputies, armed with rifles, revolvers, and clubs and wearing white armbands to distinguish them from their victims, began their Wobbly hunt. By 6:30 a.m., the posse had collected about twelve hundred people in Bisbee and nearby Lowell. Along with Wobblies, the sweep had netted IWW sympathizers—including three women—and anyone who could not adequately explain his reasons for being in Bisbee. Among those snared were businessmen, property owners, and Liberty Bond subscribers. One mem-

---

*According to a presidential commission that later investigated the Bisbee deportations, the rationalization for the expulsions was that the strikers were contemplating violence, but in reality, the commission found, this pretext had "no justification" (*Report on the Bisbee Deportations*, p. 5).

ber of the Citizens' Protective League and one miner were killed during the roundup.

According to one detainee's account, his group was herded by men in an automobile, who trained a machine gun on their captives. The prisoners were marched to a baseball field, where they were held under the broiling desert sun for several hours, then moved at bayonet point and gunpoint onto a freight train of about two dozen cattle cars and boxcars provided by the El Paso and Southwestern Railroad. A little after noon, the train pulled out, bound for Columbus, New Mexico, with scant provisions of bread, crackers, and water. There were armed guards on top of each car, and the train was shadowed for miles by gunmen in automobiles.

At Columbus, the townspeople refused to let the train discharge its passengers, so it returned to the small town of Hermanas, where they were unceremoniously dropped off and left to fend for themselves. After two days without food, the refugees were escorted by soldiers to an Army camp in Columbus; there the government provided for them for two months, until the middle of September.

The Arizona State Federation of Labor demanded that President Wilson take immediate action in returning the miners to their homes, asking, "Are we to assume that Phelps Dodge interests are superior to the principles of democracy?" Wilson took umbrage at the implication, considering it "unjust and offensive."[47] Rather than condemning the vigilante deportations in a tough and decisive manner, Wilson wired his tepid displeasure to Governor Campbell. "May I not respectfully urge the great danger of citizens taking the law into their own hands, as your report indicates their having done," wrote the president. "I look upon such action with grave apprehension. A very serious responsibility is assumed when such precedents are set."[48]

Unruffled by the president's criticism, Sheriff Wheeler defiantly told the attorney general of Arizona that if he and his posse were "guilty of taking the law into our own hands, I can only cite to you the Universal Law that necessity makes . . . I would repeat the operation any time I find my own people endangered by a mob composed of eighty percent aliens and enemies of the Government."[49] Not even the presence of federal troops, sent in to maintain order after the deportations, could intimidate Wheeler, as he maintained a vigilante government in Bisbee for the next three months, in flagrant defiance of the law.

The mainstream press roundly praised Wheeler's actions in the deportations. Although, said *The New York Times*, "a Sheriff who makes his own law is on dangerous and indefensible ground . . . [t]he Sheriff of Bisbee was on the right track." The *Los Angeles Times* stated that "the citizens of Cochise county, Arizona, have written a lesson that the whole of America would do well to copy. In these days America cannot afford to trifle with rioters . . . If there ever was a case where the doubtful expedient of taking the law into the hands of those not lawfully authorized to execute it, this is one."[50]

Wheeler had contended, and in this he was undoubtedly acting as the mouthpiece of the mine owners: "This is no labor trouble. We are sure of that; but it is a direct attempt to embarrass the government of the United States."[51] However, the future Supreme Court justice Felix Frankfurter, who served as legal counsel to the presidential commission on Bisbee, told Congress that there was a "total want of justification on the part of those who participated in the deportations . . . It is easy to disregard economic abuses, to insist on the exercise of autocratic power by raising the false cry of 'disloyalty.' "[52]

The deportations were clearly nothing more than a strikebreaking tactic, cloaked in the disguise of patriotic fervor and tacitly sanctioned by the state. Despite the known identity of the perpetrators, and the commission's finding that "the deportation was wholly illegal and without authority in law, either State or Federal," nobody was ever punished for the outrage.[53]

As the government looked the other way, depredations against Wobblies continued, the most grievous being the murder of Frank Little by a masked and armed vigilante mob in Butte during the early morning hours of August 1. Small, frail, blind in one eye, and walking on crutches as a result of an earlier beating, Little, a thirty-eight-year-old half Cherokee, was a member of the IWW's General Executive Board and a widely traveled organizer whose radical speeches had gained him a fair degree of notoriety.

He arrived in Butte on July 19, direct from the Arizona strikes, and immediately earned the enmity of mine owners, the local press, law-enforcement officials, and the Pinkerton detectives who had been called in to break the strike. After delivering at least two inflammatory talks to thousands of strikers, Little was abducted from his rooming house in the middle of the night, clad only in his underwear. He was tied to the rear bumper of a car and dragged to a railroad bridge outside town, where he was beaten and tortured, then hanged to death from the trestle. The murderers left a note pinned to his underwear that said, "Others Take Notice. First and Last Warning."[54]

Frank Little's murder was never solved. In its aftermath, federal troops were sent to Butte, as cries now went up demanding that the government squash the IWW. "The Federal authorities should make short work of these treasonable conspirators against the United States," said an August 4 *New York Times* editorial. *The Independent* wrote, "It is time for the American public to take them in hand, put them behind the bars and break their organization."[55]

President Wilson apparently agreed and appointed the District of Columbia federal judge J. Harry Covington to investigate the IWW with a view toward prosecution. Bill Haywood immediately invited Covington to Wobbly headquarters in Chicago to examine the union's books and papers, offering him "all the assistance possible in the inquiry."[56] Covington ignored the offer, for there was a bigger plan in the works. "Under the direction of the Attorney General something quite effective is under way with respect to the I.W.W. situation," Assistant Attorney General William C. Fitts told Senator Albert Fall of New Mexico. "I do not think you or any of your western friends will be disappointed if the results which we hope to obtain are achieved."[57]

It had been a devastating summer for minority voices. Writing about the events of July 1917—which included the trial of Emma Goldman and Alexander Berkman, the shuttering of the Socialist press, and the Bisbee deportations—John Reed said, "In America the month just past has been the blackest month for freemen our generation has known. With a sort of hideous apathy the country has acquiesced in a regime of judicial tyranny, bureaucratic suppression and industrial barbarism."[58]

But the event of July 1917 that would have the most serious long-term consequences was one that Reed had no way of knowing about. On the twenty-sixth day of the month, a young law-school graduate and lifelong District of Columbia resident named John Edgar Hoover went to work for the Department of Justice. Hoover, who had been employed as a cataloger at the Library of Congress, was an ambitious and gifted bureaucrat with an innately conservative nature and a decided penchant for power. Within a year and a half, he would make his presence felt in the Justice Department, and over the next half century he would become the most adroit expert in the practices of secret government and surveillance of citizens that the United States has ever known.

CHAPTER 4

A Peculiar Sort of Mental Hysteria

By mid-August 1917, it was all-out war on the IWW. In contravention of the Posse Comitatus Act of 1878, which restricted the use of the Army for law enforcement, the War Department sent federal troops to occupy the mining towns of Arizona and Montana, as well as the timber regions of the Pacific Northwest, where lumber industry production continued to be seriously curtailed by union activity. Working with local businessmen, soldiers broke up IWW picket lines and demonstrations, established unauthorized martial law, conducted illegal searches and seizures, and arrested Wobblies, 90 percent of whom were U.S. citizens. In Seattle, federal, state, and city officials teamed with Army officers to circumvent the problem of habeas corpus: by having the military commander take charge of any detainees being held on shaky legal grounds, they were able to ignore any habeas corpus petitions for those individuals. In commenting on this arrangement, the U.S. attorney for Seattle conceded that "the troop commanders [may] have been urged to extend their authority beyond what was intended, but the plan meets with public approval."[1]

The Labor Department was also moving against the IWW. On July 21, the Idaho immigrant inspector W. J. McConnell wrote to Anthony Caminetti, the commissioner general of immigration (the Bureau of Immigration was part of the Labor Department), to ask whether alien Wobblies could be deported under the new Immigration Act that had taken effect on May 1.[2] In addition to imposing a literacy requirement on new immigrants over sixteen years of age, the law excluded various categories of undesirables, including the mentally retarded, the insane, alcoholics, paupers, vagrants, tuberculars, polygamists, and "anarchists, or persons who believe in or advocate the overthrow by force or violence of the Government of the United States."[3] Moreover, the statute stipulated that any alien who preached anarchy or the overthrow of the government could be taken into custody and deported. Perhaps the most insidious aspect of the law was its guilt-by-association provision, which provided that anybody in any way affiliated with an organization that believed in anarchism could be excluded from the United States.

After McConnell's letter, Caminetti—citing the old canard about the IWW's being under "German influence and possibly backed with German funds"—urged Assistant Secretary of Labor Louis F. Post to immediately undertake a vigorous campaign against alien leaders among the Wobblies.[4]

It was quickly recognized that while court proceedings against the Wobblies could be expensive, time-consuming, and of dubious outcome, deportation presented a quick and efficient solution to the IWW problem. The idea was to target a few select leaders and thereby produce a chilling effect on the union.

Labor Secretary William B. Wilson instructed Caminetti to obtain various IWW publications and determine if the plan suggested by McConnell was feasible. After reading an assortment of the organization's literature, Caminetti concluded that the Wobblies' willingness to "combat organized government, or the representatives thereof, is hinted at," and he endorsed McConnell's scheme to arrest and deport some of the leaders.[5]

While the War and Labor departments were carrying on their operations, the Justice Department opened a third front of attack against the IWW. On July 16, even before President Wilson authorized Judge Covington's investigation of the union, Attorney General Gregory had instructed all U.S. attorneys to undertake "an extraordinary effort . . . to ascertain the future plans of all Wobblies, as well as the names, descriptions, and history of the IWW's leaders, the sources of its income, the nature of its expenses, copies of all IWW publications, and any data that might possibly incriminate the Wobblies."[6] Gregory also suggested that any Wobblies who were German aliens and had violated the Espionage Act should be apprehended so that warrants for their detention could be prepared.

If the investigations turned up nothing, it was only because the Wobblies were guilty of nothing—at least not in terms of their actions. Certainly, they had always preached "revolution, anti-militarism, and anti-patriotism," but their activities were within the framework of the law, despite the countless unproven allegations to the contrary.[7] So, when the investigations found nothing for which the IWW could be prosecuted, the Justice Department went to Plan B, the "something quite effective" that Assistant Attorney General Fitts alluded to in his letter to Senator Fall.[8] In late August, Gregory wrote to Wilson, "You know of the intended action I have in mind with respect to the I.W.W."[9]

On August 19, in a precursor of what was soon to follow, troops raided IWW headquarters in Spokane, Washington, and arrested twenty-seven union members, all of whom were subsequently interned. The major assault, planned and carried out with military precision, came on September 5, when federal agents made simultaneous raids in thirty-three cities, hitting virtually every IWW office in the country, as well as a number of homes of IWW officers. Although "it was said that the move was not against the organization per se,"[10] the real reason for the raids was known full well, as Francis F. Kane, U.S. attorney for Philadelphia, revealed in a letter to Gregory when he wrote, "our purpose being, as I understand it, very largely to put the I.W.W. out of business."[11]

In Chicago, eight different locations were raided, including the national headquarters of the Socialist Party, the offices of two German-language newspapers, and the residences of several IWW leaders. Among the many items agents confiscated at the home of Ralph Chaplin, editor of the IWW newspaper *Solidarity*, were three bundles of love letters Chaplin had written to his wife years earlier. The eight Chicago raids alone yielded more than five tons of correspondence, records, books, pamphlets, equipment, office supplies, furniture, and miscellany.

With and without search warrants, the raids continued throughout the rest of the month, as federal agents sought additional incriminating "evidence." They found plenty, all of it circumstantial. In IWW literature, they encountered revolutionary rhetoric; in IWW correspondence, they came across open discussions of industrial sabotage and firebombs; in official and personal documents, they located countless antigovernment and antiwar diatribes.

On the basis of this evidence discovered in the confiscated documents, a Chicago federal grand jury indicted 166 IWW leaders, including Bill Haywood and Ralph Chaplin, on charges ranging from interfering in numerous ways with the war effort, to conspiring to obstruct the Selective Service Act, to violating various provisions of the Espionage Act. That many of the offending passages cited as evidence were written before the war, and thus before the Selective Service and Espionage acts were law, was of no consequence.

Similar indictments soon followed in other cities, including Cleveland, Fresno, Omaha, Sacramento, San Francisco, and Wichita. It was the beginning of the end for the IWW.

The following month, Congress passed the Trading with the Enemy Act, which increased the censorship powers of the postmaster general by requiring that foreign-language newspapers submit, for Post Office Department approval, English translations of all articles pertaining to the government, the conduct of the war, or any of the belligerent nations.

The new law gave Postmaster General A. S. Burleson virtually absolute censorship powers.* On October 9, he served notice that "if newspapers go so far as to impugn the motives of the government and thus encourage insubordination, they will be dealt with severely." He went on to specify what would not be tolerated:

> Papers may not say that the Government is controlled by Wall Street or munition manufacturers, or any other special interests. Publications of any news calculated to urge the people to violate law would be considered grounds for drastic action. We will not tolerate campaigns against conscription, enlistments, sale of securities, or revenue collections. We will not permit the publication or circulation of anything hampering the war's prosecution or attacking improperly our allies.[12]

The Trading with the Enemy Act was aimed squarely at the German-language press. Given the limited resources of most of these

---

*Less than a week after the passage of the Trading with the Enemy Act, Wilson issued an executive order establishing the Board of Censorship, which was ruled over by Burleson, who used his new power to read the private correspondence of antiwar dissidents, as well as to collect information on what a Seattle censor referred to as "Bolsheviki, Industrial Workers of the World, Socialists, or other organizations whose aims are antagonistic to this government" (see James R. Mock, *Censorship 1917*, p. 130).

publications, the law was a de facto gag rule, forcing papers to either toe the government line or close down, which many did.

The attack on the ethnic German press was merely the latest in the continuing campaign against German-Americans and German-American culture. Across the country, the names of parks, streets, schools, and even whole towns were renamed to remove any hint of Germanic influence. East Germantown, Indiana, became Pershing; officials in Berlin, Iowa, renamed their town Lincoln; and in Nebraska, Germantown was changed to Garland in honor of a local soldier who died in combat. Sauerkraut became "liberty cabbage"; hamburger went by "liberty steak." German language courses were removed from school curricula, and in a number of cases teachers of German were summarily dismissed. The renowned violinist Fritz Kreisler was forced to retire from public appearances for the duration of the war, while the German-born Dr. Karl Muck, the conductor of the Boston Symphony Orchestra and a Swiss citizen, was interned. Thousands of German families living in restricted areas were required to relocate, and thousands of others were confined to their neighborhoods, as untold numbers lost their jobs as a result. German-Americans were further stigmatized on November 16, when President Wilson issued eight additional enemy alien regulations, including the required registration of all male German aliens over the age of fourteen.

Despite Gregory's instructions that arrests of aliens "should be exercised with great care, so that innocent and harmless alien enemies may not be disturbed," local authorities and citizen groups proceeded to make hundreds of unauthorized arrests, including many of non-enemy aliens, who were apprehended along with Germans.[13] After posting bond and finding a sponsor who was an American citizen, most German aliens were released on parole within a few weeks, but many were held in jail for months while their cases were decided. Those deemed too dangerous for release—a large percentage of whom were Socialists, Wobblies, and union organizers—were handed over to the War Department for internment, either at Fort Douglas, Utah, or Fort Oglethorpe, Georgia. Grounds for internment included "anti-American remarks, failure to purchase Liberty Bonds, membership in the I.W.W.,* possessing pacifist or anti-war literature, or even information given by an anonymous informer to local officials for the pur-

---

*In July 1917, Gregory ordered internment of all German aliens who were Wobblies.

pose of eliminating a rival."[14] Through the end of October 1917, at least 895 alien enemies had been arrested on presidential warrants and 295 interned; by the end of the war, there would be nearly 6,300 warranted arrests and about 2,300 internments, many of which were for minor infractions.[15] Ninety percent of those interned were labor leaders, leftists, IWW members, and anarchists. Countless thousands more were arrested without warrants.

The arrests and internments were carried on as secretly as possible. According to John Lord O'Brian, "Government operations should remain a mystery so the arrest of a few would have the greatest possible impact on the many."[16]

Another element of this approach was the confiscation of alien enemy property. The alien property custodian, A. Mitchell Palmer, who would shortly succeed Gregory as attorney general and lend his name to one of the most flagrant violations of civil liberties in U.S. history, took possession of the holdings of interned aliens, claiming that the government was "merely protecting and conserving the property of the allies of the enemy."[17]*

The number of enemy aliens rose dramatically when the United States declared war on Austria-Hungary on December 7. In the century preceding the war, close to four million Austro-Hungarians had immigrated to the United States, making them the fourth-largest ethnic group in the country, outnumbered only by Germans, Irish, and Italians. Concentrated in the industrial cities of the Northeast, two million Austro-Hungarian men were now in the same boat as German aliens.

The lines were becoming increasingly blurred when it came to the varieties of the "disloyal"—that is, those who opposed the war on any grounds, be they moral, political, cultural, or religious. Socialists, anarchists, Wobblies, pacifists, and Germans were all lumped together and reviled. In a caveat to all "traitors," Gregory issued a stern warning: "May God have mercy on them, for they need expect none from an outraged people and an avenging Government."[18]

---

*Later, in the midst of the postwar red scare hysteria that he played a major part in unleashing, Palmer would reveal a more honest and more accurate acknowledgment of the insidious implication of these seizures when he wrote, "No feature of the great war was so radical a departure from precedents . . . as the invasion of private rights and private property" ("Why We Seized German Property," *Forum*, Dec. 1919, p. 584).

Since the beginning of the war, pacifists had been denigrated as unpatriotic and lumped in the same category as "slackers," that is, draft dodgers. Physical assaults on pacifists were not uncommon. One of the most highly publicized was the kidnapping of the Reverend Herbert Bigelow, a prominent Cincinnati pacifist and Socialist who had nevertheless publicly declared his support for the war on many occasions. Bigelow was seized by a gang of men before a scheduled speech in Newport, Kentucky, directly across the Ohio River from Cincinnati; he was forced into a car and driven out of town, where a gang of two or three dozen men "wearing white masks and aprons or skirts of the same material" removed his coat and vest and bullwhipped him "in the name of the women and children of Belgium and France."[19] After the flogging, they cut off locks of his hair and poured crude oil over his head. Before they drove off, the leader warned him to leave Cincinnati within thirty-six hours and stay away for the remainder of the war. Bigelow was hospitalized for a week.

On July 2, 1917, the day after the Boston peace parade was broken up, a new organization was introduced, with one of its main functions being "the defense of men who refuse to fight on the ground that they are 'conscientious objectors.' "[20] The National Civil Liberties Bureau was an outgrowth of the American Union Against Militarism and the People's Council of America for Democracy and Peace, two staunch antiwar organizations.* Its formation was a watershed moment in U.S. history, as the NCLB would become the American Civil Liberties Union soon after the war.

Part of the need for defending conscientious objectors was that the Selective Service Act had granted CO status only to members of the traditional antiwar churches, such as the Quakers and Mennonites. Others who opposed the war on humanitarian, political, or ethnic grounds were left to try to convince skeptical draft boards of the sincerity of their beliefs. Even among those who received CO status, many were subjected to the harshest kind of treatment—because there was no official policy regarding alternate service before March 1918,

---

*On July 4, *The New York Times*, which just one month earlier had hastened to defend freedom of speech when the Espionage Act threatened to restrict the press (see Chapter 2, above), now published an editorial titled "Jails Are Waiting for Them," denigrating the National Civil Liberties Bureau as a "little group of malcontents" who "make the mistake of believing that speech can be literally and completely free in any civilized country."

conscientious objectors were until that time inducted into the Army and sent to boot camp, where they were held while the government decided what sorts of noncombatant roles were acceptable. In Army camps, COs often faced harangues, beatings, hosings, mock hangings, handcuffings, and other forms of physical and mental abuse. A few died from the mistreatment; a handful committed suicide. Of the close to twenty-one thousand conscientious objectors who were inducted into the Army, nearly seventeen thousand wound up accepting combat status rather than endure the continued abuse. Conscientious objectors who refused any sort of cooperation or noncombatant work were sentenced to prison terms of up to thirty-five years, though most were released by 1920.

Through the winter and spring of 1918, the mood of the country turned increasingly ugly. In December, Vice President Thomas Marshall declared that Congress should confiscate the property and "take away the citizenship of every disloyal American—every American who is not in support of his Government in its crisis . . . This is no time for pacifists to be running loose."[21] In January, in a speech before the National Security League, Representative Julius Kahn of California, who had led the House fight on the draft law, proposed that "a few prompt trials and a few quick hangings would prove most salutary at this point."[22] In March, Senator Warren Harding suggested putting German spies "against the wall,"[23] and the following month, on the day before Robert Prager was lynched in Collinsville, Illinois, former president Taft, while cautioning against mob rule, similarly expressed the opinion that spies should be court-martialed, lined up, and shot.[24]

The reaction to the Prager murder was a demand for more stringent laws—not against mob rule but against the "disloyal." On the day of the killing, Collinsville's mayor, John Siegel, sent Senator Lee Overman of North Carolina a telegram urging him to do all he could to speed the passage of new legislation, believing "it would have a wholesome effect on those tending to be disloyal."[25] Expressing the logic of prevailing sentiment, Attorney General Gregory agreed, saying, "While the lynching of Prager is to be deplored, it cannot be condemned. The department of justice has repeatedly called upon Congress for the necessary laws to prevent just such a thing as happened in the Illinois town."[26] In other words, if dissent had been more forcefully restricted, a mob would not have had to take it upon itself to enforce vigilante justice. "Mob violence, in this view," the historian David Kennedy has astutely observed, "was strangely transformed into the visible sign of a healthy society, vigorously rooting out criminal—or at least less than 'decent'—elements from its midst."[27] Indeed, as *The Washington Post* editorialized, "Enemy propaganda must be stopped, even if a few lynchings may occur."[28] The fact that there was no evidence of Prager's having been a spy or a traitor never entered the discussion, nor did the distinction between truly dangerous spies and saboteurs and those who simply opposed the war.

In response to the demand for harsher legislation, Congress immediately sped up work on two pending bills. The Sabotage Act, passed on April 20, provided penalties for the destruction of property. But it was the Sedition Act, an amendment to the Espionage Act of 1917, that provided truly draconian limitations on freedom of speech and would come to be regarded as one of the most repressive laws ever enacted in the United States.

According to Gregory, a new law was necessary because the Espionage Act "did not reach the individual casual or impulsive disloyal utterances."[29] That is, there was no way to prosecute the person who offhandedly said, "Damn this war," or, "To hell with the government."

The Sedition Act made it unlawful to "utter, print, write, or publish any disloyal, profane, scurrilous, or abusive language about the form of government of the United States," the Constitution, the flag, and the military forces or their uniforms.[30] The irony of prohibiting any negative word about the Constitution by abridging the right of free speech guaranteed therein was lost on the supporters of the Sedition Act.

The bill also made it illegal "to incite, provoke, or encourage resistance to the United States, or to promote the cause of its enemies." One provision of the law forbade anyone to advocate any curtailment of a war-related product, leading the Georgia senator Thomas W. Hardwick to conclude that "the real—in fact, practically the only—object of this section is to get some men called I.W.W.'s."[31] The maximum penalties for any of these offenses were a $10,000 fine and/or twenty years in prison.

Finally, the legislation empowered the postmaster general, "upon evidence satisfactory to him," to return to the sender any mail that he suspected of being in violation of the act, with the words " 'Mail to this address undeliverable under Espionage Act' plainly written or stamped upon the outside." Burleson now held absolute power over every publication in the country. By the end of the war, he would in one way or another impede or completely shut down seventy-five different publications, more than half of which were Socialist.

If there was any type of dissent not already squelched by the Espionage Act, the Sedition Act took care of it. Even Theodore Roosevelt was appalled, calling the bill "unconstitutional," "sheer treason," and "a proposal to make Americans subjects instead of citizens."[32]

Yet there was very little resistance to the bill in Congress. Hiram Johnson of California, one of the few senators to argue against it, called it the result of "a peculiar sort of mental hysteria."[33] The Republican conservative Henry Cabot Lodge declared he could not go along with the bill's repressive extremes, arguing that the law was aimed not at curbing sedition but "at certain classes of agitators . . . in different parts of the country."[34]

Senator Miles Poindexter of Washington, on the other hand, could not understand his colleagues' uneasiness with the Sedition Act, or why they attached more value to "the right to talk as they choose and express all sorts of opinions than they do to the right of life and the right of property and the right of trade."[35] Representative William Bell Walton of New Mexico thought the measure did not go far enough, saying, "I would have voted for it much more readily if it carried the death penalty."[36]

The strongest opposition stand came from the Maryland senator Joseph I. France, who was of the opinion that such a repressive law had not "been enacted in any country since the dark ages" and introduced an amendment that stated "nothing in this act shall be construed as limiting the liberty or impairing the right of any individual to publish or speak what is true, with good motives, and for justifiable ends."[37] The Senate passed the France amendment unanimously, but the House-Senate conference committee killed it on the advice of the director of the Emergency War Division, John Lord O'Brian, who cautioned that "the most dangerous type of propaganda in this country is religious pacifism" because it was virtually impossible to impugn on the basis of motive.[38]

The final version of the Sedition Act passed in the Senate by 48–26 (21 senators did not vote), and 293–1 in the House, where the New York Socialist Meyer London cast the lone vote against. On May 16, Wilson signed it into law. With few exceptions, editorial pages coast-to-coast hailed the Sedition Act as a welcome and long-overdue measure.

The *Harvard Law Review*, however, wrote that the law left

> little room for any public discussion adverse to the war policies of the national government . . . and if [it] is held to be constitutional, the power of Congress to abridge the time-honored right of freedom of speech will seem well established . . . Freedom of speech, being a constitutional guaranty, cannot be abridged in times of stress and strain any more than when the country is at peace . . . [T]rue patriotism consists as much in protecting the legal and constitutional rights of individuals as it does in giving the government an undivided and whole-hearted support.[39]

When the Sedition Act became law, the trial of the Chicago Wobblies had been going on for a month and a half. The judge in the case was Kenesaw Mountain Landis, who would soon become the first commissioner of baseball following the 1919 Black Sox scandal, a post he would hold until his death in 1944, during which time he would use the power of his office to keep organized baseball racially segregated.

Of the 166 Wobblies who had been arrested, 53 were released for lack of evidence. The remaining 113 were each charged with four counts of conspiring to hinder the draft and interfere with the U.S. war program by disrupting industrial production. After a month of jury selection, the actual trial phase finally got under way on May 1.

The defendants never had a prayer. Relying more on public opinion than on hard evidence, the government concentrated on IWW philosophy, its criticisms of capitalism, various antiwar literature, written discussions of sabotage, and advocacy of the general strike. In effect, the prosecution put the IWW on trial rather than the 113 defendants. After almost four months of testimony, the jury took just fifty-five minutes to find 96 men guilty on all four counts. With 113 defendants each charged with four counts, the jury had spent an average of 29.2 seconds per defendant and 7.3 seconds per count. The prison sentences ranged from a few days to the maximum twenty years, and the fines from $20,000 to $30,000. Bill Haywood and Ralph Chaplin were among the 14 who got twenty years.

. . .

With Haywood and Emma Goldman out of circulation, the federal government had silenced the two most dynamic and influential leaders of the IWW and anarchist movements. Now it targeted the last of the big three, the Socialist Party leader Eugene V. Debs.

When the government went after the charismatic Debs in June 1918, two other important Socialist leaders had already been convicted of Espionage Act violations. In December 1917, Debs's close friend Kate Richards O'Hare was sentenced to five years for an antiwar speech she had delivered in North Dakota the previous July.[40] Six months later, Rose Pastor Stokes, who had resigned from the Socialist Party after its April 1917 antiwar proclamation only to rejoin the following February, received a ten-year sentence for writing, in a March letter to *The Kansas City Star*, "No government which is for the profiteers can also be for the people, and I am for the people, while the Government is for the profiteers."[41]

After O'Hare's conviction, Debs, an electrifying speaker, was increasingly outspoken in his defense of those serving prison sentences for violating the Espionage Act, and in his criticism of Wilson and the war. On June 16, he delivered a passionate and defiant speech at Canton, Ohio, that would go down in the annals of great American oratory. He began by saying, "It is extremely dangerous to exercise the constitutional right of free speech in a country fighting to make democracy safe in the world . . . I must be exceedingly careful, prudent, as to what I say, and even more careful how I say it." Debs then proceeded to throw all caution to the wind, inviting the wrath of the government upon himself:

Wars throughout history have been waged for conquest and plunder . . . The master class has always declared the war; the subject class has always fought the battles. The master class has all to gain and nothing to lose, while the subject class has had nothing to gain and all to lose—especially their lives . . .

[T]he working class who fight all the battles, the working class who make the supreme sacrifices, the working class who freely shed their blood and furnish the corpses, have never yet had a voice in either declaring war or making peace. It is the ruling class that invariably does both. They alone declare war and alone make peace . . .

They are continually talking about your patriotic duty. It is not *their* but *your* patriotic duty that they are concerned about. There is a decided difference. Their patriotic duty never takes them to the firing line or chucks them into the trenches . . .

War makes possible all . . . crimes and outrages. And war comes in spite of the people. When Wall Street says war the press says war and the pulpit promptly follows with its *Amen*.[42]

Debs was indicted on June 19 and tried in September. The prosecuting attorney called him "the palpitating pulse of the sedition crusade."[43] He was convicted and sentenced to ten years.

Throughout the spring and summer of 1918, the American Protective League, working with local law-enforcement agencies and/or military personnel, had been carrying on "slacker" raids to ferret out draft dodgers in cities across the country. In large sweeps, they stopped men on the street, in saloons, at ballparks, in movie theaters, in restaurants, and demanded to see proof of their draft status. Those lacking draft registration cards—which the Selective Service Act required registrants to have in their possession at all times—were arrested, often at bayonet point by soldiers or at gunpoint by APL agents, and held in custody while their draft boards were wired for verification of their status; in some cases, it was weeks before confirmation was received and the men were released. At least one raid, and more typically a series, was carried out in Birmingham, Boston, Cleveland, Davenport, Dayton, Detroit, Galveston, Louisville, Minneapolis, Philadelphia, San Francisco, and St. Louis.

By July 1, an estimated 100,000 men had been arrested and detained.[44] The government and the APL justified the raids on the basis of the 20,000 slackers apprehended, with no mention of the 80,000 innocent men who were taken into custody. In Chicago, a three-day July offensive carried out by ten thousand APL members canvassed 150,000 men and arrested 16,000, of whom only 1,200 were draft dodgers and 265 deserters. By the end of August, the raids had netted 30,000 slackers.

The raiders saved the New York City area for last. On September 3 and 4, with the war already winding down, a force of Justice Department agents, APL members, a thousand sailors, and several thousand soldiers swept New York City and five northern New Jersey cities.

Newspaper accounts gave differing numbers, but according to *The New York Times* a staggering 60,187 men were arrested or temporarily detained.[45] The *Times* reported that 16,500 were slackers, but the actual number of draft dodgers was only about 1,300; the rest were delinquents whose records were out of date for one reason or another.[46]

The sheer magnitude and widespread press coverage of the New York raids raised a cry of outrage in the press and in the Senate. Frank Cobb, editor of the *New York World* and a confidant and unwavering supporter of Wilson, was irate, calling the raids a "lawless proceeding," a "monstrous invasion of human rights," and "a shameful abuse of power."[47]* The *Nation* denounced the Wilson administration for allowing "arrests without warrants, mostly by striplings in uniform and irresponsible agents of a volunteer self-appointed protective (!) league."[48] Even *The New York Times*, ordinarily the establishment's inveterate apologist, decried "the press gang method adopted" and cautioned, "The appearance of infringing personal liberty should be sedulously avoided."[49]

Senators Charles Thomas, Henry Cabot Lodge, Hiram Johnson, George Chamberlain of Oregon, William Calder of New York, Reed Smoot of Utah, and others strongly condemned the New York raids. The Illinois senator Lawrence Y. Sherman demanded to know "whether bayoneting men around when there is no martial law proclaimed, when civil law is in full effect in New York City . . . whether there is any difference between democracy in the United States and Kaiserism in Berlin?"[50]

Senators Miles Poindexter, Lee Overman, and William Kirby of Arkansas were among those who found nothing alarming in what had occurred. Kirby thought it far better that "some individuals are inconvenienced or individual rights are infringed . . . than that the law shall not be enforced,"[51] while Poindexter insisted, "There is no showing that any great hardship has been imposed upon a single individual."[52]

In a letter of response to Wilson's request for an explanation, Attor-

---

*Cobb also wrote to the president's secretary to say, "I can think of nothing that will have a worse effect on public opinion and war sentiment in this city than this action of . . . arresting tens of thousands of patriotic and law-abiding citizens at the point of the bayonet and driving them through the streets under armed guards to remain under arrest until they prove their innocence" (Cobb to Joseph P. Tumulty, Sept. 5, 1918, Wilson Papers, LOC).

ney General Gregory accepted "full and entire responsibility" for initiating the raids and defended the practice, including the use of APL members and military personnel.[53] The only misgiving he expressed was that the arrests were illegally carried out by soldiers, sailors, and APL members out of an "excess of zeal for the public good." That detail aside, Gregory upheld slacker raids as necessary and legitimate and informed Wilson that he intended to continue with the project unless directed otherwise. Wilson released Gregory's letter to the press, thereby giving his tacit approval to the procedure.

Meanwhile, J. Edgar Hoover had begun his meteoric rise through the ranks of the Department of Justice. By December 1917, after less than five months at the agency, he had been chosen by John Lord O'Brian for the War Emergency Division's Alien Enemy Bureau.

That same month, in Wilson's State of the Union message to Congress, the president proposed that the alien enemy regulations be extended to cover women, including American citizens who had demonstrated their disloyalty by marrying alien enemy men, thus giving the government reason enough to take away their citizenship. When the new rules went into effect the following April, 220,000 German women and 2 million Austro-Hungarian women were required to register, bringing the total number of alien enemies in the United States to between 4 and 4.5 million.[54]

Hoover was the Justice Department's point man for the registration of these new female alien enemies. In addition to working on alien enemy registration for the rest of the war, he was entrusted with the responsibility of evaluating the legal issues and making decisions in particular cases.

It was here in the Alien Enemy Bureau that Hoover learned the methods that he would later employ with such imperious force. As his biographer Richard Gid Powers has observed, "Hoover's wartime experience . . . accustomed him to using administrative procedures as a substitute for the uncertainties and delays of the legal process. The enemy status of the aliens Hoover supervised had stripped them of the protection of the Constitution, and so he got his first taste of authority under circumstances in which he could disregard the normal constitutional restraints on the power of the state."[55] Less than a year after the war ended in November 1918, Hoover would already be exercising these lessons to devastating effect.

. . .

"World War I . . . brought an internal sacrifice of civil liberty more serious than any the American people had suffered before," observed one historian in 1944. "The record of our behavior with respect to civil liberties during World War I is not one in which the thoughtful citizen can take much pride or satisfaction."[56]

The World War I years left a legacy in the United States that would change the Republic in two fundamental ways. First, the ascendancy of the military-industrial complex gave arms manufacturers enormous influence in governmental affairs. Second, the birth of the surveillance state created a self-perpetuating infrastructure that enabled and encouraged spying on civilians; as a result, surveillance would quickly seep into the bedrock of American life, and governmental secrecy would increasingly become an operational norm. These would prove instrumental in the postwar red scare.

CHAPTER 5

The Gravest Menace
to the Country

At the break of dawn on the morning of December 21, 1919, a lone ship slipped unceremoniously out of New York harbor, bound for an unknown destination. Dubbed the "Soviet Ark" by the press, the vessel was the *Buford*, a venerable five-thousand-ton troop transport ship on loan from the War Department to the Department of Labor for the purpose of conveying 249 aliens being deported to Soviet Russia.

The impending departure of the Soviet Ark had been keenly anticipated in the press as the purging of "scores of Bolsheviki, anarchists, I.W.W.'s and other . . . dangerous Reds" from U.S. shores.[1] One hundred eighty-four of the deportees had been swept up in a November 7 nationwide raid on the Union of Russian Workers, a "revolutionary" group with a national membership of between four thousand and seven thousand.[2] Fifty-one others were supposed "anarchists" whose banishment had been previously decreed, the most prominent of whom were Emma Goldman and Alexander Berkman. The other fourteen outcasts were garden variety "undesirables"—aliens who had become public charges or been convicted of crimes of moral turpitude.

As ever, Goldman was defiant. "I do not consider it a punishment to be sent to Soviet Russia," said Red Emma, dressed entirely in black, and one of only three women in the group. "On the contrary, I consider it an honor to be the first political agitator deported from the United States . . . I am coming back . . . I insist that I am an American."[3]

In an editorial, *The New York Times* bade good riddance to bad garbage: "With the general American gratification at the departure of these unclean spirits may well be mingled something of shame to remember how long they were suffered to afflict us."[4]

According to Department of Justice officials on hand to witness the *Buford*'s sailing, the deportations were merely the tip of an iceberg of sixty thousand radicals residing in this country. As J. Edgar Hoover, now head of the Bureau of Investigation's new General Intelligence (that is, antiradical) Division, promised, "The Department of Justice is not through yet, by any means. Other 'Soviet Arks' will sail for Europe just as often as it is necessary to rid the country of dangerous radicals."[5]

To hear government officials talk of it, the mass deportation had rid the country of the most dangerous revolutionary leaders in the United States. According to the Bureau of Investigation's director, William J. Flynn, the *Buford* carried off "the brains of the ultra-radical movement."[6] The reality was a far cry from that.

Following the armistice of November 11, 1918, international events continued to shape U.S. domestic affairs. The Bolshevik revolution of October 1917 in Russia had created seismic waves of anxiety among the ruling classes of Europe and the United States, and when the new Soviet government signed the peace treaty of Brest-Litovsk with Germany and the Central powers on March 3, 1918, the Russians were vilified for betraying the Allied cause. Compounding the insult, the new Bolshevik government called for an end to all fighting and a worldwide proletarian revolution to hasten the demise of capitalism. Communism—or Bolshevism, as it was also known—now took its place alongside anarchism and socialism as the archenemies of democracy.

The Soviets' withdrawal from the conflict meant that Germany was no longer forced to carry on a two-front war. In response, the Allies sent troops to northern Russia and Siberia to keep up the fighting on Germany's eastern front while also attempting to destabilize the Soviet government. American troops landed at Vladivostok and in northern Russia in August and September; by the end of the year, the United States had seven thousand troops stationed on Russian soil. At the same time, it appeared that Bolshevism was making serious inroads in Europe, as Austria, Germany, Hungary, Poland, and Bavaria either were flirting with or had already established Soviet-style governments. The red menace seemed to be spreading.

In September, George Creel's Committee on Public Information released to the press a series of documents smuggled out of Soviet Russia by the CPI representative Edgar Sisson. The documents "proved" that the Soviet leaders Vladimir Lenin and Leon Trotsky were German agents, that the Bolshevik revolution was financed by the German government, and that the Soviet government was "not a Russian government at all, but a German government acting solely in the interests of Germany and betraying the Russian people."[7] When serious doubts about the documents' authenticity were raised—they were, in fact, later proven to be forgeries—two academics, one of whom knew no Russian, were engaged to study them. The men were pressured into declaring the documents genuine, and in October, despite lingering questions, the CPI published them in a pamphlet called *The German-Bolshevik Conspiracy*, thereby putting the federal government's imprimatur on the bogus papers.

With the link between Germans and Bolsheviks thus firmly established, and with the memory of "radical" opposition to the war fresh in the public mind, the stigmatization and hostility that had been aimed at German-Americans and other minorities during the war were swiftly and easily redirected toward Russians, Bolsheviks, and "reds" of every sort. The intolerance of the postwar years was a direct outgrowth of the tone set during the war—the target shifted, but the scapegoating was the same.

The federal government, in concert with the leaders of big business and the press, now triggered a red scare, giving the federal surveillance program an urgent new impetus that would have severe and lasting repercussions on civil liberties in the United States.* As Frank J. Donner has written in *The Age of Surveillance*, "If World War I created a climate favorable to the federalization of intelligence, the 1917 Bolshevik Revolution gave it a permanent *raison d'être*, constituency, and mission . . . The twin traumas of war and revolution at once consolidated a nationwide countersubversive constituency and made intelligence its spokesman."[8]

---

*Regin Schmidt, author of *Red Scare*, conducted an exhaustive search of the Department of Justice files at NARA and found that the government was instrumental in creating the red scare hysteria, rather than simply reacting to the pressure of public opinion, as earlier writers had concluded. Schmidt's work is invaluable in documenting early DOJ and BI involvement in the creation of the red scare, but even without those sources an examination of the chronology of the unfolding of the process belies the theory that the government acted only when public opinion demanded a crackdown on the radical movement.

The marshaling of the new hysteria began just two months after the signing of the armistice, with a Senate subcommittee chaired by North Carolina's Lee Overman. The panel had been investigating German influences in the brewing industry, and with the war over it appeared that the group would soon be out of business.

On January 9, 1919, however, the outgoing Bureau of Investigation director, A. Bruce Bielaski, introduced during his testimony the issue of Bolshevism and other left-wing radical activity in the United States, and Overman saw the red peril as an opportunity to breathe new life into his moribund committee. The problem was how to segue from German brewers to Russian Bolsheviks to American radicals.

The answer was provided on January 22 by Archibald E. Stevenson, a New York lawyer and supposed expert on the radical movement in the United States, who presented himself to the committee as a BI agent and an operative of the Military Intelligence Division.[9] The rabidly anti-Communist Stevenson informed the committee: "The Bolsheviki movement is a branch of the revolutionary socialism of Germany. It had its origin in the philosophy of Karl Marx and its leaders were Germans . . . German socialism . . . is the father of the Bolsheviki movement in Russia, and consequently the radical movement which we have in this country to-day has its origin in Germany." Bolshevik propaganda, he warned the committee, is "the gravest menace to the country today."[10]

For two days, Stevenson lectured the committee about the dangers of Bolshevism. The following exchange among Stevenson, Overman, the Minnesota senator Knute Nelson, and the War Department representative Major E. Lowry Humes is representative of the quality of Stevenson's information:

HUMES: What are the forms and requirements for marriages and divorces under the Soviet government in Russia?
STEVENSON: Simply a statement before the proper commissary that they want to be married or that they want to be divorced.
OVERMAN: Do they have as many wives as they want?
STEVENSON: In rotation.
HUMES: Polygamy is recognized, is it?
STEVENSON: I do not know about polygamy. I have not gone into the study of their social order quite as fully as that.
NELSON: That is, a man can marry and then get a divorce when he gets tired, and get another wife?

STEVENSON: Precisely.

NELSON: And keep up the operation?

STEVENSON: Yes.

OVERMAN: Do you know whether they teach free love?

STEVENSON: They do.

HUMES: Can a divorce be secured upon the application of one
party to the marriage, or has it to be by agreement?

STEVENSON: I think by one party.

HUMES: By either party?

STEVENSON: By either party.

HUMES: They can renounce the marital bond at will?

STEVENSON: Precisely.

HUMES: Do you know whether or not the element that is active
in this country is advocating the same thing here in their
public speeches, or their literature?

STEVENSON: In considerable of the literature some of the
element has done so. I will not say that all have.[11]

Apart from the opéra-bouffe aspects of Stevenson's testimony, he
managed to do some real damage. Using the same tactic of guilt by
smear and innuendo that Senator Joseph McCarthy would employ so
effectively thirty-five years later, Stevenson provided the committee
with a "Who's Who in Pacifism and Radicalism" that he had compiled.[12] The list contained the names of about two hundred "clergy-
men, professors, lawyers, writers, Socialists, labor leaders, architects,
an I.W.W. agitator, and one former publisher of a New York newspaper" who were "active in movements which did not help the United
States when the country was fighting the Central Powers." After going
over the names in executive session, the committee eliminated more
than 70 percent of the people on the list, whittling it down to sixty-
two. The names that were entered into the record included such
prominent Americans as the social reformer Jane Addams; the econo-
mist Emily Greene Balch; the National Civil Liberties Bureau director
Roger Baldwin; the historian Charles Beard; the IWW leader Elizabeth Gurley Flynn; the Socialist attorney Morris Hillquit; the U.S.
commissioner of immigration for New York Frederic C. Howe; the
former Stanford University president David Starr Jordan; Rabbi
Judah L. Magnes; the peace activist Scott Nearing; the Socialist Kate
Richards O'Hare; the attorney Amos Pinchot; the Reverend Norman

Thomas; the *Nation* editor Oswald Garrison Villard; the sociologist Lillian D. Wald; and of course Eugene V. Debs. Baldwin, O'Hare, and Debs were serving prison sentences for violation of various wartime statutes.

Some of those named protested—"I am boiling with indignation,"[13] fumed the Brown University professor Lindsay T. Damon— while the New York attorney Gilbert E. Roe attacked Stevenson's motivation in presenting his list of names. In a letter to Overman, Roe charged that Stevenson "used the committee for giving publicity to himself" and pointed out:

> The persons mentioned on your list have only one thing in common—they have opposed the Prussianization of the United States . . . Most of them, I think, were opposed to the passage of the espionage law . . . They have also been opposed to the lawlessness of which the Military Intelligence Department has been guilty, whereby . . . the emissaries of the Military Intelligence Department again and again, in disregard of every right of the citizen, without warrant or pretense of authority, have invaded homes, arrested persons, held them incommunicado for days, seized and carried away property.

Retaliation for having represented many of these individuals, Roe maintained, was "the real reason for my name appearing upon this list."[14]

Sensing the half-baked and unfounded nature of many of Stevenson's claims, the Delaware senator Josiah O. Wolcott asked him whether the radicals, "after all their efforts and agitation and the expenditure of a great deal of labor and emotional energy," had actually made "any kind of an impression at all on the plain, common-sense American people."[15]

"I think if you really mean the American people," admitted Stevenson, "I should say no, Senator."

"That is what I mean," said Wolcott. "I mean the ordinary American citizen . . . Of course, they can make some trouble here and there in spots, but, taking the great body of the American people, were they not too level headed to be influenced by this outfit?"

In his response, Stevenson reached back for the nativism that had been an undercurrent in American life for decades and had played so well during the war. "They have made a very great impression on the foreign element," he asserted.

When asked by Overman his opinion of U.S. immigration laws, Stevenson said, "I think they ought to be very much more stringent."[16]

"Would it do to pass a law that no person should enter this country unless he is a white man—an Anglo-Saxon—for the next 10 years?" asked the chairman.

"If it could be done I think it would be a good thing," responded Stevenson.

"You think it would be a good law to pass?" pressed Overman.

"Yes, sir," maintained Stevenson.

"So do I," Overman agreed.

Stevenson's testimony breathed new life into the Overman Committee. Abandoning its inquiry into Germans and the brewing industry, the group requested and received Senate permission to extend its investigation, in order to concentrate on Bolsheviks and others who sought to change the government and/or the economic system.

Throughout its investigation, the committee enjoyed the close cooperation of the Bureau of Investigation. Overman was already well-known to the BI, having acted as an informant during and after the war.* Accordingly, Attorney General Gregory granted the committee access to Justice Department files and assigned Special Agent William R. Benham to help the committee conduct its investigation. The committee, in turn, gave the information it acquired to the bureau.

From February 11 to March 10, the Overman Committee, assisted by Benham, amassed information and statistics on the radical movement, investigated individual radicals and monitored their activities, and collected and analyzed radical literature, while a parade of witnesses provided a litany of by-now-familiar lurid descriptions of the horrors of life in Soviet Russia. Despite all its digging, however, the committee never produced any remotely convincing evidence concerning either the prevalence of Bolshevik propaganda in the United States or the danger posed by the radical movement in this country.

---

*Among the items Overman had supplied to the bureau were a letter charging that the Germans controlled American Jewish organizations and an unsubstantiated claim that German and Austrian arms manufacturers in the United States were providing the radical movement with weapons. Minnesota's senator Nelson was also a BI informant (see Schmidt, *Red Scare*, p. 142).

One witness, Raymond Robins, who had led an American Red Cross mission to Soviet Russia and was an outspoken opponent of Bolshevism, expressed the opinion that repression was not the best way to combat radicalism in the United States. "I have faith enough in our institutions," said Robins, "to believe that we will throw that foreign culture, born out of a foreign despotism, back out of our land, not by treating it with the method of tyranny, not by a witch hunt, nor by hysteria, but by strong intelligent action."

Overman took umbrage. "What do you mean by 'witch hunt'?" he demanded.

"I mean this, Senator," responded Robins. "You are familiar with the old witch-hunt attitude, that when people get frightened at things and see bogies, then they get out witch proclamations, and mob action and all kinds of hysteria takes place."[17]

The months following the signing of the armistice were fraught with economic insecurity. As industry began the conversion to a peacetime economy, the nine million Americans formerly employed in war-related work faced an uncertain future. Also, four million returning servicemen glutted the job market. Inflation soared as prices and the cost of living doubled from what they had been before the war.

Labor and management were on a collision course. Organized labor, which had enjoyed tremendous gains during the Progressive Era, had for the most part patriotically suspended its agenda in support of the war effort. Aside from the IWW copper and lumber strikes, most labor actions during the war had been small and localized. With the conflict now over, the labor movement was eager to claim its due in the form of increased wages, improved working conditions, and, most important, collective bargaining. The business interests, on the other hand, which were quite content with the general lack of opposition they had enjoyed during the war years, were equally determined to not only hold the line against new demands but to reverse the gains that labor had made in the years leading up to the war. Collective bargaining, in particular, was not negotiable.

The resulting clash between labor and management would become one of the primary fronts on which the government waged its new battle against radicalism. In this campaign, the Department of Justice, the Bureau of Investigation, and the General Intelligence Division would function as outright instruments of capital, defending management against the upstart ambitions of labor and fanning the public's fears of radicals. As Frederic C. Howe, the immigration commissioner in charge of Ellis Island during the red scare, later wrote, "There was a concerted determination on the part of employers to bring wages back to pre-war conditions and to break the power of organized labor. This movement against alien labor leaders had the support of the Department of Justice. Private detective agencies and strike-breakers acted with assurance that in any outrages they would be supported by the government itself . . . The government borrowed the agent provocateur from Old Russia; it turned loose innumerable private spies."[18]

The first skirmish in the labor-management conflict took place in Seattle, a hotbed of union activity, where the BI had been keeping tabs on IWW and Socialist activity since 1915. After the war, the bureau continued its surveillance of labor radicals as informants from patriotic groups like the American Protective League and the Minute Men and strikebreaking outfits like the Pinkerton National Detective Agency infiltrated various labor organizations and fed biased information to the bureau.

In December 1918, with a shipyard strike brewing in Seattle, BI informants depicted the cause of the unrest as being due to the presence of radical agitators. According to a typical APL informant named Walter R. Thayer, who had infiltrated the Seattle Central Labor Council, "The ignorant worker . . . falls an easy victim to the Bolshevists because there is no . . . restraint on the agitator, no restraint on the tons of damnable literature they are selling openly on the streets of Seattle." Thayer claimed that a shipyard strike would result in the imposition of martial law, which "would be the beginning of the end of permanent peace in this country," as the aim of the strike's leaders was to set off a revolution. As Thayer saw it, "The Bolshevist spirit will control industry in the United States in a few years as certain as sunrise."[19]

An evaluation of Thayer's assessment of the labor movement's motives, which would become the dominant view during the ensuing struggle, reveals three mistaken, interrelated premises that would underlie the government's mind-set in dealing with the red scare. The first was trusting in the reliability of intelligence provided by informants, a basic fallacy that would persist for decades, as the bureau and the General Intelligence Division—and later the FBI—would time and time again act against individuals and organizations on the basis of concocted and prejudiced information furnished by informants.

The second error was the literal reading of radical propaganda, which led officials to overestimate the extent of radical influence in the labor force. In the aftermath of the Bolshevik revolution, radicals in the United States were convinced that, like the Bolsheviks in Russia, they could take over the government with a tiny minority. This delusion led to the publication of wildly optimistic literature with all manner of far-fetched revolutionary rhetoric. The business community and the government took this propaganda at face value, seeing in it the threat of imminent overt action, even though organized labor, led by the American Federation of Labor's staunchly antiradical Samuel Gompers, assiduously dissociated itself from any taint of radical sway.

The third faulty notion in this pre–Great Depression era was that the American economic system, though subject to minor flaws, was essentially infallible and that any criticism of capitalism by workers could only be the result of agitation by radicals. Little credence was given to the possibility that the fundamental causes of discontent could be rooted in the conditions of millions of laborers, especially immigrants, who were overworked, underpaid, and living in poverty and in general constituted an underclass in America. As government and big business saw it, otherwise contented—or at least complacent—workers were always being stirred up and manipulated by radical troublemakers.

Thus, when thirty-five thousand Seattle shipbuilders walked off the job on January 21, 1919, Seattle's mayor, Ole Hanson, saw the strike as an attempt at revolution by miscreants who "want to take possession of our American Government and try to duplicate the anarchy of Russia."[20] According to *The New York Times*, Hanson was a reformed radical who had called himself "the friend of the 'under dog,' " until "radical elements" refused to let him run for office on their ticket. After repeated snubs, Hanson changed his views to the degree that "he found favor with the Business Men's party" and won the mayoralty as their candidate.[21]

In support of the shipyard workers, the Seattle Central Labor Council, representing 110 unions, called for a general strike—the first ever in the United States—to begin at ten o'clock on the morning of February 6. The city was thrown into a state of excitement and alarm. The labor council paper, the *Seattle Union Record*, boasted, "We are undertaking the most tremendous move ever made by LABOR in this country, a move which will lead—NO ONE KNOWS WHERE!"[22] On the other side, in a simultaneous plea and threat, *The Seattle Star* cautioned potential strikers to "STOP BEFORE IT'S TOO LATE . . . You are being urged to use a dangerous weapon—the general strike . . . This is America—not Russia."[23]

To defend against the insurrection, Mayor Hanson telegraphed Secretary of War Newton Baker on February 5 to request federal troops. The following morning, driving his flag-draped auto, the mayor personally escorted a contingent of fifteen hundred soldiers from Camp Lewis into Seattle. The troops were equipped with machine guns and hand grenades and had orders to "shoot to kill at first sign of rioting."[24] Augmenting the military force were fifteen hundred policemen.

Some sixty thousand workers joined the general strike on February 6, virtually shutting down the city, except for essential services such as garbage collection and food and fuel deliveries. "REDS DIRECTING SEATTLE STRIKE," screamed a headline in the *Los Angeles Times*, which labeled the work stoppage "a real Bolshevik movement."[25] Nevertheless, despite the press's portrayal of the strike as Bolshevik-inspired and "The Rule of the Mob,"[26] there was no violence, and not one strike-related arrest was made.[27]

On February 7, a bill was prepared in the state legislature appropriating $100,000 "for the use of the Government in suppressing strikes and maintaining order during labor troubles." The same day, Hanson warned the strikers that unless they ended their action by eight o'clock on the morning of the eighth, he would place the city under martial law. "The time has come," he proclaimed, "for every person in Seattle to show his Americanism . . . The anarchists in this community shall not rule its affairs."[28]

The labor council did not heed Hanson's threat, but by the end of the day on February 8 it was apparent that the strike was not going to succeed. The AFL undercut the effort by calling upon its Seattle locals to withdraw their support, and the hard line adopted by Hanson resonated with the public. On February 11, the Seattle general strike ended.

As the man who had broken the strike, Hanson declared:

This was an attempted revolution which they expected to spread all over the United States. It never got to first base, and it never will if the men in control of affairs will tell all traitors and anarchists that death will be their portion if they start anything . . . Any man who owes a higher allegiance to any organization than he does to the Government should be sent to a Federal prison or deported. Let the National Government stop pandering to and conciliating the men who talk against it. Let us clean up the United States of America.[29]

Not everybody agreed with Hanson's assessment. The Bureau of Investigation agents R. O. Samson and F. W. Byrn Jr., who were assigned to investigate the strike, telegraphed Washington that it had been a "purely local labor trouble" and, as such, did not affect the government any more than any other strike.

Hanson's view became the prevailing one. Addressing a conference of governors and mayors on March 3, Secretary of Labor William Wilson declared that the Seattle general strike was "not industrial, economic [in] origin," but rather a "deliberate attempt . . . to create a social and political revolution that would establish the soviet form of government in the United States and put into effect the economic theories of the Bolsheviki of Russia."[30]

Six months after the strike ended, Ole Hanson resigned as mayor of Seattle and undertook a profitable lecture tour of the nation, speaking on the dangers of Bolshevism. By that time, the red scare would be in full swing.

The Overman Committee concluded its hearings on March 10 and issued a twelve-hundred-page report with the unlikely title *Brewing and Liquor Interests and German and Bolshevik Propaganda*. The Seattle general strike had solidified the committee's opinion that the United States was under siege, and its recommendations included more rigorous enforcement of deportation laws, the passage of tougher sedition legislation, and a campaign of patriotic propaganda to counteract the Bolshevik literature that was supposedly flooding the nation. Overman declared, "We must bring home to the people the truth that a compromise with Bolshevism is to barter away our inheritance."[31]

The press bought it whole. From coast to coast, headlines broadcast the looming Bolshevist menace. "EXTREMISTS HERE PLAN

A REVOLT TO SEIZE POWER," cried *The New York Times.* "I.W.W., ANARCHISTS, SOCIALISTS, IN CONSPIRACY TO OVERTHROW GOVERNMENT," proclaimed the *Los Angeles Times.*[32]

At the end of March, the New York State Legislature took up the cause, authorizing the creation of a committee to investigate and report on "the scope, tendencies, and ramifications of . . . seditious activities."[33] The state senator Clayton R. Lusk was named chairman of the new committee, and Archibald E. Stevenson, who had dazzled the Overman Committee with his "expertise" on radicals, was appointed chief counsel. Hearings were scheduled to begin July 1.

That same month, the red scare gained momentum when the Third International meeting in Moscow called for a worldwide revolution, thereby confirming the worst fears of the U.S. government and the business community.

At 2:00 a.m. on April 30, the New York postal employee Charles Caplan was reading the newspaper as he rode the subway home after working the swing shift.[34] His eye was drawn to an article about a bomb that had been delivered by mail to the home of the former Georgia senator Thomas W. Hardwick; the device had exploded, blowing off both hands of the Hardwicks' maid and inflicting serious injuries on Mrs. Hardwick as well.

What struck Caplan was the description of the package—it was wrapped in straw-colored glazed paper and bore the return address of Gimbel Brothers department store. Just the day before, *The New York Times* had reported a similar package having been delivered to the office of Ole Hanson, who was out of town; only an accidental mishandling of the packet by Hanson's staff had caused the sulfuric acid to leak out and thereby fail to set off the enclosed dynamite caps.

Three days earlier, Caplan had processed sixteen similar items at the post office and set them aside because the seals on either end of the parcels made them first-class mail, and as such they lacked the proper amount of postage. Alarmed, Caplan got off the train at the next stop and returned to the post office in midtown Manhattan, where he and the night superintendent retrieved the packages, which were alike in every detail to the description of the Hardwick and Hanson parcels. They immediately called the chief of postal inspection for New York City. It took six hours for the bomb squad to dismantle one of the bombs, which the inspector in charge of the operation said was "the work of an expert," adding that "he had never examined a bomb of more skillful construction or deadlier possibilities."[35]

The addressees on the sixteen packages included Postmaster A. S. Burleson; the Post Office Department solicitor, William Lamar; the Supreme Court justice Oliver Wendell Holmes; Judge Kenesaw Mountain Landis; John D. Rockefeller; J. P. Morgan; the U.S. commissioner general of immigration, Anthony Caminetti; the immigration commissioner for New York, Frederic C. Howe; and A. Mitchell Palmer, the former alien property custodian who had succeeded Thomas Gregory as attorney general on March 5.

In the next few days, it was discovered that bombs had also been mailed to, among others, senators Overman and William H. King, Secretary of Labor Wilson, and the district attorneys who had prosecuted the Chicago IWW case and the Tom Mooney case in San Francisco.* In all, as many as thirty-six men had been targeted.

Suspicion naturally centered on Bolsheviks and the IWW, particularly since the bombs appeared to be intended for delivery on May 1, the day celebrated throughout the world as a labor holiday. Without a shred of evidence, *The New York Times* and *The Washington Post* concluded in editorials that radicals were to blame. Hanson, now a national celebrity for his role in quashing the Seattle strike, warned of a "widespread, national effort to overthrow the Government and society by violence" and proclaimed that the government was "on the wrong track in starting conferences instead of cemeteries in dealing with the I.W.W. . . . I trust Washington will buck up and clean up and either hang or incarcerate for life all the anarchists in the country. If the Government doesn't clean them up I will. I'll give up my mayorship and start through the country. We will hold meetings and have hanging places . . . The conspiracy to overthrow the Government is widespread. It permeates every State in the Union."[36]

On May 1, newspaper coverage of the bomb plot played up the May Day angle, and in several major cities the day's labor parades, meetings, and rallies were set upon by patriots and the police. In Boston, a police officer was fatally stabbed, one civilian and three other policemen were shot, and scores of "radicals" were injured in riots in two different locations. The 116 people arrested were all Socialists. In New York, the Russian People's House and the offices of the Socialist *New York*

*For the Tom Mooney case, see Chapter 1 n. 18, above.

Call newspaper were stormed by soldiers, sailors, and civilians who broke up meetings and beat the participants, about twenty of whom required medical attention. The worst incidents took place in Cleveland, where Army tanks and troop transport trucks were used to restore order after a parade, a Public Square meeting, and Socialist Party headquarters were attacked; 1 Socialist was killed, 25 wounded, and 106 arrested.

Notwithstanding that in virtually every case the violence had been initiated by antiradicals and/or the police, the "radicals" were blamed, as the demand grew for "further repression of them and their activities."[37] Congress promptly announced that it would drop "the policy of tolerance" and consider legislation "to curb Bolshevism."[38]

New York City police and Justice Department detectives worked around the clock on the mail bomb case. Two thousand radicals were placed under investigation as authorities proceeded from the assumption that "the conspirators . . . will be found among these agitators." A high-up, albeit unidentified, federal official guaranteed: "It may be several days, a week or even a month, but I am confident that we will land every person concerned. No matter how long it takes, this investigation will continue until this case is solved. We already have several good clues, and we have made very good progress to date."[39]

Rumors and hearsay abounded. A federal undercover agent cited an imaginary "Committee of Five," considered the "most desperate band of anarchists" in the nation, as the perpetrators of the bomb plot.[40] Another report claimed that "the police had twenty-one 'Spanish anarchists' " and that arrests were imminent.[41] One detective who first believed the whole thing to be the work of a crackpot soon changed his opinion, concluding that it was "a gigantic conspiracy by an organized gang."[42]

On May 12, despite almost daily "breakthroughs" in the case, police announced that after two weeks of investigation, they had no clues and offered a reward for information. Evidence indicates, however, that the BI had actually tied the bombs to a small group of fanatic Italian anarchists—no more than fifty or sixty individuals—known as the Galleanists, but chose to keep this knowledge quiet, instead representing the bombs as part of a national conspiracy, which created greater alarm and allowed for a wider crackdown on radicals.*

---

*For the case that the federal government, including President Wilson, knew the Galleanists were behind the bombings, see Schmidt, *Red Scare*, pp. 148–50.

On the evening of June 2, the mail bombs became almost insignificant when a new series of bombs exploded in seven cities. The blasts in Cleveland, Paterson, Boston (two), Philadelphia (two), and Pittsburgh (six) caused extensive destruction of property, but nobody was injured. In New York, however, an explosion killed a night watchman guarding the home of Judge Charles C. Nott.

The most sensational explosion occurred in Washington, D.C., where the home of Attorney General Palmer suffered extensive damage. None of the residents was harmed, but the bomber apparently tripped on the steps leading up to the front door of the house and blew himself up before he could plant the bomb. Pieces of his body were found as far as two blocks away.

Law-enforcement officials and the press once again quickly assumed that radicals were behind the bombings. The BI's director, William Flynn, announced that the perpetrators were "connected with Russian bolshevism, aided by Hun money."[43] Similarly, *The New York Times* concluded, "These crimes are plainly of Bolshevist or I.W.W. origin."[44] Palmer himself called them "nothing but the lawless attempt of an anarchistic element in the population to terrorize the country."[45]

The conclusion that the bombings were the work of radicals and were tied to the May 1 plot was based on copies of a leaflet found near Palmer's house. The flyer, titled "Plain Words," was a tirade filled with the most incendiary revolutionary rhetoric and threats:

> There will have to be bloodshed; we will not dodge; there will have to be murder; we will kill, because it is necessary; there will have to be destruction; we will destroy to rid the world of your tyrannical institutions.
>
> We are ready to do anything and everything to suppress the capitalist class; just as you are doing anything and everything to suppress the proletarian revolution.

The screed ended with "Long live social revolution! Down with tyranny!" and was signed, "THE ANARCHIST FIGHTERS."[46]

Once again, the papers were filled with reports of swift developments in cracking the case. Though police worked twenty-four hours a day on it, they came up empty-handed.

Assistant Labor Secretary Louis Post, who would play perhaps the single most crucial role in bringing the red scare to a close, later wrote, "The lack of real 'leads' is remarkable . . . How was it possible for so gigantic a conspiracy of revolutionaries, if that is what it was, or so desperate an outburst of proletarian passion, if it was that, to have escaped detection when most of the detective agencies of the country, public and private, regardless of expense and frequently of lawful methods, were pursuing the perpetrators of its crimes with tireless zeal?"[47]

In fact, although neither the May Day nor the June 2 plot was ever officially solved, there is evidence that the Bureau of Investigation knew they had both been carried out by the Galleanists. The Justice Department instead characterized the bombings as part of a vast, nationwide conspiracy by a consolidated force of radicals, what Palmer labeled "a combined and joint effort of the lawless classes of the population to injure, if not destroy, the Government," cynically manipulating the threat of such an invented insurrection in order to ignite public fears and power the antiradical/antilabor engine that drove the red scare.[48]

Several consequences of the June 2 bombings kicked the red scare into a higher gear. The most significant was that Palmer, a pacifist Quaker who had turned down the position of secretary of war in Wilson's first cabinet before later accepting the alien property custodian post, was understandably shaken by the attempt on his life, and set out with a vengeance to eradicate the "anarchistic element" responsible for the bombings. Palmer announced a plan he had been working on for two months—the reorganization of the Justice Department to facilitate the hunt for radicals.[49] He had already selected William J. Flynn, former head of the Secret Service, whom the attorney general called "the greatest anarchist-expert in the United States," to replace Bruce Bielaski as director of the Bureau of Investigation;[50] Frank Burke, former manager of the New York Secret Service office, as BI assistant director; and Francis P. Garvan, an experienced investigator who had worked with him in the alien property custodian's office, for assistant attorney general in charge of overseeing the hunting of reds. Immediately after the bombings, their appointments became public. Palmer, Flynn, Burke, and Garvan, along with J. Edgar Hoover, would become five major players in the unfolding red scare.*

*The significance of Garvan's appointment would become clear only half a year later, after the deportation of the 249 radical aliens aboard the "Soviet Ark" on

Palmer, Flynn, and Garvan wasted no time in raising the specter of an imminent radical uprising. Appearing before the House Committee on Appropriations on June 13 to ask for an increase in the Justice Department budget, the attorney general said, "We have received so many notices and gotten so much information that it has almost come to be accepted as a fact that on a certain day in the future, which we have been advised of, there will be another serious and probably much larger effort of the same character which the wild fellows of this movement describe as revolution, a proposition to rise up and destroy the Government at one fell swoop."[51]

Flynn and Garvan identified the "certain day in the future" as July 4,[52] which had been designated by radical labor as the day for a general strike to free Tom Mooney, the San Francisco Socialist who had been convicted on trumped-up charges in the 1916 Preparedness Day bombing that killed ten people and injured forty others in San Francisco.[53] Law-enforcement officials in the nation's large cities began planning in order to crush the anticipated Fourth of July uprising.

A second consequence of the June 2 bombings was that the Lusk Committee in New York moved up its hearings from the beginning of July to June 12. On the day of its initial session, police and private detectives under the committee's jurisdiction raided the Manhattan offices of the Russian Soviet Bureau, the unofficial embassy of the Soviet government. The bureau was run by Ludwig C. A. K. Martens, the unofficial Soviet ambassador, who had established the headquarters in January, ostensibly to set up trade relations with U.S. companies while also fostering close ties to American left-wing groups. Martens had presented his credentials to the State Department in March but was refused on the basis that the United States did not recognize the Bolshevik government.

In the raid on the bureau's offices, the police took possession of virtually every piece of paper in the place and brought Martens and his associates in for questioning by the Lusk Committee. In defense of

---

December 21. As *The New York Times* reported the following day, "The action that ended yesterday had its beginning when Mr. Garvan joined the staff of Attorney General A. Mitchell Palmer, it was said yesterday. He took office determined to stamp out the Red menace. The first results of this determination were the wholesale raids of the Department of Justice on Nov. 7 . . . Two hundred who went out yesterday . . . were the fruits of these raids."

these actions, Lusk said the committee had information that "representatives of the Russian Soviet Government had an establishment in this city from which propaganda was being circulated advocating the Soviet form of government as it exists in Russia under the Bolsheviki."[54]

Nine days later, similar raids were conducted at the Rand School of Social Science, the offices of the Left Wing Socialists, and the New York City headquarters of the IWW. When Lusk was asked about the purpose of these incursions, he answered, "Names!—Names of all parlor bolsheviki, IWW, and socialists. They will be a real help to us later on."[55]

CHAPTER 6

A Skimming of the Great American Melting-Pot

As July 4, 1919, approached, the press parroted Justice Department officials' warnings, issuing dire alarms about the forecast revolutionary uprising. "REIGN OF TERROR PLANNED," blared a *New York Times* headline, while on the opposite coast the *Los Angeles Times* proclaimed, "RED RISING ORDERED."[1]

The new BI director, William Flynn, met with law-enforcement officials from major cities across the country in order to coordinate federal, state, and local efforts to contain the impending revolt. Two companies of federal soldiers were sent to Chicago to assist the police department, which was also bolstered by a thousand volunteers. In New York, the entire eleven-thousand-man police force was assigned to twenty-four-hour duty, guarding all government buildings as well as the New York Stock Exchange and the homes of prominent citizens, while the state militia and hundreds of specially sworn deputies stood by on alert. Armed soldiers guarded the Federal Building in Boston, and police officers filled the streets of many American cities. In Oakland, California, police rounded up known radicals and held them in jail for the duration of Independence Day. Across the bay in San Francisco, police raided the local IWW headquarters and arrested three men, despite Captain John O'Meara's assurance, "We have had secret details working among the alleged radical elements and reports show there is nothing to be apprehensive of."[2]

O'Meara's assessment was entirely accurate, the extravagant predictions of Palmer, Flynn, and Garvan notwithstanding. When the Fourth of July came and went without so much as a hint of an attempted revolution, Palmer and other law-enforcement officials attributed it to their security measures. *The Christian Register,* on the other hand, believed that the projected July 4 revolt "had been considerably over-emphasized in an attempt to impress public opinion with the gravity of an ultimate danger."[3]

Scarcely had the fictitious threat of a Bolshevik insurrection passed when a rather more substantial crisis unfolded. On July 19, inflamed by reports of attacks by black men on white women, a mob of soldiers, sailors, and marines on leave in Washington, D.C., invaded an African-American neighborhood, severely beating one black man and threatening several others before police could stop them. The incident touched off four nights of race riots in the nation's capital, leaving six people dead and a hundred injured.

The Washington race riots were not the first that year—there had already been smaller disturbances in other cities, including Charleston, South Carolina, in May, and Longview, Texas, earlier in July—but the D.C. disturbances were of a significantly greater magnitude and, taking place as they did in the nation's capital, focused national attention on the issue of race relations in the United States.

The great migration of half a million African-Americans from the rural South to the industrial North during World War I had created friction between blacks and whites over housing and employment, and employers exacerbated the strains by hiring unemployed blacks as strikebreakers. Tensions were further intensified by the return of nearly 400,000 African-American soldiers, many of whom were determined to claim their civil rights as their due for having served the country in the war, which contributed to a growing resolve among blacks to resist and fight back against lynchings and other virulent manifestations of racism.

In the heat of summer, animosities sizzled, and the antagonism finally erupted in the streets. Twenty-five cities experienced major race riots, as more than 120 people were killed during what came to be known as the Red Summer of 1919.

The worst riots took place in Chicago. Five days after Washington quieted down, the Windy City exploded. The immediate cause was the death of Eugene Williams, an African-American youth who, while swimming in Lake Michigan, inadvertently crossed an invisible line dividing white and black beaches. Whites on the shore began pelting Williams with rocks, one of which hit him in the head, and he drowned. When police arrived, they refused to arrest the man responsible and instead took a black man into custody, triggering a weeklong rampage, during which fifteen whites and twenty-three blacks were killed, more than five hundred people injured, and close to a thousand people, many of them immigrants, left homeless by the fires that burned in South Side neighborhoods. It took the arrival of the state militia to stabilize the situation.

As was the case with the Seattle general strike, the government pinned the source of the trouble on radical agitators, who had been actively recruiting, with notably little success, among African-Americans. This view was given authority by Robert A. Bowen, director of the Justice Department's Bureau of Translations and Radical Publications in New York. Three weeks before the Washington riots, in a report titled "Radicalism and Sedition Among the Negroes as Reflected in Their Publications," Bowen, a South Carolinian, warned that African-Americans were being led down the primrose path by radical black editors in a "concerted effort, abetted by certain prominent white publicists, to arouse in the negro a well-defined class-consciousness, sympathetic only with the most malign radical movements."[4]* The government could not, Bowen warned, ignore such a trend.

Just as in the Seattle situation, the press jumped on the bandwagon. "Reds Accused of Stirring Up Negro Rioters," cried the *New York Tribune*, while *The New York Times* quoted an unnamed federal official who said, "It is an agitation which involves the I.W.W., Bolshevism and the worst features of other extreme radical movements." A *Times* editorial revealed how readily the stigma of disloyalty had been redirected after the war: "We know that in the early days of the war there was a pro-German and pacifist propaganda among the negroes, which may well have turned into a Bolshevist or at least Socialist propaganda since."[5] The editorial went on to say that "the situation presupposes intelligent direction and management"—the clear implication being that African-

*Bowen concluded that service in the armed forces during the war had led to the radicalization of African-Americans. President Wilson, a southerner, had himself expressed a fear of this when he told his personal doctor, on March 10, that "the American negro returning from abroad would be our greatest medium in conveying Bolshevism to America" (Link, *Papers of Woodrow Wilson*, vol. 55, p. 471).

Americans, like laborers, were not, in and of themselves, capable of finding dissatisfaction with their condition, and therefore only some "intelligent direction and management" by outside agitators could explain the underlying discontent that found expression in the form of race riots or labor strikes.

For months, the Bureau of Investigation had been carrying out surveillance of prominent black radicals on both the right and the left, including the black nationalist Marcus Garvey, the outspoken NAACP leader and *Crisis* editor W. E. B. Du Bois, and the Socialist editors A. Philip Randolph and Chandler Owen. Now, two days into the Chicago rioting, the new BI assistant director, Frank Burke, ordered the Chicago field office to begin an inquiry into whether radicals had been instrumental in causing the outbreak. Although this and other Justice Department investigations failed to produce any direct link connecting the riots and either radical propaganda or activities, J. Edgar Hoover kept the issue alive in an internal BI memo that, while offering no evidence, insisted that radicals were somehow implicated.

In the official Justice Department report issued after riots occurred in a number of other cities, Bowen went a step further, insisting that the very occurrence of the riots proved that "there can no longer be any question of a well-concerted movement among a certain class of Negro leaders of thought and action to constitute themselves a determined and persistent source of a radical opposition to the Government, and to the established rule of law and order."[6]

Initially, Palmer disagreed, stating that the riots "were due solely to local conditions and were not inspired by Bolshevik or other radical propaganda."[7] But the Justice Department continued to peddle the fabrication that radicals were behind the uprisings, as *The New York Times* reported that "according to information now in the hands of the Department of Justice . . . I.W.W. and Soviet influence were at the bottom of the recent race riots in Washington and Chicago."[8] The effect of such baseless charges was to keep suspicions of both radicals and African-Americans on the front burner and to reinforce the notion that the red menace was reaching into every sector of American life.

Palmer, whose well-known presidential ambitions were, at least to begin with, well served by his anti-red crusading, soon came to the conclusion that radical propaganda was indeed corrupting the African-American population. "These radical organizations have endeavored to enlist Negroes on their side, and in many respects have been successful," he told Congress.[9] Just as a few months earlier all Germans and German-Americans had been suspect, all African-Americans were now worthy of suspicion.

By midsummer, Palmer had begun to discern "a bolshevist plot in every item of the day's news."[10] To deal with the perceived threat, he created, on August 1, the General Intelligence Division to coordinate antiradical activities and tapped the rising Justice Department star J. Edgar Hoover as its head. The GID, better known as the Radical Division, quickly turned into the hub of the Bureau of Investigation, and the crusade against radicals became the BI's main pursuit, as Hoover and the bureau's director, Flynn, deftly exploited the red scare to increase the BI's influence and funding.

Using the skills he had learned as a cataloger at the Library of Congress, Hoover established a cross-referenced index-card system called the "Editorial Card Index" that by the end of 1920 contained "over 200,000 cards, giving detailed data not only upon individual agitators connected with the ultraradical movement, but also upon organizations, associations, societies, publications, and special conditions existing in certain localities."[11] Within months of the GID's creation, its work expanded to cover general intelligence work, including "economic and industrial disturbances" as well as international issues. Hoover received weekly reports from the field offices and issued a confidential weekly bulletin to select government officials, covering "the entire field of national and international operations and . . . all situations at home or abroad" that were worthy of scrutiny.

It was during the red scare following World War I that the foundation of the later, all-powerful FBI was laid, as Hoover's Editorial Card Index mushroomed to 450,000 cards by December 1921,[12] containing what Palmer called "a remarkable record of facts, available for future use at the hands of the Government."[13]

A month after the establishment of the GID, two new radical organizations arose that commanded the division's attention. The Bolshevik revolution had splintered the Socialist Party, as the more radical members advocated the overthrow of the U.S. government and the establishment of a dictatorship of the proletariat, while the moderates continued to favor the slower approach of evolutionary change and working to change capitalism from within. By the time the party's annual convention opened in Chicago on August 30, a majority of the more than 100,000 members backed the first group, which was itself split into two factions: the American-born, who sought to establish a uniquely U.S. variety of Communism, and the immigrants, who saw the Russian model as the only viable alternative.

Both dissident groups split from the Socialist Party, with the foreign-born bloc, which represented 90 percent of the insurgents, founding the Communist Party, thus aggravating already well-developed xenophobic attitudes, and the native-born circle forming the Communist Labor Party.

The combined defections reduced Socialist Party membership by over two-thirds, to about thirty thousand, but the establishment of the two new Communist parties reinforced the government's belief that the numbers and influence of radicals were on the rise everywhere, even though the combined membership of the two Communist parties was between forty thousand and seventy thousand—at the most, less than one-tenth of 1 percent of the adult population of the United States.[14] Characteristically, out of fear of the radical ideas posed by these parties, the government grossly overestimated the actual threat they posed.

Because the Sedition Act was no longer in effect after the war, the Justice Department could not prosecute radicals for simply advocating the overthrow of the government. Instead, the strategy became the deportation of alien radicals under the Alien Act of October 16, 1918. This statute, which superseded the already stringent immigration law that had gone into effect in May 1917, allowed the government to deport, with a warrant from the secretary of labor, any alien belonging to an anarchist organization. A classic example of the principle of guilt by association, the 1918 law made it possible for an alien to be deported for simply being a member of the IWW, even without having engaged in any illegal activity. As John Higham wrote in *Strangers in the Land*, his classic study of American nativism, the Alien Act was a reflection of the widespread "impression that radicalism permeated the foreign-born population, that it flourished among immigrants generally and appealed to hardly anyone else."[15]

The deportation policy enacted in late 1919 had actually been formulated much earlier. On January 8 of that year a headline in the *New*

York World declared, "MEET 'RED' PERIL HERE WITH A PLAN TO DEPORT ALIENS." The story below stated, "Announcement was made in Washington that there is a definite plan to round up and deport all the alien 'Reds' in the United States and that the Departments of Labor and Justice are co-operating in preparing a list of every person in the country who has been drawn into the Bolshevik movement."

The government lost no time in putting the plan into action. On the morning of February 6, two hours before the Seattle general strike was scheduled to begin, immigration officers swept up forty men,[16] described by the *Chicago Tribune* as a "motley company of I.W.W. supporters, bearded labor fanatics, and Bolshevist agitators," loaded them into two heavily guarded sleeper cars, and shipped them east for deportation.[17] According to one immigration official traveling with the train, the agency had been working on the project for more than a year.

That the red scare was, to a significant degree, a government move against labor can be clearly seen from the *Tribune*'s prophetic evaluation of the situation, as it noted that "the train blazed a trail which, immigration authorities agree, will entirely solve the greatest danger of an industrial unrest during the reconstruction period."[18]

As the train made its way to the East Coast, one newspaper after another cheered "such a skimming of the great American melting-pot."[19] The *Seattle Times* thought it high time that "the interference of foreigners in the affairs of this country be curbed" and that immigrants be made to understand that "this is a country of Americans, by Americans, and for Americans." *The Washington Post* applauded the "serious cleaning up" of "bewhiskered, ranting, howling, mentally warped, law-defying aliens" and "international misfits."

Few and far between were voices like *The Duluth Herald*, which expressed concern over "those who are trying to make the fight against Bolshevism broad enough to cover everything that doesn't appeal to them," and the Socialist *New York Call*, which believed that the deportations struck at "the whole question of the right to think differently from the powers that be."

The government was moving steadily and decisively toward wholesale deportations of aliens and prosecution of citizens, as *The New York Times* revealed after the discovery of the May Day mail bombs. "The expected round-up of anarchists and other radicals who are agitating for the overthrow of this Government did not begin yesterday," said the *Times* on May 2. "The authorities [are] moving slowly, but thoroughly," with the expectation that "all agitators of alien citizenship will be deported, while those of American citizenship will be held for criminal prosecution in the Federal courts."

The distinction was a crucial one, for while proceedings against citizens were judicial, against aliens they were administrative, and therefore not only required a significantly lesser degree of proof but also were not subject to the lengthy delays of the judicial process. As New York's immigration commissioner, Frederic Howe, pointed out, "In deportation cases it is not necessary to provide a preponderance of testimony, or to convince the court of the justice of the charge; all that the government needs to support its case is a 'scintilla' of evidence, which may be any kind of evidence at all. If there is a bit of evidence, no matter how negligible it may be, the order of deportation must be affirmed."[20]

A week after the June 2 bombings, Wilson's cabinet discussed "deportation of aliens who advocated changing [the] government by force."[21] Attorney General Palmer proposed "very stringent alien & sedition laws," which he thought would "make it possible to reach radical socialists who did not resort to force," but whom he considered nonetheless dangerous. In a series of ensuing meetings, officials of the Labor Department, which had jurisdiction over immigration and deportation, and officials of the Justice Department agreed to "the closest cooperation and harmony" regarding matters of deportation.[22]

By August, when the GID came into existence, the plan to deport alien radicals was moving relentlessly toward implementation. On August 12, the BI's director, William Flynn, issued a directive ordering "a vigorous and comprehensive investigation" of anarchists, Bolsheviks, and others who advocated changing the government by force or violence; the emphasis was to be on aliens, "with a view of obtaining deportation cases."[23] Two weeks later, Hoover and Assistant Attorney General John T. Creighton met with the immigration commissioner general, Anthony Caminetti, and they agreed to arrest fifty targeted aliens who had been under investigation.[24]

At the same time, the war between capital and labor continued unabated. Whereas the largest strike of 1918 had involved 60,000 machinists, 1919 saw nine separate labor disturbances that involved more than 60,000 workers. By the end of August, there had been the Seattle general strike and the New York City building trades strike in February (60,000 and 125,000 workers, respectively); the Chicago building trades lockout in July (115,000); the Chicago stockyards strike (65,000) and the nationwide railroad shop workers strike in August (250,000).[25]

The fall of 1919 saw three landmark labor strikes, each of which was seized upon by the government, business interests, and the press as evidence of a radical conspiracy in the labor movement, thereby adding further fuel to the already hotly blazing red scare.

The first strike involved a most unlikely group of employees. For some time, members of the Boston police force had been discontented with their working conditions, long hours, and inadequate pay. In the spring, they were given a meager raise, but their other two issues remained unaddressed.

In June, when the Boston Social Club, a police officers' association, announced plans to unionize and affiliate with the American Federation of Labor, they were merely following the same course of action as police in more than three dozen other American cities, including Chattanooga, Los Angeles, Topeka, Tulsa, and Washington, D.C. But the Boston police commissioner and former mayor, Edwin U. Curtis, forbade such a move, saying that "a police officer cannot consistently belong to a union and perform his sworn duty."[26] Undaunted, BSC leaders defied Curtis and asked the AFL for a charter, which was granted on August 15. Less than two weeks later, Curtis tried nineteen BSC officials for violating orders; they were found guilty and given suspended sentences.

In an attempt to find a middle ground, a citizens' committee appointed by Boston's mayor, Andrew J. Peters, declared that the police should not affiliate with the AFL but were free to form an independent union of their own. Commissioner Curtis's response was to reverse his prior ruling and dismiss the nineteen convicted officers from the force on September 8. The Boston Social Club called an emergency meeting and, by a vote of 1,134–2, approved a strike for the following evening. As local newspapers condemned the decision, business owners recruited a volunteer police force from among their employees, Harvard University students, and former servicemen and American Legionnaires.

But when 1,117 of Boston's 1,544 officers walked off the job at

5:45 p.m. on Tuesday, September 9, the volunteer force, working together with the non-striking policemen, were overwhelmed, as bands of toughs roamed the city, smashing shopwindows, looting, roughing up private citizens, and holding public dice games. At midnight, a contingent of servicemen from the Boston Navy Yard was called in to maintain order.

The Boston papers wasted no time in labeling the strike a radical conspiracy. The *Herald* decried the "Bolshevist nightmare," while the *News Bureau* called the strike an "attempt at sovietizing Boston." The *Evening Transcript* published photographs of looted stores, comparing the mayhem to the Russian Revolution and praising the volunteer police for keeping "the State's collective will supreme over Bolshevism."[27]

Although Mayor Peters called out five thousand soldiers of the State Guard to protect the city, the night of September 10 was worse than the previous one. Riots broke out at a number of places, and there were several deaths, but by the morning of Thursday the eleventh, the State Guard and volunteer police force had managed to get the situation under control.

In Washington, the mood was decidedly apprehensive. The *Boston Evening Transcript* reported that lawmakers were "giving close attention to the Boston police strike . . . One senator said that . . . if the police should win the patrolmen of other cities would immediately attempt to affiliate with labor organizations."[28] On September 11, President Wilson, who was barnstorming the country to drum up support for the Treaty of Versailles and the League of Nations, issued a statement calling the strike "a crime against civilization." That same day, the Democratic senator Henry L. Myers of Montana took the floor of the Senate to denounce the "growing unrest throughout the country" and predict that "unless some branch of the Government stops this tendency, there will be no need of holding an election in 1920 [because] a Soviet Government will have been organized by that time."[29]

Despite the generally acknowledged conservative political leanings of law-enforcement officers, newspapers nationwide agreed that the Boston police strike constituted an outbreak of revolution. "Lenine [*sic*] and Trotsky are on their way in the United States," cried *The Wall Street Journal*, while in Philadelphia the *Evening Public Ledger* declared, "Bolshevism in the United States is no longer a specter . . . If [the nation] ever was vague in its conception of the Bolshevik horror its vision is clean-cut now."[30]

Mayor Peters, a Democrat, suggested arbitration to settle the strike, but Police Commissioner Curtis and Massachusetts's governor, Calvin Coolidge, both Republicans, refused. "The men are deserters," said Coolidge. "This is not a strike. These men were public officials. We can not think of arbitrating the government or the form of law."[31]

On September 12, the head of the AFL, Samuel Gompers, urged the strikers to put their faith in mediation and return to work. The Boston Social Club voted unanimously to follow Gompers's suggestion, but the following day Curtis fired the striking officers and announced that a new police force would be formed.

In a September 14 telegram to Gompers, Governor Coolidge declared unequivocally, "There is no right to strike against the public safety by anybody, anywhere, any time,"[32] a phrase that, as he later wrote, "caught the attention of the nation," catapulting him to the 1920 Republican vice presidential nomination, and ultimately, with the death of Warren Harding, the presidency.[33]

Meanwhile, the Bureau of Investigation's assistant director, Frank Burke, wired the Boston field office: "Make thorough investigation in police strike situation and ascertain whether radical elements or I.W.W.'s are in any way responsible for situation."[34] In their reports, BI agents offered some generalized accusations about radical involvement but could come up with nothing specific linking any radical individuals or organizations to the strike.* Nevertheless, the BI kept supposed radical instigators under surveillance and investigation after the strike ended.

The Boston police strike was broken, and even though the striking officers had demanded nothing more radical than shorter hours and better working conditions, the perception of a revolutionary uprising persisted. *The New York Times* commended Boston for "giving Bolshevism a salutary lesson," while the *Boston News Bureau* expressed relief over the defeat of the "attempt at sovietizing Boston."[35]

. . .

*One undercover agent heard "considerable radical talk" at strike headquarters, and another thought that since the Communist *New England Worker* newspaper supported the strike and distributed copies among the strikers, it was "the first step on the part of the radicals to participate in the strike" (Schmidt, *Red Scare*, p. 217).

A week after the police strike ended, a second momentous strike began when more than 275,000 steelworkers throughout the country walked off the job on September 22. Steel was the watershed industry in the battle between capital and labor; the business community feared that if steel became unionized, the trend would quickly spread to the rest of the mass-production sector.

As with all heavy industry, the backbone of steel manufacturing was immigrant labor. Wages were low, working conditions perilous, and hours inhumanely long—the average workweek was close to seventy hours, and many steelworkers labored twelve hours a day, seven days a week.

In August 1918, a meeting of twenty-four AFL unions in Chicago formed the National Committee for Organizing Iron and Steel Workers, with Gompers as honorary chairman. In June 1919, the committee wrote to the board chairman of the United States Steel Corporation, Judge Elbert H. Gary, proposing a conference to discuss industry conditions and the plight of steelworkers. When Gary failed to answer, the committee sent a strike ballot to local unions, and they unanimously approved it. On August 21, the committee announced twelve demands that would be made, including the right to collective bargaining, an eight-hour day and six-day week, the abolition of twenty-four-hour shifts and company unions, increased wages, and double pay for overtime, Sundays, and holidays.

The committee then asked Judge Gary for an arbitration conference to address their differences. He responded, "As heretofore publicly stated and repeated, our corporation and subsidiaries, although they do not combat labor unions as such, decline to discuss business with them. The corporation and its subsidiaries are opposed to the 'closed shop.' They stand for the 'open shop.' " Refusing to meet, Gary asserted, "In wage rates, living and working conditions, conservation for life and health, care and comfort in times of sickness or old age, and providing facilities for the general welfare and happiness of employees and their families, the corporation and subsidiaries have endeavored to occupy a leading and advanced position amongst employers."[36]

In an effort to head off a steel strike, President Wilson, in his August 31 Labor Day message, called on organized labor to join the government in combating radicalism, in exchange for which he vowed to call a conference to discuss "fundamental means of bettering the whole relationship of capital and labor."[37] The president's promise apparently carried little weight, for on September 10, the second day of the Boston police strike, the AFL announced the impending action against the steel companies. Citing "the intolerable and brutal conditions under which the men are compelled to work," the AFL named September 22 as the day a nationwide steelworkers' strike would begin.[38]

The timing could not have been worse. The antilabor climate, which had been building since the Seattle general strike, had sharply intensified as a result of the police strike, and when the steelworkers left the job, the mainstream press quickly dragged out the specter of "Bolshevism." The *New York Tribune* called the steel strike "another experiment in the way of Bolshevizing American industry," and the *New York World* said the strike had "some of the aspects of an economic revolution." *The Wall Street Journal* saw only "well-paid, satisfied workers" who were being led astray by "I.W.W. influences . . . and Russian Bolshevists." The *Chicago Tribune* regarded the steel strike as a tipping point: "In the end the decision means a choice between the American system and the Russian—individual liberty or 'the dictatorship of the proletariat' . . . The American people ought to do some serious thinking in these days forced upon them by radicals and aliens. Is the American system worth keeping? Are American ideas as good as German or Russian?"[39]

Steel officials, seeing the opportunity to turn public opinion in their favor, began a disinformation and smear campaign against the strikers. Newspapers carried stories, based entirely on industry sources, claiming that workers were abandoning the strike and returning to their jobs in droves. "CONDITIONS ALMOST NORMAL IN ALL STEEL PLANTS," read a banner headline in the *Los Angeles Times* on September 23, the same day union leaders estimated that 284,000 steelworkers were walking the picket lines. "STRIKE CRUMBLING," proclaimed *The Christian Science Monitor* a week later, at a time when the number of strikers had actually grown to more than 365,000, almost three-quarters of the industry workforce.

In Pittsburgh, the epicenter of the steel industry and ground zero of the strike, the city's seven newspapers functioned as the mouthpiece of the steel companies. As the Interchurch World Movement, an ecumenical group that conducted an independent investigation of the steel strike, later reported, the Pittsburgh press created the perception that "the strikers were foreigners striking in support of demands which would enable them to get control of the steel industry . . . Undiscriminating readers must have gained the impression that the men on strike in the steel industry were disloyal and un-American by virtue of entertaining some revolutionary economic theory."[40]

Reinforcing the idea that radical beliefs were un-American, the Justice Department, working with local law-enforcement agencies in many communities, arrested hundreds of radical steelworkers, most of whom were noncitizens and therefore deportable under the Alien Act of October 1918. Senator William S. Kenyon of Iowa, chairman of a Senate committee to investigate the strike, announced that it was high time the United States became a "one-language nation."[41]

Strike leaders came under heavy attack, as moderates were overshadowed by firebrands like the National Committee for Organizing Iron and Steel Workers' chairman, John Fitzpatrick, who attempted to rally his constituency with remarks like "We are going to socialize the basic industries of the United States," and "The strike won't stop until the steel workers become the lawmakers, at Washington, D.C."[42] Critics of the strike cited Fitzpatrick's rhetoric as proof that the strikers to a man sought to overthrow the government.

But it was the committee's secretary-treasurer, William Z. Foster, who became the lightning rod for the anti-union campaign. Foster was a seasoned organizer who had participated in his first strike in 1894, at age thirteen. He was later affiliated with the Socialist Party and the IWW but eventually decided to stay with organized labor and work at "boring from within," which he characterized as "the policy of militant workers penetrating conservative unions, rather than trying to construct new, ideal, industrial unions on the outside."[43] Returning to the AFL, he worked on campaigns to organize railroad workers and meatpackers before being appointed to the National Committee for Organizing Iron and Steel Workers. The National Association of Manufacturers, a rabidly anti-union group representing big business, disdainfully referred to him as "the well-known 'Red' Foster."[44]

The Bureau of Investigation, which had been keeping tabs on the leaders of the National Committee for Organizing Iron and Steel Workers for at least six months prior to the strike, discovered a 1911 pamphlet titled *Syndicalism*, co-authored by Foster, which was filled with revolutionary doctrine and rhetoric. The work stated, among other things, that a syndicalist "considers the State a meddling capitalist institution . . . He is a radical opponent of 'law and order' . . . He recognizes no rights of the capitalists to their property, and is going to strip them of it, law or no law."[45]

Foster's words were also turned against the movement as a whole. The pamphlet, which had long been out of print, suddenly began appearing everywhere, and newspapers were quoting from it at length. Despite Foster's subsequent wartime record of patriotic service as a speaker at Liberty Bond drives and Gompers's defense of him, Foster's words and radical philosophy as expressed in the 1911 pamphlet were now depicted as the driving forces behind the steel strike.

On September 24, the House Military Affairs Committee chairman, Julius Kahn, who during the war had recommended "a few prompt trials and a few quick hangings" as a solution to the problem of dissent,[46] now met with Attorney General Palmer to suggest that since there had been a number of steel-strike-related deaths, Foster should be arrested for murder. Moreover, if it could be shown that the killers had been influenced by Foster's writings, he should also be considered an accessory before the fact.

In the Senate, Montana's Henry Myers labeled Foster "an enemy of this Government and of organized society," and Charles Thomas of Colorado accused him of intending "to keep the revolution going until [he] may become in America even as Lenin and Trotski [*sic*] have become in Russia."[47]

On October 3, Foster appeared before the Senate committee investigating the steel strike and refused to completely repudiate his earlier writings. "The last piece," wrote the labor historian David Brody, "had been fitted in place to complete the picture of the steel strike as a dangerous radical movement."[48]

The National Committee for Organizing Iron and Steel Workers understood they had been discredited. What the committee did not know was the key part played by the Bureau of Investigation in tarnishing the strike leadership and, by extension, the strike itself. It was the BI that created the fiction of the strike's being engineered entirely by Foster and the Wobblies, as a way of getting rid of the relatively conservative leadership of the AFL, in order to form "the greatest revolutionary labor movement the world has ever seen."[49] In fact, there was no evidence of radical or revolutionary action on the part of Foster or other committee leaders during the course of the strike, but as Hoover wrote in an internal Justice Department memo in October, the bureau's smear tactics "quite apparently had a very salutary effect upon the failure of the radical elements in the steel strike."[50]

From the beginning, the steel strike was plagued by violence, due in no small part to collusion between the steel companies and the law-enforcement agencies in striking communities. Indeed, in the great majority of cases, the violence was initiated by the police—sometimes on horseback—as union meetings were raided, picket lines broken up, and strikers mercilessly beaten.

In many cases, the companies provoked ethnic and racial strife among strikers. One detective agency hired by the Illinois Steel Company, a subsidiary of U.S. Steel, instructed its employees to "stir up as much bad feeling as you possibly can between the Serbians and Italians."[51] In Donora, Pennsylvania, two men were shot and many more were injured in a battle between striking steelworkers and imported African-American strikebreakers. Predictably, however, press reports made it seem as if the strikers were responsible for the violence and the steel companies were merely defending themselves against the lawlessness of the workers.

In the process of saving western Pennsylvania from this "revolution," the authorities gratuitously swept aside civil liberties, as the constitutional rights of free speech and assembly were denied to union members in many localities, most of which had experienced no previous violence as a result of public meetings. In a number of places, the ban on public assembly actually began before the strike had even started.

The worst violence occurred in Gary, Indiana, where five thousand striking workers battled with strikebreakers and police on October 4. Fifty were injured and another fifty jailed, as eleven companies of state militia were called in but were unable to keep order, despite the support of five hundred special police and three hundred deputies. When Indiana's governor, James P. Goodrich, appealed for federal troops after two days of hostilities, General Leonard Wood arrived with a thousand soldiers armed with cannons, machine guns, and rifles. The general's first step was to declare the city under martial law.

Wood, who had presidential aspirations of his own, saw his duty as not only to suppress the rioting but also to make a contribution to "the rounding up of the Red element," and ordered an investigation by Army Intelligence of the radical influence among steelworkers in Gary.[52] Amid "wholesale seizures of firearms, radical literature and red flags,"[53] one of the items that turned up was a handbill, supposedly issued by the Communist Party, urging "overthrow of the military in Gary." Four copies of this flyer were found in the possession of a striker, leading Colonel W. S. Mapes to tell reporters, "This is the most dangerous piece of literature that has ever come to my attention . . . Before we leave we intend to clean Gary of Red agitators."[54]

Nonetheless, despite a determined effort, Army Intelligence was unable to prove the strike was a "red" plot, and a Senate Labor and Education Committee report, published while the strike was still on, concluded that while radicals were attempting to use the strike to their advantage, "it would be unfair to say that they were the leading force behind the strike."[55]

An Interchurch World Movement report was more emphatic: "Charges of Bolshevism or of industrial radicalism in the conduct of the strike were without foundation."[56]

Over a hundred striking Gary steelworkers called a press conference to refute the notion that the strike was controlled by radicals and foreigners. These men were all U.S. citizens and skilled laborers at the top end of the salary scale. "We expect to continue until we win," they told reporters, "but at no time do we intend to resort to violence or other methods that would discredit us in the eyes of the Constitution."[57]

No matter. By that time, the impression had been firmly planted and carefully cultivated in the public mind that the steelworkers' walkout was, in the words of Portland's *Oregonian*, "an attempted revolution, not a strike."[58] The mayor of Gary declared, "Deportation is the answer, deportation of these leaders who talk treason in America and deportation of those who agree with them and work with them."[59]

On October 6, the same day that General Wood arrived in Gary and declared martial law, the National Industrial Conference, as promised by Wilson at the end of August, convened in Washington. Unfortunately, it convened without the president.

Since the end of the war, Wilson's focus had been on foreign affairs, as he campaigned nonstop seeking public support for American ratification of the Treaty of Versailles and participation in the League of Nations. In September, he undertook an extended train tour of the country, speaking in several towns daily from the train's rear platform.

The stress of the effort took a sharp toll on his health. He began to experience severe headaches and asthma attacks, and in Wichita on September 26 the president's doctor insisted that the train return to Washington. Six days later, Wilson suffered a debilitating stroke that impaired his vision and paralyzed the left side of his body.

Wilson's withdrawal from domestic affairs had already helped create the climate in which the red scare flourished. Now, with his inability to fulfill the functions of office, the cabinet was left to run the country, a development that created an even greater opening for those who found it politically advantageous to further exploit the red scare.

The industrial conference itself was a fiasco. It was composed of representatives from three sectors: capital, labor, and the public. That the deck was stacked may be surmised from the fact that the twenty-two-member contingent representing the "public" contained eighteen men with corporate affiliations, including John D. Rockefeller Jr. and, most incongruously, U.S. Steel's chairman, Judge Elbert Gary. Upon learning the composition of the "public" group, the *United Mine Workers Journal* asked mischievously, "Then for the love of Mike who will represent the employers?"[60]

As expected, the issue of collective bargaining became the line in the sand. On behalf of the labor group, Gompers introduced a resolution proposing, in part, the right of workers to organize in unions and to bargain collectively. After days of debate and suggested revisions, the resolution was voted down by the employers' group. Incensed, Gompers walked out of the conference on October 22, and the talks collapsed.

A week before the industrial conference broke down, Senator Miles Poindexter of Washington, yet another man with designs on the presidency, declared to the Senate his belief that the increasing number of strikes around the country was "based on a desire to overthrow our Government, destroy all authority, and establish communism." Poindexter offered the conviction that "the Government should take vigorous action to stamp out anarchy and lawlessness. There is grave danger that a government will be overthrown when it ceases to defend itself. This is no time for sensitiveness on the part of public officials."[61]

In a grandstanding move aimed at both boosting his own presidential profile and putting pressure on the Wilson administration,

Poindexter introduced a resolution requiring the attorney general to inform the Senate why the Justice Department had not taken legal action against "the various persons within the United States who . . . have attempted to bring about the forcible overthrow of the Government . . . , who have preached anarchy and sedition, who have advised the defiance of law and authority, . . . and openly advocated the unlawful destruction of industry and . . . property."[62] Three days later, the Senate adopted Poindexter's resolution.

In fact, Palmer and the Justice Department had been working on that very scheme since the previous January; the heat from the Poindexter resolution now brought things to a head. Two days after Poindexter's motion, *The New York Times* reported that "a Federal official . . . estimated that there were at least 50,000 aliens in the United States who were openly or secretly working for a Bolshevist form of government in this country . . . The evidence of the activities of these foreigners is now in the possession of the Federal authorities, and there is reason for stating that a strict enforcement of the deportation laws against these alien trouble makers is among the possibilities of the near future."[63]

Days before the Justice Department plan was scheduled to start, the third great strike of the fall began, giving Palmer yet one more justification for putting his deportation program into action.

Although the coal industry, like the steel industry, had realized enormous profits during the war, the wages of miners had remained stagnant. After the war, coal companies refused to negotiate a wage increase, claiming that the wage agreement of September 1917, which was supposed to expire when the war ended—but no later than April 1, 1920—was still in effect because, while fighting had stopped, the war could not be officially considered over until a treaty had been signed. When the conservative United Mine Workers union declined to support miners' calls for action, wildcat strikes broke out in mines around the country. Finally, in September 1919, UMW officials put forth a proposal for a new contract that included a 60 percent pay increase, a six-hour workday, and a five-day workweek. Union leaders also set a deadline of November 1 for the signing of a new agreement, hoping that with winter approaching, the need for coal would be a strong bargaining chip in their favor.

The mine owners would agree to no more than a modified wage increase, and that only under pressure from Secretary of Labor William Wilson, himself a former miner. In response, the UMW called a strike for November 1, labeling it "the greatest enterprise in the history of trade unionism in America."[64]

From his sickbed, President Wilson condemned the impending strike, and three days before it was to begin, he met with Palmer. Without consulting the rest of the cabinet, the two decided to seek an injunction. Palmer applied to Judge Albert B. Anderson of the Indiana District Court, and on October 31, Anderson issued a temporary order prohibiting the leadership of the UMW from involvement in the strike. Union leaders, while officially complying with the order, refused to call off the action. On November 1, nearly 400,000 coal miners across the country left the job.

In announcing the strike, the UMW anticipated and tried to head off the inevitable red-baiting. "In calling this strike, the United Mine Workers have but one object in view," said the *UMW Journal*, "and that is to obtain just recognition of their right to a fair wage and proper working conditions. No other issue is involved here and there must be no attempt on the part of anyone to inject into the strike any extraneous purposes."[65]

Their plea had no effect. Just as in the Seattle general strike, the Boston police strike, and the nationwide steel strike, the cry of "Bolshevism" went up immediately. The coal company spokesman T. T. Brewster issued a press release asserting—with no evidence—that Lenin and Trotsky had ordered and financed the strike.[66] The *Seattle Times* referred to striking miners as "the I.W.W.'s, the American followers of Bolshevism and the anarchist syndicalists."[67]

"Thousands of them," reported the *New York Tribune*, "red-soaked in the doctrines of Bolshevism, clamor for the strike as the means of syndicalizing the coal mines . . . and even as starting a general red revolution in America. The public has no conception of the way in which a large element among the miners has absorbed the Bolshevik economy and the theory of soviet control."[68]

Palmer condemned the leaders of the coal and steel strikes as ultraradicals "who have no sympathy for our form of Government and no respect for our institutions. They would transplant the chaos of Russia to American soil."[69]

Just as it had in Seattle and Boston, and the steel strikes, the Bureau of Investigation secretly watched union leaders, including tapping their phones without warrants, reading all telegrams to and from the UMW's acting president, John L. Lewis, and gaining confidential access to UMW bank accounts.* The bureau, moreover, falsely discredited the coal strike as a radical revolt, despite BI agents' reports that the action was not controlled by radicals, and ultimately assisted in breaking the strike, as BI accusations of radical influence were used to justify the need for government intervention.[70]

With the steel strike in its second month, the coal strike under way, and the Poindexter resolution turning up the pressure on the Justice Department, the plan that had been afoot for almost a year was now unleashed, and the "skimming of the great American melting-pot" began in earnest.

---

*About radical labor leaders, Palmer said, "We . . . have our spying system and know every one of them and by and by some of them are going to get hurt. I would advise them to go into the hills somewhere and shoot themselves" (*New York World*, Nov. 7, 1919).

CHAPTER 7

A Lawless Government

History has come to know them as the Palmer raids. They started on November 7, 1919, six days after the beginning of the coal strike, when the Department of Justice marked the second anniversary of the Bolshevik revolution with nationwide raids on the offices of the Union of Russian Workers, an organization that Attorney General Palmer described as being "even more radical than the bolsheviki."[1] In eighteen cities, including Buffalo, Chicago, Cleveland, Detroit, Newark, New Haven, New York, Philadelphia, Pittsburgh, and St. Louis, federal and local agents invaded URW headquarters and indiscriminately swept up everyone in sight, members and nonmembers, aliens and citizens alike.

When the Union of Russian Workers was founded by exiled Russian anarchists in New York in 1907, its "Fundamental Principles" urged "the toiling masses [to] make themselves masters of all the riches of this world by means of a violent social revolution." The URW was declared to be "a broad revolutionary organization of workers carrying on a direct struggle against all the institutions of capitalism and Government," whose purpose was to "educate the working class to take the initiative and exercise power themselves in all their undertakings, thus developing the consciousness of the absolute necessity and inevitability of a general uprising—social revolution."[2]

A dozen years later, the URW had evolved into a tame, loosely affiliated group of local chapters that functioned as a social, educational, and mutual-aid society for Russian immigrants, with between four thousand and seven thousand members, the great majority of whom had joined the organization with no inkling of or interest in the subversive fundamental principles.[3] The group's anarchist leadership had returned to Russia after the Bolshevik revolution, and in 1919 URW offices were places where recent immigrants could attend a dance on the weekend; take night classes in subjects like English, math, automobile repair, and driver's education; and generally commiserate about life in a new country as they downed a glass of vodka with fellow expatriates. In 1923, an investigator who had studied the URW wrote that "no disorder, no crime, no preparation for crime, even, has been traced to any group of the Union of Russian Workers. Their sin, such as it is, has consisted in talk only."[4]

Despite the organization's benign existence, the Bureau of Investigation, insisting on a literal interpretation of the fundamental principles, had been monitoring the URW for well over a year before the November 1919 raid. By February 1919, anticipating the deportation of URW members, the BI had infiltrated the Russian People's House (the URW's national headquarters in Manhattan) on the conviction that it was a camouflage for an anarchist underground. With a minimum of accurate investigative effort, the BI could undoubtedly have determined that the URW had evolved into little more than an ethnic fraternal organization, but the bureau's view, skewed by its determinedly antiradical bent, was inclined to see revolutionaries under every rock and attribute far more power to them than they actually possessed.

In March, however, the Labor Department instructed its personnel to "avoid technicality or literalness in the enforcement" of the Alien Act of 1918,[5] and in July the Immigration Bureau told the Justice Department that no individual should be arrested or deported for mere membership in the URW, but rather that "the alien must be an active Worker in order to be subject for deportation."[6] Not to be denied, the BI contended the opposite, that an alien's membership in the organization was indeed grounds for deportation, and with its greater funding and increasing influence the Justice Department was able to force its will on the Labor Department.

On August 14, the Lusk Committee raided the Russian People's House, a four-story brownstone on East Fifteenth Street, confiscating hundreds of copies of the URW journal *Bread and Freedom* and taking fourteen men into custody, three of whom were held on $10,000 bail. The next day, apparently inspired by the committee's example, J. Edgar Hoover suggested a similar raid on the Russian People's

House to the BI's assistant director, Frank Burke; the following month, he again proposed the idea to Burke, saying it would be a way of getting the names of the people connected with the organization, in preparation for "a simultaneous raid" on URW facilities across the country.[7] At the end of October, he informed the commissioner general of immigration, Anthony Caminetti, that the BI was organizing a nationwide roundup of URW members and requested that the Bureau of Immigration furnish arrest warrants. Caminetti complied, issuing five hundred warrants.

On November 7, under orders from the BI chief, William Flynn, to "leave no stone unturned to end all symptoms of anarchy in the United States,"[8] Justice Department and local law-enforcement agents swept down on URW headquarters around the country and, despite having only five hundred arrest warrants, took 1,182 individuals into custody.[9] Of those, just 439 were held for deportation hearings, in some cases for extended periods of up to five months. In a number of circumstances, prisoners were physically and mentally abused and even tortured.[10] Bails were set at $10,000 and up.

The largest haul of people, literature, and office equipment was made at the Russian People's House, where 360 "anarchists" were arrested—308 were soon released[11]—and "tons of literature" confiscated.[12] According to press accounts, law-enforcement officials meted out gratuitous violence in the raid on the Russian People's House. "A number of those in the building," said *The New York Times*, "were badly beaten by the police during the raids, their heads wrapped in bandages testifying to the rough manner in which they had been handled." The *New York World* story noted that despite the display of force, "little resistance was offered." When thirty-five of the arrestees were transported to Ellis Island the following day, the *Times* reported, "most of them . . . had blackened eyes and lacerated scalps as souvenirs of the new attitude of aggressiveness which has been assumed by the Federal agents against Reds and suspected Reds."[13]

Ostensibly, the raids were to root out the perpetrators of the June bombings. Although the Justice Department almost certainly suspected the Galleanists by this time, the official line was still that authorities had not found "the faintest clue" to indicate who was behind the bombings and that these raids would sooner or later yield leads.[14]

But the real reasons for the raids were twofold. The first purpose

President Woodrow Wilson leading a Preparedness Day parade in Washington, D.C., during the spring of 1916, a year after the sinking of the *Lusitania*.

Library of Congress, Prints and Photographs Division, LC-USZ62-109786

Progressive Republican senator Robert La Follette of Wisconsin, a staunch peace advocate and opponent of the preparedness movement. La Follette and other minority voices opposed to preparedness and America's entry into the war were vilified as traitors.

Library of Congress, Prints and Photographs Division, LC-USZ62-14109

SHOWING THEM UP.—SEE THE HERALD'S ENEMY ALIEN LIST.

Between December 3 and 28, 1917, *The New York Herald* published a complete list of the names and addresses of all German and Austro-Hungarian "enemy aliens" living in the city.

Library of Congress, Prints and Photographs Division, LC-USZ62-42611

On the night of April 4, 1918, German immigrant Robert Paul Prager was lynched by a mob outside Collinsville, Illinois. Eleven men were tried for his murder; the jury deliberated for forty-five minutes before acquitting all the defendants. In addition to ethnic Germans, pacifists, Wobblies, Socialists, anarchists, Mennonites, and Irish-Americans also suffered scapegoating during the war.

St. Louis Post-Dispatch Archives, photograph by International Film Service Co., Inc.

When the Wobblies led strikes in southwestern copper mines in 1917, they were called traitors for sabotaging the war effort. In Bisbee and Lowell, Arizona, the local sheriff and a deputized posse rounded up twelve hundred Wobblies, marched them out of town, deported them by train, and dropped them off in the desert to fend for themselves.

Library of Congress, Prints and Photographs Division, LC-USZ62-63631

In February 1919 a Seattle general strike was labeled "an attempted revolution" by mayor Ole Hanson. Hanson became a national celebrity when he used fifteen hundred federal troops to break the strike.

Library of Congress, Prints and Photographs Division, LC-DIG-GGBAIN-28168

In September 1919, when 275,000 steelworkers walked off the job, local law enforcement agencies, working in collusion with the steel companies, incited violence and arrested many strikers.
Library of Congress, Prints and Photographs Division, LC-USZ62-23690

Right: Attorney General A. Mitchell Palmer, one of the main perpetrators of the post–World War I red scare.
Library of Congress, Prints and Photographs Division, LC-DIG-NPCC-19136

Left: Palmer appointed former Secret Service chief William J. Flynn to head the Bureau of Investigation; Flynn deftly exploited the red scare to increase the BI's influence and funding, turning the BI into a de facto secret police force.
Library of Congress, Prints and Photographs Division, LC-DIG-HEC-03690

On December 21, 1919, in the midst of the Palmer raids, scores of radicals were deported from New York City to Soviet Russia. They sailed aboard the transport ship *Buford*, pictured here; it was dubbed the "Soviet Ark" by the press.
Library of Congress, Prints and Photographs Division, LC-USZ62-40635

Among the group of 249 aliens deported on the *Buford* were the two most prominent anarchist leaders in the country, Alexander Berkman (second from left) and Emma Goldman, shown here in custody, with Uncle Sam looking down on them.

Library of Congress, Prints and Photographs Division, LC-DIG-GGBAIN-24437

Right: Assistant Secretary of Labor Louis F. Post played a crucial role in bringing the red scare to a close.

Library of Congress, Prints and Photographs Division, LC-DIG-GGBAIN-13593

Left: Harlan Fiske Stone (right) was sworn in as attorney general in April 1924. Though politically conservative, Stone was a steadfast civil libertarian who had spoken out publicly against the red scare and the Palmer raids. Stone announced a reorganization of the BI and a reordering of its priorities, including an end to illegal surveillance and persecution of civilians for their political beliefs.

Library of Congress, Prints and Photographs Division, LC-DIG-NPCC-10893

J. Edgar Hoover joined the Bureau of Investigation in 1917 and soon began a meteoric rise to the top of the agency. He is pictured here in 1924, when Harlan Fiske Stone appointed him BI director.

Library of Congress, Prints and Photographs Division, LC-USZ62-92411

Right: This was the scene on March 8, 1932, when four trains carrying men, women, and children left Los Angeles's Central Station for Mexico. Between a half million and a million people, many of them United States citizens or otherwise legal residents, were deported or "voluntarily repatriated" during the Depression.
Herald-Examiner Collection, Los Angeles Public Library

Left: In the weeks following the Japanese attack on Pearl Harbor, nearly seven thousand German, Japanese, and Italian aliens were arrested and subsequently interned in Department of Justice camps. At the camp in Crystal City, Texas, a combined crew of Japanese and German aliens built housing.
USAFA McDermott Library
MS 52, Jacobs Collection

Right: Major Karl R. Bendetsen, aide to the Army's provost marshal, authored the plan to carry out the evacuation and relocation of more than 112,000 Japanese on the West Coast.
Photograph by Mark Kauffman, Time & Life Pictures/ Getty Images

Left: The Japanese-American owner of this grocery in Oakland, California, placed the "I Am an American" sign in his store window the day after the attack on Pearl Harbor. The store was sold soon after President Franklin D. Roosevelt issued the evacuation order.
Photograph by Dorothea Lange, ©The Dorothea Lange Collection, Oakland Museum of California, City of Oakland; Gift of Paul S. Taylor

Evacuees, like this San Francisco group in April 1942, were allowed to take only what they could carry. They were sent first to assembly centers, then to relocation camps.

Photograph attributed to Dorothea Lange, Library of Congress, Prints and Photographs Division, LC-USZ62-24654

California representative Richard M. Nixon (upper left) and the arch-conservative committee chairman J. Parnell Thomas (second from right), at a 1948 hearing of the House Un-American Activities Committee.
Photograph by New York Times Co./Getty Images

Wisconsin senator Joseph R. McCarthy has been called "the most gifted demagogue" in American history. For all the hundreds of individuals McCarthy accused and investigated during his reign of terror, he never discovered or revealed a single Communist or any instance of espionage.
Photograph by Hank Walker/Time & Life Pictures/Getty Images

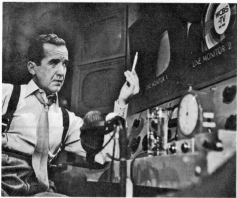

The tide began to turn against McCarthy when television journalist Edward R. Murrow devoted the entire March 9, 1954, installment of his nationwide *See It Now* program to exposing the senator's deceit and fabrications.
Photograph by Hulton Archive/Getty Images

Below: One of the most vicious and vindictive FBI COINTELPRO campaigns was conducted against the Reverend Martin Luther King Jr.
Photograph by Popperfoto/Getty Images

Above: Joseph Welch, representing the army against Senator McCarthy, uttered the celebrated line, "Have you no sense of decency, sir?", causing the audience to burst into applause.
Photograph by Hank Walker/Time & Life Pictures/Getty Images

In May 1964, President Lyndon B. Johnson (right) signed an executive order exempting J. Edgar Hoover from the mandatory retirement age of seventy for federal employees, effectively ensuring that Hoover would remain in his position as FBI director for life.
Photograph by Rolls Press/Popperfoto/Getty Images

COINTELPRO–Black Nationalist Hate Groups was an across-the-board attack on emerging African-American awareness and black pride, but the Black Panther Party, members of which are shown here in a 1969 New York City protest, bore the brunt of the assault.
Photograph by David Fenton/Getty Images

COINTELPRO–New Left targeted the anti–Vietnam War movement and other left groups, particularly Students for a Democratic Society. This photograph was taken during the protests at the 1968 Democratic convention in Chicago. Photograph by Leslie H. Sintay/Bettmann/Corbis

In 1975 and 1976 a Senate committee to study government intelligence activities, chaired by Idaho senator Frank Church, issued more than fifty thousand pages of reports detailing abuses by the FBI and other United States intelligence agencies that dated back decades.
Photograph by Central Press/Getty Images

was to round up alien "radicals" for deportation, as evidenced by the fact that citizens who were arrested were quickly released, whereas aliens were detained. The second purpose was as a trial run for a much larger operation that would soon be launched. "This is the first big step," announced the attorney general's office, "to rid the country of these foreign trouble makers."[15] Three days after the URW raids, the Department of Justice confirmed "that the Government's war on these alien agitators and conspirators is just getting under way and that there will be no letup until the country has been rid of them. Other important arrests in various parts of the country are known to be pending."[16]

In the days after November 7, there were a series of follow-up raids on URW centers and the headquarters of other radical groups. On November 8, another 250 arrests were made in Detroit and 60 in Bridgeport. The same day in New York City, a force that included "members of the anarchist, narcotic and Italian squads, plainclothes men, 700 men in uniform, agents of the Department of Justice, inspectors of the Immigration Service, and the State Constabulary," all under the direction of the Lusk Committee, stormed over seventy reported Communist Party centers throughout the five boroughs, confiscating twenty-five tons of literature and arresting more than 1,000 individuals, only 35 of whom were held and charged with criminal anarchy. "Prisoners were taken in droves, the dangerous Reds to be divided later from the innocent bystanders." Senator Lusk issued a statement that said, in part, "The time has come for the people of this country to take a definite stand on this question in order that we may know who our enemies are and deal with them as they deserve."[17]

Palmer became an overnight hero. The *Ohio State Journal* out of Columbus called him "A Strong Man of Peace . . . in these troubled days a tower of strength to his countrymen," while *The Atlanta Constitution* said Palmer brought "thrills of joy to every American," and *The Pittsburgh Post* dubbed him "The Fighting Attorney General."[18]

A week after the URW raids, the attorney general sent a letter and report to the Senate in which he responded to the accusations of the Poindexter resolution, detailing the Justice Department's efforts against radical aliens.[19] In the letter, Palmer recommended a peacetime sedition law that would make it possible to clamp down on radical aliens and citizens alike, and though none would ever be enacted, the next several months saw the introduction of some seventy such bills in Congress.

. . .

November 11 was Armistice Day, the first anniversary of the end of the fighting in Europe, and all across the country parades were held to commemorate the occasion. In the logging town of Centralia, Washington, a typical procession was planned.

The businessmen and law-enforcement officials of Centralia had been engaged in a long-standing campaign to eliminate the IWW presence from their town. In 1918, at least two Wobblies—one a blind newspaper vendor—had been abducted and severely beaten, and during a Red Cross parade on Memorial Day a mob had raided and forced the shutting of the local IWW hall. The office reopened in September, prompting a group of local businessmen to form the Centralia Protective Association, for the purpose of preventing further IWW activity in Centralia. After the Centralia Post of the American Legion announced the planned Armistice Day parade, rumors began circulating that the event would be the occasion of a repeat attack on IWW headquarters.

Founded in Paris by twenty World War I veteran officers on February 15, 1919, the American Legion was conceived as a patriotic support group for military veterans. It grew by staggering leaps, and within a year the membership rolls would increase to 840,000 men. The Legion was not only the largest of the patriotic organizations; it was also the most violent. Legionnaires, with the tacit approval of law-enforcement officials, were instrumental in breaking up public meetings, busting picket lines, and raiding the offices of radical groups. As one historian of the organization notes, without the contribution of the American Legion, "the Red Scare of 1919–20 might not have so effectively stopped American radicalism in its tracks."[20]

The Armistice Day parade route was scheduled to pass by the reopened IWW office, which, given the rumors, was evidence enough to the Wobblies that their suspicions of an attack were well-founded. Arming themselves with rifles and pistols, six men occupied the office, four were stationed in two hotels across the street, and three more waited on a hill about a quarter of a mile away.

At about 2:00 p.m., the parade left the city park, led by the local Elks Lodge, which included two prominent Centralians—the city postmaster and the former mayor, an ex-clergyman—who carried long pieces of rope, "as a joke," as the latter would later testify under oath.[21] The Elks were followed by a marching band, a contingent of

Boy Scouts, and three distinct blocs of servicemen and veterans in uniform: first, a group of marines and sailors, then the American Legion Post from nearby Chehalis, and finally the Centralia American Legion Post. Bringing up the rear were several automobiles carrying uniformed Red Cross nurses.

When the marchers passed the IWW hall without incident, it appeared that violence would be averted, but after about a block the paraders suddenly did an about-face and headed back toward Wobbly headquarters. When the Centralia Legionnaires reached the office, they stopped.

What happened next has never been definitively determined, but within seconds a fusillade of bullets poured down on the Centralia Legionnaires from all directions. The Legionnaires later claimed they were fired on without cause; the Wobblies insisted that several of the Legionnaires rushed the building and had forced open the front door before the shooting began. Whatever triggered the gunfire, three Legionnaires fell dead in the cross fire. Among those killed was Warren O. Grimm, the Centralia Legion post commander and a prominent member of the Centralia Protective Association.

Eleven Wobblies were quickly arrested, and another, Wesley Everest, himself a World War I veteran who had fought in Europe, escaped and fled the town. He was pursued by a posse, and after a firefight in which a fourth Legionnaire was mortally wounded, Everest was captured and beaten. That night, the lights went out throughout Centralia; during the blackout, a mob dragged Everest from his jail cell, beat him again, threw him into a car, and drove him out of town. En route, he was emasculated and, in a stark reenactment of the Frank Little lynching, hanged from a railroad bridge.

The Centralia killings touched off a fierce wave of reaction across the country. Senator Miles Poindexter sounded his theme of governmental indulgence of radicals, saying, "Instead of deporting and otherwise punishing as the laws provide this miserable human vermin which seeks to destroy civilization, the government has shown them many favors."[22] His fellow Washington senator, Wesley L. Jones, told the Senate, "The shots that killed these boys were really aimed at the heart of this Nation by those who oppose law and seek to overthrow our Government."[23] Meanwhile, the press cried out for vengeance. "It reads like an atrocity of the Huns," said *The Pittsburgh Press*. "The sooner the firing squad is got into action the better." The *Boston*

Evening Transcript called it "an act of war against the United States" and insisted that "the I.W.W. organization . . . be throttled." The *United Presbyterian* demanded that "every Bolshevist in this land change his course or swing at the end of a rope."[24]

In Washington, D.C., the BI's assistant director, Frank Burke, wired the special agents F. D. Simmons and F. W. McIntosh of the Seattle field office, instructing them to begin a complete investigation. In their initial response the day after the incident, the two agents reported that the IWW attack had been unprovoked. Several days later, however, having had more time to investigate, they learned from eyewitnesses that before any shots were fired, the parade had come to a halt and a Legionnaire had left the march, approached the IWW office, and attempted to open the door. Failing, he turned back to his fellows and said, "Come on, boys," prompting several more Legionnaires to leave the parade and move toward the hall. The first man managed to open the door, whereupon the firing began. The agents concluded that the tragedy was not a result of premeditated action on the part of either the Wobblies or the Legionnaires, but rather had its roots in the animosity that had existed between the union men and the townspeople for months and arose spontaneously out of the heat of the occasion. "What was done by the ex-soldiers appears to have been done on the spur of the moment, on impulse," said Agent McIntosh's report, "and the previous feeling existing generally between the two factions made the first move a signal for rather concerted action by those within available reach."[25]

Nevertheless, despite Agent Simmons's acknowledgment of the fact that these momentous findings shed "new light on matter," he advised that they "be kept absolutely confidential by Department at this time as I believe County Prosecutor will resent publication as an interference with his case."[26] Not only did the Bureau of Investigation never reveal what it had discovered about the Centralia shootings, but it actually aided the prosecution in its case and even advised the county prosecutor on how to rebut the testimony of the eyewitnesses who maintained that the Legionnaires had opened the door of the IWW office and were about to enter before the shooting started. Moreover, the bureau would later point to the Centralia incident as evidence that proved the IWW was engaged in a crusade of "sabotage and lawlessness."[27]

Of the ten Centralia Wobblies who were tried the following March, two were acquitted, one was found insane, and the rest were given sentences of twenty-five to forty years. In an affidavit taken after the trial, the juror E. E. Torpen declared, "I verily believe . . . that if these men had not been affiliated with the I.W.W. organization they would never have been convicted."[28] Other jurors confirmed this sentiment.

Shortly after the Centralia killings, the House Committee on Immigration discovered that of the nearly seven hundred hundred aliens who had been arrested on anarchy charges between February 1917 and November 1919, only sixty had actually been deported. This was largely attributable to the compassion and decency of Frederic C. Howe, the New York commissioner of immigration and administrator of Ellis Island. In his autobiography, *The Confessions of a Reformer*, Howe explained:

> Men and women were herded into Ellis Island. They were brought under guard and in special trains with instructions to get them away from the country with as little delay as possible. Most of the aliens had been picked up in raids on labor headquarters; they had been given a drum-head trial by an inspector with no chance for defense; they were held incommunicado and often were not permitted to see either friends or attorneys, before being shipped to Ellis Island. In these proceedings the inspector who made the arrest was prosecutor, witness, judge, jailer, and executioner. He was clerk and interpreter as well. This was all the trial the alien could demand under the law . . .
>
> I was advised by the Commissioner-General to mind my own business and carry out orders, no matter what they might be. Yet such obvious injustice was being done that I could not sit quiet . . . Members of Congress were swept from their moorings by an organized propaganda, and demanded that I be dismissed because I refused to railroad aliens to boats made ready for their deportation. I took the position from which I would not be driven, that the alien should not be held incommunicado, and should enjoy the right of a writ of habeas corpus in the United States courts, which was the only semblance of legal proceedings open to him under the law.[29]

With lawmakers and the newspapers calling for his head, Howe responded, "If it has been charged that I have released radicals or any one else held for deportation, the charges are entirely false. I had no power to release anybody and did not release anybody. All releases were made at Washington."[30] It made no difference, and Howe chose to resign. "There were some orders I would not carry out," he wrote in his autobiography. "And I wanted to be rid of political office that compelled compromise."[31] His successor, Byron Uhl, would be constrained by no such lofty concerns.

While the Howe drama was playing out, the Bureau of Investigation announced that in a return raid on the Russian People's House, agents had discovered a "bomb factory" that had somehow been missed in the earlier raids. Inspector Owen Eagan of the Bureau of Combustibles called the find "the most deadly and dangerous assortment of explosives and bomb ingredients I have seen in many a year."[32] Eagan estimated that a hundred bombs could be made from the confiscated ingredients, which allegedly included TNT as well as "muriatic acid, sulphuric acid, ammonia hydrate and glycerine sulphate." He implied that such chemicals may have been used in the May mail bombs, and agents also stated that "the bottles had not been standing idly for any length of time." Strangely enough, however, no other mention of the bomb-making materials was ever made, making it just one more in a series of sensational accusations in the bombing cases that went nowhere.

The imaginary bomb factory, combined with the Howe hysteria, added more steam to the red scare. The Department of Labor now reversed its earlier position and ruled that mere membership in the Union of Russian Workers was indeed grounds for deportation under the Alien Act, and when the *Buford* sailed out of New York harbor on December 21 with its cargo of deportees, 184 of its 249 passengers were URW members who had been apprehended in the November 7 raids. By Assistant Secretary of Labor Louis Post's count, "no less than 175 such persons" were guilty of nothing more than their URW membership.[33] One deportee who did not even belong to the group but was simply enrolled in a math course that happened to be in progress at the time of the raid, was swept up along with the others and, despite a total lack of incriminating evidence at his deportation hearing, wound up bound for Russia on the *Buford.*

.   .   .

The November roundups were just a dress rehearsal, and on January 2, 1920, the Justice Department engineered a second and far more extensive set of raids. The targets of these new attacks were the Communist Party and the Communist Labor Party.

In December, Hoover's Radical Division sent Anthony Caminetti in the Immigration Bureau a classic example of the type of flawed and falsified intelligence that was later to become a hallmark of Hoover's tenure as head of the FBI. Although its own investigations had found otherwise, the division's report on the Communist Party claimed that the organization had been both a major influence in the labor disturbances of 1919 and an instrumental force in provoking the previous summer's race riots. The day after the *Buford*'s departure, Hoover sent Caminetti a list, supposedly based "upon careful and thorough investigations," of more than fifteen hundred alien CP members for whom arrest warrants were requested.[34] In fact, these "careful and thorough investigations" were nothing more than the word of informers, accepted whole cloth with no corroborating evidence.

Hoover asked for the warrants by December 27, all but ensuring that the understaffed and underfunded Immigration Bureau would be unable to review every case in the allotted five days. On December 24, Labor Secretary William Wilson agreed that alien CP members were deportable, and by the end of the month Hoover's number of requested warrants had grown to three thousand. Then, without seeking Labor Department confirmation, Hoover decided that alien Communist Labor Party members were also deportable. "The Communist Party," he wrote to Caminetti on the same day of the labor secretary's decision, "is exactly similar to the Communist Labor Party . . . It is therefore the intention of this office to treat the members of the Communist Labor Party in the same category as those of the Communist Party."[35]

It was all blatantly illegal. To begin with, deportation rulings were strictly within the province of the Labor Department, which housed the Immigration Bureau. Nevertheless, as the Massachusetts district court judge George W. Anderson wrote in his ruling on a habeas corpus case brought by a group of detainees, "The general conduct and control of this wholesale deportation undertaking [was] assumed by the Department of Justice."[36] Moreover, the Bureau of Investigation's annual appropriation from Congress was expressly for the detection and prosecution of crimes against the United States, and deportation measures were administrative, not criminal proceedings.* Most decisively, neither the Communist Party nor the Communist Labor Party was outlawed at the time, and the Justice Department's pursuit of them was clearly outside its purview. Hoover, of course, knew all this and later admitted as much, writing to the BI's assistant director, Frank Burke, in February that there was "no authority under the law permitting this Department to take any action in deportation proceedings relative to radical activities."[37]

Palmer was also aware of the illegality of the plan. Louis Post recounts a meeting in which the attorney general instructed Labor Department representatives that they were obliged to issue any arrest warrants he requested without his being required to produce any proof of sufficient cause.[38] When the Labor Department employee A. Warner Parker protested, Palmer challenged him. "Do you mean to tell me," demanded Palmer, "that there is no law under which you can issue a warrant for the arrest of an alien when I certify that he is subject to deportation?"

"Mr. Attorney General," responded Parker calmly, "not only is there no such law, but no such law would be Constitutional if there was one."

But the legalities were clearly of little concern. Undercover infiltrators were ordered to have their groups arrange meetings for the evening of January 2, and on December 27 Palmer issued guidelines to Justice Department agents who would be carrying out the upcoming raids.

One more crucial step in preparation for the raids was a change in the rules governing an alien's right to counsel. On December 31, under pressure from Hoover, John W. Abercrombie,† who was acting secretary of labor while Secretary Wilson was ill and Assistant Secretary Post was engaged with other business, changed the wording of Rule 22 of the Labor Department guidelines for deportation hearings.

---

*The Justice Department also misspent federal funding by providing newspapers with plates of preprinted material "without charge, carriage prepaid." The material included articles with headlines like "U.S. DEPARTMENT OF JUSTICE URGES AMERICANS TO GUARD AGAINST BOLSHEVISM MENACE" and "TO 'CONQUER AND DESTROY STATE,' U.S. COMMUNISTS CALL FOR LABOR REVOLT." See *Nation*, March 6, 1920, p. 299, for a facsimile of one such page.

†Abercrombie was the Labor Department solicitor; he was appointed—as were all departmental solicitors—by the attorney general and, as such, maintained a close relationship with the Justice Department.

Rule 22, which had been changed in the aliens' favor by Labor Secretary Wilson the previous March, provided that at the beginning of a deportation hearing, an alien had to be informed of the right to counsel. Hoover complained to Caminetti that the attorneys who defended aliens were advising them not to make any statements about their activities or organizational affiliations. Caminetti, in turn, suggested to Abercrombie that it would be better to revert to an earlier version of Rule 22 that allowed an alien to testify "without being hampered by the advice of counsel."[39] Abercrombie immediately changed the wording of the rule to say that the alien should be apprised of the right to counsel "preferably at the beginning of the hearing," or when the hearing had "proceeded sufficiently in the development of the facts to protect the Government's interest."[40]

On the last day of 1919, in a New Year's message to the nation, Palmer assured the American public that he fully intended "during the forthcoming year to keep up an unflinching, persistent, aggressive warfare against any movement, no matter how cloaked or dissembled, having for its purpose either the promulgation of [radical] ideas or the excitation of sympathy for those who spread them."[41] As Palmer framed it, then, the anti-red campaign was not against criminal activity but against the spread of ideas.

Louis Post, intensely disturbed by what he saw developing, wrote in a New Year's entry in his journal, "At present there are signs of an overthrow of our Government as a free government. It is going on under cover of a vigorous drive against 'anarchists,' an anarchist being almost anybody who objects to government of the people by tories and for financial interests."[42]

The January 2 operation was carried out in thirty-three cities, with *The New York Times* reporting 5,483 arrests.[43] Of those, 2,435 were turned over to immigration officials for deportation proceedings, but since the Department of Justice had hijacked the entire process, Immigration's role was merely to apply a rubber stamp.

The most authoritative overview of the Palmer raids comes from Post. His ringside seat as assistant secretary of labor, together with his unswerving commitment to the principles of constitutional democracy, makes his account by far the most convincing. About the January 2 raids he wrote:

Toward public law and private rights, these raids were if possible more defiantly reckless than those of November . . . [T]hey involved lawless invasions of peaceable assemblies—public and private, political, recreational and educational. Meetings wide open to the general public were roughly broken up. All persons present—citizens and aliens alike without discrimination—were arbitrarily taken into custody as if they had been burglars caught in the criminal act. Without warrants of arrest men were carried off to police stations or other temporary prisons, subjected there to secret-police inquisitions commonly known as the "third degree," their statements written categorically into mimeographed question blanks, and they required to swear to them regardless of their accuracy. The sole excuse for these outrages was the mere presence of the victims at these open and lawful meetings.[44]

Most of these meetings, of course, were organized by undercover agents provocateurs.

Among the reported discoveries netted in the raids were "drawings alleged to represent the mechanism of bombs" in New Brunswick, New Jersey;[45] four iron balls, alleged to be bombs, at a Newark location; and what Palmer characterized as "large quantities of revolutionary documents . . . together with many firearms."[46] Only the "revolutionary documents" turned out to be as described. The "bomb mechanism" drawings were sketches of phonograph inventions. The iron ball "bombs," which were submerged in water and displayed for reporters, who unquestioningly reported their explosive capabilities, were bowling balls. And aside from three pistols capable of firing—two of which were .22 caliber—the "many firearms" were a bunch of stage props discovered in a raid on an amateur theatrical society. "At no place in all that nation-wide raiding of January, 1920," wrote Post, "were any weapons or explosive materials or destructive mechanisms discovered from which an inference of projected crime, private or political, could be reasonably drawn. Even as to criminal thoughts the proof was flimsy—absurdly so in contrast with the severity of the raiding."[47]

Agents broke into meeting halls and private homes without search warrants, tore apart offices and residences, and forced detainees to stand against the walls of meeting halls and searched them—all of which prompted the Massachusetts judge George Anderson to observe that "a mob is a mob, whether made up of government officials acting under instructions from the Department of Justice, or of criminals, loafers, and the vicious classes."[48] In many cities, the raids were "disgraceful legal travesties . . . in defiance of the law by officers of the law."[49] Countless arrestees were beaten and held incommunicado. Bails were established at $10,000, a gross violation of the Eighth Amendment. Citizens caught in the net were handed over to local law-enforcement departments for prosecution under criminal syndicalist laws. In Boston, eight hundred prisoners were marched through the streets in chains, and photographs of the procession appeared in newspapers as evidence of their violent and menacing nature. In Hartford, ninety-seven men were held in near-solitary confinement for five months, "practically buried alive."[50]

The worst outrages took place in Detroit, where eight hundred aliens and citizens were held for six days in a windowless corridor on the fifth floor of the Justice Department building. They had the use of just one toilet and one sink, with no bedding, and, except for two biscuits and a cup of coffee twice a day, no food except what their friends or relatives brought them. The longtime journalist Frederick R. Barkley, who was sent by his newspaper, *The Detroit News*, to investigate, reported: "The heat was sickening, and the stench was almost overpowering . . . The conditions were such . . . that Mayor Couzens . . . informed the City Council that they were intolerable in a civilized city." Barkley noted that the men were "fairly well-dressed for workingmen—not dirty looking fellows," as "we have been led to believe bolshevists look like."[51]

The situation in Detroit was so extreme that a citizens' committee of prominent individuals—including businessmen, professionals, and the Episcopal bishop of eastern Michigan—was formed to look into the situation. Its findings were summed up by Bishop Charles D. Williams in a sermon in April 1921:

> Businessmen are seeing "red." They commenced seeing "red" with their drive on radicalism. They branded every one who had a progressive thought as a "parlor bolshevist," and persons have been secretly arrested by paid spies on manufactured information and often reported without cause. I investigated several of these cases in Detroit, and found persons supposed to be dan-

gerous radicals to be but simple, ignorant foreigners, unaware of what was being done to them. It is the foulest page in American history. The very principles of Americanism have been undermined by this hysteria and panic.[52]

The red scare was at its peak, as the avalanche carried away the nation's lawmakers. On January 5, the various sedition bills under consideration in the House were combined into one piece of legislation by George S. Graham of Pennsylvania. Two days later, the New York State Legislature, whose Lusk Committee on seditious activities had been operating with unmatched zeal since the previous March, voted 140–6 not to seat five new Socialist members, who had been elected the previous November. On January 10, a Senate sedition measure sponsored by South Dakota's Thomas Sterling passed and was sent along to the House.

The same day, the House of Representative voted for a second time not to seat Victor L. Berger, the Socialist newspaper publisher and activist from Milwaukee. In 1911, Berger had become the first Socialist to serve in Congress, and in 1918, while under indictment for violation of the Espionage Act for his antiwar crusading, he was returned to the House after an absence of six years. After indignantly holding up his swearing in for nearly a year, the House—with only Representative Edward Voigt of Wisconsin voting in Berger's favor—refused to seat him, which resulted in a special election in Wisconsin's Fifth District. Running against a Democratic-Republican coalition candidate, Berger won again, and again on January 10 the House voted to exclude him, this time by a count of 330–6.

On January 12, Francis Kane, U.S. attorney for eastern Pennsylvania, who had protested the proposed raids to Palmer before they were undertaken, sent a letter of resignation to President Wilson. "I feel out of sympathy with the anti-radical policies of Mr. Palmer and his methods of carrying them out," wrote Kane, whose district included Philadelphia, where the January 2 raids netted two hundred people.

I am strongly opposed to the wholesale raiding of aliens that is being carried on throughout the country . . . I am also utterly opposed to the enactment of a new espionage act "with teeth in it" now that we are, to all intents and purposes, at peace. I believe that the enactment of such a new act as Mr. Palmer has proposed would lead to an entirely unnecessary repression of free speech and interference with the liberty of the press. I could not conscientiously and whole-heartedly take part in the enforcement of such a law.[53]

Although Kane's objections to a new bill would ultimately prevail, at the moment panic was carrying the day. On January 14, the House Judiciary Committee merged the Graham and Sterling measures and began hearings on the combined Graham-Sterling bill.

Meanwhile, the Palmer raids continued. As late as January 20, "truck loads of alleged Reds" were arrested in Seattle;[54] of the 316 taken into custody there, only 27 were held for deportation hearings.

Although Labor Secretary Wilson ruled on January 25 that membership in the Communist Party was a deportable offense, it was the Justice Department that drove the entire process. As Post described it, throughout January and February, "agents of the Department of Justice, contemptuous of the exclusive authority of the Department of Labor and using the machinery of the Bureau of Immigration pretty much at their own will and for their own ends, were dealing dictatorially with the whole subject as if all authority had through some subterranean channel been passed along to them."[55] At deportation hearings, BI agents variously served as guards, stenographers, prosecutors, defense attorneys, and interpreters.

Two months after the January 2 raids, Acting Labor Secretary Abercrombie abruptly resigned, and the mantle fell to Louis Post. At seventy-one years old, Post was at the end of a long and distinguished career in public life. He was an unabashed progressive, an advocate of free speech and gender equality, and an opponent of imperialism, trusts, and racial discrimination, who had nevertheless supported the war effort despite its inconsistency with his beliefs.

When Post took command of the Labor Department on March 6, he discovered a staggering backlog of case files that had languished since reaching the Immigration Bureau. Post immediately threw himself into the quagmire, relieving Caminetti of any involvement with the cases and ordering that all records be sent to his office for his personal review. He declared that membership in the Communist Labor Party was not in itself a deportable offense, thereby directly negating Hoover's previous decision on the CLP. Moreover, he canceled the warrants for the hundreds of former Socialist Party members whose names had been automatically transferred to the CP rolls without their knowledge. Post also ruled that the contention by Palmer, Hoover, and Caminetti that constitutional safeguards did not apply in these cases was indefensible, and he restored the detainees' rights to counsel, habeas corpus, and reasonable bail and the right to confront their accusers. Finally, he reduced the excessive $10,000 bails to $1,000.

Between March 6 and April 10, Post and his assistants reviewed as many as a hundred cases a day. Of the approximately 1,600 individuals whose records they assessed, Post canceled about 1,140 warrants and ordered about 460 deportations. Of those he had deported, Post wrote, "I had no alternative under the law but to order their deportation if proof of membership in the Communist Party were clear, however innocent the individual might have been."[56]

Bound by Labor Secretary Wilson's decree that CP membership was a deportable offense under the 1918 Alien Act, Post was nonetheless clearly troubled by the mandatory deportations:

> I could not sleep at night for thinking of some of the cases where the men had to be sent out. They were good, hard-working and useful men, who would have made good citizens; but it was proved that they were members of this organization, even though they did not know what its purpose was; even though they thought they were joining an organization of men from their own country; even though they thought that they were going to school. I have deported such men, because the evidence showed that it was clear that they belonged to the organization.[57]

All told, in the thirty-seven hundred to four thousand cases he oversaw, Post canceled 75 percent of the warrants, ordering only about seven hundred deportations, the overwhelming majority of which were for nothing more than membership. Not surprisingly, Post's actions earned him the enmity of Palmer and Hoover, who undertook a campaign to discredit him. Hoover ordered a BI investigation of Post and assembled a file on him that ran to 350 pages, but when no real incriminating evidence was found, Congress took up the crusade. On April 15, the Kansas representative Homer Hoch submitted a resolution of impeachment against Post.

. . .

At the end of April, Palmer made one more attempt to ramp up the red scare with the announcement of another May Day "plot." On April 30, in a three-column headline, *The New York Times* warned, "NATION-WIDE PLOT TO KILL HIGH OFFICIALS ON RED MAY DAY REVEALED BY PALMER." According to the attorney general, the two Communist parties and the IWW were working together as part of a "worldwide plan" to assassinate "Federal and State officials and other prominent figures in national life," as well as to bring about a general strike. In a replay of the previous summer's July 4 "plot," state militias were dispatched to guard public buildings and the homes of prominent citizens. In Chicago, police rounded up 360 radicals and held them in custody for the day. When May 1 came and went without a single "radical" disturbance, Palmer naturally attributed it to the police presence, but he had cried wolf once too often, and public opinion quickly began to turn against him.

The nonexistent May Day plot and the call for Post's impeachment were the turning points in the red scare frenzy, as people who opposed Palmer's methods but had perhaps been reluctant to protest in public now began to speak out. In New York, the former Republican president William Howard Taft condemned the "wholesale deportation of aliens."[58] In the House of Representatives, the Alabama congressman George Huddleston admonished his colleagues, saying:

You gentlemen have read in the newspapers about the raids upon aliens—unconstitutional raids, raids without process of law, raids in which American citizens, women as well as men, were arrested, were beaten, were dragged to jail and held without legal process . . . Many private homes were invaded without legal process . . . Private papers were seized and carried off for evidence. There was no process of law for any of this . . . Oh, a lawless people is bad enough, but a lawless government is infinitely worse.[59]

Post demanded the opportunity to testify in his own behalf, and on May 7 and 8 he appeared before the House Rules Committee that was determining whether or not to proceed with his impeachment. The

Rules Committee was chaired by Washington's Albert Johnson, who on April 12 had entered a long and ferocious attack on Post into the *Congressional Record.*

One of the primary charges against Post was that he usurped Caminetti's authority when he relieved the commissioner general of the power to order deportations. Post quickly set the committee straight on the matter, informing them: "The Bureau of Immigration has nothing whatever to do, the Commissioner General of Immigration has nothing whatever to do with the proceedings except to act in a ministerial capacity to obey the orders of the Secretary of Labor. He, in other words, is the sheriff, as it were, of the Secretary of Labor in these matters and nothing else . . . There is no judicial power whatever vested in the commissioner general."[60] He made it perfectly clear that only the secretary of labor or himself, as acting secretary, had the authority to order deportations, and derided the House Immigration Committee—also chaired by Johnson—for being ignorant of the law in accepting such rulings from Caminetti.

Post also denounced the Department of Justice, saying despite its claim of a great armed conspiracy, the raids had yielded a mere three pistols. He further established that with regard to deportation cases, the Department of Justice had absolutely no investigative authority.

In his two days before the committee, Post acquitted himself brilliantly, impressing even his erstwhile detractors. Two conservative newspapers, Spokane's *Spokesman-Review* and Portland's *Oregonian*, characterized him as "mentally supple, quick-witted, . . . a living exhibit of vigor and sustained power. He pounced upon Attorney General Palmer one minute, then hurled a charge of 'non-lawful' performance at Anthony Caminetti, Commissioner General of Immigration, and landed a terrific wallop here and there to the House immigration committee . . . The impression created by Mr. Post was altogether favorable to himself."[61]

By the end of Post's testimony, North Carolina's Edward W. Pou, one of his main congressional critics, was thoroughly won over, to the point of declaring, "I want to say, Mr. Secretary, that my feeling is that in what you have done, speaking for myself, I believe you have followed your sense of duty absolutely."[62] When Pou then walked out of the hearings, it was a sure indication that the impeachment of Post was going nowhere.

. . .

The spotlight now shifted to Palmer. On May 28, the National Popular Government League published a sixty-seven-page pamphlet called *To the American People: Report upon the Illegal Practices of the United States Department of Justice*. It was a devastating indictment authored by twelve leading attorneys, including Francis Kane, Felix Frankfurter, and Zechariah Chafee Jr. The charges were both wide-ranging and specific, referring to "the utterly illegal acts which have been committed by those charged with the highest duty of enforcing the laws—acts which have struck at the foundation of American free institutions, and have brought the name of our country into disrepute."[63]

At the Rules Committee's invitation, Palmer appeared on June 1 to defend himself and his department. He was defiant, denying any wrongdoing and blasting both Post and the authors of the NPGL report. He denigrated the former for "his habitually tender solicitude for social revolutionists and perverted sympathy for the criminal anarchists of the country." The latter he contemptuously called "12 gentlemen said to be lawyers [who] have either been woefully deceived or have deliberately declared their political convictions rather than their judgment as reasoning men."[64]

Palmer's performance was as unimpressive as Post's had been stirring. *The New York Times* defended the attorney general, but most newspapers around the country reflected the public's growing skepticism toward the red scare. "The country will be slow to accept at face value everything that Mr. Palmer says," wrote *The Indianapolis News*, "not because it doubts his veracity, but because it has come to feel that, on the Red question, he is something of an alarmist." *The Christian Science Monitor* said, "In the light of what is now known, it seems clear that what appeared to be an excess of radicalism on the one hand was certainly met with something like an excess of suppression."[65]

The red scare balloon was rapidly deflating, but the purposes behind the witch hunt had been accomplished. First, the radical movement had been squashed. Membership in the two Communist parties took a precipitous drop from seventy thousand to sixteen thousand, and the parties were driven underground. The IWW was all but finished. The Socialist Party moved toward the center and ceased to be a factor in American politics.

Equally important, the government and big business had inflicted a crushing setback on the labor movement. The Seattle general strike and the Boston police strike were disasters. The steel strike dragged on for months, until January 8, 1920, when, with only a hundred thousand steelworkers still out, the National Committee for Organizing Iron and Steel Workers voted to call off the strike. Twenty men had died, workers had lost $12 million in wages, and the strikers had not gained any of their original twelve demands.

The coal miners fared a bit better. On November 8, Palmer had submitted a motion to the Indiana judge Albert Anderson to make permanent the temporary injunction against the coal strike, which the latter did, ordering the UMW leaders to withdraw their strike call by the evening of November 11. After an all-night session on November 10–11, union officials reluctantly complied. "We do it under protest," said the acting president, John L. Lewis. "We are Americans. We cannot fight our government."[66] President Wilson proposed a flat 14 percent wage increase and promised miners that a commission would be established to arbitrate their other demands. Many miners refused to return to the job, however, and the strike limped along for another month. On December 10, with eighty-four UMW officials, including Lewis, under citation for violating the injunction, the miners finally accepted Wilson's offer, and the strike officially came to an end. Three months later, the arbitration commission recommended an increase of 27 percent but made no proposal for shorter hours or improved working conditions, and on March 31, 1920, a two-year contract was signed.

Though its effects would be felt for years, the red scare was essentially over. Not even another horrific bombing on September 16, 1920, on New York City's Wall Street, the symbolic heart of capitalism, could elicit renewed panic from the American public. Although Palmer and Flynn depicted the attack, which killed more than thirty people and wounded over two hundred others, as "a challenge to the American Government," the public was no longer responsive.[67] "The usual pinch of salt must be used," cautioned the *Rocky Mountain News*.[68] The Justice Department devoted great time and effort to the Wall Street bombing, but, like the May Day and June 2 bomb plots, it was never officially solved, although it was almost certainly, like the other two cases, the work of the small Italian anarchist group known as the Galleanists.[69]

"The whole 'red' crusade stood revealed as a stupendous and cruel fake," wrote Louis Post.[70] It was a monstrous abuse of power, a cynical and sordid manipulation of the American public by government and business leaders, working in concert to solidify their power and repress minority opinion.

The implications of the red scare provide a sobering lesson. "Under Palmer's assaults," wrote the historian Robert K. Murray, "the inner light of freedom was made dimmer for *everyone;* not just his intended radical victims, but American society as a whole was the loser."[71] In summing up the effects of the red scare, Murray concluded, "Civil liberties were left prostrate, the labor movement was badly mauled, the position of capital was greatly enhanced, and complete antipathy toward reform was enthroned."[72]

There was one more result. The most far-reaching outcome of the red scare was the institutionalization of the Bureau of Investigation as a political tool for spying on civilians, thereby fulfilling Palmer's promise that the bureau's intelligence gathering during the red scare would pay off as a resource "for future use at the hands of the Government."[73] By the time Warren Harding was elected president in November 1920, the BI was securely positioned to become the secret police force of the United States.

During the red scare, the assault on democratic values came not from radical subversives but from government repression. In order to defeat the threat of Bolshevist tyranny in the United States—a threat hardly of the magnitude portrayed by the Justice Department and the press—the government employed the very methods of tyranny it supposedly condemned. The "cure" brought on the very affliction it was purported to prevent.

Senator William Borah of Idaho saw the danger clearly when he warned, "The safeguards of our liberty are not so much in danger from those who openly oppose them as from those who, professing to believe in them, are willing to ignore them when found inconvenient for their purpose; the former we can deal with, but the latter, professing loyalty, either by precept or example undermine the very first principles of our Government, and are far the more dangerous."[74]

Louis Post was equally alarmed about the corollary, "those pagan patriots who, without malice, without evil designs of any kind, but heedlessly, support any cause, however menacing it may be to American ideals, if its promoters decorate it richly enough with the American flag."[75]

CHAPTER 8

Grave Abuses and Unnecessary Hardships

At the beginning of 1921, a Senate subcommittee spent six weeks investigating allegations of illegal activities by the Justice Department during the red scare. For more than a year after the hearings, the subcommittee's chairman, Thomas Sterling, stonewalled any move to bring the results to the Judiciary Committee's attention. When Sterling at last offered a report, it was an unqualified defense of Palmer and the methods employed by the Department of Justice throughout the red scare.

A strongly critical minority report by the subcommittee's Thomas J. Walsh of Montana, a progressive Democrat, echoed the charges made in the National Popular Government League pamphlet. Walsh maintained that although the Palmer raids took place in "a time of high feeling, approaching hysteria," that reality offered no justification for the abuses committed by the government. On the contrary, Walsh argued:

> It is only in such times that the guarantees of the Constitution are of any practical value. In seasons of calm no one thinks of denying them; they are accorded as a matter of course. It is rare except when the public mind is stirred by some overwhelming catastrophe or is aghast at some hideous crime, or otherwise overwrought, that one is required to appeal to his constitutional rights. If, in such times, the Constitution is not a shield, the encomiums which statesmen and jurists have paid it are fustian.[1]

Neither Walsh's report nor Sterling's version was taken up by the Judiciary Committee until February 5, 1923, nearly two years after the end of the hearings, and then only because Walsh finally forced a vote. When the committee chose to submit no report at all, Walsh made certain that both reports were published in the *Congressional Record*.[2]

After President Harding took office in March 1921, he appointed his friend and campaign manager, Harry M. Daugherty, as the new attorney general. Daugherty, in turn, brought in his old buddy William J. Burns, head of one of the most successful detective agencies in the country, to replace William Flynn as BI chief, and Burns promoted J. Edgar Hoover to assistant director.

Despite the crushing blow that had been dealt to the radical movement, Burns continued to play the red card, claiming that the absence of radical activity was proof positive of underground plotting. In March 1922, he told a House subcommittee on appropriations that "radical activities have increased wonderfully [*sic*]," and although "very little is ever said in the newspapers about it, . . . we are in very close touch with it, and it is stronger now than it ever was . . . [I]t is all underground work, and a great deal of it is going on." In making his pitch for increased funding to combat radicals, Burns urged, "I can not impress upon you too much how dangerous they are at the present moment."[3] To the same subcommittee two years later, he averred, "Radicalism is becoming stronger every day in this country. They are going about it in a very subtle manner . . . I dare say that unless the country becomes thoroughly aroused concerning the danger of this radical element in this country we will have a very serious situation." The underlying antidemocratic bent of the BI is evident in Burns's complaint to the subcommittee: "These parlor Bolsheviks have sprung up everywhere, as evidenced by this American Civil Liberties Union of New York. They have also organized a civil liberties union on the coast. Wherever we seek to suppress these radicals, a civil liberties union promptly gets busy."[4]

Harry Daugherty presided over the Justice Department during one of the most corrupt and scandal-plagued administrations in the nation's history, and he was under constant fire during his three-year tenure as attorney general. In late 1922, he survived an impeachment attempt, but in February 1924 the Montana senator Burton Wheeler called for an investigation into the Justice Department's failure to prosecute both antitrust cases and the celebrated Teapot Dome case, in which Secretary of the Interior Albert Fall received $400,000 for secretly leasing U.S. Navy oil reserves in Wyoming and California to private oil companies. In March, the Senate appointed a committee chaired by the Iowa Republican Smith W. Brookhart to investigate the allegations. Hearings began on March 12, with Wheeler as the committee's prosecutor.

Before the hearings started, Daugherty directed the BI's chief, William Burns, to dig up something on Wheeler, and on April 8 a federal grand jury in Montana indicted the senator on charges of receiving $2,000 from a Montana oilman after being elected to office. It was clearly a politically motivated indictment—a Senate investigation chaired by William Borah fully exonerated Wheeler, and he was also later acquitted in a criminal trial in Montana in which the government's main witness was utterly discredited on the stand. One Washington correspondent wrote that the BI agents who found the "evidence" against Wheeler simply fabricated their story. According to another account, "Hoover was very active in that case."[5]

Among the revelations brought to light by the Brookhart Committee was that the Bureau of Investigation, with Daugherty's blessing, had been investigating congressional critics of the Justice Department since 1921; those who had been probed included Wheeler, Walsh, La Follette, and Borah, among others.* The list of legislators whose offices, homes, and private lives were surreptitiously turned inside out was apparently so extensive that Wheeler, in questioning Gaston B. Means, a former BI detective who had been involved in the covert investigations, remarked that another senator had suggested to him that he could save time "by asking you what Senators you have not investigated."[6]

---

*Legislators were not the only victims of unwarranted spying. In two other notable examples, the BI continued its surveillance of the former assistant secretary of labor Louis Post after he left office and conducted extensive investigations of the twelve lawyers who authored the National Popular Government League's 1920 report on the Justice Department's illegal practices; the BI even went so far as to become involved in the unsuccessful attempt to have one of the attorneys, Zechariah Chafee, dismissed from his teaching post at Harvard (see David Williams, "The Bureau of Investigation and Its Critics, 1919–1921," *Journal of American History*, Dec. 1981, pp. 570–74).

Wheeler asked Means whether the purpose of searching La Follette's offices was to stop the senator from his investigation of the Teapot Dome case.

> MR. MEANS. Well, how it was going to be used, I don't know, except this way I would interpret it: If you found something damaging on a man you would quietly get word to him through some of his friends or otherwise that he had better put the soft pedal on the situation. That is the way the information is generally used when you find it.
>
> SENATOR WHEELER. In order to deter him in going ahead with his work in the Senate, is that correct?
>
> MR. MEANS. Work in the Senate or anywhere else, before his constituents, wherever he was, stop him—it doesn't make any difference. Use it again afterward if he attempted to do anything else.
>
> SENATOR WHEELER. And when you spoke about having somebody to go through Senator La Follette's office, what do you mean by going through his office?
>
> MR. MEANS. Oh, search his—find out all the mail that comes in, all the papers, anything that he has got lying around. Find out in his home. Just like you would take—the same principle that you pursue, Senator, when you make a criminal investigation. There is a servant working in this house. If she is a colored servant, go and get a colored detective woman take her out; have this colored detective woman to entertain her, find out the exact plan of the house, everything they discuss at the table, the family, write it down, make a report. And any information you find that is . . . damaging, why, of course it is used.[7]

Brookhart, the committee chair, asked the forty-five-year-old Means, "When did this terrific spy system start in the United States; by what official authority, if you know?"

> MR. MEANS. I have been investigating since I was 21. It had been going on prior to that time. I never saw a candidate that loomed up, any little candidate for town marshal, that they didn't go out and make an inquiry about him . . .

THE CHAIRMAN. And that gang, then, that is behind those investigations of that nature is the same gang that I have denominated as the Nonpartisan League of Wall Street, is that the crowd?

MR. MEANS. I think that President Wilson gave them the best designation: "Invisible Government."

THE CHAIRMAN. Well, that is the same gang.[8]

In the wake of the Brookhart Committee hearings, President Calvin Coolidge, who had inherited the Oval Office after Harding's death the previous August, asked for Daugherty's resignation, and on March 28, 1924, the beleaguered attorney general stepped down. In his place, Coolidge appointed Harlan Fiske Stone, an esteemed jurist and former dean of Columbia Law School, who would later serve on the U.S. Supreme Court. Though politically conservative, Stone was a steadfast civil libertarian who had publicly spoken out against the red scare and the Palmer raids and had denounced the New York State Legislature for refusing to seat five elected Socialists in January 1920.

Six weeks after becoming attorney general, Stone asked the BI chief, Burns, to resign and moved Hoover up to acting director, intending it as an interim appointment. Stone also announced a reorganization of the bureau and a reordering of its priorities, declaring, "There is always the possibility that a secret police may become a menace to free government and free institutions because it carries with it the possibility of abuses of power which are not always quickly apprehended or understood." Vowing that both illegal surveillance and persecution of civilians for their beliefs and ideas would cease, he said, "The Bureau of Investigation is not concerned with political or other opinions of individuals. It is concerned only with their conduct and then only with such conduct as it is forbidden by the laws of the United States. When a police system passes beyond these limits, it is dangerous to the proper administration of justice and to human liberty, which it should be our first concern to cherish."[9]

With the expiration of the Espionage Act at the end of the war and no peacetime sedition act to take its place, the BI had altered its mode of attack on radicals, turning instead to the many state laws enacted during the red scare that forbade such ambiguous activities as "sedition," "criminal anarchy," and "criminal syndicalism." The appropriations act that funded the BI gave it no authority to investigate violations of local statutes, but that did not deter the bureau. In 1922, federal agents were instrumental in the securing of over a hundred state convictions under these laws, the most celebrated of which resulted from the raid on a secret meeting of Communist Party officials in Bridgman, Michigan, in August. Not surprisingly, Hoover was involved in the management of the Bridgman case.[10]

In pronouncing an end to illegal spying and the persecution of minority opinion, Stone intended to reverse entrenched Justice Department and Bureau of Investigation practice. Unfortunately, in J. Edgar Hoover, he chose the wrong man to carry out the new program.

Hoover's early tenure as BI director offered no indication that he had ever been one of Palmer's right-hand men in executing the illegal and repressive policies of the red scare, or that he had subsequently assisted Burns in keeping red hunting on the bureau's front burner.[11] On the contrary, seeing the chance to advance his career, Hoover suddenly became the champion of civil liberties and tolerance. Following Stone's game plan, he reformed bureau procedures, fired incompetent agents, abolished the General Intelligence Division, and called a halt to the bureau's antiradical activities. On October 18, he frankly admitted the illegality of past BI actions in the surveillance, arrest, and prosecution of radicals when he wrote to Assistant Attorney General William J. Donovan that "the activities of the Communists and other ultra-radicals have not up to the present time constituted a violation of the Federal statutes, and consequently, the Department of Justice, theoretically, has no right to investigate such activities as there has been no violation of the Federal laws."[12]

Hoover gained the ringing endorsement of the American Civil Liberties Union by persuading its head, Roger Baldwin, that he had been an unwilling accomplice in the excesses of Palmer's reign as attorney general and Burns's stewardship of the Bureau of Investigation. Baldwin wrote to Stone to say he had misjudged Hoover, and the ACLU went so far as to issue a public statement of support for the newly configured bureau.

On December 10, Attorney General Stone, having been unsuccessful in his attempt to enlist John Lord O'Brian as BI director, made Hoover's appointment permanent. It was a choice that would have devastating long-term consequences for the future of civil liberties in the United States.

. . .

The world war and the red scare were history. The last German alien enemy internees were released in April 1920, and the last political prisoners jailed under the Espionage Act went free in December 1923.

The prosperity of the 1920s brought with it a relatively open and tolerant time, especially when compared with what had gone before. Women achieved suffrage. A literature of social criticism flourished, exemplified by the novels of Sinclair Lewis. The decade saw the emergence of jazz music, the Art Deco movement, and the Harlem Renaissance.

But the phantoms of the xenophobia and antiradical hysteria unleashed during the war and red scare were not completely laid to rest. That they still stalked the land was confirmed by the Sacco and Vanzetti case.

Nicola Sacco and Bartolomeo Vanzetti were two Italian-American anarchists who were associated with the Galleanists and may have played a part in the three major bombings of 1919–20. However, as in the instance of the Haymarket "conspirators" and the IWW organizer Joe Hill, Sacco and Vanzetti were prosecuted, convicted, and executed more for their political beliefs and previous activities—as well as for the deterrent effect—than for the murder of which they stood accused. At their trial, in talking to the jury about Vanzetti, the judge said, "This man, although he may not have actually committed the crime attributed to him, is nevertheless culpable, because he is the enemy of our existing institutions."[13] As in the Haymarket and Joe Hill cases, the evidence against Sacco and Vanzetti in the 1920 robbery-related killing for which they were tried was far from conclusive, and despite a worldwide plea for clemency the two were executed in August 1927.

In the early and mid-1920s, the lingering hostility to immigrants also manifested itself in other ways: the eugenics movement; the rebirth of the Ku Klux Klan; a virulent anti-Semitic campaign spearheaded by Henry Ford; a successful California ballot initiative forbidding Japanese ownership of land; and the passage of a new law in 1924 that restricted immigration from eastern and southern Europe and put an end to immigration from more than a dozen Asian countries, including China, Japan, and India.

Toward the end of the decade, a new anti-alien campaign got under way, and especially after the stock market crash of October 1929, as the

United States slid into the depths of the Great Depression and the nation returned to crisis mode—in this case, economic—the specter of nativism took on renewed life. The emotions behind the new crusade were all too familiar, the latest version of the resentment of immigrants that had been an undercurrent in American life for more than a hundred years. This time the target was Mexicans.

Immigration from Mexico had begun a steady climb in the 1880s. The first large wave came in the opening decade of the twentieth century, driven by the labor needs of the railroad companies; by 1909, the nine western railroads were employing just under six thousand Mexican workers, about 17 percent of their unskilled workforce.[14] The following year, the Mexican Revolution sent people fleeing across the border, and with the urgent need for seasonal labor that accompanied the burgeoning expansion of agriculture throughout the Southwest, the large influx of Mexican immigrants was a boon. The migration continued during World War I, when Mexican workers shored up a depleted labor supply in the copper mines. After the war, the great numbers of African-Americans moving from the rural South to the industrial North created a dearth of field hands, and to fill the void, every year from 1917 to 1920 the Labor Department exempted fifty thousand Mexicans from the literacy test and head tax established by the Immigration Act of 1917.[15] Mexican immigration peaked in 1924, as nearly ninety thousand people headed for *el Norte*, and then leveled off at about fifty thousand annually.[16] By the end of the 1920s, the number of Mexicans working for the railroads had increased to almost twenty-three thousand, close to 60 percent of the industry's unskilled laborers,[17] and the mobility of American society enabled significant numbers of Mexican workers to also find employment all across the country in such diverse arenas as the automotive, canning, construction, meatpacking, mining, and steel industries.

With the 1924 bill that restricted influx from southern and eastern Europe and ended immigration from Asia, entrants from Mexico suddenly became a greater percentage of the total number of immigrants, and when the large numbers known to be coming over the border illegally were factored into the equation, the quantity of people crossing the Rio Grande now seemed enormous. Predictably, there was a backlash, as organized labor, patriotic societies, and eugenics advocates sent up cries calling for restrictions on immigration from Mexico.

The campaign for a quota was spearheaded by Texans. According to the Lone Star congressman John Box, the low wages and primitive living conditions of Mexican immigrants would "drive American labor to the deepest poverty and ultimately to extermination."[18]* Moreover, the restrictionists argued, Mexicans exacted a heavy social price. "A nation can not survive when the necessities of life are produced by an inferior and servile race," another Texan told Congress. "Such a system, long continued, will destroy the fertility of the soil, abolish rural community life, and destroy our patriotic standards. The influx of Mexican peons is already taxing our schools beyond their capacity; it is lowering our educational standing; it is putting an extra burden upon our native people and taxpayers; it is creating an unhealthy political condition, and will ultimately result in the most serious consequences."[19] According to the Texas congressman Eugene Black, Mexicans were "germ-carriers, inassimilable, a people . . . of moral and financial pauperism, incapable of development away from that condition, whose influence is toward the breaking down of our social fabric."[20] Worst of all, Box stated, they were "a bad racial element" who would "create the most insidious and general mixture of white, Indian, and negro blood strains ever produced in America."[21]

It was this last factor, wrote Robert A. Divine in his study of American immigration policy, that was at the heart of the push for quotas on Mexicans. "While undoubtedly organized labor was concerned with the effect of Mexican immigration on the wage scale," observed Divine, "the drive for restriction represented primarily the desire to keep out what many considered an undesirable ethnic group. The economic and social arguments tended to be window dressing."[22]

Until a quota might be set, deportation was seen as a viable alternative. During the summer of 1928, accordingly, the Border Patrol, which had been created as an arm of the Bureau of Immigration in 1924, began carrying out deportation raids on the ethnic Mexican community of the lower Rio Grande valley, invading homes without

---

*The restrictionists were opposed by the powerful southwestern agricultural interests, which maintained that a quota on Mexican immigrants would cripple not only their industry but the economy of the entire Southwest. Any concerns over the social costs of Mexican immigration, they insisted, were far outweighed by economic factors.

warrants, and creating fear and insecurity among the population. Anybody involved in labor organizing was a particular target.

By the following summer, rumors were circulating to the effect that the government would soon deport all Mexicans. One area newspaper reported that most Mexicans were so frightened they were saving money in order to return to Mexico as soon as possible.

The Mexican government, needing a reconstituted labor force to rebuild the country after the revolution, encouraged their return. As incentives, returnees were offered financing for the purchase of land, as well as a discount on import duties, including exemptions on farm equipment, household goods, and $100 per family in provisions.

By the spring and summer of 1930, Mexicans were being deported "en masse" from southern Texas. According to one newspaper, "The Mexican people of the valley were in a state of virtual panic, expecting to be deported by the thousands, and thousands of them were leaving rather than wait to be arrested."[23]

As the Depression worsened, the notion that illegal aliens were occupying jobs that would otherwise go to American citizens took on increased currency. As one historian of the Mexican deportation and repatriation writes, "The idea that aliens were holding down jobs and that by giving those jobs to Americans, the depression could be cured, runs through the depression years as a cure-all with little foundation in fact."[24]

On January 6, 1931, the newly appointed Secretary of Labor, William N. Doak, told the Senate that there were about 400,000 illegal aliens in the United States, and that 100,000 of them were deportable under existing immigration laws. He also suggested that those laws be stiffened to make deportations easier. Doak's comments were published in the nation's newspapers, and one of the people who read them was Charles P. Visel, head of the Los Angeles Citizens Committee on Coordination of Unemployment Relief.

Visel immediately sent a telegram to Colonel Arthur Woods, national coordinator of the President's Emergency Committee for Employment, offering a scheme to get Doak's suggested deportations under way in Southern California. "Figure four hundred thousand deportable aliens United States," said Visel. "Estimate five per cent in this district. We can pick them all up through police and sheriff channels . . . You advise please as to method of getting rid. We need their jobs for needy citizens."[25]

Visel was using code: in Los Angeles, "deportable aliens" meant, above all, Mexicans, who constituted by far the largest ethnic minority in the area. With nearly 100,000 Mexican immigrants, Los Angeles was home to the largest concentrated Mexican ethnic population outside of Mexico City.

Visel followed up his January 6 telegram to Woods with a letter to the Los Angeles Chamber of Commerce's Crime and Unemployment Committee, saying that since illegal aliens were breaking the law by being in this country, "it would be a great relief to the unemployment situation if some method could be devised to scare these people out of our city."[26]

On January 8, Woods answered Visel, telling him, "There is every willingness at this end of the line to act thoroughly and promptly." Encouraged, Visel wired Doak, asking the secretary of labor to send Immigration Bureau agents from other cities to Los Angeles in order to create a climate of fear. "This apparent activity," said Visel, "will have tendency to scare many thousand alien deportables out of this district which is the result desired."[27] Doak responded warmly, thanking Visel for his efforts and instructing him to put his plan into action directly.

Visel's strategy, as he outlined it, was to first use local newspapers and radio stations to broadcast an imminent roundup of illegals by immigration officials, and then arrest some "prominent deportable aliens."[28] The arrests would be accompanied by heavy media coverage, which would intimidate "an army of aliens" into leaving the United States, thereby supposedly opening up job opportunities for unemployed American citizens.

The ball was rolling, and on January 12 anti-Mexican sentiment gained momentum when the Los Angeles County Board of Supervisors endorsed proposed legislation to prevent illegal aliens from establishing residence, holding a job, or conducting any type of business. Disputing Doak's numbers, Supervisor John R. Quinn claimed that there were actually between 2.5 million and 3 million aliens residing in the United States, and that California was home to between 200,000 and 400,000 of them, making his upper estimate of the state's illegal population equal to Doak's nationwide figure. "If we were rid of the aliens who have entered this country illegally," said Quinn, "our present unemployment problem would shrink to the proportions of a relatively unimportant flat spot in business."[29] He also claimed that purging the illegal aliens would cause crime rates to plummet. Finally, playing on the old fears that aliens and radicalism were closely associated, Quinn turned the issue into one of national security, asserting that "most of the so-called 'Red problem' " would also be solved.

After Doak agreed to send a special officer and eighteen agents from neighboring districts to Los Angeles to work on the project, Visel issued the press release announcing the deportation drive. His statement emphasized that law-enforcement agents from the city police force, the county sheriff's office, and the San Francisco, San Diego, and Nogales offices of the Bureau of Immigration would all be participating in the effort. The release was intended for publication in all L.A.-area papers, "especially foreign language newspapers." In a letter to Woods, Visel wrote, "It is the opinion of the Immigration authorities here that these articles will have the effect of scareheading [*sic*] many thousand deportable aliens."[30]

On January 26, a headline on the front page of the *Los Angeles Times* announced, "UNIFIED EFFORT TO OUST ALIENS BEING EVOLVED." An article in the *Illustrated Daily News* the same day warned, "Aliens who are deportable will save themselves trouble and expense . . . by arranging their departure at once," while the *Examiner* darkly cautioned, "Deportable aliens include Mexicans, Japanese, Chinese, and others."

On the twenty-ninth, the leading Spanish-language newspaper, *La Opinión*, ran a lengthy story quoting from Visel's press release, as well as from the articles that had appeared in the English-language papers. The banner headline—"PROXIMA RAZZIA DE MEXICANOS"—left no doubt in readers' minds that the deportation drive was first and foremost aimed at them, and although the Immigration Bureau's district director, Walter E. Carr, insisted that the drive on illegals was not directed "against any one race," the message was clear enough, as waves of fear rippled through the Los Angeles Mexican and Mexican-American community.[31]

On February 9, President Herbert Hoover got into the act, announcing "a vigorous alien deportation drive to . . . conserve employment for American labor" and asking Congress for half a million dollars to add 245 patrolmen to the force engaged in deportation work.[32]

Since Labor Secretary Doak's January 6 declaration of war on illegals, a series of raids in the New York City area had yielded five hundred deportable aliens, resulting in "Ellis Island's detention pens . . .

being taxed to capacity." In the most notorious raid, eighteen "deportables" had been apprehended at a Saturday night dance in Manhattan when a squad of Immigration Bureau officers descended on the Finnish Workers' Education Association and blocked the doors, forcing the musicians to stop playing and ordering the one thousand attendees to produce proof that they were in the United States legally. "In an atmosphere of hysteria tinged with indignation," all but sixteen men and two women "passed the test."[33] As a result of these types of wanton raids, Doak was dubbed "The Deportation Chief" as expulsions reached an all-time, one-year peak of 18,142 in 1931.[34]

President Hoover's National Commission on Law Observance and Enforcement—commonly known as the Wickersham Commission— condemned these raids in its 1931 report, saying, "The apprehension and examination of supposed aliens are often characterized by methods unconstitutional, tyrannic, and oppressive." The report confirmed that little had changed in the processing of deportation cases since the red scare more than a decade earlier, with the Bureau of Immigration still acting as "investigator, prosecutor, and judge, with despotic powers," inflicting "grave abuses and unnecessary hardships."[35] In addition to unjustified raids, those abuses included star-chamber proceedings, third-degree interrogations, and summary deportations.

Writing in *The New Republic*, the Baltimore lawyer Reuben Oppenheimer, the chief author of the Wickersham Commission report, further summarized its findings:

> The action of the Department of Labor is final. There is no probation, no pardon, no effective way to mitigate undue hardships. The suspect has no regular method of appeal. The remedy of habeas corpus is insufficient and, in the great majority of cases, unavailing because of the suspect's ignorance or poverty . . .
>
> Under the present system, . . . foreign-born residents of this country live in a constant state of apprehension that they will suddenly be made a subject of administrative process, carried on without their knowledge . . . Anonymous communications are largely relied upon in apprehending suspects. Proceedings are carried on in secret by immigration officials, who, while generally honest and hardworking, are, for the most part, never personally interviewed or investigated before the Department of Labor employs them . . .
>
> [I]t is often customary for the immigrant inspectors to jail

suspects without any warrant; . . . both the persons and effects of many supposed aliens are searched without a warrant . . .

[I]n some instances the suspect is definitely discouraged by immigration authorities from procuring a lawyer.[36]

The Wickersham Commission's report was issued at about the time the deportation crusade was getting under way in Los Angeles, where immigration officials took thirty-five deportable Mexicans into custody during the first week of February. The first large-scale operation took place in the small city of El Monte on February 13, as sheriff's deputies and immigration agents stopped and questioned three hundred people and netted thirteen illegals, twelve of whom were Mexicans, which would appear to belie the district director Carr's contention that the roundups were not directed "against any one race." The L.A. County sheriff, William Traeger, and federal agents announced that they would continue "nightly raids on suspected quarters" until they were satisfied that "all parts of the county offering a safe haven for unwanted foreigners have been covered."[37]

In the San Fernando and Pacoima areas, immigration agents conducted warrantless door-to-door searches, requiring that Mexicans and Mexican-Americans produce proof of legal residency, and those who could not were arrested. A central premise underlying the dragnet approach to finding illegals was the notion that "a Mexican is a Mexican,"* and any person of Mexican ethnicity, whether an illegal Mexican national, a legal-resident Mexican national, or a U.S. citizen, was therefore justifiably subject to search and seizure. The fact that many of those apprehended for deportation were identified by paid informers contributed to the terror, as Mexicans and Mexican-Americans were never sure who might finger them to the authorities.

In the first three weeks of February 1931, agents came up with only 225 deportable aliens, 64 of whom agreed to "voluntary departure" to Mexico, thereby avoiding arrest and deportation and giving them the option of reentering the country legally at a later date. The rest, who were held for formal hearings, included Chinese, Japanese, and Euro-

---

*This attitude was institutionalized. During the 1930 census, for example, census takers were instructed that "all persons born in Mexico, or having parents born in Mexico, who are not definitely white, Negro, Indian, Chinese, or Japanese, should be returned as Mexicans" (*Fifteenth Census of the United States: 1930, Population, Special Report on Foreign-Born White Families by Country of Birth of Head*, p. 27).

peans, but according to the Immigration Bureau supervisor William F. Watkins, who had been brought in to manage the Los Angeles operation, it was "the Mexican element that predominates."[38]

Despite the Mexican government's protests, the raids continued. The most flagrant one took place on the afternoon of February 26, when a force of about thirty Immigration Bureau agents and Los Angeles police officers surrounded the city plaza park and sealed it off for an hour while they questioned about four hundred individuals.[39] According to eyewitnesses, a number of Mexicans were struck by police in the course of the proceedings. The raid, which was not covered by the English-language newspapers, netted eleven Mexicans, five Chinese, and one Japanese. One of the arrested Mexicans produced his passport, showing that he had entered the country legally, but he was taken into custody nonetheless. Nine of the eleven apprehended Mexicans were later released.

By the third week of March, 230 people had been deported, 110 of whom were Mexicans. Another 159 captured Mexicans had departed voluntarily, making Mexicans 69 percent of those expelled in the Los Angeles crusade to rid Southern California of illegal aliens.

Law-enforcement officials had by now rounded up and interrogated between 3,000 and 4,000 individuals in order to get rid of 389 illegals. But the number of deportations was not the point. The real purpose behind the deportation drive was to instill fear in the ethnic Mexican population, which in turn would hopefully cause many to return to Mexico. On that level, the crusade was a ringing success. As Visel wrote to Labor Secretary Doak, "The exodus of aliens deportable and otherwise who have been scared out of the community has undoubtedly left many jobs which have been taken up by other persons (not deportable) and citizens of the United States and our municipality. The exodus continues. We are very much impressed by the methods used and the constructive results steadily being accomplished."[40]

Not everyone was so favorably impressed. Between March 13 and 25, the *Los Angeles Record* ran a hard-hitting series that underscored the abridgment of aliens' civil liberties. Headlines in the series cited "Inquisition Methods," "Terror Reign," and "Deportation Mania." *The Nation* called it "an outrage that the Immigration Bureau officials should be investigators, prosecutors, judges, and a final court of appeals in deportation cases, and take their orders from men of the type of William N. Doak."[41] And James H. Batten, the executive director of the Inter-America Foundation, made headlines when he spoke out against the deportation campaign, saying, "We are suffering from an epidemic of hysteria against aliens which finds expression in rigid enforcement of the law governing deportations . . . The present deportation activities . . . are actually scaring bona fide resident Mexicans out of the country."[42]

Alarmed at the wholesale abrogation of civil liberties, the constitutional rights committee of the Los Angeles Bar Association appointed a subcommittee to study the deportation of aliens in the area. The subcommittee's report discovered blatant civil liberties violations that were virtually identical to those described in the Wickersham Commission's report.

The criticism had little, if any, effect. By the time the funding for Visel's office expired on March 31, the deportation crusade in Los Angeles had triggered the desired evacuation of Mexicans, and the low-yield deportation drive had merged with the far more effective "voluntary" departure program—now euphemistically called "repatriation"—to produce a mass evacuation of Mexicans and Mexican-Americans from Southern California.

If the claim behind the deportation campaign was to free up jobs for American citizens, the stated rationale for the repatriation crusade was to reduce the welfare rolls, which, in fact, were populated in the greatest part not by illegals—who tended to avoid applying for public assistance for fear of being detected*—but by lawful residents and U.S. citizens. Moreover, there was no pretense here of claiming that the repatriation effort was not directed "against any one race." This measure was clearly aimed at Mexicans.

The journalist and author Carey McWilliams was at Central Station when the first trainload of 350 "repatriates" left Los Angeles for El Paso on March 23. "The loading process began at six o'clock in the morning," wrote McWilliams. "*Repatriados* arrived by the truckload—men, women, and children—with dogs, cats, and goats; half-open suitcases, rolls of bedding, and lunchbaskets."[43] Another observer noted, "The majority of the men were quiet and pensive. Most of the women and children were crying."[44]

---

*A Border Patrol inspector was quoted as saying, "It has been found from experience, an alien who is unlawfully in the United States does not apply for relief unless he finds it absolutely necessary, through fear that he will be found and deported" (See Hoffman, *Unwanted Mexican Americans*, p. 122).

Many of the émigrés had been in the United States for well over a decade—having entered at a time when the law did not provide any penalty for illegal entry—and were hardly eager to return to Mexico. Moreover, their U.S.-born children were fully Americanized, English-speaking U.S. citizens. In some instances, families were torn apart when the husband left but the wife stayed behind in order to avoid displacing the children, who had no experience of Mexico and no desire to live there.

In the middle of April, *The New York Times* reported that since the beginning of the year, thirty-five thousand Mexicans had left Southern California and returned to Mexico.[45] Anti-Mexican sentiment now spread all across California, and a new state law made it virtually impossible for a contractor to use Mexican workers on a public job.

In Texas, meanwhile, the continued deportations drove the repatriation campaign. The *Hidalgo County Independent* reported, "Arrests by agents have terrified the Mexicans, acting in accord with orders issued from Washington to deport every deportable alien. It is obvious only a small fraction of the number returning to Mexico would be deportable, but ignorance of the law and fear of arrest has added to the movement across the border."[46]

By this time, the deportation/repatriation campaign had spread across the country. The Immigration Bureau pressed the deportation operation, while local governments, welfare bureaus, and private charitable agencies encouraged local Mexican and Mexican-American residents to return to Mexico voluntarily. Free railway transportation was offered as an incentive, which, combined with the Mexican government's tender of land, persuaded scores of thousands to undertake the move. Coercion and deception were used as well, as the Inter-American Foundation's James Batten cited cases of welfare workers persuading Mexicans to repatriate voluntarily, under the false assurance that they could return to the United States at will. Others were told that if they refused the offer of free transportation, they would be cut off from further welfare assistance and their cases closed with the notation "Failed to cooperate."[47] McWilliams cited instances of invalids being removed from Los Angeles County Hospital and "carted" across the border.[48]

All across the United States, Mexican immigrants pulled up stakes and streamed south. Mexicans from Chicago, Denver, Detroit, Gary, Kansas City, New Orleans, New York City, Oklahoma City, Phoenix,

Pittsburgh, San Francisco, Seattle, St. Louis, Terre Haute, and other locations boarded trains and ships and made the journey. Untold thousands more fled in automobiles and trucks without informing any authorities of their leaving. By the beginning of December, *The New York Times* reported that "112,407 Mexican repatriates have returned [to Mexico] this year, most of them from the United States," and predicted that the total for the year could exceed 150,000.[49]

Although 1931 was the peak of the deportation/repatriation exodus, it was not the end. According to *The New York Times*, by the summer of 1932, a quarter of a million Mexicans had been repatriated from the United States.[50] While the intensity of the movement ebbed after Franklin Delano Roosevelt assumed the presidency in 1933, the migration back to Mexico continued for the rest of the Depression decade, as the lack of employment opportunities and the fear created by the deportation drive combined to send Mexicans and Mexican-Americans across the border in droves. At least 250,000 of them were from Texas.

Estimates of the total who returned between 1929 and 1939 vary.[51] The two most authoritative studies of the subject offer quite different numbers. In *Unwanted Mexican Americans in the Great Depression*, Abraham Hoffman estimates 500,000, while in *Decade of Betrayal*, Francisco Balderrama doubles the figure to 1 million.[52] Whichever number is closer to accurate, either one is staggering.

In 1931, Jane Perry Clark summed up the tendency to persecute minorities during crises. "In time of stress," she wrote, "as in the deportation raids of 1920, and again in the economic depression of 1930 with its renewed deportation raids and activity, anti-alien sentiment so manifests itself that fundamental rights guaranteed by the Constitution may be completely disregarded."[53]

The book was barely closed on the Great Depression, with its deportations and repatriation of Mexicans and Mexican-Americans, when the next crisis arrived, unleashing another round of scapegoating, surveillance, and the curtailment of civil liberties.

CHAPTER 9

The Utmost Degree of Secrecy

Following the reorganization and reprioritization of the Bureau of Investigation as mandated by Attorney General Harlan Fiske Stone in 1924, the agency was supposedly converted from a witch-hunting unit into a crime-fighting corps. Theoretically, the BI would no longer be keeping tabs on people for political reasons. The era of covert spying on and overt hounding of "subversives," typified by the former BI chief Burns's vow to "drive every radical out of the country and bring the parlor Bolsheviks to their senses," was purportedly over.[1]

Certainly, the greatest part of what the American Civil Liberties Union had called "The Nation-Wide Spy System Centering in the Department of Justice" was dismantled.[2] But it was not completely eliminated. The ACLU—despite its enthusiastic public endorsement of Hoover and the "new" bureau—continued to be the object of covert BI attention. "They never stopped watching us," said the ACLU founder, Roger Baldwin, decades later, when files released under the Freedom of Information Act in the 1970s revealed the BI's ongoing surveillance of the ACLU.[3]

Nor was the ACLU the only group that the BI kept tabs on. Bureau agents continued to provide Hoover with reports about organizations like the Communist Party, as well as with information about hundreds of suspected individual "subversives," indiscriminately lumping those who may have posed some actual threat with those who simply ran afoul of Hoover's notions of what constituted loyalty.

Until Stone's 1924 edict, Hoover had carried on a secret exchange of information with the Army's Military Intelligence Division, supplying MID with reports and carrying out investigations when asked, and receiving intelligence gained from foreign sources in return. While Hoover ended this practice after Stone's decree, he continued to pass along any information regarding specific violations of federal law that he thought might interest military intelligence. In 1929, he also established a working agreement with the retired Army major general Ralph Van Deman, who is often called the father of U.S. military intelligence.[4] After retiring from the Army, Van Deman maintained a private intelligence network with which the BI exchanged confidential information.

Moreover, although the Bureau of Investigation had been largely reined in and its main focus and activity were now fighting organized crime, it still carried out investigations of radicals where there appeared to be a violation of federal laws, or when such investigations were specifically requested by the State Department. The BI also collected "intelligence-type information" when it was "volunteered by some outside force." Thus, the bureau emerged from its pre-1924 rogue status to become "the recognized instrument of the Federal Government for the investigation" of radical activities.[5]

Publicly, at least, Hoover did refuse a number of requests during this period for BI involvement in investigations of radicals, citing the lack of any violation of federal law on the part of such individuals and groups. For example, when the New York congressman Hamilton Fish Jr., who, as chair of a House committee investigating Communist and radical activities in December 1931, introduced legislation that would empower the BI to "investigate the revolutionary propaganda of communists in the United States, and of all entities, groups or individuals who teach or advocate the overthrow by force and violence the republican form of government," Hoover opposed the bill, arguing that "it would be better to make it a crime to participate in such activities."[6]

Hoover's reluctance to let the bureau be used for such purposes appears to have been based as much on a fear of criticism as on any principled concern for preserving civil liberties. Recalling, no doubt, the censure leveled at the Justice Department and the BI after the red scare, he told Attorney General William D. Mitchell that if the BI were to take up such actions, "the Department and the Bureau would undoubtedly be subject to charges in the matter of alleged secret and undesirable methods in connection with investigative activities, as well as to allegations involving charges of the use of 'Agents Provocateur' [sic]."[7]

Even as Hoover kept the bureau from becoming too deeply involved in investigations of radicals between 1924 and 1934, other developments during these years combined to increase the BI's scope and power: it became the clearinghouse for fingerprints and other identification records; an organized program to train new agents was developed; and a new, state-of-the-art crime laboratory was created. As part of his continuing professionalization of the agency, Hoover instituted uniform reporting rules for agents in the bureau's field offices, which were located in strategic cities around the country. Also, in the spring of 1934, a spate of new federal crime bills bestowed greater responsibilities on the bureau. As a 1976 Senate committee report concluded, although these factors did not confer any explicit power to carry out intelligence investigations, they unquestionably created "an organization with all the assets, composition, and capabilities for conducting such investigations if so directed."[8]*

With this structure in place, it was inevitable that the bureau would be so directed. In the second year of Franklin D. Roosevelt's first term, the directive arrived.

Just as the Russian Revolution had raised alarms in the United States in 1917, the rise of Fascism and Nazism in Europe now caused similar concerns. As Mussolini and Hitler solidified their power, Fascist and Nazi groups began springing up in this country. In January 1934, Secretary of War George H. Dern had informed Attorney General Homer Cummings of the "definite indication" that foreign espionage was afoot in the United States, and of the probability that there would be an eventual attempt to undermine U.S. military capability.[9] Dern recommended establishing a civilian counterespionage service to collect information about potential espionage or sabotage activities, a throwback to the American Protective League and the other "patriotic" organizations that had flourished during World War I.

On May 8, FDR assembled a group at the White House to discuss the budding Nazi movement in the United States. Of particular con-

---

*In addition to these advances, the Editorial Card Index—which by the time of Stone's reform order contained more than half a million entries—still existed, and while Stone's edict made the index unusable, it lay dormant, waiting, as the former attorney general Palmer had put it, "for future use at the hands of the Government" (see Chapter 6 n. 13, above).

cern to him was Fritz Kuhn's German-American Bund, an organization that enjoyed the backing of several powerful businessmen, including Henry Ford. The White House conference was attended by Attorney General Cummings, Secretary of Labor Frances Perkins, Secretary of the Treasury Henry Morgenthau, Secret Service chief W. H. Moran, and the BI director, J. Edgar Hoover. According to Hoover's memo on the meeting, the president asked the various agencies to cooperate in a very thorough investigation of the Bund and other domestic Nazi groups, particularly to determine whether the German embassy and consulates might be connected to the movement.

Hoover immediately sent confidential instructions to the BI field offices, directing them to begin such an investigation and informing them that the inquiry was for the purpose of providing the president with information, rather than for purposes of prosecution. As such, it was a distinct break with Stone's policy stating, "The activities of the Bureau are to be limited strictly to violations of law."[10]

While FDR's directive to the Bureau of Investigation constituted a clear-cut departure from Stone's guidelines, the parameters of the investigation ordered by the president were intended to be limited to the connection of German diplomats in this country to the domestic Nazi movement, particularly vis-à-vis the German-American Bund. Roosevelt requisitioned "an intelligence investigation within specified guidelines," but Hoover lost no time in extending the study into a more "sweeping and general assignment . . . which by necessity, involved aliens and United States citizens."[11]

Pandora's box was open. With Stone's policy thus superseded, it was an easy step to discarding it altogether. The Bureau of Investigation was on the threshold of reclaiming its role as the nation's secret police force.

When Hoover stopped in at the White House on the morning of August 24, 1936, for a confidential meeting at Roosevelt's request, he had little idea of just how far-reaching the effects of their talk would be. According to Hoover's top-secret summary of the meeting, FDR had summoned him to discuss "the question of subversive activities in the United States, particularly Fascism and Communism."[12]

The director of the now-renamed Federal Bureau of Investigation spent most of the time talking about Communist activities, going into detail about the control of the San Francisco longshoremen's union by Harry Bridges, the activities of the Newspaper Guild headed by Heywood Broun, and the doings of suspected Communists in the federal government. Hoover's information in these areas was extensive, indicating that the FBI, while lacking official authorization to conduct intelligence operations, had nevertheless been involved in collecting information on left-wing groups. Hoover informed the president that officially there was no governmental agency engaged in gathering "general intelligence information" in this area.[13]* When Roosevelt expressed his desire to get "a broad picture of the general movement and its activities as may affect the economic and political life of the country as a whole," Hoover, ever eager to extend his web of control, sprang at the opening. Roosevelt appeared to be offering a justification for further undermining Stone's order prohibiting the bureau from conducting intelligence investigations. Such investigative authority could prove a quantum leap forward for the FBI, bestowing upon it a power and influence it had not enjoyed since 1924.

There was a problem, though. The current appropriations statute funding the bureau limited its activities to investigating and prosecuting crimes. Hoover saw a way around that. The appropriations statute of 1916, which was still on the books, allowed the bureau to use its funds for investigations requested by the secretary of state, even if no violations of law had yet occurred, and since the investigation Roosevelt was outlining involved international movements, the matter should be of clear interest to the State Department. If Roosevelt wanted to get the ball rolling on such a broad-ranging investigation, all it would take would be a request from Secretary of State Cordell Hull to bring it within the bureau's purview as set down by the 1916 law.

The following day, Hull joined FDR and Hoover at the White House. Again, according to Hoover's confidential record of the meeting, Roosevelt told Hull of his concerns about domestic Communist and Fascist activity and informed him that the Justice Department could undertake an investigation of these at the secretary of state's request.[14] Hull, in turn, asked if the request should be in writing, but

---

*The Secret Service of the Treasury Department had agents working in every Communist group, but their function was limited to discovering potential assassination plots aimed at Roosevelt.

the president, fearing a potential leak to the press by State Department personnel, indicated that he preferred to keep the matter confidential. Hull then asked for an FBI investigation.

Involving Hull through the 1916 statute was clearly nothing more than a pretext to execute an end run around the existing appropriations restrictions on FBI activities. In his analysis of the August 1936 meetings, Frank Donner points out that the 1916 appropriations statute "contemplated limited, closed-end investigations related to foreign affairs (the dynamiting of a consulate, the suspicious movements of a diplomatic attaché), not the extended domestic political probe that the President apparently had in mind." Moreover, suggests Donner, FDR's request for "a broad picture of the general movement" was not a demand for specifics like "dossiers, identifications, linkages requiring penetrative surveillance."

Donner concludes that Roosevelt, Hoover, and Hull deliberately "deceived Congress for what the President regarded as a justifiable end . . . Congress was doubly deceived: the launching of the probe was kept secret, and its funding authority deliberately misused."[15]

Whatever Roosevelt's intentions, the significance of these two meetings cannot be overstated, for in sanctioning such secret investigations of "subversives," FDR started Hoover down a path the FBI director would zealously pursue for the next four decades, a path that would soon lead to serious abuses of power and invasions of privacy by the FBI as it carried out covert and often illegal scrutiny of tens of thousands of individuals and organizations, the vast majority of whom were guilty of absolutely nothing. "No one," writes Donner, "could persuasively claim—although the Bureau has not hesitated to do so—that Secretary Hull requested an investigation in 1936 which permanently empowered it to conduct domestic intelligence operations."

Yet Hoover interpreted the Roosevelt/Hull request as a carte blanche license to reinstitute the freewheeling counter-subversive investigations of the pre-Stone era. On September 5, he sent a memo to FBI field offices, instructing agents "to obtain from all possible sources information concerning subversive activities being conducted in the United States by Communists, Fascists, representatives or advocates of other organizations or groups advocating the overthrow or replacement of the Government of the United States by illegal methods."[16] Tellingly, Roosevelt and Attorney General Cummings were not among the recipients of this memo,[17] and Hoover apparently never informed them of his unilateral broadening of the investigative boundaries beyond the Communist and Fascist movements.

Athan Theoharis, author of numerous books on J. Edgar Hoover and the FBI, has observed that the pattern was now set for "certain basic characteristics of federal surveillance policies after 1936: the ineffectiveness of executive supervision over the internal security bureaucracy; the indifference of federal officials, particularly within the FBI, to constitutional and legal principles; and the arrogance of FBI officials who either ignored, misinformed, or selectively informed responsible elected officials about bureau policies and procedures."[18]

In the spirit of the 1934 suggestion by Secretary of War Dern to establish a civilian counterespionage service, the bureau began within days to put together a corps of informants, as well as reports on "prominent subversives" and daily memos for Hoover on "major developments in any field" of subversive activity.[19] To facilitate the new mission, Hoover resurrected the bureau's General Intelligence Division, which had been disbanded in 1924, and renamed it the General Intelligence Section.

For the next two years, as Hoover reported to Roosevelt in October 1938, the special agents in charge of the FBI field offices collected information on subversive activities in the following categories: "maritime; government; industry (steel, automobile, coal mining, and miscellaneous); general strike; armed forces; educational institutions; Fascisti; Nazi; organized labor; Negroes; youth; strikes; newspaper field; and miscellaneous."[20] Using this information, Hoover created a new version of the Editorial Card Index, which by the fall of 1938 contained twenty-five hundred names. The bureau also developed an extensive collection of periodicals, pamphlets, and other publications and, in accordance with Roosevelt's instructions at the August 24, 1936, meeting, "developed a close and coordinated plan of operation" with the Office of Naval Intelligence and the Military Intelligence Division.[21]*

In Hoover's October 1938 memo to the president, he appealed for additional funding and expanded authority, requesting $35,000 each for MID and ONI and $300,000 for the FBI. He maintained that the established protocol, whereby the secretary of state requested investi-

---

*As noted, Hoover had enjoyed a secret arrangement with MID since the early 1920s.

gations, was "sufficiently broad to cover any expansion of the present intelligence and counter-espionage work." He also argued that in expanding the intelligence structure, they had to proceed "with the utmost degree of secrecy in order to avoid criticism."[22]

When Roosevelt gave his imprimatur on November 2 to the proposal for a secret expansion of domestic intelligence operations, it further reinforced the clandestine approach established in 1936, as FDR, Hoover, and Cummings continued to deceive Congress about the FBI's highly questionable and ever-increasing intelligence-gathering activities.[23] The old pre-Stone Bureau of Investigation—"The Nation-Wide Spy System Centering in the Department of Justice"—was small potatoes in comparison to the organization that Hoover was now putting together.

The late 1930s saw an escalation of tensions around the globe, as German, Italian, and Japanese aggression posed rising threats in Europe, Asia, and Africa, and caused heightened concerns about sabotage and espionage in the United States. Following the signing of a Germany-Soviet nonaggression pact in August 1939, Hitler invaded Poland on September 1.

The following day, Hoover—on his own authority, apparently[24]—sent a memo to the field offices, instructing them to prepare reports on "persons of German, Italian, and Communist sympathies," as well as on others "whose interest may be directed primarily to the interest of some other nation than the United States."[25] These included subscribers to and officers of all German- and Italian-language newspapers, foreign-language Communist newspapers, and other foreign-language and English papers "of pronounced or notorious Nationalistic sympathies"; members of all German and Italian fraternal and other organizations; and members of "any other organization, regardless of nationality, which might have pronounced Nationalistic tendencies." As his authority for such investigative activity, Hoover cited the Foreign Agents Registration Act of 1938, which required agents of foreign governments to publicly disclose their relationship with those governments. But, as Athan Theoharis points out, since the law makes no mention of U.S. citizens, Hoover's plan "entailed the abrupt abrogation of the constitutional rights of every American citizen affected by it."[26]

Four days after Hoover's unilateral decree, Roosevelt issued a directive appointing the FBI "to take charge of investigative work in matters relating to sabotage, espionage and violations of the neutrality regulations."[27] Local law-enforcement agencies were instructed to turn all intelligence in these areas over to the FBI. In the same week, it was revealed that for the past year, FBI agents had been receiving "intensive secret training in the technique of uncovering espionage, sabotage and subversive activities."[28]

On November 9, Hoover asked the FBI's assistant director, Edward A. Tamm, to begin compiling a list of individuals whose "presence at liberty in this country in time of war or national emergency would constitute a menace to the public peace and safety of the United States Government."[29] A month later, Hoover sent out a lengthy memo to the special agents in charge of the forty-nine regional field offices, giving them six months to compile extensive information on these individuals, stressing that under no circumstances should the investigations become known to anyone outside the FBI.

It would seem that six months was hardly an adequate amount of time to conduct careful and thorough investigations of thousands of suspects, especially in an era before the advent of computers and centralized, instantly accessible databases. Nevertheless, in the middle of June 1940, Hoover asked the SACs to supply the lists of individuals in their districts "who should be considered for custodial detention . . . in the event of a national emergency."[30]

The legal basis for "custodial detention" could be found in the Alien Enemies Act of 1798 and its updated World War I version, the Alien Enemies Act of 1918.[31] There was, however, absolutely no legal basis during peacetime for amassing such a catalog of names or for the FBI's clandestine investigations of those individuals whose names appeared therein.

The catalog was officially called the Custodial Detention Index and was maintained by the bureau's Special Defense Unit, but the names submitted by the SACs came to be known as the "ABC list" for the three designations of enemy aliens described: the "A" list of supposedly irrefutably dangerous individuals; the "B" list of the potentially dangerous; and the "C" list of those who merely merited surveillance. Whereas holding a leadership position in an ethnic organization was enough to qualify a person for the "A" list, an individual could land on the "C" list for nothing more than having made a donation to a cultural society. All three lists included many prominent business, cultural, and religious leaders, but given the sources used and the time allotted, it was not surprising that the methods employed in researching these names were less than airtight, as would become clear in due time.

Nor was there any legal basis for Roosevelt's secret order of May 21, 1940, authorizing Attorney General Robert Jackson to conduct wiretaps of "persons suspected of subversive activities against the Government of the United States, including suspected spies." The admonition "to limit these investigations . . . to a minimum and to limit them insofar as possible to aliens" would prove meaningless.[32]

Emboldened by the new surveillance parameters and with the ABC list being compiled, Hoover wrote to Assistant Attorney General Matthew F. McGuire in August 1940, proposing that the Department of Justice draft legislation "with reference to the internment of dangerous alien enemies in event of war" and advocating that such legislation "permit the taking into temporary custody of individuals" who were suspected of seditious activity "pending further investigation."[33]

On June 28, 1940, two months before Hoover suggested legalizing wartime custodial detention of aliens, Congress had passed the Alien Registration Act, also known as the Smith Act. The legislation made it a crime for anyone to advocate the overthrow of the government, or to belong to any organization that advocated such an end. The law also required all aliens to register and be fingerprinted and photographed at a U.S. post office. This process was overseen by Solicitor General Francis Biddle, who would soon be attorney general, and Earl G. Harrison, an up-and-coming Philadelphia lawyer, whom Biddle had tapped for commissioner of the Immigration and Naturalization Service, which had been transferred from the Department of Labor to the Department of Justice on June 14. By the end of the year, nearly 5 million aliens were registered, including close to 700,000 Italians, over 300,000 Germans, and more than 90,000 Japanese.

The war in Europe was almost a year old, and Americans had watched from across the Atlantic as Hitler swept through the continent, reportedly aided by fifth-column movements in many countries. Declaring it "an acknowledged reality" and "an established fact" that such a movement was now menacing America, Hoover used the specter of a fifth column in the United States to create fear and tighten the grip on alien control. "A Fifth Column of destruction," he declared, "following in the wake of confusion, weakening the sinews and paralyzing it with fear can only be met by the nationwide offensive of all law enforcement." He identified the supposed fifth columnists only as "the vilifying Communist and the espouser of alien philosophies."[34]*

By this time, the Immigration and Naturalization Service, despite no funds having yet been allotted for such a purpose, had already begun preparing detailed plans for internment camps to house those "A" list individuals in the Custodial Detention Index who would presumably be apprehended and interned when war broke out. In January 1941, Fort Stanton, on the site of an abandoned Civilian Conservation Corps camp in southern New Mexico, was the first internment camp to go into operation, providing housing for more than four hundred seamen from the German luxury liner *Columbus*, which had scuttled off the east coast of the United States. By April, Fort Missoula, in Montana, and Fort Lincoln, near Bismarck, North Dakota, both military facilities, were being converted for service as internment camps.

The FBI, meanwhile, working together with ONI and MID, was zealously adding names to the Custodial Detention Index and carrying out secret investigations of individuals on the list. Concerned that these illegal methods might jeopardize the prospect of convictions in court cases, Attorney General Jackson wrote to Hoover early in the spring of 1941 to question these activities. Citing the 1924 Stone guidelines, Jackson pointed out that "the Federal Bureau of Investigation . . . cannot be used except for the investigation of crimes and subversive activities which amount to overt acts rather than matters of opinion." He set out a proposed list of rules that the bureau should observe, including: "The subject matter of investigations which the FBI has authorized to undertake do not extend beyond charges of sus-

---

*In fact, there was never a serious fifth-column threat in the United States during World War II; the few acts of sabotage and espionage that were carried out were isolated incidents bearing no connection to a centralized plan. One of the more sensational cases occurred in February 1938, when the FBI broke up a German spy ring in New York City. Despite the ineptitude of the German agents involved and the government's reassurances that no vital national secrets had been compromised, the media attention accompanying the case served to inflame fifth-column fears.

picion of crime, or of definite subversive activity which does not consist of views or expressions of opinion, but of overt acts of incriminating relationships."[35]

Hoover responded on April 1 with a long defense of the investigations and list keeping, saying,

> Had we refrained from gathering such information . . . this Bureau would not be in a position today to furnish to the Department the names of individuals who should be considered for either internment or prosecution in the event of the declaration of a complete national emergency. None of these persons today has violated a specific Federal law now in force and effect, but many of them will come within the category for internment or prosecution as a result of regulations and laws which may be enacted in the event of a declaration of war. To wait until then to gather such information or to conduct such investigations would be suicidal.[36]

Paying no heed to Jackson's concerns or instructions, Hoover continued with the investigations and compiling of lists. On April 30, he sent a thirteen-page single-spaced memo to the SACs, instructing them to "continue to submit to the Bureau the names of persons who you believe should be considered for custodial detention pending investigation in the event of emergency."[37] The memo went on to delineate in minute detail how the investigations should proceed, what types of materials should be collected, and how the gathered intelligence should be presented.

In July, with war appearing increasingly inevitable, the Department of Justice and the War Department agreed to a set of procedures regarding the roundup of alien enemies. The FBI would carry out the arrests of "dangerous" aliens, who would then be held in INS camps as temporary "detainees." The Justice Department would conduct their hearings, and those found worthy of internment would be handed over to the War Department for incarceration in camps managed by the provost marshal general. The INS would retain custody of any women and children who were ordered interned. The attorney general's office also prepared a series of presidential proclamations authorizing the pending roundups of German, Japanese, and Italian aliens, to be issued upon the outbreak of hostilities.

The machinery was in place. The stage was set for the inevitable.

It arrived just before 8:00 a.m. on Sunday, December 7, 1941, when the Japanese air force unleashed a surprise attack on the U.S. naval base at Pearl Harbor on the island of Oahu. Upon receiving the news, Roosevelt immediately issued the already-written Presidential Proclamation 2525, regarding Japanese alien enemies, which laid out the "conduct" and "regulations" that Japanese aliens were to follow. Their movements were restricted to certain areas, and the list of items they were forbidden to possess included firearms, ammunition, bombs, shortwave radios, transmitters, signal devices, and cameras. Most important, "alien enemies deemed dangerous to the public peace or safety of the United States by the Attorney General or the Secretary of War" were subject to "summary apprehension," and arrested aliens were subject to "confinement."[38]

The FBI swung into action, making warrantless arrests of Japanese, German, and Italian aliens, even though the presidential proclamations regarding Germans and Italians would not be issued until the following day, December 8, and the United States would not officially be at war with Germany and Italy until December 11. As Francis Biddle, who was now attorney general, would later write in his memoir, "On that Sunday night Hoover was authorized to pick up several hundred without warrants, and this procedure was followed for a short time until the more dangerous had been apprehended."[39]

On December 8, Roosevelt issued Presidential Proclamations 2526 and 2527, dealing with German and Italian aliens, respectively. The same day, Hoover sent a telegram to the SACs canceling the earlier categories denoted in the ABC list:

Immediately take into custody all German and Italian aliens previously classified in groups A, B, and C, in material previously transmitted to you. In addition, you are authorized to immediately arrest any German or Italian aliens, not previously classified in the above categories. In the event you possess information indicating the arrest of such individuals necessary for the internal security of this country. Above procedure applies only to German and Italian aliens, and not to citizens.[40]

Despite Hoover's instruction that citizens were not to be arrested, a number were. "We were jittery," the Alien Enemy Control Unit chief, Edward Ennis, later admitted. "We did not know what to expect . . . Our policy was to act first and explain afterward."[41] By December 10, three days after Pearl Harbor, nearly 2,300 individuals had been taken into custody, including 1,291 Japanese, 857 Germans, and 147 Italians.[42] On December 17, Hoover officially widened the net to include U.S. citizens.

Those arrested in the days and weeks following Pearl Harbor included community leaders, Buddhist priests, owners of businesses that catered to ethnic interests and tastes, martial arts masters, newspaper editors and publishers, ordinary workers, and thousands of other utterly harmless individuals. Peter Greis, a chemist who had been living and working in Milwaukee since 1923, was taken from his home at 3:00 a.m. on December 10, and his family had no word of him for six weeks. George Teikichi Kojima, a bookstore owner in Oahu, Hawaii, was arrested in the middle of his wife's funeral at the Nichiren Shu Buddhist Temple on December 7, after which his fifteen-year-old daughter, Mary Mariko, parentless and penniless, wound up living at the temple for the next eight months. The San Jose salesman Filippo Molinari, taken into custody on the wintry night of December 11, was not permitted even to take his overcoat or to remove his house slippers and put on his shoes. Describing the period immediately following December 7, Jerre Mangione, a special assistant to the INS, wrote, "Civil liberties took a back seat in those days; in the name of national defense expediency became the order of the day."[43]

Certainly, there were genuine subversives nabbed in the roundups. The Chicago Bund leader Dr. Otto Willumeit and his fellow Bund officer Gerhard Wilhelm Kunze were arrested for providing U.S. defense secrets to Germany and Japan. In Southern California, the U.S. Navy lieutenant commander Kenneth D. Ringle worked with the FBI for forty-eight consecutive hours to round up 450 bona fide Japanese intelligence agents, whose names had been garnered by Ringle when he carried out an audacious nighttime break-in at the Japanese consulate in Los Angeles the previous spring.* Other

* The raid resulted in the June 1941 arrest and deportation of two Japanese spymasters and the neutralizing of the West Coast Japanese spy network, which, as docu-

detainees, while having engaged in no seditious activity, harbored undeniable nationalistic feelings for their homelands and may have been capable of carrying out espionage work in time. But the vast majority of those taken into custody were guilty of nothing more than their ethnicities.

By March 20, 1942, when the head of the Alien Enemy Control Unit, Edward Ennis, testified before a House subcommittee of the Committee on Appropriations, there were approximately sixty-seven hundred alien enemies in custody. "We thought we were off to a pretty good run," Assistant Attorney General James Rowe Jr. would later recall.[44]

Following arrest, the case of each detained individual came before an Alien Enemy Hearing Board, composed of prominent citizens, one of whom was usually a lawyer. In setting up these panels, Ennis, who had a reputation as a civil libertarian,* was supposedly carrying out Biddle's express belief that "everyone in our country, whatever his racial or national origin, should be treated with fairness. We did not want people pushed around."[45]

Nevertheless, at alien enemy board hearings, the deck was heavily stacked in the state's favor. The local U.S. attorney's office represented the government, and the evidence presented had been gathered by the FBI in the course of its investigation of the detainee. For the majority of detainees, who understandably had no idea why they were in custody, this was the first time they were informed of the reason for their detention. The detainee could present his own evidence but had no right to object to questions put to him, and was allowed representation by a friend or relative but not by a lawyer—"an exclusion," according to Biddle, "that greatly expedited action, saved time, and put the procedure on a prompt and common-sense basis."[46] As Rowe later noted, "It went much better, much faster without lawyers."[47]

Many hearings were simply kangaroo courts. Ennis acknowledged as much to the House subcommittee when he said, "Every effort has been made to get away from costly time consuming judicial procedures . . . If there is substantial reason to sustain the charges against the alien, every doubt at this time must be resolved against him and in favor of the Government. The man cannot be given anything like a

---

ments secured in the break-in clearly showed, was dedicated to intelligence gathering rather than to acts of sabotage or a fifth-column strategy.

*Ennis would later serve as president and chairman of the board of the American Civil Liberties Union.

jury trial on these issues." He further admitted the antidemocratic nature of the custodial detention program as it was being carried out. "The underlying principle of the whole program is that it is preventive," he testified. "I think we are bound to intern some people on suspicion in order to resolve all doubts in favor of safety. In some instances there will be injustice done. A man may be interned because of his associations, while he himself would do nothing at all against the country."[48]

The hearing board could recommend one of three courses—unconditional release, parole with conditions, or permanent internment—and after review by the Department of Justice, the final outcome was determined by the attorney general. The criteria applied by the hearing boards and in the review process, however, were decidedly inconsistent and frequently baffling.

One detainee who was a former German army officer, for example, had been a member of the National Socialist Party of Germany in 1936–37 and had distributed propaganda brochures in the United States that sang Hitler's praises. At the time of his arrest, he was a Bund member, the secretary of Friends of New Germany, and an employee of the German consulate in Cleveland. This man received the board's recommendation for outright release, but the attorney general decided instead upon parole. Another German alien, who had written letters in which he called Hitler "beloved Fuehrer" and expressed his joy that after the war Germany would rule the world, was deemed "potentially dangerous to the security of the United States" and recommended for internment by the hearing board, but the review section of the Department of Justice recommended "parole under fairly strict sponsorship." The attorney general paroled the man.[49]

Carmelo Ilacqua, on the other hand, had come to this country in 1924 after serving in the Italian navy, as an ally of the United States, during World War I. For more than ten years before Pearl Harbor, he worked as a clerk at the Italian embassy in San Francisco, where he was required to keep his Italian citizenship and join the Fascist Party as two conditions of employment. As a veteran of World War I, Ilacqua was also a member of the Federation of Italian War Veterans, known as the Ex Combattenti, a social organization that functioned as a support network for its members. When the U.S. government ordered the closing of the Italian consulate in June 1941, Ilacqua chose to stay in this country with his wife—a naturalized U.S. citizen—and their six-year-old daughter. Despite no shred of evidence that he had ever engaged in any activity that could be even remotely classified as subversive, Ilacqua was arrested on December 17 and, for the next year and nine months, was moved from one internment camp to another before being released.

Similarly, Taichi Fujimoto, a carpenter and farmer from the Wakayama Prefecture of Japan, had been in the United States since 1927. He settled in Wapato, a thriving Japanese-American farming community in Washington's Yakima valley. By the late 1930s, the Japanese ethnic community around Wapato had grown to about a thousand people, and a new, ambitious community center was planned. With his expertise in carpentry, Fujimoto was put in charge of construction and the training of volunteers. His work on the center made him a community leader but also a marked man. He was arrested on January 19 and, with no indication on his part of disloyalty to the United States, interned at Fort Missoula, Montana.

Fujimoto was finally paroled nearly a year later, on December 29, 1942, but it was not to freedom, and his reunion with his family was not in the Yakima valley. By that time, Fujimoto's wife, Ayako, and their five children, along with the entire Japanese and Japanese-American populations of the West Coast—approximately 112,000 people, almost 70 percent of whom were U.S. citizens—had been "relocated" to ten inland concentration camps, in what the historian A. Russell Buchanan has aptly called "the most widespread disregard of personal rights in the nation's history since the abolition of slavery."[50]

A Jap Is a Jap

The forced relocation and incarceration of 112,000 ethnic Japanese under the auspices of the War Relocation Authority is generally regarded as having sprung independently and full-blown in direct reaction to the bombing of Pearl Harbor. On the contrary, the WRA program was part of a larger, more encompassing process—a natural and direct outgrowth of the groundwork that had been laid with its antecedent, the Alien Enemy Control Program. This is clearly spelled out in the government's official 1943 publication *Final Report: Japanese Evacuation from the West Coast, 1942.* "The ultimate decision to evacuate all persons of Japanese ancestry from the Pacific Coast under Federal supervision," states the report, "was not made coincidentally with the outbreak of war between Japan and the United States. It was predicated upon a series of intermediate decisions, each of which formed a part of the progressive development of the final decision. At certain stages of this development, various semi-official views were advanced proposing action less embracing than that which finally followed."[1]

The process began at least five years before Pearl Harbor, with concerns over national security, and was originally aimed at Communists, Fascists, and Nazis. By December 1939, it had evolved into hysteria directed at German, Italian, and Japanese aliens, as J. Edgar Hoover began compiling the notorious ABC list. After Pearl Harbor, the idea of rounding up all the Japanese aliens and Japanese-Americans on the West Coast gained incremental acceptance.

Moreover, the commonly accepted understanding of the relocation and internment as having been based exclusively on racism—a constantly perpetuated interpretation—is one of the most serious misunderstandings of World War II domestic history. While racism was clearly and undeniably a key motivating factor, it is not the entire explanation. A fuller picture emerges only when the ethnic Japanese situation is seen in the total context of the internment of the three alien enemy groups. A cloud of suspicion hung over all three communities, based in large part on the assumption and fear that aliens' loyalties were necessarily divided between the United States and their countries of origin, and therefore their allegiance to this country was questionable, regardless of how long they had lived here.

Identifying racism as the sole cause of the Japanese and Japanese-American relocation and incarceration distorts the historical record and obscures the other, equally critical factors that were responsible for not only the Nikkei internment but the internment of German and Italian enemy aliens as well. Those factors were rooted in national security fears and hysteria, and in the long-standing history of nativism in this country.

Suspicion and surveillance of Japanese aliens and Japanese-Americans had been building for decades. As early as 1920, when the Bureau of Investigation's General Intelligence Division was responsible for monitoring the Nikkei community in the United States, the BI conducted extensive investigations of Japanese nationals and Japanese-Americans throughout the West, South, and Southwest—not for having committed any illegal activity but merely for being of Japanese descent. In Seattle, for example, a study was made of all Japanese landowners, while a similar investigation in San Antonio concluded that "an organized effort is being made by Japanese to obtain agricultural lands in the Rio Grande territory for the purpose of colonizing them with Japanese from California."[2] In New Orleans, an investigation was made of all Japanese who bought cameras, and in Galveston, Texas, every Japanese resident's name was indexed. In California, where the Japanese community was largest, the BI investigated Japanese-language schools, Japanese-owned businesses, and Japanese fishermen, who were assumed to be spies. One California BI agent deduced that the Japanese would become "a real menace to the American people unless this Government makes strict legislation governing them." In fact, California had already attempted to do exactly that, passing the Alien Land Act of 1913, which forbade the immigrant issei generation—who were already barred from citizenship by the Naturalization Act of 1790—to own land, and a second law seven years later that prevented all Asian immigrants from even holding long-term leases.*

In hearings before the Senate Committee on Immigration in March 1924, witness after witness spoke in denigrating terms of the ethnic Japanese.† The Sacramento businessman V. S. McClatchy complained, "They have driven white labor off the farms," and, "They have displaced the whites in business."[3] California's attorney general, U. S. Webb, called the Japanese "an unassimilable people," telling the committee, "They are different in color; different in ideals; different in race; different in ambitions; different in their theory of political economy and government. They speak a different language; they worship another God. They have not in common with the Caucasian a single trait."[4]

After the Japanese invasion of Manchuria in 1931, diplomatic relations between the United States and Japan chilled. By the following year, the Office of Naval Intelligence, the Military Intelligence Division, the State Department, the Commerce Department, and the Justice Department were all involved in secret, cooperative surveillance of the ethnic Japanese population.

In 1934, suspecting that in the event of war, the Japanese and Japanese-American community would harbor a fifth-column threat, President Roosevelt had the State Department look into the potential of Japanese espionage and sabotage on the West Coast. The investigation concluded that "when war breaks out, the entire Japanese population on the West Coast will rise and commit sabotage."[5]

At the same time, Hawaii, with its large ethnic Japanese population, came under scrutiny. Japanese-Hawaiians had long been regarded as a latent threat, with the assumption being that they would back a Japanese invasion of the islands. In the early 1920s, the Army's War Plans Division developed a strategy for defending Oahu. The plan was produced by the division's assistant chief of staff, the then colonel John L. DeWitt, who two decades later, as the commanding general of the Fourth Army and Western Defense Command, would be one of the architects of the Japanese relocation and internment. DeWitt's

*To get around these restrictions, Japanese immigrants often purchased land in the names of their children or a Caucasian friend.

†The hearings were part of the lead-up to the passage of the Immigration Act of 1924, which, among other restrictions, banned all immigration from Japan (see Chapter 8, above).

plan for Oahu called for the imposition of martial law, suspension of habeas corpus, and registration and selective internment of Japanese aliens. In 1933, the Hawaiian branch of MID produced a fifteen-volume report that portrayed the Japanese-Hawaiians as disloyal, fanatical, duplicitous, arrogant, morally inferior, and highly likely to support Japan—including committing acts of sabotage—if an invasion occurred. In 1936, DeWitt's original defense plan was amended to incorporate intelligence activities, including broad-based surveillance of the Japanese-Hawaiian population.

In May of that year, a Joint Planning Committee report noted that the crews of Japanese commercial ships docking in Oahu made regular contact with local Japanese-Hawaiians, in order to "advance Japanese nationalism and to cement bonds of loyalty."[6] FDR's response, on learning of this, was that any Japanese or Japanese-Hawaiian who had any contact with these ships "should be secretly but definitely identified and his or her name placed on a special list of those who would be the first to be placed in a concentration camp in the event of trouble."[7]

By this time, the Japanese were being blamed for sowing the very same seeds of discontent that left-wing agitators had been accused of planting in the 1920s. Intelligence reports claimed that Japanese agitators were inciting minorities—particularly African-Americans—and radicals to labor unrest, racial strife, and other nefarious unpatriotic activities and attitudes. The FBI and MID undertook a fruitless investigation of relations between Japanese and African-Americans, conducting covert surveillance of associations like the Washington, D.C.-based New Negro Alliance, a direct-action civil rights group, and the National Negro Congress, a broad-based lobbying coalition of African-American organizations, for indications of Japanese influence. With no evidence, the bureau also blamed Japanese agitators for a rash of strikes that were triggered by the 1935 National Labor Relations Act, a piece of New Deal legislation that guaranteed the rights of workers to form labor unions, conduct collective bargaining, and participate in strikes.[8]

After the Japanese invasion of northern China in mid-1937 and the conquest in December of Nanking, which resulted in widespread atrocities by the Japanese army, U.S. relations with Japan seriously deteriorated. By October 1940, with war appearing a certainty, Navy Secretary Frank Knox sent FDR a list of fifteen actions that should be undertaken "to impress the Japanese with the seriousness of our preparations" for armed conflict.[9] The twelfth item was "Prepare plans for concentration camps."

With anti-Japanese feelings on the rise throughout the country, the sentiment for internment was gaining in currency. In August 1941, the president received a letter from John D. Dingell, a New Deal congressman from Michigan, who proposed that if the Japanese took any action against American citizens in Japan, the United States should retaliate by placing ten thousand Japanese-Hawaiians in concentration camps, and be prepared to do the same to the entire U.S. ethnic Japanese population.

In October, Attorney General Biddle, concerned by increasing anti-Japanese attitudes and recalling the excesses of World War I, condemned the "type of hysteria" that arises during national emergencies and often leads to the persecution of "innocent people."[10] Less than a month later, he reassured a group of West Coast Japanese who had traveled to Washington to register their "concern about the strained relations between the United States and Japan" and to profess their loyalty to the United States.[11] "I promised them they would receive fair treatment," said Biddle, "if they do not violate any laws." At the same time, however, he also revealed plans for the control of alien enemies that ranged from supervised parole to detention.

In November 1940, the FBI's Honolulu office, which had recently reopened after having been closed for six years, furnished a report refuting the Joint Planning Committee's conclusion that Japanese-Hawaiians were disloyal and should be considered a security risk.[12] The bureau report contended that only a small group of about a thousand teachers, Buddhist and Shinto priests, and consular agents warranted surveillance, while the vast majority of Japanese-Hawaiians were steadfastly loyal to the United States.

Faced with conflicting intelligence reports from the military and the FBI, Roosevelt secretly assigned his adviser John Franklin Carter, a journalist who wrote under the pen name Jay Franklin and had been a speechwriter for FDR's 1940 reelection campaign, to establish an independent intelligence network that would investigate the fifth-column threat in Hawaii, as well as on the West Coast, where more than 95 percent of the Japanese and Japanese-American population of the United States lived.* The two areas appeared vulnerable to a Japanese

---

*Of the 127,000 ethnic Japanese in this country, more than 112,000 resided in California, Oregon, and Washington, with almost 94,000 in California alone.

attack that—so the thinking went—would be aided by a fifth-column movement of alien, immigrant-generation issei and their children, the American-born nisei, who were U.S. citizens. Carter asked Curtis Munson, a Chicago businessman and special representative of the State Department, to assess and report on the West Coast and Hawaiian situations.

Munson submitted his report a month before Pearl Harbor. While acknowledging that there would likely be some sabotage by paid Japanese agents, he found overwhelming evidence that "there is no Japanese 'problem' on the West Coast. There will be no armed uprising of Japanese . . . There will be no wholehearted response from Japanese in the United States . . . We do not believe that they would be at the least any more disloyal than any other racial group in the United States with whom we went to war."[13] In Hawaii, Munson found, the Japanese were overwhelmingly faithful to the United States, and the FBI and Navy intelligence had the potentially disloyal individuals under surveillance. On the contrary, Munson's main concern was not the disloyalty of the ethnic Japanese but the very real possibility of violence directed against them after war broke out.

While Munson was conducting his study, Lieutenant Commander Kenneth Ringle, who spoke Japanese and was well known in the Los Angeles Japanese-American community, was carrying out a similar investigation for the ONI. Ringle's break-in at the Japanese consulate the previous spring had yielded documents showing that Japan mistrusted the issei and nisei as being too Americanized to be of use as espionage agents. His report, submitted on January 26, 1942, more than six weeks after Pearl Harbor, concluded, "The entire 'Japanese Problem' has been magnified out of its true proportion, largely because of the physical characteristics of the people. It should be handled on the basis of the *individual*, regardless of citizenship, and *not* on a racial basis."[14]

Cooler heads like Munson and Ringle were not destined to prevail. Immediately after the bombing of Pearl Harbor, Secretary of the Navy Knox went to Hawaii to consult with naval officers and inspect the devastation. When he returned to Washington on December 15, he met with Roosevelt to report his findings and then held a press conference, at which he declared, "I think the most effective fifth-column work of the entire war was done in Hawaii, with the possible exception of Norway."[15] Knox's remark, which had no factual basis, appeared in newspapers across the country, effectively indicting the Japanese-

Hawaiian community for complicity in the attack. Concerned that the misinformation could lead to reprisals against the ethnic Japanese, John Franklin Carter asked Roosevelt to issue a public statement refuting Knox's claim, but FDR remained silent on the matter.

As FBI agents went about the business of rounding up alien enemies around the country, attention also focused on the West Coast, which, along with Alaska, was officially designated a "theater of operations," that is, a war zone. The Fourth Army there was commanded by Lieutenant General John DeWitt, who had been the author, in the 1920s, of the defense plan for Oahu that called for martial law, suspension of habeas corpus, and registration and internment of select alien Japanese.

Biddle characterized DeWitt as "apt to waver under popular pressure, a characteristic arising from his tendency to reflect the views of the last man to whom he had talked."[16] On one matter, however, DeWitt was unwavering. In his attitude toward Japanese aliens and Japanese-Americans, he was unabashedly racist. "A Jap's a Jap," he declared flatly on more than one occasion, adding, "It makes no difference whether he is an American citizen or not."[17]

In the wake of Pearl Harbor, DeWitt fully expected another Japanese attack, and he was determined not to be blindsided. On December 9, he hotly scolded San Franciscans for their casual attitude toward a blackout the previous night, after the supposed sighting—actually a false alarm—of a squadron of Japanese warplanes over the Bay Area.

From his San Francisco headquarters, DeWitt passed along to the War Department unsubstantiated rumors of espionage and sabotage by Japanese-Americans on the West Coast, including an undocumented account of an impending revolt of twenty thousand Japanese-American San Franciscans and a report of regular communications between Japanese spies and submarines off the coast that had led to attacks on "practically every ship that has gone out."[18] These intelligence reports turned out to be either wildly exaggerated or simply false, leading one of DeWitt's under-generals to refer to his commanding officer in a diary as a "jackass."[19]

Right after Pearl Harbor, DeWitt recommended the creation of a military zone, running a hundred miles inland from the coast, from which dangerous enemy aliens—German, Italian, and Japanese alike—would be barred. On December 19, he went a step further, proposing that all alien enemies over fourteen years old be moved away from the coast and relocated inland.

At the beginning of January, Biddle sent Assistant Attorney General Rowe to San Francisco to meet with DeWitt. DeWitt pressed for the registration of all West Coast enemy aliens, for the designation of military exclusion zones that enemy aliens could enter only with a pass, and for the raiding of issei residences. In a January 4 meeting with DeWitt, Rowe and the chief West Coast FBI agent, Nat Pieper, agreed that the Justice Department would undertake these actions.

Although DeWitt mistrusted Japanese aliens and Japanese-Americans in equal measure—"I have no confidence in their loyalty whatsoever," he told Rowe—he initially opposed any mass evacuation and incarceration of them.[20] "I'd rather go along the way we are now . . . rather than attempt any such wholesale internment," he informed the Army's provost marshal general, Allen Gullion, adding, "An American citizen is, after all, an American citizen."[21]

Gullion was frustrated with Biddle's temperate approach to the alien enemy question, which was based both on the attorney general's constitutional concerns and on the various intelligence reports that affirmed that the West Coast issei and nisei were no threat. Impatient with what he regarded as Biddle's foot-dragging, Gullion asked his aide, Major Karl R. Bendetsen, a thirty-five-year-old Stanford Law School graduate, to draft a memo to the president recommending that the Alien Enemy Control Program be transferred from the Justice Department to the War Department.

The struggle for management of the Alien Enemy Control Program was the latest manifestation of the turf war that had been brewing since Roosevelt had directed the FBI, ONI, and MID to cooperate and coordinate intelligence gathering in 1936. In June 1940, the three agencies had agreed to a division of labor that gave the FBI responsibility for investigating cases of civilian espionage, counterespionage, and sabotage in the United States and American territories, while MID's purview was military espionage and sabotage, including instances involving civilians employed by the Army, and ONI was to handle investigations of cases involving naval personnel, including the Navy's civilian employees.

When the FBI also assumed direction of the civilian organizations that would be used to combat any fifth-column activity, Hoover ran into a dispute with MID, which had defined a fifth column as a military entity, "essentially a part of military operations," whose activities "are coordinated . . . with those of the uniformed forces of the enemy."[22]

MID accordingly considered the supervision of anti-fifth-column groups to be within its domain, not the FBI's. A month after the agreement that delineated each agency's areas of responsibility, MID began planning its own operation to counter fifth-column activity. Hoover disdained the Army's intelligence unit as being prone to "hysteria and lack of judgment" and protested to Roosevelt that MID was usurping the FBI's authority.[23] After six weeks of negotiations, Hoover finally prevailed, and the bureau hung on to its control of anti-fifth-column operations.

Now the Justice and War departments again locked horns over the Alien Enemy Control Program. The War Department's goal of gaining control of the program was pushed dramatically forward by the January 25 publication of the report of the Roberts Commission, which was issued as part of the joint congressional committee hearings investigating Pearl Harbor.[24]

The report concluded—incorrectly, it would later be proved—that there had been espionage leading up to the attack, by both "Japanese consular agents and other . . . persons having no open relations with the Japanese foreign service," a conclusion that was widely and mistakenly interpreted to be confirmation of Navy Secretary Knox's claim of sabotage and fifth-column activities.[25] Reaction to the Roberts Commission report was vehement, as anger toward the ethnic Japanese population, which on the West Coast was remarkably restrained in the immediate aftermath of Pearl Harbor but had been gradually gaining momentum, now swung violently against everything Japanese.

Even before the report was published, the Los Angeles Chamber of Commerce had called for the removal of all Japanese aliens and Japanese-American citizens. Congressman Leland M. Ford of California had also gone on record as being in favor of moving all Japanese, aliens and citizens alike, to concentration camps. In letters to Hoover and the secretaries of war and the Navy, as well as in a statement to the press, Ford argued that any loyal ethnic Japanese should be willing, even eager, to acquiesce, since "other loyal Americans are enlisting in the Army and Navy and Air Forces and are willing to give their lives for their country, and if these men are willing to make their contribution to the safety and welfare of the country . . . it is not asking too much of the Japanese to make theirs in the form of permitting themselves to be placed in concentration camps, although they may be loyal."[26]

After the publication of the Roberts Commission report, mass evacuation and internment became the rallying cry of the day. The Los Angeles County Board of Supervisors' demand for the removal of aliens on January 27 was followed by similar resolutions in seventeen more counties around the state and from the statewide County Supervisors Association.

The *San Francisco Examiner* columnist Henry McLemore advocated "the immediate removal of every Japanese on the West Coast to a point deep in the interior. I don't mean a nice part of the interior either. Herd 'em up, pack 'em off and give 'em the inside room in the badlands. Let 'em be pinched, hurt, hungry and dead up against it . . . Personally, I hate the Japanese. And that goes for all of them."[27]

In the *Los Angeles Times*, W. H. Anderson argued, "A viper is nonetheless a viper wherever the egg is hatched . . . So a Japanese-American, born of Japanese parents, nurtured upon Japanese traditions . . . almost inevitably and with the rarest of exceptions grows up to be a Japanese, not an American."[28]

California's governor, Culbert Olson, urged DeWitt that federal intervention was needed immediately, warning that the danger of vigilante action was imminent. California's attorney general, Earl Warren—soon to be the state's governor and later chief justice of the U.S. Supreme Court—also publicly came out in favor of mass evacuation.

Prominent among those calling for the removal of the ethnic Japanese were powerful agricultural interests, who saw the chance to put their competitors out of business and buy up their lands. Over the decades, Japanese immigrants had purchased millions of acres on the coast and in the inland valleys, becoming a considerable agricultural and economic presence. The Western Growers Protective Association, the Grower-Shipper Association of Central California, and the White American Nurserymen of Los Angeles were all vociferous in their advocacy of mass evacuation. "We trust that your office will make a sincere effort to eliminate as many of these undesirable aliens as possible at this time," one official of the WGPA wrote to Warren.[29] The managing secretary of the GSACC was even more blunt, saying, "We're charged with wanting to get rid of the Japs for selfish reasons. We might as well be honest. We do. It's a question of whether the white man lives on the Pacific coast or the brown men. They came into this valley to work and they stayed to take over . . . If all the Japs were removed tomorrow, we'd never miss them in two weeks, because the white farmers can take over and produce everything the Jap grows. And we don't want them back when the war ends, either."[30]

The public outcry aided Bendetsen and Gullion, who had been exerting heavy pressure on DeWitt to support the wholesale removal of the ethnic Japanese community. Now DeWitt started coming around. The day after talking to Governor Olson, he told Assistant Secretary of War John J. McCloy that the predominant sentiment on the West Coast boiled down to "a Jap is a Jap" and that "the question of the alien Japanese and all Japanese presents a problem in control, separate and distinct from that of the German or Italian."[31] The latter groups, said the general, "you don't have to worry about . . . as a group. You have to worry about them purely as certain individuals."

On January 29, Biddle issued an order requiring all enemy aliens to leave the West Coast restricted zones by February 24, and the attorney general further designated dozens of additional zones of exclusion. Faced with immediate relocation, at least four Italian aliens in northern California, all over fifty-seven years of age, committed suicide rather than comply, the stigma of disloyalty being too much for them to bear.[32]

Also on the twenty-ninth, Bendetsen met with the California congressional delegation, which unanimously approved a plan of action that called for the evacuation of enemy aliens and "dual" citizens but made no mention of any specific ethnic group. When Bendetsen briefed Gullion on his meeting with the legislators, however, he represented their proposal as "calling for the immediate evacuation of all Japanese from the Pacific coastal strip including Japanese 21 years of age and under."[33]

On February 4, Biddle met with Bendetsen, Gullion, and McCloy. The attorney general's refusal to consider evacuating American citizens without a suspension of habeas corpus angered the War Department group. McCloy, a lawyer and banker, had the aplomb and temerity to tell the attorney general, "If it is a question of the safety of the country [and] the constitution . . . why the constitution is just a scrap of paper to me."[34] Biddle insisted that the Justice Department would have nothing to do with violating the rights of U.S. citizens—if that was to happen, it would have to be the War Department that carried it out.

This was the opening the military men were waiting for. That very day, Bendetsen submitted a memo to Gullion recommending that the president issue an executive order giving the secretary of war control of alien enemies and the power to "requisition the services of any and all other Federal agencies," that is, the Justice Department, in carrying out whatever measures he deemed necessary. Bendetsen recommended the removal of "both Japanese aliens and American citizens of Japanese extraction or parentage" from the West Coast and their relocation to "the Zone of Interior in uninhabited areas where they can do no harm under guard . . . [M]ass evacuation is a course which, if followed, will largely relieve the necessity for eternal vigilance." As Bendetsen saw it, the only problem—aside from the daunting mechanics of such a huge undertaking—was that "no one has justified fully the sheer military necessity for such action."[35]

Bendetsen was arguably the most fanatical and racist of the War Department group. Because it was DeWitt who submitted the February 14 "Final Recommendation" memo suggesting mass evacuation, then signed the order for it and oversaw its execution on the ground, he is often regarded as having been responsible for its conception. On the contrary, it was Bendetsen, following Gullion's general orders, who bears the responsibility both for writing the "Final Recommendation" memo signed by DeWitt and for devising and administering the specifics of the evacuation. After the war, Bendetsen would boast that he was awarded the Distinguished Service Medal for being the one who "conceived method, formulated details, and directed evacuation of 120,000 persons of Japanese ancestry from military areas."[36] In 1949, Father Hugh T. Lavery of the Catholic Maryknoll Center in Los Angeles would write of him, "Colonel Bendetsen showed himself to be a little Hitler. I mentioned that we had an orphanage with children of Japanese ancestry, and that some of these children were half Japanese, others one-fourth or less. I asked which children should we send to the relocation center . . . Bendetsen said: 'I am determined that if they have one drop of Japanese blood in them, they must go to camp.' "[37] For his work, Bendetsen was promoted twice in a ten-day period—to lieutenant colonel on February 4 and to full colonel on February 14. Coincidentally or not, these were the respective dates of Bendetsen's memo to Gullion recommending mass evacuation and of DeWitt's "Final Recommendation" memo—which was also, as noted, written by Bendetsen—to Secretary of War Henry L. Stimson, urging the same.

. . .

As the situation on the West Coast grew more tense, anger at Japan was increasingly directed at the ethnic Japanese. By the middle of February, there were at least five murders and twenty-five other serious crimes committed against Japanese nationals and Japanese-Americans in the Pacific states.[38]

The national cry for evacuation and incarceration of the West Coast ethnic Japanese was reaching a crescendo. Such disparate and influential syndicated newspaper pundits as the measured liberal Walter Lippmann and the acerbic conservative Westbrook Pegler both came out in favor of removal. In a piece called "The Fifth Column on the Coast," Lippmann argued for "a policy of mass evacuation and mass internment," and three days later Pegler fulminated, "The Japanese in California should be under armed guard to the last man and woman right now—and to hell with habeas corpus until the danger is over."[39]

Three days after his meeting with the War Department group, Biddle had lunch with Roosevelt and expressed his opinion that mass evacuation was ill-advised, that the Justice Department was not equipped to carry it out, and that the Army had made no convincing argument for it as a military necessity. Biddle further "emphasized the danger of the hysteria . . . moving east and affecting the Italian and German population in Boston and New York." Roosevelt's response, that he was "fully aware of the dreadful risk of Fifth Column retaliation in case of a raid," indicated either that he had swallowed as true the bogus accusations of sabotage and espionage made by Navy Secretary Knox, the Roberts Commission report, and countless others or that he simply found it politically expedient to go along with them.[40]

Without Roosevelt's support, Biddle began to cave in. In a February 9 letter to Secretary of War Stimson, he again expressed the same desire to wash his hands of the entire matter that he had voiced to McCloy, Gullion, and Bendetsen five days earlier. "The proclamations directing the Department of Justice to apprehend and, where necessary, evacuate alien enemies do not, of course, include American citizens of Japanese race," wrote Biddle. "Should they have to be evacuated, I believe that this would have to be done on the military necessity in the particular area. Such action, therefore, should in my opinion be taken by the War Department and not by the Department of Justice."[41]

Stimson, however, had his own doubts about the legality of such a drastic measure. "I am afraid it will make a tremendous hole in our constitutional system," he wrote in his diary.[42]

On February 11, Stimson and McCloy asked Roosevelt for a decision on the evacuation question.[43] "Is the President willing to authorize us to move Japanese citizens as well as aliens from restricted areas?" Stimson wanted to know.[44] FDR avoided answering the question directly, instead putting the onus of the decision back on Stimson. In his diary account of their conversation, Stimson wrote that Roosevelt "told me to go ahead on the line that I had myself thought the best."[45]

McCloy immediately called Bendetsen to tell him they had "carte blanche" as far as Roosevelt was concerned.[46] Overstating FDR's order, McCloy said that Roosevelt had specifically authorized the evacuation of citizens and had acknowledged that while such action was likely to have some repercussions, the situation had to be dictated by military necessity.

Bendetsen was in San Francisco, having been sent there to assist DeWitt in the writing of the "Final Recommendation" regarding "evacuation of Japanese and other subversive persons from the Pacific Coast," which was due on the thirteenth. In justifying the military necessity for mass evacuation, Bendetsen employed the same logic that the BI chief William Burns had used when he told a House subcommittee in 1922 that the absence of any radical action was proof of clandestine plotting.[47] The Bendetsen/DeWitt "Final Recommendation," dated February 14, insisted, "The very fact that no sabotage has taken place to date is a disturbing and confirming indication that such action will be taken."[48]

Perverse as it may have been, this was enough to set the machinery for mass evacuation in motion, and on February 17, Roosevelt gave approval to the War Department's plan. Stimson and McCloy avoided notifying Biddle, who, that same day, sent FDR a memo providing him with information on the subject of a possible West Coast evacuation for his upcoming press conference.[49] Biddle's memo informed the president that while arguments in favor of evacuation were based on a supposedly imminent Japanese attack on the West Coast and sabotage on the part of the region's ethnic Japanese, intelligence reports from the FBI and the War Department indicated that neither supposition was true. Evacuation was, therefore, not only unnecessary but also certain to hurt agricultural production. When Roosevelt then advised Biddle that he had already approved the mass evacuation of Japanese aliens and Japanese-American citizens, the attorney general's resistance ended.

That evening, in his living room, Biddle met with Gullion; McCloy; Bendetsen; Rowe; the head of the Alien Enemy Control Program, Edward Ennis; and Assistant Attorney General Tom C. Clark. Unaware that Biddle had already capitulated, Rowe and Ennis engaged the War Department group in debating the issues and presenting the constitutional case against evacuation of citizens, while the attorney general simply looked on and said little. After a time, Gullion impatiently reached into his pocket and extracted a piece of paper on which was written an order giving the War Department the authority to evacuate aliens and citizens alike.

"I laughed at him," said Rowe eight months later. "The old buzzard got mad. I told him he was crazy . . . But in another minute I thought that I was crazy. Because the Attorney General immediately wanted to get to work polishing up the order." Rowe and Ennis were devastated. "[Biddle's] attitude amazed me," Rowe said. "Ennis almost wept. I was so mad that I could not speak at all myself and the meeting soon broke up."[50]

On February 19, Roosevelt issued Executive Order 9066, which authorized the secretary of war and his designated military commanders to prescribe areas from which, at their discretion, "any or all persons may be excluded."[51] The order was specifically worded to avoid any mention of the ethnic Japanese, but there was no doubt at whom it was directed. Italians, whom Roosevelt referred to after Pearl Harbor as "a lot of opera singers,"[52] and hence not treacherous, were not to be evacuated except by Stimson's order, and then only on an individual basis.[53] Germans, who Roosevelt thought were "different, they may be dangerous," were theoretically in the same category as Japanese, but the War Department made an exception for "bona fide" German refugees, which postponed the evacuation of German aliens until DeWitt could determine who the true German refugees were.[54]

The evacuation of all ethnic Japanese on the West Coast began on March 31, 1942, conducted by DeWitt and the newly created War

Relocation Authority, an agency of the Department of the Interior. Despite his acquiescence, Biddle was appalled: "I thought at the time that the program was ill-advised, unnecessary, and unnecessarily cruel . . . [T]he *Nisei*, American citizens from the day they were born in this country like any other Americans, were . . . treated like aliens . . . Their constitutional rights were the same as those of the men who were responsible for the program."[55] The bitter irony, of course, was the incongruity of fighting Fascism and racism abroad while incarcerating tens of thousands of American citizens at home for no other reason than their ethnic identity.

In its 1982 report, *Personal Justice Denied*, the Commission on Wartime Relocation and Internment of Civilians stated, "The promulgation of Executive Order 9066 was not justified by military necessity, and the decisions which followed from it—detention, ending detention and ending exclusion—were not driven by analysis of military conditions. The broad historical causes which shaped these decisions were race prejudice, war hysteria and a failure of political leadership."[56] These conclusions are true as far as they go, but there were other factors operating as well.

Morton Grodzins, whose groundbreaking 1949 study of the relocation and internment laid down the foundation for all subsequent investigations, points out, "Virtually every statement made concerning the special danger of the Japanese minority could also have been made against Germans and Italians." As Grodzins notes, there were over eighteen thousand more Italian than Japanese aliens in California, and over seven thousand more foreign-born Italians than the entire ethnic Japanese population of the state.[57] DeWitt and others, in fact, pushed hard for the removal of all West Coast alien enemies. Why, then, aside from the obvious motive of racism, were only the ethnic Japanese as a whole removed and incarcerated, and not the Germans and Italians as well? Again, the state of New York was home to more German aliens than the total number of ethnic Japanese on the West Coast, yet no outcry was made for the removal of German aliens from the East Coast.

The historian Stephen Fox argues that the evacuation of the West Coast ethnic Japanese but not the German or Italian alien population of either coast was based on pragmatic concerns, that is, sheer numbers. Practically speaking, not only were there too many Italian and German aliens, but interning them, says Fox, would have angered hundreds of thousands, perhaps millions of Italian- and German-Americans, which might well have provoked a serious domestic crisis.[58] Indeed, Biddle alerted Roosevelt that the hysteria on the West Coast was having an effect on the morale of East Coast ethnic Germans and Italians, and he also cautioned Stimson that "the evacuation of all enemy aliens would . . . present a problem of very great magnitude."[59] A group of lawyers whom the attorney general engaged to study the legality of evacuating Japanese-American citizens advised that "persons of Japanese descent constitute the smallest definable class" and were therefore the easiest group to evacuate.[60] As Fox concludes, "Who should or should not be removed came down to a question of the number of people involved."[61]

Moreover, there was no economic motivation to intern the West Coast German and Italian aliens. Unlike the ethnic Japanese, neither of these groups were large-scale landowners. As Grodzins writes, "For three decades previous to the war, farm organizations had expressed regret at the penchant of Japanese to shift from a laboring to an entrepreneur status."[62] The outbreak of war finally provided these powerful agricultural interests with the opportunity to eliminate their competitors and seize their land.

Finally, there was the attitude of President Roosevelt toward the ethnic Japanese, an attitude in line with the prevailing belief that racial characteristics were innate and that being born in the United States, speaking English as a native language, and growing up surrounded by American culture did not mitigate the fact of having Japanese ancestry. It was essentially the same as Bendetsen's opinion that "while many second and third generation Japanese born on United States soil, possessed of United States citizenship, have become 'Americanized,' the racial strains are undiluted."[63] Or DeWitt's blunter assessment, "A Jap's a Jap." In Roosevelt's writings from the 1920s, he referred to the ethnic Japanese as people of "oriental blood" and therefore "unassimilable," a mind-set that he carried forward through the next decades, and that predisposed him to believe Navy Secretary Knox's fabricated statement and the insinuations of the Roberts Commission report about Japanese-Hawaiian complicity in Pearl Harbor, as well as the rash of other unsubstantiated rumors concerning subversive activities by West Coast ethnic Japanese.[64]

Roosevelt also believed that immigrant groups in general should not be permitted to cluster together. As the 1920 Democratic vice presidential candidate, he had declared, "Our main trouble in the past has been that we have permitted the foreign elements to segregate in colonies. They have crowded into one district and they have brought congestion and racial prejudices to our large cities. The result is that they do not easily conform to the manners and the customs and the requirements of their new home. Now, the remedy for this should be the distribution of aliens in various parts of the country."[65]

So, by removing the ethnic Japanese from the West Coast, Roosevelt successfully broke up the Little Tokyos that existed in every major city in California, Oregon, and Washington. The historian John Howard also plausibly argues that the postwar resettlement of Japanese-Americans constituted a deliberate attempt on the part of the government to disperse the Nikkei community, to "Americanize" its members, and to decrease their geographical proximity to Japan.[66]

There is no evidence that Roosevelt agonized greatly, if at all, over the decision to forcibly uproot the lives of 112,000 people. "I do not think he was very much concerned with the gravity or implications of this step," said Biddle in his 1962 memoir. "He was never theoretical about things." According to Biddle, the fact that 70 percent of these people were American citizens also did not cause the president to lose sleep. "Nor do I think that the constitutional difficulty plagued him," wrote the former attorney general.[67]

The evacuation and internment of the West Coast ethnic Japanese is a serious blot on Roosevelt's legacy, but it is in keeping with his often cavalier disregard for civil liberties. As Frank Donner points out in *The Age of Surveillance*, "The President's record as a social reformer has obscured his anti-libertarian tendencies, reflected not only in his policies on such issues as wiretapping and Japanese relocation but in his prior career in public life. One need only recall his praise, in his 1920 campaign for the vice-presidency, of the raid the previous year by American Legionnaires on the Centralia, Washington, headquarters of the IWW as a 'high form of red-blooded patriotism.' "[68]

. . .

Meanwhile, the arrests and detentions of domestic alien enemies continued. In all, 8,004 Japanese-Americans, 6,847 German-Americans, and 2,991 Italian-Americans were taken into "custodial detention," and in some cases held up to three years after the end of the war. Hundreds of others were "repatriated" to Germany and Japan in prisoner-of-war exchanges, among them many U.S.-born children—American citizens—who were sent "home" with their immigrant parents. In the end, not a single person arrested and interned under the Alien Enemy Control Program was convicted of committing a war-associated crime against this country.

German, Italian, and Japanese aliens and West Coast Japanese-Americans bore the main brunt of government scapegoating during World War II, but they were not the only ones to be persecuted. Conscientious objectors whose opposition to the war was based on religious conviction were assigned either noncombatant status in the armed forces or, in the case of those unwilling to wear the uniform, a form of alternative service, but draft resisters, political dissenters, and those whose religious beliefs did not qualify for CO status went to jail. Approximately fifty-five hundred men, more than three-quarters of them Jehovah's Witnesses, were thus imprisoned.

Hawaiians lived under martial law for almost three years following Pearl Harbor, as the federal government put into effect the Army's decades-old plan, first formulated by DeWitt in the early 1920s and updated in 1936. Until October 1944, habeas corpus, trial by jury, and other basic civil liberties were suspended in Hawaii. In 1942 alone, there were more than twenty-two thousand military trials, resulting in a 99 percent conviction rate, with sentences that included prison terms, fines, required donations of blood, and mandatory purchases of war bonds.[69]

Japanese aggression in the Aleutian Islands in 1942 prompted the federal government to forcibly evacuate close to nine hundred native Aleutian Unangan people from their homes and destroy the dwellings for fear that Japanese troops would occupy the buildings and use the islands for a base. They were relocated to internment camps in southeastern Alaska, where living conditions were appallingly squalid—no electricity, heat, laundry, or bathing facilities, contaminated water. Illness was rampant, and close to seventy-five individuals died from disease during the three years of internment.

As in World War I, there were prosecutions for sedition, but instead of leftists and pacifists, the defendants were now anti-Semites and Nazi and Fascist sympathizers. In July 1942, William Dudley Pelley, founder and leader of the Silver Legion of America, a Fascist organization that numbered fifteen thousand members at its height in 1934, was convicted under the 1917 Espionage Act and sentenced to fifteen years, for little more than making inflammatory statements about the president, the government, and the war. The same month, twenty-six American Fascists were indicted under both the 1917 law and the Smith Act, for conspiring to undermine the morale of the armed forces. Despite an outcry from such notables as Zechariah Chafee, Roger Baldwin, and senators Robert A. Taft and Burton Wheeler, the group of twenty-six went on trial in April 1944. After seven months, the presiding judge died, and the charges were dismissed.

But the most egregious and far-reaching program occurred in Latin America, where, in flagrant violation of international law, the United States conspired with the governments of more than fifteen Latin American countries to identify, arrest, and deport to the United States, with little or no evidence and no legal proceedings, more than sixty-two hundred Latin Americans of German, Japanese, and Italian ancestry, including eighty-one German Jews, some of whom had spent time in Nazi concentration camps.* The deportees, who were interned in the same camps as domestic alien enemies, consisted of both immigrant residents and citizens of those Latin American countries from which they were deported. As with domestic alien enemies, they included only a tiny percentage of Nazis and Nazi sympathizers, and virtually no dangerous Japanese. The greatest majority by far were utterly innocent.

The ostensible aim of the Latin American program was hemispheric security, but there were as well other, darker purposes behind the plan. The Japanese Latin Americans faced racial prejudice and economic resentment, particularly in Peru, from which more than 80 percent of the Japanese internees came. The generally more pros-

---

*The countries that participated in the program included Bolivia, British Honduras (now Belize), Chile, Colombia, Costa Rica, Cuba, the Dominican Republic, Ecuador, El Salvador, Guatemala, Haiti, Honduras, Mexico, Nicaragua, Panama, Paraguay, Peru, and Venezuela.

perous and longer-established German community had challenged American economic dominance in Latin America, and the deportations were designed to help American businesses reassert their supremacy.

The most sinister objective of the agenda, however, was the intended use of the deportees for the purpose of prisoner exchange, as expressed in an internal State Department memo of November 1942, which noted, "Nations of Central America and the Caribbean islands have in general been willing to send us subversive aliens without placing any limitation on our disposition of them. In other words, we could repatriate them, we could intern them or we could hold them in escrow for bargaining purposes."[70]

Many of those "repatriated" in the prisoner exchange program had been born in Latin America and had never seen the countries to which they were "returned." Those who were not "repatriated" either made their way back to Latin America or stayed in the United States and began anew here.

The exclusion of Japanese aliens and Japanese-Americans from the West Coast was lifted in September 1945. Six months later, the last functioning internment camp closed.

Most, but not all, alien enemy internees were released as "restricted parolees" at the end of the war. In July 1947, Senator William Langer of North Dakota introduced S. 1749, "A Bill for the Relief of All Persons Detained as Enemy Aliens," proposing the release of the remaining internees. It failed to pass in the Senate.

A group of German-Americans were still in custody when the Crystal City, Texas, family internment camp closed in late 1947. They were transferred to the Ellis Island detention center; in the course of the next year, some were repatriated to Germany, while others were paroled or released.

Finally, in August 1948, more than three years after the war with Germany ended, the last internees were freed from Ellis Island. Camp employees and released internees alike signed secrecy oaths, vowing never to reveal their experiences on either side of the Alien Enemy Control Program.

. . .

The end of World War II marked another turning point in American life, as our World War II ally the Soviet Union once again became our adversary. America and Russia now locked in Cold War combat, and a new red scare brought about the most prolonged and intense period of political scapegoating this nation has ever known.

CHAPTER II

Scare Hell Out of the Country

The end of the war brought with it certain momentous advances in civil liberties. The GI Bill made it possible for millions of returning veterans to attend college or learn a trade and to buy homes through low-interest, no-down-payment government loans. In 1946, Jackie Robinson broke the color line in organized baseball, playing for the Montreal Royals; the following season, he moved up to the Brooklyn Dodgers, changing forever the complexion of the game and spelling the beginning of the end of racial segregation in the United States.

At the same time, civil liberties came under heavy attack, as the Soviet Union's aggression in Eastern Europe caused a wave of fear and intolerance, unleashing more than a decade of persecution of the American political left.

With the war over, tensions between the United States and the U.S.S.R. began to increase. After FDR's death in April 1945, Assistant Secretary of State Archibald MacLeish sought to reassure Americans and Russians alike regarding the future of U.S.-Soviet relations. In a May 26 radio broadcast, MacLeish invoked the late president, saying, "There is no necessary reason . . . why the United States and the Soviet Union should ever find themselves in conflict with each other . . . What underlies the current talk of inevitable conflict between the two nations . . . is nothing real, nothing logical. The basis of the fear is only fear itself."[1]

In general, Americans continued to hold a hopeful outlook regarding the possibility of a peaceful coexistence with the U.S.S.R. In a survey taken in September 1945, a striking 70 percent of those questioned were in favor of continued friendly relations with the Soviets.[2] By the end of the decade, however, public opinion had shifted drastically, unleashing an avalanche of mistrust and paranoia that opened the door for McCarthyism and set the pattern for the government's persecution of the American left for the next quarter century—until well after any threat, real or imagined, from the American Communist Party had long since faded.

Early in 1946, J. Edgar Hoover sent a memo to President Harry S. Truman, warning him about Communist espionage activities in the United States, particularly within the federal government. The president immediately instructed Hoover to make the investigation of such activities a top priority and approved the use of wiretapping in pursuing this investigation.

In February, FBI executives met in conference to plan the implementation of Truman's directive. The Bureau's assistant director, D. Milton Ladd, proposed reinstituting the old policies of "investigating all known members of the Communist Party" and preparing "security index cards" on them. He further recommended asking the attorney general to study the legal options regarding the potential need for mass detentions, pointing out that "the greatest difficulty" in carrying out a roundup of Communists in the case of an emergency would be "the necessity of finding legal authorization."[3]

Ladd also suggested a second program, this one to be kept secret from the attorney general. The plan involved preparing and distributing "educational material" for the purpose of convincing Americans that Communism was "the most reactionary, intolerant and bigoted force in existence." Equally important, the program was also designed to drive a wedge between Communists and more moderate liberals, who traditionally had defended the rights of their radical leftist colleagues. "The Party earns its support by championing individual causes which are also sponsored by the Liberal elements," reasoned Ladd, so this concentrated propaganda campaign would also serve to undermine the party's backing from " 'Liberal' sources," "labor unions," and "persons prominent in religious circles." As Ladd conceived it, the overarching effect of this "educational" effort would be to counteract an anticipated "flood of propaganda from Leftists and so-called Liberal sources" should it become necessary to carry out "extensive arrests of Communists."[4]

Ladd's recommendations dovetailed neatly with Hoover's long-standing obsession with Communism. In 1920, as head of the Justice Department's General Intelligence Division (better known as the Radical Division), Hoover had written a "Brief on the Communist Party" as well as a "Memorandum on 'The Revolution in Action,' " both of which were submitted to the House Rules Committee in defense of the Justice Department's actions during the Palmer raids. In the latter document, Hoover concluded, with a typical hyperbolic flourish, that in Communism "civilization faces its most terrible menace of danger since the barbarian hordes overran West Europe and opened the Dark Ages."[5] During the first red scare and intermittently throughout the 1930s, the bureau promoted the threat of Communism to influence government policy and create fear in the public, and in 1936, when President Roosevelt summoned the FBI director to talk about "the question of subversive activities in the United States, particularly Fascism and Communism," Hoover had predictably focused primarily on the latter.[6]

With the alliance of the United States and the Soviet Union during World War II, a moratorium was observed, and the FBI—while continuing to secretly investigate and keep files on American Communists—temporarily suspended public harassment of them. Now, however, with Fascism defeated and the Russian bear flexing its muscles, Hoover enthusiastically embraced Ladd's proposals. He wrote to Attorney General Tom Clark, who as an assistant to Francis Biddle had been a minor player in the decision to evacuate the ethnic Japanese from the West Coast. Hoover told Clark that the FBI had found it necessary to step up its investigation of CP activities and Soviet espionage cases, and to start compiling a list of all Communist Party members and others who might prove dangerous in the event of a crisis between the United States and the Soviet Union. Such a crisis, suggested Hoover, might make it necessary "to detain a large number of American citizens," and he urged Clark to undertake a study of what legislation was available or needed for "effective action," when and if an emergency situation should occur.[7]

Hoover also put Ladd's secret propaganda plan into effect, in what would become an unflagging, orchestrated crusade to destroy traditional liberal acceptance and defense of radical dissent, as well as to eradicate any influence American Communists might have in labor unions. In so doing, the FBI, while hiding behind its supposedly non-partisan investigative function, carried out Hoover's personal political agenda and helped pave the way for the rise of Wisconsin's senator Joseph McCarthy and his reign of terror.

Like the secret prewar investigations and subsequent scapegoating of German, Italian, and Japanese aliens, the genesis of the second great red scare in America can be traced to the FBI. In fact, there is a direct line of descent, starting with the original Custodial Detention Index (the ABC list), which the bureau began compiling in December 1939 to catalog individuals who could be dangerous in time of war or national emergency. In addition to the aliens on the list, the Custodial Detention Index included the names of many Communists.

In 1943, Attorney General Biddle ordered Hoover to stop using the index, noting that such activity went beyond the bureau's statutory authorization. In an act of covert insubordination, Hoover defied Biddle's order, sending out a confidential memo to FBI field agents instructing them to change the name of the list to the "Security Index" and to keep the program top secret. It stayed that way until the end of World War II—by which time the FBI had vastly increased both its size and its influence, going from 898 agents in 1940 to 4,886 in 1945—and with the intensified postwar investigations of Communists, the Security Index assumed a major new import.

The FBI's powerful ally in the secret campaign to influence public opinion and undercut liberal tolerance for American Communists was the House Un-American Activities Committee, the first incarnation of which was created in 1938 as a special committee, with the conservative Democrat Martin Dies of Texas as its chairman. Originally intended to investigate the German-American Bund, the committee, with its staff of thirty investigators, soon shifted its attention to the left, depicting the New Deal and the Roosevelt administration as parts of a monstrous Communist conspiracy. "Communists have infiltrated the government," Dies declared in October 1939. "There are Communists in high positions. This is particularly true of the New Deal agencies."[8]

Soon after HUAC's creation, Vice President John Nance Garner predicted, "The Dies Committee is going to have more influence on the future of American politics than any other committee of Congress."[9] In its first set of hearings alone, HUAC identified 640 organizations, 483 newspapers, and 280 labor unions as being under Communist control, and about a thousand individuals as being members of the party. The groups named included such "subversive" organizations as the Boy Scouts, the Camp Fire Girls, the ACLU, the Congress of Industrial Organizations, the National Catholic Welfare Conference, and the American Society of International Law. Dies later also provided names and occupations of "2,000 of the 4,700 Communists in the Chicago area";[10] the names of more than 500 federal employees who were supposedly members of the American League for Peace and Democracy (many were not), which Dies labeled "a Communist front"; and a list of 1,121 federal employees he accused of being either "Communists or affiliates of subversive organizations."[11] As Robert Griffith wrote in *The Politics of Fear*, "Martin Dies named more names in one single year than Joe McCarthy did in a lifetime."[12]

A symbiotic relationship quickly developed between HUAC and the FBI, as FBI agents were allowed unrestricted access to HUAC files, while the bureau secretly provided purportedly confidential reports to HUAC. Despite strained relations between Hoover and Dies— the bureau director considered the committee chairman an amateur investigator—Hoover nevertheless told the Montana representative James F. O'Connor that the bureau was in favor of HUAC's continuation and that his agency and the committee were "working together."[13] The FBI and HUAC continued to cooperate until the committee's term ended with the close of the Seventy-eighth Congress in December 1944.

When the new Congress convened in January 1945, Mississippi representative John Rankin—who in 1942 had advocated arresting, interning, and deporting "every Japanese in America, Alaska, and Hawaii"[14]—blindsided the Dies Committee's critics by moving to make HUAC a permanent committee of the House. In a roll-call vote, the resolution passed, 207–186, as forty New Dealers—including Lyndon Baines Johnson of Texas—were reluctant to take a stand and voted a neutral "present."

The new committee took up where Dies had left off. The committee member Karl Mundt of South Dakota spelled out HUAC's fundamentally antidemocratic mission when he talked about "dealing with factors, people, and policies of organizations engaging in actions which are un-American even though their activities are legal. Because of the extreme privilege of free press and free speech they can do much harm if the nefarious purposes and people lurking behind their high-sounding organizational names remain unexposed."[15]

For the greatest part of the next three decades, the clandestine alliance between the FBI and HUAC propped up the committee in its witch-hunting efforts, as the bureau provided a constant source of confidential reports and security information, despite officially denying such activities. When one HUAC investigator, who was himself a former FBI agent, told a *Washington Star* reporter in 1957, "We wouldn't be able to stay in business overnight if it weren't for the FBI," he was merely confirming what the then HUAC chairman, J. Parnell Thomas of New Jersey, had intimated nearly a decade earlier when he stated that "the closest relationship exists between this committee and the FBI. I think there is a very good understanding between us. It is something, however, that we cannot talk too much about."[16]

The quality of the information supplied by the FBI to HUAC may be surmised from descriptions of the committee's reports by two of its chroniclers. In *The House Committee on Un-American Activities, 1945–1950*, Robert K. Carr wrote that these reports "contain so many obvious errors and grossly unfair attacks upon persons of undoubted non-Communist standing that it is often difficult to single out or evaluate the authentic information about Communists and Communist activity that they contain." Similarly, in *The Committee*, Walter Goodman noted that "the reports were marred by an unfastidious use of evidence, sloppy organization and writing, rampant emotionalism, and wild charges."[17]

On March 10, 1946, barely a month after Assistant Director Ladd had first proposed it, the secret FBI "educational" program got off the ground when Father John F. Cronin, an official of the National Catholic Welfare Conference—which had been identified by Martin Dies just seven years earlier as itself being controlled by Communists—made front-page news by charging that there were 2,000 Communists working for the federal government in Washington, D.C. Basing his accusations on material secretly supplied by the FBI, Cronin alleged that 130 of those 2,000 "were in key positions from which they could influence the policies" of the State Department, Treasury Department, and Budget Bureau.[18] Despite his refusal to reveal his sources or to identify any individuals by name, and despite immediate and adamant denials from officials of all three agencies, Cronin's unsubstantiated allegations marked the beginning of an onslaught of ferocious and prolonged red-baiting.

Representative Edward Rees of Kansas, the ranking minority member of the House Civil Service Committee, immediately announced that he intended to introduce a resolution calling for a "complete and thorough investigation."[19] The stampede was on, as elected officials and other public figures now rushed to outdo one another in staking out the strongest possible anti-Communist positions.

Anti-Communism was the stance, and red-baiting the tactic. Originally initiated by anti–New Deal Republicans seeking to recapture the government after fifteen years of Democratic control, both were soon enthusiastically embraced by liberals eager to dissociate themselves from any taint of Communist leanings or affiliations. In so doing, they validated the FBI's strategy of eliminating liberals' traditional support for radicals and radical ideas.

The FBI plan was enhanced as a result of a wave of labor turmoil that swept the country in the year and a half following the end of World War II. During the conflict, grievances had built up, and just as labor unrest had erupted following World War I, late 1945 and 1946 saw almost five thousand strikes involving more than 4.65 million workers nationwide, including general strikes in Camden, Hartford, Houston, Lancaster, Oakland, Rochester, and Stamford. The government broke an oil workers' strike in October 1945 and a packinghouse strike the following January. Truman curtailed a rail workers' strike in May by seizing the railroads, and in November, after the United Mine Workers walked off the job for the second time that year, he obtained a court injunction forcing them back to work. Charges of Communist influence in unions led to a public-opinion backlash against labor—in 1945 and 1946, ninety antilabor bills were introduced in the Seventy-ninth Congress—contributing to the darkening mood toward radicals and isolating Communists in the labor movement.

Tolerance was further shuttered by two spy scares in 1945–46. The *Amerasia* affair, though labeled an espionage case, actually involved a longtime State Department employee's leaking classified documents to a left-wing magazine editor, who then used some of the information contained therein in a story. Three people were indicted, but with no evidence that the material had been passed to a foreign government or used for any purpose other than in the magazine piece, they were charged with unauthorized possession of government documents rather than espionage. Before their trial, however, a defense attorney learned that the FBI had illegally broken into both the magazine's offices and the homes of the accused, and a plea bargain avoided a potentially embarrassing trial for the bureau. The second spy case involved the arrest of twenty-two people in Canada on charges of conspiring to steal information about the atomic bomb for the Soviets; the Canadian Royal Commission report on the incident alleged extensive Russian espionage in Canada and, according to a Soviet informer, in the United States as well.

On July 6, 1946, with concern now understandably heightened about spies in the State Department, Congress passed the McCarran rider to the Smith Act. The amendment gave the secretary of state "absolute discretion [to] terminate the employment of any officer or employee of the Department of State or of the Foreign Service of the United States whenever he shall deem such termination necessary or advisable in the interests of the United States."[20] The McCarran rider would become a permanent fixture in State Department appropriations bills and would later be attached to the appropriations bills of other government agencies as well.

Throughout the 1946 midterm election campaign, the Republicans hammered away at the red issue. The soon-to-be Speaker of the House, Joseph Martin of Massachusetts, promised that a Republican Congress would "put an end to the boring from within by subversionists high up in the government."[21] GOP candidates made baseless connections between Communism and the Democratic Party's candidates. In California, the congressional challenger Richard M. Nixon emphasized his opponent's association with the "communist-dominated" Congress of Industrial Organizations' political action committee and accused him of "consistently voting the Moscow-PAC . . . line in Congress," while in Wisconsin, the senatorial challenger Joseph McCarthy accused his opponent of enjoying "Communist support."[22] The day before the election, Martin, the House Republican leader, told Massachusetts voters their choice was the difference "between chaos, confusion, bankruptcy, state socialism or communism, and the preservation of our American life, with all its freedom and its opportunities."[23] Dispensing with all subtlety, the Republican National Committee chairman, B. Carroll Reece, advised the American people that their option in the upcoming vote was between "Communism and Republicanism."[24]

The Republicans picked up fifty-four seats in the House and eleven in the Senate. With his party now in the driver's seat, HUAC's chairman, Parnell Thomas, announced a plan to spotlight "the sorry spectacle of having outright Communists controlling and dominating some of the most vital unions in American labor," as well as to investigate "Communist influences in Hollywood," "the Communist influence in our educational system," and "Communists and Communist sympathizers in the Federal government."[25]

The tone was set. The hunt was on.

Truman now faced three daunting challenges. First, from their new position of power, the Republicans, having proven the efficacy of playing the red card, accused him of being soft on Communism, both domestic and foreign. At the same time, Truman came under attack from the left wing of his own party, led by Henry Wallace, who had been fired as secretary of commerce shortly before the election for making a speech that was supposedly too conciliatory toward the Soviet Union. The progressive Democrats criticized Truman for adopting too harsh a stance toward the Soviets and for not pursuing attempts at accommodation. Finally, the president was having difficulty selling Americans on the Marshall Plan to rebuild a war-ravaged Europe, a program that was critical to American business interests.

Truman's response to the first issue was to create, less than two weeks after the election, the Temporary Commission on Employee Loyalty to study the issue of Communists in the federal government. In its report the following February, the commission wrote that while it was "unable . . . to state with any degree of certainty how far reaching" the problem was, there was nevertheless "sufficient evidence to convince a fair minded person that a threat exists," and concluded that "the presence within the government of *any* disloyal or subversive persons . . . presents a problem of such importance that it must be dealt with vigorously and effectively."[26]

Truman tended to regard the matter as a tempest in a teapot. "I believe the issue has been blown up out of proportion to the actual number of possible disloyal persons we may have," he told an official of the Democratic National Committee.[27] In fact, he saw the entire business of the danger from domestic Communism as greatly exaggerated. "People are very much wrought up about the Communist 'bugaboo,' " he wrote to a friend in late February, "but I am of the opinion that the country is perfectly safe as far as Communism is concerned."[28]

However, with the Republicans breathing down his neck, and HUAC, led by the rabid archconservative Parnell Thomas, banging the anti-Communist drum ever more loudly and insistently, Truman saw a chance to steal their thunder on the domestic Communism issue. Following the commission's recommendation, he established, by executive order on March 21, 1947, the Employees Loyalty Program in order to provide the country "maximum protection . . . against infiltration of disloyal persons into the ranks of its employees."[29] He later frankly admitted to a confidant "that he had signed the Order to take the ball away from Parnell Thomas."[30]

The Republicans, of course, lost no time in claiming credit for the new plan. "I am glad," said the RNC chairman, B. Carroll Reece, "that the President, however belatedly, has adopted this important part of the program supported by the Republican party and its candidates in the 1946 campaign." House Speaker Martin backhandedly commended Truman, saying that it was "good to see that he has finally awakened to the truth of what we have been telling him for the last few years."[31]

The Employees Loyalty Program was in keeping with the Hatch Act of 1939, which prevented any member of an organization advocating the overthrow of the U.S. government from gaining or continuing in federal employment, as well as with the Interdepartmental Committee on Employee Investigations, created by FDR in 1943 to investigate federal employees who advocated the overthrow of the government or belonged to an organization that advocated the same.

Truman's new program called for a loyalty investigation of every potential new employee of executive branch departments and for the termination of "disloyal" employees. The standard for non-hiring or firing was "reasonable grounds . . . for belief that the person involved is disloyal to the Government of the United States," a criterion that included membership in or "sympathetic association with" any organization the attorney general designated "totalitarian, fascist, communist, or subversive."[32]

As the bureaucracy of the Employees Loyalty Program was being created, the FBI and the Civil Service Commission engaged in a power struggle over which agency would be responsible for conducting the investigations of governmental employees and job applicants. Hoover won and extended the bureau's reach yet again.

If a loyalty investigation turned up anything suspicious, a hearing was scheduled before a departmental "loyalty board" comprising employees from the same agency as the accused. In their lack of deference to due process, the procedures for hearings in these cases were disturbingly reminiscent of those employed by the Alien Enemy Hearing Boards during World War II. There was no provision, for example, for the accused to see any evidence, and therefore no way for the accused to refute any such evidence. Neither was there any stipulation that a detailed—or, in fact, any—record of the loyalty hearing be made. Nor was a loyalty board required to make a finding based on evidence—or, indeed, to make any finding at all. Appeals were directed first to departmental authorities and then, if necessary, to the Loyalty Review Board, which was part of the Civil Service Commission. The Loyalty Review Board's recommendations, however, were merely advisory; the final decision rested with the head of the agency.

The legal ramifications were ominous. In a letter to *The New York Times*, a group of four prominent legal scholars and civil libertarians, including Zechariah Chafee, addressed the shortcomings of the loyalty-hearing process. "Where is the burden of proof?" they wrote. "Is it on the accused? . . . There is an implication of surrender in the apparent abandonment of the elementary requirements that charges be supported, that issues be clearly assigned, and that an adjudication must be based upon evidence with which the defendant has been confronted." The historian Henry Steele Commager raised additional legal objections, calling the loyalty program "an invitation to precisely that kind of witch-hunting which is repugnant to our constitutional system" and pointing out, "Here is the doctrine of guilt by association with a vengeance . . . The Alien Registration Act of 1940, directed against aliens and enacted under pressure of war, for the first time wrote that odious doctrine into American law. Now, apparently, it is here to stay."[33]

There was also the fact that the departmental loyalty boards and the Loyalty Review Board, like the Alien Enemy Hearing Boards of World War II, were administrative, not judicial, bodies composed of administrative officials who were now given the power to investigate and rule on individuals' personal convictions, opinions, affiliations, and relationships.

The essence of the Employees Loyalty Program was thought control, as Alan Barth, who covered civil liberties for *The Washington Post*, pointed out in 1951: "As a rule, only the unorthodox come before loyalty boards. They come before loyalty boards because someone has charged them with expressing the 'wrong' opinions, associating with the 'wrong' people, belonging to the 'wrong' organizations, and in general criticizing or seeking to change the existing patterns of American life."[34]

But the greatest danger of the program, wrote Barth, lay in its fundamentally undemocratic underpinnings:

> The inevitable effect is a corruption of the traditional American right of privacy and the development of a dangerous police power . . . The maintenance of . . . dossiers about citizens who have never been charged with any violation of law and who have no means of refuting misinformation that may have been collected concerning them is an invitation to abuses of the gravest sort. Secret dossiers are paraphernalia of a police state. They are not proper instruments of a democratic government . . .
>
> It does not matter that these invasions of what were once deemed inalienable rights have been adopted for the sake of national security . . . Dictatorship always has its origin in the assumption that men supposed to be benevolent may be entrusted with arbitrary authority.[35]

Despite the criticism, the federal plan was used as a model for state and municipal loyalty programs, and the practice of blacklisting quickly crept into private industry as well. As opponents of the Employees Loyalty Program feared, the policy did indeed become the cornerstone of the hysteria, repression, red-baiting, and witch-hunting that pervaded American life for the next ten years.

While the Employees Loyalty Program was being established, Truman was devising a foreign policy designed both to undercut progressive Democrats' attacks on him for being too harsh on the Soviet Union and to sell the American public on the Marshall Plan, for which American business interests were clamoring. In early 1947, after Britain's decision to cut off economic aid to Greece and Turkey—the governments of which were both threatened by strong Communist movements—Truman approached skeptical Republican leaders of the new Congress to ask for $400 million in military and financial assistance to the two beleaguered countries. In a strategy session, the Republican senator Arthur H. Vandenberg of Michigan counseled, "Mr. President, if that's what you want, there's only one way to get it. That is to make a personal appearance before Congress and scare hell out of the country."[36]

Truman took Vandenberg's advice, and on March 12 the president introduced the Truman Doctrine in a speech to a joint session of Congress that was broadcast nationally on live radio. In his address, Truman began by warning about the "gravity of the situation which confronts the world today," citing the threat of worldwide Communism to American national security, and went on to announce that the United States intended to vigorously oppose Soviet expansionism in Europe, as well as the spread of Communism around the globe.[37]

"The peoples of a number of countries of the world have recently had totalitarian regimes forced upon them against their will," said Truman. "I believe that it must be the policy of the United States to support free peoples who are resisting attempted subjugation by armed minorities or by outside pressures." Although he declared that our aid should be mainly economic, Truman also asked Congress to authorize sending troops to Greece and Turkey. He raised the specter of the domino theory, warning that if Greece fell, Turkey could follow, and then "confusion and disorder" could spread throughout the Middle East.

It worked. Truman scared hell out of the country, and Congress approved the funding, with the $250 million for Greece being divided into financial and military assistance, while the funding for Turkey was designated solely as military aid. With a stroke, Truman had enlisted the support of the American people for the plan to rebuild Europe and also trumped his left-of-center Democratic critics, whose disapproval of him for being too severe with the Russians now seemed incongruous and unseemly, given the magnitude of the threat he had described. Conversely, opposing the Truman Doctrine seemed dangerous to national security.

On the day after his speech to Congress, Truman further delineated his new hard line, telling a conference of radio journalists that although he had tried his "level best to get along with our friends the Russians . . . , [t]hey understand one language, and that is the language they are going to get from me at this point."[38]

The Cold War was on.

Two weeks after the Truman Doctrine speech, J. Edgar Hoover went before HUAC to testify about Communist activities and influence in the United States. Calling the American Communist Party "a fifth column if there ever was one," whose goal was "the overthrow of our Government," Hoover charged that Communists had been "mobilizing, promoting mass meetings, sending telegrams and letters to exert pressure on Congress" in opposition to the aid package to Greece and Turkey.[39]

Thus, the view that opposition to the Truman Doctrine endangered national security became coupled to the notion that all such dissent was Communist inspired. Now the FBI plan, hatched a year earlier by Assistant Director Ladd, to undermine traditional liberal support of Communists by driving a wedge between the two groups began to truly bear results, as liberals began a desperate attempt to disengage themselves from any taint of radicalism.

In so doing, they not only abandoned their Communist and fellow-traveler friends but also allowed the FBI to frame the parameters of the Cold War debate. As a result, the argument centered not on the question of whether the government had the right to investigate law-abiding citizens who held unpopular political views but instead on who exactly was worthy of investigation and who exactly should carry out those investigations; not on whether red-baiting in itself was un-American but instead on who exactly was a permissible and appropriate target.

Because HUAC's witch-hunting tactics were so odious, liberals misguidedly put their faith in the FBI and its supposedly nonpolitical brand of red-baiting as the more acceptable and responsible alternative. In fact, the bureau's methods and agenda were every bit as antidemocratic and subversive as the committee's. As noted, the two bodies covertly worked together, sharing confidential information, with the FBI often using HUAC as a front to maintain the ruse of its own nonpolitical nature. "It is as necessary to the success of this committee that it reveal its findings to the public," said a 1948 HUAC report, "as it is to the success of the FBI that it conceal its operations from the public."[40] Or, as Hoover put it, HUAC "served a useful purpose in exposing some . . . activities which no Federal agency is in a position to do, because the information we obtain in the Bureau is either for intelligence purposes or for use in prosecution, and committees of Congress have wider latitude in that respect."[41] When the committee came to Hoover for help with its investigation of the movie industry in mid-1947, the director—after receiving the committee chairman Thomas's assurance that such assistance would not be made public—wrote an internal memo to his assistants, saying, "I do think that it is long overdue for the Communist infiltration in Hollywood to be exposed, and as there is no medium at the present time through which this Bureau can bring that about on its own motion I think it is entirely proper and desirable that we assist the Committee of Congress that is intent upon bringing to light the true facts in the situation."[42]

In choosing the FBI over HUAC, liberals thus willingly forsook certain key, bedrock principles. As Kenneth O'Reilly points out in *Hoover and the Un-Americans*, "In this new climate, mainstream liberalism abandoned a tolerant set of beliefs for an ideology that denied traditional First Amendment rights to Communists and, to a lesser extent, fellow travellers."[43] In the process, postwar liberals helped open the door to McCarthyism and became its red-baiting allies as they sought to dissociate themselves from their more radical colleagues on the left. Such liberal bastions as the American Civil Liberties Union, Americans for Democratic Action, the Congress of Industrial Organizations, the National Association for the Advancement of Colored People, and many more, along with such liberal luminaries as Francis Biddle, Sidney Hook, Irving Kristol, Dwight Macdonald, Reinhold Niebuhr, Walter Reuther, Arthur M. Schlesinger Jr., Norman Thomas, Diana Trilling, Roy Wilkins, and countless others, all joined the red-baiting rush to draw the distinction between themselves and the Communists. Ironically, their efforts were hardly well served, for in the end Hoover had a file on every one of them, and many, despite their support for the bureau, were classified by the FBI as enemies all the same.

In *The Nightmare Decade*, Fred J. Cook observes that repressing Communists was merely "the smoke screen" and that liberals were the "true target" all along. "The real foe," writes Cook, "was always the American liberal—the New Dealer, the innovator, the idealist who saw the injustices in American society and advocated the use of the instrumentalities of democratic government to effect reforms. To the emperors of the status quo, such shakers and movers were dangerous men."[44] Through intimidation, the great majority of these voices were silenced.

The climate was chilling rapidly. In the first weeks of the new Eightieth Congress, over two hundred antilabor bills were introduced, and on June 23 the crushingly restrictive Taft-Hartley Act was passed over Truman's veto. By the middle of 1947, the ACLU described "an atmosphere increasingly hostile to the liberties of organized labor, the political left and many minorities . . . Excitement, bordering on hysteria, characterized the public approach to any issue related to Communism."[45]

In June, the Senate Appropriations Committee wrote to Secretary of State George C. Marshall to warn that the State Department was the target of "a deliberate, calculated program being carried out not only to protect Communist personnel in high places but to reduce security and intelligence protection to a nullity."[46] Marshall quickly set up the Personnel Security Board to formulate a set of security guidelines for the agency. That same month, the McCarran rider to the State Department appropriations bill, which gave the secretary of state absolute discretion to terminate an employee in the interests of national security, was used to summarily dismiss ten State Department workers, without benefit of charges, evidence, or hearings.

In October, HUAC's investigation of the movie industry, secretly supported by confidential information from the FBI, resulted in the Hollywood blacklist, as accused Communists who refused to deny allegations about themselves were shut out of work. In December, the Attorney General's List of Subversive Organizations was made public.* The civil libertarian Alan Barth condemned it as "a kind of official blacklist," which represented "perhaps the most arbitrary and far-reaching power ever exercised by a single public official in the history of the United States," as it gave the attorney general the ability to "stigmatize and, in effect, proscribe any organization of which he dis-

---

*The list consisted of more than seventy groups and schools, including the Communist Party, the Ku Klux Klan, the National Negro Congress, the Protestant War Veterans, and the Washington Bookshop Association.

approves."[47] The publication of the list, observed Richard M. Freeland in *The Truman Doctrine and the Origins of McCarthyism*, was "a deliberate attempt by the Department of Justice to neutralize various political organizations that were, among other subversive things, impeding the Administration's efforts to win support for Cold War foreign policy."[48]

The cumulative effect of these types of actions was a pervasive stifling of dissent, as Americans became increasingly reluctant to question or criticize the government and increasingly intolerant of anyone who did. The February 1948 Communist coup in Czechoslovakia further amplified paranoia, as the Russians appeared to be bent on unlimited expansion through satellite governments. As the prominent Republican attorney Richard Scandrett commented in a letter to a friend, "Even to suggest in a whisper here nowadays that every Russian is not a cannibal is to invite incarceration for subversive activities." In mid-1948, the ACLU reported "a confusion and uncertainty over the basic principles of civil liberty unmatched in years."[49]

Developments during one week in the summer of 1948 cast even greater doubt over the state of civil liberties in the United States. First, on July 28, a federal grand jury in New York indicted twelve high-level Communist Party officials, charging them with violating the Smith Act. The charge against them was not *attempting* or *advocating* the overthrow of the government, not *conspiring* or *instructing how* to overthrow the government, but *conspiring to advocate* the overthrow of the government. In effect, Communists were now being indicted simply for being Communists, even though the Communist Party was not outlawed. In fact, the previous March, at a HUAC hearing on "bills to curb or outlaw the Communist Party of the United States," Hoover himself had advised against any such bills, expressing "grave doubts" about "restrictive legislation that might later be declared unconstitutional."[50]

Three days after the New York indictments, with the presidential election looming, the Republican-controlled HUAC—whose staff had increased from ten in 1947 to forty-seven in 1948—launched a sensational inquiry into espionage within the federal government. Most of the individuals subpoenaed had been identified by Elizabeth Bentley and Whittaker Chambers, two former Communist Party members who professed to having themselves previously been engaged in espionage, although their reliability as witnesses was questionable. Many of the accused individuals had also been subpoenaed the previous spring by the same New York federal grand jury that later charged the twelve Communist leaders, but when not one was indicted in the New York hearings, HUAC stepped in and took over.

Bentley, often called the "blond spy queen" in the press, accused dozens of current and former government employees—including FDR's administrative assistant Lauchlin Currie and Treasury Secretary Morgenthau's former assistant Harry Dexter White, who had been the principal architect and executive director of the International Monetary Fund. The biggest fish named by Chambers, an editor at *Time*, were White and Alger Hiss, who had been a law clerk for the Supreme Court justice Oliver Wendell Holmes, had held various positions in the Roosevelt administration, and at the time of Chambers's revelations was serving as president of the Carnegie Endowment for International Peace.

An irate White demanded to appear on his own behalf and, in his testimony, vehemently denied his accusers' allegations. He suffered from a weak heart, and the humiliation and stress of his appearance before HUAC were too much for him. White died three days after testifying.

Hiss, a former Roosevelt protégé and confirmed New Dealer, was a perfect pawn for HUAC and the Republicans, who were out to associate the Democrats and the New Deal with Communism going into the election. (Chambers himself adamantly believed that the New Deal was "a genuine revolution" and every bit as extreme a movement as international Communism.)[51] As Alistair Cooke noted in his account of the Hiss case, "The House Committee wanted to prove that the New Deal was a calculated flirtation with Communism, and . . . thus succeeded, before he ever came to trial, in making a large and very mixed public identify Hiss with what was characteristic of the New Deal."[52]

Hiss was indicted. The first of two high-profile trials ended in a hung jury, but in the second he was convicted—not of espionage but of perjury—and sentenced to five years.

As a junior member of HUAC, Richard Nixon found the Hiss case a perfect vehicle to ride to national prominence. Just as the committee had been covertly aided by the FBI in its investigation of the movie industry, Nixon was now clandestinely supplied with confidential FBI information on Hiss. His tough questioning of Hiss catapulted him to the forefront of anti-Communist crusaders, and he used his newfound celebrity to advance both himself and the cause. "Like the exposed tip of an iceberg," Nixon solemnly lectured the American public, "the Alger Hiss case is only a small part of the whole shocking story of Communist espionage in the United States."[53]

On August 3, three days after the HUAC hearing began, the Justice Department submitted to the FBI an emergency detention plan it had been developing since Hoover, following Assistant Director Ladd's suggestion, originally proposed such a program early in 1946. In the course of developing the plan, the department had rejected Hoover's request for a bill that would justify widespread detentions, saying, "The present is no time to seek legislation. To ask for it would only bring on a loud and acrimonious discussion."[54] Ladd tended to agree, telling his boss that what was needed instead was "sufficient courage to withstand the courts . . . if they should act."[55]

The top-secret Justice Department plan—only three copies were made, two of which were kept by the FBI and the other by the Justice Department—was referred to as "the Department's Portfolio." According to Ladd, the guidelines laid out in the Portfolio were the basis of the FBI's "entire planning and operational procedure to appre-hend individuals contained in our Security Index."[56]

The Portfolio has never been made public, but a 1952 memo from Ladd to Hoover, which has been published, outlines its stipulations in detail.[57] It provided for suspending habeas corpus; arresting all individu-als on the Security Index under one "master warrant," without any criminal charges needing to be filed; and carrying out searches and seizures of contraband. Detainees could be held incognito for forty-five days, after which hearings would be conducted, but they would not be bound by "the rules of evidence." Appeals could be made only to the president and not through the courts. Moreover, just three years after the end of the war that saw the internment of well over a hundred thousand aliens and citizens, the Portfolio endorsed the establishment of what the civil liberties champion Frank Wilkinson called "the ultimate weapon of repression: concentration camps to intern potential troublemakers" in the event of some future "national emergency."[58]

In its intentions and provisions, the Justice Department Portfolio was a blueprint for a police state.

. . .

As the election approached, it appeared a certainty that the Republicans would both win the White House and retain control of Congress. The support for Henry Wallace, who had broken with the Democrats to run for president on the Progressive Party ticket, seemed certain to split the Democratic vote and doom the Democrats' chances. Accordingly, Truman and the liberals adopted a policy of red-baiting Wallace in order to undermine his support.

Truman's main campaign strategist, Clark Clifford, had spelled out the strategy a year earlier, when Wallace was still contemplating a third-party candidacy. In a memo to the president, Clifford wrote, "Every effort must be made . . . to identify him and isolate him in the public mind with the Communists," by enlisting "prominent liberals and progressives—*and no one else*—to . . . point out that the core of the Wallace backing is made up of Communists and the fellow-travellers."[59]

Truman took up the theme, alluding to "Wallace and his Communists," and legions of liberals jumped in to add their voices.[60] The social critic Dwight Macdonald called Wallace the "mouthpiece of American communism," while the columnist Dorothy Thompson said, "The Communist Party—let's tell the truth—initiated the movement for Wallace." The labor leader Walter Reuther declared, "It is tragic that he is being used by the Communists the way they have used so many other people . . . They write your speeches, attend your meetings, applaud what you say and inflate your ego. That's what is wrong with Henry Wallace." (While it was true that many members of the Communist Party enthusiastically supported Wallace, the party's chairman, William Foster, scoffed at the notion that the party was running Wallace's campaign, saying, "Who but a fool can believe that the Communist party had or believed it had any such power over Wallace?")[61]

But it was the Americans for Democratic Action that did the most complete and effective hatchet job on Wallace, collecting, producing, and distributing a plethora of materials, including a pamphlet called *Henry A. Wallace: The First Three Months*, that portrayed the Progressive Party candidate—and all other opposition to the Truman Doctrine—as Soviet inspired and unpatriotic.

The tactic succeeded brilliantly. Wallace's support evaporated, and in the most stunning upset of American electoral politics not only did Truman defeat Thomas E. Dewey, who had soft-pedaled his red-baiting of Truman during the campaign, but the Democrats recaptured both houses of Congress.

Throughout 1949, the hysteria quickened as fears of espionage were highlighted by both domestic and international events. At home, Americans' fears were kept alive by the ongoing Hiss case, which commanded daily headlines, and by the March arrest and subsequent trial of the Justice Department employee Judith Coplon, who was charged with copying and delivering FBI reports to the Russians.*

Internationally, there was the triumph of the Chinese revolution in August, for which Republicans blamed the State Department, portraying the agency as a viper's nest of traitors, dominated—as the Ohio senator Robert Taft put it—by "a left-wing group who . . . were willing . . . to turn China over to the Communists."[62] When the Soviet Union detonated its first atomic bomb in September, the prevailing view in the United States was that the only way the Russians could have obtained the necessary knowledge for such a feat would have been through espionage. The successes of the Chinese revolution and the Soviet A-bomb program, thus seen as having been aided and abetted by Communist agents in the United States, translated into yet an even more severe clampdown, as the twin threats to national security were now perceived to be both an external power and unpatriotic and disloyal Americans.

Truman played an active role in feeding the fears, publicly denouncing as traitors the twelve CP leaders who were being tried under the Smith Act and endorsing, together with the U.S. commissioner of education, Earl J. McGrath, the National Education Association's stand that "members of the Communist Party shall not be employed in the American schools."[63]

By now, most Americans were convinced that there were Communists hiding under every rock. "They are everywhere," warned Attor-

---

*Although none of the reports were related to national security, they did reveal the FBI's proclivity for spying on civilians, particularly New Deal liberals, progressives, and radicals. Coplon's conviction was eventually overturned when it came to light that the evidence against her had been obtained through illegal wiretaps and that the bureau had destroyed evidence in order to protect the agent who lied on the stand about not having tapped Coplon's telephone.

ney General J. Howard McGrath (no relation to the education commissioner), "in factories, offices, butcher stores, on street corners, in private businesses. And each carries in himself the germ of death for society."[64]

The ACLU annual report of August 1949 was titled *In the Shadow of Fear* and declared:

> The imagined insecurity of the strongest democracy in the world in the face of the cold war with Communism has created an atmosphere in which fear makes the maintenance of civil liberties precarious. Not only the liberties of real or suspected Communists are at stake. Far beyond them, the measures to protect our institutions from Communist infiltration have set up an unprecedented array of barriers to free association, of forced declarations of loyalty, of black-lists and purges, and most menacing to the spirit of liberty, of taboos on those progressive programs and principles which are the heart of any expanding democracy.[65]

The scene was set. Enter Joe McCarthy, stage right.

CHAPTER 12

A Neurotic Nightmare

At the beginning of 1950, Joseph McCarthy was halfway through his first term in the Senate, and with very little to show for it. In three undistinguished years of service, the forty-one-year-old junior senator from Wisconsin had earned a reputation as an uncouth, hard-drinking, publicity-seeking troublemaker who demonstrated little regard for the Senate's elaborate conventions of decorum, procedure, and seniority. McCarthy's sustained efforts on behalf of the soft-drink lobby had earned him the derisive nickname the Pepsi-Cola Kid, and senators of both parties made a point of distancing themselves from him. Frustrated by his failure to gain recognition and casting about for an issue that would bolster him in his upcoming reelection campaign, McCarthy hit upon the theme of Communists in the federal government, a subject that was at once topical, sensational, apparently long-lived, and in keeping with his earlier track record of red-baiting.

The perjury conviction of Alger Hiss on January 21 had propelled the matter of Communists in the government onto the front pages of newspapers and into the minds of the American public. Four days later, after Hiss had been sentenced to five years in prison, Secretary of State Dean Acheson initiated a furor when he stated, "I do not intend to turn my back on Alger Hiss."[1] Although Acheson went on to explain that his motivation came from Christ's Sermon on the Mount,* the secre-

---

*Acheson referred reporters to the following passage: "For I was an hungred, and ye gave me meat: I was thirsty, and ye gave me drink: I was a stranger, and ye took me in: Naked, and ye clothed me: I was sick, and ye visited me: I was in prison, and ye came unto me . . . Inasmuch as ye have done it unto one of the least of these my brethren, ye have done it unto me."

tary of state's intended magnanimity created a public relations disaster, as he foolishly left himself and the Truman administration open to attack for being soft on Communism.

With his Ivy League background and his aloof—some called it arrogant—patrician bearing, Acheson rankled many conservatives, who had been gunning for him since China was taken over by Mao Zedong's forces the previous August. After the Chinese Communists' triumph, the New Hampshire senator Styles Bridges had called on Congress to investigate the State Department, charging Acheson with "what might be called sabotage" of Chiang Kai-shek's government.[2] Now Republicans and southern Democrats seized on Acheson's statement of loyalty to Hiss as proof that Communist sympathizers occupied positions of influence at the very top levels of the federal government, and that American foreign policy was being created by such men.

It was McCarthy who informed the Senate of Acheson's remark, labeling it "a fantastic statement."[3] Richard Nixon, who had played a major role in Hiss's original indictment, called it "disgusting"[4] and cautioned that "the great lesson which should be learned from the Alger Hiss case is that . . . traitors in the high councils of our own government make sure that the deck is stacked on the Soviet side of the diplomatic table."[5] The Republican Robert F. Rich of Pennsylvania opined, "I don't know if we have anybody working for Joe Stalin more than the Secretary of State,"[6] and the Democrat Edward E. Cox of Georgia, though finding Acheson's statement to be "no surprise," added that it very well "might be terrifying to the American people."[7]

The outrage over Acheson's indiscretion had hardly died down when Truman announced on January 31 that since the Soviets were also now in possession of the A-bomb—having successfully carried out their first atomic test four months earlier—the United States would begin work on "the so-called hydrogen or super-bomb," thus escalating the arms race and reinforcing the idea that we had much to fear from our adversaries.[8] Three days later those concerns were confirmed when the British government announced that the English physicist Dr. Klaus Fuchs, who had worked on the Manhattan Project, had confessed to having passed atomic secrets to the Soviets.

It was in this charged atmosphere, then, that McCarthy traveled to West Virginia on February 9 to address the Women's Republican Club of Wheeling, as part of the annual nationwide Lincoln Day appearances by Republican legislators.* It was the first of a five-stop speaking tour that would also take McCarthy to Reno, Las Vegas, Salt Lake City, and Huron, South Dakota—a hinterlands itinerary that reflected his lowly status in the Republican hierarchy.

In his Wheeling speech to an audience of almost three hundred, McCarthy went directly for the jugular, claiming that America was at a disadvantage in international affairs, "not because our only powerful potential enemy has sent men to invade our shores, but rather because of the traitorous actions of those who have been treated so well by this Nation." Zeroing in on his target, he said, "The bright young men who are born with silver spoons in their mouths are the ones who have been the worst . . . In my opinion the State Department, which is one of the most important government departments, is thoroughly infested with Communists." He singled out Acheson, calling him a "pompous diplomat in striped pants with a phony British accent."9

Then McCarthy uttered the sentence that would almost overnight transform him into a household name and soon thereafter make him the most feared man in America. "And ladies and gentlemen, while I cannot take the time to name all the men in the State Department who have been named as active members of the Communist Party and members of a spy ring, I have here in my hand a list of 205—a list of names that were made known to the Secretary of State as being members of the Communist Party and who nevertheless are still working and shaping policy in the State Department."

There was no list. There were no names. McCarthy's charges were loosely based on information in a July 1946 letter from Secretary of State James Byrnes to the Illinois representative Adolph Sabath that had been entered into the *Congressional Record*.10 The letter had to do with the screening of 3,000 federal employees who were transferred to the State Department after the war. Of these, 285 were not recommended for permanent employment, and 79 of that group had been terminated for unspecified reasons. By some fuzzy math and even fuzzier logic, McCarthy came up with 205 "active members of the Communist Party," even though the letter contained no names or any reference to Communist Party membership.

---

*The Wheeling talk was delivered the same day that Nixon, speaking in Ogden, Utah, called the Alger Hiss case "only a small part of the whole shocking story of Communist espionage in the United States" (see Chapter 11, above).

McCarthy's allegations were pure hokum, but nobody, certainly not McCarthy himself—who from all indications had no idea what he was getting into[11]—could have predicted the fallout.

Aside from the expected coverage in the local Wheeling paper, McCarthy's speech attracted little attention at first. The Associated Press sent out a brief three-paragraph piece to newspapers across the United States, but only eighteen publications carried the story on February 10, and of those, only three, most notably *The Denver Post*, gave it front-page placement. The *Chicago Tribune* ran it on page 5. Most large metropolitan dailies, including *The New York Times*, *The Washington Post*, and the *Los Angeles Times* did not publish the article at all.

During a thirty-minute stopover in Denver on his way to Salt Lake City on the tenth, McCarthy was surprised to find himself surrounded by reporters who confronted him with a State Department press release that categorically denied his accusations, characterizing them as "entirely without foundation."[12] The senator sneered at the agency's denial and told the newsmen he had "a complete list of 207 'bad risks' still working in the state department."[13] Where this new number came from is unclear, but when the reporters asked to see the list, McCarthy was caught off guard. Stalling for time, he opened his briefcase and made a show of digging around for the list, but as *The Denver Post* reported, he quickly "discovered he had left it in his baggage on the plane." The paper also published a staged-looking photograph of the senator rifling through the briefcase, with the caption "Left Commie list in other bag."

By the time McCarthy landed in Salt Lake City, he had devised a further refinement of his assertions, displaying the techniques that he would use to dazzle, deceive, and intimidate so many members of Congress, the press, and the American people for the next four years. Weaving the beginning strands of what would become a vast web of half-truths, fictions, and outright lies—demonstrating what the historian Robert Griffith terms "his exceptional talent for compounding distortion upon distortion"—McCarthy informed the press that there were actually *two* lists.[14] The first, which he had alluded to in Wheeling, was composed of 205 "bad risks" who were still employed by the State Department. The second, and even more threatening list, he now revealed, contained the names of 57 "card-carrying Communists" who worked at the agency.[15]

As with the original 205, the source of this new number was vague and outdated. The information came from the testimony of the House Appropriations Subcommittee investigator Robert E. Lee, who had reported in March 1948 that after reviewing the cases of 108 past, present, and prospective State Department employees who had been investigated as possible loyalty or security risks, 57 were at that time still working for the department. Not only were there no names on Lee's list—the cases were referred to by numbers—but in the two years since it had been presented, four committees of the then-Republican-controlled Congress had reviewed the cases and had not lodged a charge of disloyalty against a single State Department employee. Many of the 108 individuals listed had simply been the targets of malicious gossip and rumor.

In Reno on February 11, McCarthy delivered the same speech he had given in Wheeling, but changed the 205 to 57. He also named four names, only one of whom, John Service, worked for the State Department at the time, and Service had been cleared of all charges against him on multiple occasions.

While in Reno, McCarthy received a State Department telegram asking him to name the "card-carrying Communists" who worked in the department. McCarthy, in turn, wrote to Truman, repeating his charges, blasting the State Department's denial of them, and suggesting that of three hundred employees "certified for discharge by the President's own Loyalty Board," only eighty had been fired.[16] He went on to condemn Truman's 1948 order forbidding the release of any State Department employee's loyalty records to members of Congress. "Despite this blackout," McCarthy wrote, "we have been able to compile a list of 57 Communists in the State Department." The actual number, he insisted, was much larger and could be obtained from the secretary of state.

The State Department responded with an unqualified denial of McCarthy's charges, saying that never had three hundred of its employees been designated by the Loyalty Review Board as disloyal, nor had eighty such workers ever been dismissed; in fact, the Loyalty Review Board had never recommended the dismissal of even one State Department employee.

By the time McCarthy returned to the Senate on the evening of February 20, he was the subject of front-page headlines from coast to coast. He was aware that the Democratic majority leader, Scott W. Lucas of Illinois, had announced that there would be no votes taken that evening, and when he sauntered to the microphone toting an overstuffed briefcase, there were fewer than ten senators in the chamber. "Mr. President," announced McCarthy in his nasal monotone, "I wish to discuss tonight a subject which concerns me more than does any other subject I have ever discussed before this body, and perhaps more than any other subject I shall ever have the good fortune to discuss in the future. It not only concerns me, but it disturbs and frightens me."[17]

For the next five hours, McCarthy harangued the Senate chamber, citing cases from the two-year-old Lee list without ever identifying it as his source, but claiming instead that his information came directly from State Department files that had been provided by "some good loyal Americans." The entire speech was a bluff, one of the most fraudulent and mendacious presentations ever witnessed on the floor of the U.S. Senate. McCarthy read 81 of the 108 cases on the Lee list, exaggerating, distorting, and lying, as he changed information, omitted conclusions, and added fabrications in the most flagrant and irresponsible manner imaginable. Robert Taft, Republican of Ohio, one of the conservative stalwarts of the Senate, called it "a perfectly reckless performance."[18]

Nevertheless, two days later, the Senate adopted Resolution 231, authorizing the Senate Foreign Relations Committee to investigate whether there were disloyal employees in the State Department. At the insistence of Senate Republicans, the resolution called for the committee to subpoena the loyalty and employment files of all State Department personnel and of all employees in other suspect agencies.* A subcommittee of five was appointed, chaired by the Democrat Millard E. Tydings of Maryland, a stalwart conservative and anti–New Dealer serving his fourth term in the Senate. Hearings began on March 8.

In the meantime, McCarthy, apparently realizing just how deep a hole he had dug for himself, was scrambling behind the scenes to find some

---

*This set up a head-on collision with Truman, who refused to allow the files to be removed from the State Department's archives; instead, in a compromise, he ruled that committee members would be allowed to examine individual files at State Department headquarters.

concrete evidence of something, anything, that he could use to support his claims. In the aftermath of the Wheeling speech, he had phoned J. Edgar Hoover and asked for help. "This caused headlines all over the country, and I never expected it," McCarthy told Hoover, "and now I need some evidence to back up my statement that there are Communists in the State Department."[19] Hoover gave McCarthy "unshirted hell" for his recklessness but immediately issued instructions to FBI staff to review the files for anything that might be of assistance to the senator.[20]

Hoover also suggested that McCarthy engage Donald Surine, a hard-nosed ten-year FBI veteran whom the director had recently been forced to fire for becoming involved with a prostitute during the course of an investigation. McCarthy promptly hired Surine as his investigator and set him to work collecting information on suspected State Department employees. Surine quickly became one of McCarthy's most trusted aides, and every week during the time he worked for the senator, the two of them had lunch with Hoover to share information and compare notes.

The wave of publicity that attended McCarthy's February 20 Senate speech thrust him into the role of standard-bearer for the red-baiters and witch-hunters. Few newspapers adopted a critical stance similar to that of *The New York Times*, which accused McCarthy, in a February 22 editorial, of conducting a "campaign of indiscriminate character assassination." On the contrary, the typical press accounts of the proceedings made him sound rather reasonable, and in no way conveyed the manic, chaotic, semi-deranged quality of his live presentation. McCarthy suddenly appeared to be a populist champion of ordinary Americans, a dedicated crusader acting out of pure patriotism in order to expose a confirmed spy ring, rather than a calculating demagogue deviously exploiting an undercurrent of fear.

Immediately picking up on the momentum of the unexpected outpouring of popular support, Republicans rallied behind McCarthy and latched onto his coattails. Within a matter of weeks, Senator Taft, who had criticized the February 20 talk as "perfectly reckless," encouraged McCarthy to keep on with his accusations, telling him, "If one case doesn't work, try another."[21]

Appearing before the Tydings Committee, McCarthy was combative, defiant, and abusive. When Senator Theodore F. Green of Rhode

Island refused to allow him to obfuscate in answering a question and persisted in attempting to pin him down, McCarthy shouted, "You be quiet until I finish."[22] When Tydings demanded the names of the "good loyal Americans" in the State Department who had supposedly furnished the list of suspects, McCarthy countered:

> You are not fooling me, Senator. I know what you want. I know what the State Department wants. They want to find out who is giving out information on these disloyal people so their heads will fall, and so far as I am concerned, gentlemen, no heads of any loyal people in the State Department will fall . . . I am very surprised and disappointed, Senator, that this Committee would become the tool of the State Department, Senator, not to get at the names, the information, of those who are bad security risks, but to find out for the Department who may have given me information so those people can be kicked out of their jobs tomorrow.[23]

Realizing he had to come up with something concrete, McCarthy named Dorothy Kenyon, a New York City lawyer and former municipal judge who had never worked for the State Department but had served a U.S. delegate to the United Nations Commission on the Status of Women from 1947 to 1949. The sixty-two-year-old Kenyon was a long-standing, distinguished liberal who had been affiliated over the decades, however loosely, with a number of liberal and left-of-center organizations that the Dies Committee had designated as Communist fronts. There was no evidence whatsoever that Kenyon had ever belonged to the Communist Party.

Kenyon responded immediately, calling McCarthy an "unmitigated liar" and demanding to appear before the committee.[24] In her testimony, she stated, "I am not, and never have been disloyal. I am not, and never have been a Communist. I am not, and never have been a fellow traveler." At the same time, she also articulated the plight of so many caught in the web of the witch hunts. "Literally overnight," said Kenyon, "whatever personal and professional reputation and standing I may have acquired after many years in private practice and some in public office, they have been seriously jeopardized, if not destroyed by the widespread dissemination of charges of Communistic leanings or proclivities that are utterly false."[25]

McCarthy's next target was the State Department's ambassador at large Dr. Philip C. Jessup, whom the senator accused of having an "unusual affinity for Communist causes."[26] This second attempt was similarly wide of the mark. Jessup denounced McCarthy for making "false and irresponsible" charges that demonstrated a "shocking disregard" for the national interests of the United States, and the committee's chairman, Millard Tydings, read into the record strong letters of support for Jessup from the former secretary of state Marshall and General Dwight D. Eisenhower.[27]

His first two supposedly "big names" having amounted to nil, McCarthy was on the spot to produce something that would stick. Confronted by reporters on March 21, he impulsively told them that he had just given the committee "the name of the man—connected with the State Department—whom I consider the top Russian espionage agent in this country."[28]

It was another con. Meeting with the committee in executive session, McCarthy fingered Dr. Owen Lattimore, a widely published author and recognized authority on Far Eastern affairs. Though a confirmed leftist and even a fellow traveler in the 1930s and 1940s, Lattimore was neither a spy nor a Communist and, except for a brief four-month stint five years earlier, had never been a State Department employee—aside from that service, his only affiliation with the department consisted of two speeches he had given there. McCarthy was undaunted, however, telling the committee, "If you crack this case, it will be the biggest espionage case in the history of this country."[29]

McCarthy identified Lattimore as "one of the principal architects of our far eastern policy [whose] record as a pro-Communist goes back many years."[30] He claimed that Lattimore enjoyed "free access" to the State Department and even had a desk there. In truth, Lattimore had no direct influence on foreign policy, had no desk at the State Department, and, before McCarthy's accusation thrust him into the national limelight, was unknown to Secretary of State Acheson.

Employing his trademark offensive tactic of innuendo, McCarthy implied under questioning that Lattimore's FBI file would confirm everything he was saying. When the Connecticut Democrat Brien McMahon jumped in and tried to pin him down, McCarthy demonstrated his patented defensive technique of evasiveness:

McMahon: Have you seen the FBI files?
McCarthy: I think I know what is in them.

McMahon: That is not the question. Have you seen them?

McCarthy: I will tell you, Senator McMahon, do not worry about whether I have seen them or not.

McMahon: I am worried. You will either answer or you will not. You have or you have not.

Tydings: Nobody is going to ask you for your sources.

McCarthy: Senator McMahon, let me tell you this.

McMahon: Do not tell me anything. I am not interested in a single thing. That technique you have is not going to work on me. If you cannot answer the question, that you have or you have not, then I am not interested in anything else you are going to say. That is the question: Have you seen the FBI file or have you not.

McCarthy: I heard your question.

Tydings: Let me say this—

McMahon: You refuse to answer?

McCarthy: No; I don't refuse to answer.

Tydings: We do not want to know your sources. But what I think we are entitled to know is, is this a speculation or have you had some contact with the files in one way or another that makes you think you have some accurate information?

McCarthy: I am about as certain as I could be of anything as to what those files will show. As to whether I have seen them, who might have helped me get information, or things like that—

Tydings: I do not want to know that.

McCarthy: I know you do not . . . I might say I have not seen the original FBI files.

McMahon: The original FBI files. Have you seen a copy of them?

McCarthy: I think, Senator, whether I have seen a copy or not, not having seen the original I would have no way of knowing whether I saw a copy unless I compared it with the original.

Tydings: Have you seen what purports to be a copy, or have you got your evidence from somebody who has seen the files? That is all.

McCarthy: Let me say this. To the best of my knowledge, and I think it is good, I think it has been proven so far in dates and places that I have been giving the committee, the FBI file will show in detail not the case merely of a man who happens to favor Russia, not the case of a man who may disagree with what we think about Russia, but a man who is definitely an espionage agent.

McMAHON: See how he goes away from the question?[31]

Sticking to his bluff, McCarthy told the committee that the Lattimore case "will prove that I am completely wrong or it will prove I am 100 percent right."[32] A few days later, despite a State Department denial of the charges against Lattimore, McCarthy assured reporters, "I am willing to stand or fall on this one. If I am shown to be wrong on this I think the subcommittee would be justified in not taking my other cases too seriously. If they find I am 100 percent right—as they will—it should convince them of the seriousness of the situation."[33]

From Afghanistan, where he was on a United Nations mission, Lattimore cabled the Associated Press, calling McCarthy's "rantings pure moonshine" and vowing to return to the United States as soon as he was able. "Delighted his whole case rests on me," read Lattimore's cable, "as this means he will fall flat on his face."[34] In Lattimore's absence, his wife asked that he be granted an appearance before the Tydings Committee.

In the interim, Truman ordered Hoover and Attorney General McGrath to prepare a confidential summary of Lattimore's FBI file for the committee members. As Tydings would later inform Lattimore during his appearance, "There was nothing in that file to show that you were a Communist or ever had been a Communist, or that you were in any way connected with espionage information or charges, so that the FBI file puts you completely . . . in the clear."[35]

On March 30, McCarthy delivered a four-hour speech to the Senate, supposedly detailing the proof of Lattimore's treason. It was typical McCarthy "evidence," full of half-truths, distortions, and lies. Lattimore's attorney, the future Supreme Court justice Abe Fortas, would later point out more than a hundred factual errors and misstatements in the speech.

On April 5, the day before Lattimore was scheduled to appear, the committee heard from the State Department's Loyalty and Security Board chairman, Conrad E. Snow, and the Civil Service's Loyalty Review Board chairman, Seth W. Richardson. The former had been a brigadier general in World War II; the latter had served as an assistant attorney general in Herbert Hoover's administration. Both were lifelong Republicans. Snow told the committee, "If there are any Communists in the State Department, the Loyalty Security Board is uninformed of their existence." Richardson testified, "The FBI has considered nearly 3,000,000 files. More than 10,000 of those cases have been given a field investigation by the FBI. Not one single case, or evidence directing toward a case, of espionage has been disclosed in that record . . . [N]ot one single syllable of evidence has been found by the FBI . . . indicating that a particular case involves the question of espionage."[36]

This was consistent with the committee's findings. With Richardson on the stand, Tydings announced that four weeks into the hearings, the committee had "not yet received the names or the evidence of any card-carrying Communist from any source, including Senator McCarthy, . . . now in the State Department, up to the present time."[37]

The following day, Lattimore began his testimony by reading a prepared statement that took an hour and three-quarters. Calling McCarthy's charges "base and contemptible lies," he vowed to show "in detail" the speciousness of those accusations, and in turn accused the senator of having "flagrantly violated" the responsibility of his office.[38] Invoking his "right and duty to list these violations," he specifically charged McCarthy with:

> impairing the effectiveness of the United States Government in its relations with its friends and allies, and . . . making the Government of the United States an object of suspicion in the eyes of the anti-Communist world, and undoubtedly the laughing stock of the Communist governments.
>
> . . . [I]nstituting a reign of terror among officials and employees in the United States Government, no one of whom can be sure of safety from attack.
>
> . . . [W]ithout authorization us[ing] secret documents obtained from official Government files.
>
> . . . [V]ilif[ying] citizens of the United States and accus[ing] them of high crime, without giving them an opportunity to defend themselves.
>
> . . . [R]efus[ing] to submit alleged documentary evidence to a duly constituted committee of the Senate.

In the conclusion to his prepared statement, Lattimore challenged the underlying principle of the Cold War red scare, that is, the suppression of dissent. "If the people of this country," he said, "can differ . . . only at the risk of the abuse to which I have been subjected, freedom will not long survive."[39]

For most of the rest of the day, Senator Bourke B. Hickenlooper of Iowa—McCarthy's staunchest supporter on the committee—badgered Lattimore, trying to pin the blame for the fall of China on him. Lattimore acquitted himself eloquently and convincingly, bringing a depth of knowledge to the discussion that made Hickenlooper appear uninformed and overmatched.

The parade of witnesses in the weeks that followed made a mash of the charges against Lattimore, and Lattimore himself, appearing again on May 2 and 3, put to rest any lingering notion that he was "the top Russian espionage agent in this country."

McCarthy was 0 for 3, and the Lattimore case on which he was "willing to stand or fall" had been revealed as a sham, but it made no difference. All at once, the junior senator from Wisconsin was the man of the hour and in great demand as a speaker. Intoxicated with the media attention and emboldened by the backing of his Republican colleagues, he stepped up his attacks. Addressing the American Society of Newspaper Editors, McCarthy called the former secretary of state George Marshall "a pathetic thing . . . completely unfit" for the office and branded Dean Acheson "completely incompetent." He condemned "the Reds, their minions and the egg-sucking phony liberals who litter Washington with their persons" and belittled "the pitiful squealing of those who would hold sacrosanct those Communists and queers who have sold 400,000,000 Asiatic people into atheistic slavery and have the American people in a hypnotic trance, headed blindly toward the same precipice."[40] Speaking to the Midwest Council of Young Republicans, he defended doing "a bare-knuckle job" and derided Tydings and McMahon as Truman's "political puppets," saying they knew "little or nothing of Communist techniques—even less about how to conduct an investigation," and labeling the Tydings Committee hearings "Operation Whitewash."[41]

It was almost three months since the Wheeling speech, and not a single one of McCarthy's accusations had been credibly proved. Referring to the Wheeling talk, Representative Frank M. Karsten, Democrat from Missouri, called for an "inquiry . . . as to whether or not a hoax, a deceit, or a fraud, has been practiced somewhere, by someone, upon the American people."[42] The Republican Kenneth S. Wherry of Nebraska, another of McCarthy's loyal backers in the Senate, angrily defended his ally, saying, "The American people want an investigation not of Mr. McCarthy but of subversives in the State Department."[43]

On May 4, at the urging of Tydings, Truman decided to allow the committee members to examine the FBI files of all eighty-one individuals McCarthy had accused in his February 20 Senate speech. The president had resisted opening the files on the advice of J. Edgar Hoover, who had sanctimoniously told the committee on March 27, "I would not want to be a party to any action which would smear innocent individuals for the rest of their lives. We cannot disregard the fundamental principles of common decency and the application of basic American rights of fair play in the administration of the Federal Bureau of Investigation."[44]*

Tydings, however, pointed out to Truman that the dossiers had already been examined earlier by Republican-controlled congressional committees, who had found nothing incriminating in them. Accordingly, the president agreed to allow members of the Tydings Committee to review the files at the White House. The senators could not bring any staff, and they would not be allowed to take notes. As anticipated, the files revealed nothing damaging to any of the eighty-one cited individuals.

McCarthy charged that the files had been altered and became even more strident, widening his accusations, painting the reputed Communist conspiracy in ever broader strokes, and in the process keeping himself on the front pages of the nation's newspapers. Most Republicans in Congress backed him.

Only a handful of seven Republican moderates repudiated McCarthy. On June 1, the freshman senator Margaret Chase Smith of Maine, the chamber's only woman, read the seven senators' "Declaration of Conscience" to the Senate.† The statement began by expressing concern over "the growing confusion that threatens the security and

---

*Hoover's lofty defense of civil liberties was self-serving and hypocritical—at the time, the FBI had files on seventy million Americans, and the bureau regularly supplied HUAC with derogatory, and frequently unproven, information about people, which HUAC then made public in its hearings, often causing great and undeserved personal damage to reputations, livelihoods, and personal relationships.

†In addition to Smith, the six others were George D. Aiken (Vt.), Robert C. Hendrickson (N.J.), Irving M. Ives (N.Y.), Wayne L. Morse (Ore.), Edward J. Thye (Minn.), and Charles W. Tobey (N.H.).

stability of our country" and blaming the source of that confusion on the Truman administration's "lack of effective leadership" and "complacency to the threat of communism here at home." But it quickly went on to denounce "certain elements of the Republican party [who] have materially added to this confusion in the hopes of riding the Republican party to victory through the selfish political exploitation of fear, bigotry, ignorance and intolerance." In her speech accompanying the statement, Smith lamented that the Senate "recently . . . has too often been debased to the level of a forum of hate and character assassination sheltered by the shield of Congressional immunity."[45]

That only one other Republican, H. Alexander Smith of New Jersey, publicly expressed his support of the "Declaration of Conscience" was a measure of how powerful McCarthy had become in the space of just three months. In fact, except for Wayne L. Morse of Oregon, who left the Republican Party to become an Independent in 1952 and then a Democrat three years later, all the signers and supporters of the "Declaration of Conscience" would soon abandon their criticism of McCarthy.

But Joe McCarthy was just getting started. The fear that he inspired would continue to build for four more years before his reign of terror was finally brought to a halt.

The Tydings Committee hearings ground on, but on June 25, 1950, they suddenly became page 2 news when North Korean soldiers crossed the border and attacked South Korea. Two days later, the United Nations Security Council passed a resolution calling on member nations to provide military assistance to South Korea, and two days after that Truman instructed General Douglas MacArthur, as head of the UN Command, to invade North Korea. With the outbreak of the Korean War, the red scare intensified, as the anti-Communists and red-baiters shifted the hysteria into overdrive. "The greatest Kremlin asset in our history," proclaimed Senator Taft, "has been the pro-Communist group in the State Department who promoted at every opportunity the Communist cause in China."[46]

The Tydings Committee concluded its hearings on June 28 and released its report on July 17. Meticulously scrutinizing and analyzing the evidence, the report found McCarthy's charges of espionage and disloyalty in the State Department to be "false," "irresponsible," and "unwarranted." The report also offered a blistering indictment of McCarthy, calling his accusations and methods "what they truly are: A fraud and a hoax perpetrated on the Senate of the United States and the American people. They represent perhaps the most nefarious campaign of half-truths and untruth in the history of this Republic. For the first time in our history, we have seen the totalitarian technique of the 'big lie' employed on a sustained basis."[47] The report was signed by the committee's three Democrats; the Massachusetts senator Henry Cabot Lodge Jr. submitted a short minority report, while Bourke Hickenlooper of Iowa remained silent.

McCarthy immediately went on the counterattack. "The Tydings-McMahon report is a green light to the Red fifth column in the United States," he maintained. "It is a signal to the traitors, Communists, and fellow travelers in our Government that they need have no fear of exposure from this Administration . . . [T]he Tydings-McMahon half of the committee has degenerated to new lows of planned deception. The result of their work is a clever, evil thing to behold. It is gigantic in its fraud and deep in its deceit."[48]

The timing of the Tydings Committee report could not have been worse. The same day it was released, the FBI announced the arrest in New York of the electrical engineer Julius Rosenberg, the fourth American apprehended in an atomic spying case that developed out of the arrest of Klaus Fuchs in Britain. In June and July, nine U.S. citizens, including Rosenberg's wife, Ethel, and her brother David Greenglass, were arrested on charges of passing atomic secrets to the Soviets. Although none of the arrestees was affiliated with the State Department, the very fact of apparent atomic espionage was enough to lend credibility to McCarthy's charges that the Tydings Report had been a whitewash. Not only did the Tydings investigation fail to slow McCarthy down, but his power and influence were actually enhanced in the process.

The atomic spy case further fueled the new wave of panic ignited by the Korean War. In this frantic environment, Congress passed the Internal Security Act of 1950 on September 12. Also known as the McCarran Act for its chief sponsor, the Democratic senator Pat McCarran of Nevada, the ISA was, as one historian puts it, "one of the most massive onslaughts against freedom of speech and association ever launched in American history."[49] Among other things, the broad-spectrum bill required the registration of Communist-action and Communist-front groups; established the Subversive Activities Control Board, which could designate any organization as a Communist action or Communist front if it failed to voluntarily register; and prohibited members of any so-designated organizations from working for the government or for a private company engaged in defense work.

The most ominous aspect of the law, however, was the provision for a preventive detention program—proposed by seven liberal Democratic senators, including Hubert Humphrey of Minnesota, Estes Kefauver of Tennessee, and Herbert Lehman of New York—that empowered the president, in time of national emergency, "to detain . . . each person as to whom there is reasonable ground to believe . . . probably will engage in, or probably will conspire with others to engage in, acts of espionage or of sabotage."[50]*

The ISA passed in the Senate by 70–7; the House approved it by 354–20. To his credit, Truman vetoed the bill, but Congress overrode his veto, 57–10 in the Senate and 286–46 in the House. On December 21, the Senate Internal Security Subcommittee was established to oversee the administration and enforcement of the ISA. With McCarran as its chairman, SISS became the Senate version of HUAC and, like the House committee, received secret, confidential information from the FBI in carrying out its investigations.

The Republican senator William Langer of North Dakota called the Internal Security Act of 1950 "one of the most vicious, most dangerous pieces of legislation against the people that has ever been passed." A *New York Times* editorial said it represented "a potentially serious threat to American civil liberties" in that it endangered "the freedom of thought and speech that is a vital part of the American tradition and that is, in fact, essential for the proper functioning of democratic government." *The Washington Post* feared that the new law was so vague it "might easily be applied to many organizations guilty of nothing more than a loyal opposition to Government policies or to prevailing popular opinion."[51]

---

*As portentous as this feature was, Attorney General McGrath instructed Hoover to ignore it in favor of the Justice Department's secret and more stringent police-state-style emergency detention plan of August 3, 1948 (see Theoharis, *FBI and American Democracy*, p. 69; for the Justice Department plan, see Chapter 11, above).

The *Post* also correctly identified the nature of the driving impulse behind Cold War paranoia. "Subversion," said the editorial, "is a neurotic nightmare."

The 1950 elections saw the Republicans cut into the Democratic majority in both houses. By maintaining a focus on the red threat and on the Democrats' alleged softness toward that threat, the GOP was able to pick up five Senate and twenty-eight House seats. In California, Nixon moved up to the Senate by smearing his opponent, Helen Gahagan Douglas, with accusations that she harbored Communist sympathies. McCarthy singled out Tydings, McMahon, and the Democratic Senate leader, Scott Lucas of Illinois, for retribution for their roles in attempting to expose his chicanery, and he actively supported their opponents. McMahon was politically unassailable and easily won reelection, but Tydings and Lucas were both defeated.

The Maryland campaign against Tydings featured an assortment of dirty tricks, including a doctored composite photograph of Tydings talking to the former Communist Party chief Earl Browder. The results of McCarthy's active role in the contest terrified Senate Democrats, who saw in the defeat of the influential Tydings a warning to each of them. As one powerful Democratic senator, quoted anonymously, put it, "For whom does the bell toll? It tolls for thee."[52]

The Washington Post accused McCarthy of "exploiting the popular anxieties of these fevered times . . . What he is trying to do is not new. It worked well in Germany and in Russia; all voices except those officially approved were silenced in those lands by intimidation . . . [T]he public must demand an end to the kind of thought control that Senator McCarthy is creating."[53]

By the beginning of 1951, the phenomenon that the political cartoonist Herb Block dubbed "McCarthyism" was sweeping the country. McCarthy himself, however, was merely an opportunist who hijacked an already moving train, one that had left the station soon after the end of World War II and that had been given a large boost of fuel by Truman in 1947. As the journalist and author Carey McWilliams wrote in 1950, "McCarthyism is merely a second chapter in the loyalty program which the administration officially sanctioned three years ago." With the loyalty program, McWilliams said later, "witch-hunting ceased to be a form of Congressional rabble-rousing and became a formally sanctioned aspect of the Administration's foreign policy. The loyalty programme was simply the domestic counterpart of the Truman Doctrine which was proclaimed at the same time."[54]

In 1951, four years after he privately expressed "the opinion that the country is perfectly safe as far as Communism is concerned," Truman's own view of domestic Communism had not changed.[55] In April 1950, speaking to the Federal Bar Association, he had reiterated his conviction that "the internal security of the United States is not seriously threatened by the Communists in this country . . . They are noisy and they are troublesome, but they are not a major threat."[56]

Nevertheless, just as political expediency had prompted him to establish the original Employees Loyalty Program, now, in April 1951, the Republicans' gains in the 1950 election and their continued attacks on his administration for being soft on Communism led Truman to tighten the loyalty program criteria. Whereas the initial basis for dismissal from or refusal of employment had been "reasonable *grounds*"[57] indicating disloyalty, the new standard became "a reasonable *doubt*"[58] regarding loyalty. This change, as the historian Athan Theoharis has written, "was a complete reversal of the burden of proof" and "legitimized the tactics of McCarthy," thereby contributing to "an escalatory process that could not be reversed."[59]

Ironically, Truman never appeared to understand the precedent set by his loyalty program or its connection to what followed. Speaking to the American Legion in August 1951, he declared, "Real Americanism means that we will protect freedom of speech—we will defend the right of people to say what they think, regardless of how much we may disagree with them."[60]

He went on to condemn those who were "chipping away our basic freedoms just as insidiously and far more effectively than the Communists have ever been able to do," by attacking the "basic principle of fair play that underlies our Constitution." In the strongest language, he denounced "the scaremongers and hatemongers" and called upon "every American who loves his country and his freedom to rise up and put a stop to this terrible business."

When Truman made this speech, McCarthy had been carrying out his political pogrom for a year and a half, and by the time Truman finally saw fit to take a stand against him, it was without ever mentioning McCarthy by name.

. . .

The outcry over the Republicans' campaign tactics in the Maryland senatorial race prompted the Rules and Administration Committee to appoint a subcommittee to investigate whether the winner, John M. Butler, should be unseated, and to determine McCarthy's role in the election. The subcommittee's August report, which was unanimously endorsed by the three Democrats and two Republicans on the panel, found no grounds to unseat Butler but strongly condemned "the despicable 'back street' type of campaign . . . conducted by non-Maryland outsiders . . . designed to destroy the public faith and confidence in the basic American loyalty of a well-known figure . . . The implication of such tactics as a threat to our American principles should be obvious and frightening." The report also concluded that McCarthy had been a "leading and potent force" in the campaign against Tydings.[61]

William Benton, McMahon's fellow Democratic senator from Connecticut, called for McCarthy's resignation. Knowing that he would not step down, Benton also introduced a resolution calling for a committee to investigate not only McCarthy's participation in Butler's campaign but his entire Senate record in order to determine if expulsion proceedings should be brought against him.

Benton was a political neophyte; he had been appointed to the Senate in December 1949 as a replacement for a senator who had resigned, and he was elected a year later to serve out the remaining two years of the term. When he offered his resolution to investigate McCarthy, not one other senator of either party spoke out in support of it.

Characteristically, McCarthy immediately tore into Benton, hurling personal insults and making an implicit threat about his political future: "Benton has established himself as the hero of every Communist and crook in and out of government . . . Connecticut's mental midget . . . will learn that the people of Connecticut do not like Communists and crooks in Government any more than the people of Maryland like them."[62]

In September, a subcommittee was appointed to consider Benton's motion. For the next year, McCarthy attacked Benton mercilessly and relentlessly, calling him "the chameleon from Connecticut," who, as assistant secretary of state, had surrounded himself with "a motley, Red-tinted crowd" of "fellow travelers, Communists and complete dupes" who were "very, very bad loyalty and security risks."[63] He brought a $2 million libel suit against Benton, conceding that he couldn't win but wanted to make Benton "sweat."[64] He attacked Benton on national television, had his tax records investigated, and charged that Benton, rather than himself, was the one who should be expelled from the Senate.

McCarthy succeeded. By the end of the summer of 1952, Benton acknowledged, "There couldn't be a better example anywhere to illustrate why experienced politicians don't get mixed up with fellows like McCarthy. Instead of pursuing McCarthy—I am the fellow who is being pursued."[65] The ultimate proof of the efficacy of McCarthy's strategy came when Benton was defeated for reelection in 1952.

Equally important, McCarthy's tactics and Republican stonewalling succeeded in tying up the subcommittee appointed to pursue Benton's resolution. Just before Benton left the Senate, the subcommittee issued a report saying, "Senator McCarthy deliberately set out to thwart any investigation of him by obscuring the real issue and the responsibility of the subcommittee by charges of lack of jurisdiction, smear and Communist-inspired persecution."[66] The report did not, however, recommend expulsion or even censure.

The 1952 election, in addition to putting Eisenhower in the White House, gave the Republicans slim majorities in both houses. When the new Congress was seated in January 1953, the newly reelected McCarthy was appointed chairman of both the Senate Committee on Government Operations and that committee's Permanent Subcommittee on Investigations. He was now, said *The New York Times*, "in a position of extraordinary power—in the country as well as the Senate . . . He is in undisputed control . . . of the Senate's most powerful investigative organ . . . And the Senate now knows . . . Senator McCarthy is a very bad man to cross politically."[67]

From his new position of power, McCarthy met with Hoover to request "closer cooperation and more extended use of the FBI and its facilities." Hoover instructed his assistants to covertly provide McCarthy with the information he needed, and asked Assistant Director Louis B. Nichols to act as a "close liaison" with the senator.[68] According to William C. Sullivan, a top assistant who later became the FBI's third-ranking official after Hoover and Associate Director Clyde Tolson, "We gave McCarthy all we had."[69]

McCarthy's first actual target, in February, was the State Department's communications arm, the International Information Administration, and its shortwave propaganda radio network, Voice of America. McCarthy charged that his staff had found thirty thousand books by Communist authors in IIA's overseas library catalogs. The list was actually a compilation of multiple copies by fewer than 425 "un-American" writers, some who were or had been Communists or fellow travelers, and others who clearly were not. The list included such "subversives" as the educators John Dewey and Robert M. Hutchins; the novelists Edna Ferber, Dashiell Hammett, and Lillian Hellman; the poets W. H. Auden and Stephen Vincent Benét; the philosopher Jean-Paul Sartre; the head of the NAACP, Walter White; Secretary of State John Foster Dulles's cousin Foster Rhea Dulles; and the best-selling authors Arthur M. Schlesinger Jr. and Theodore H. White.

In response, the State Department informed VOA that it could use no material by "Communists or other controversial authors" in its broadcasts.[70] A list of titles was circulated; hundreds of books were removed from IIA library shelves, and in some cases they were even burned or pulped.

Equally serious, hundreds of VOA and IIA employees were fired with no evidence, as McCarthy's aides David Schine and Roy Cohn toured Europe, cultivating a network of informers within the agencies. The VOA's deputy administrator, Reed Harris, and the acting director for public affairs of the U.S. High Commission for Germany, Theodore Kaghan, were both forced to resign as a result of words they had spoken or written in the 1930s. One VOA employee, the electrical engineer Raymond Kaplan, committed suicide, saying in a farewell note to his wife, "Once the dogs are set on you, everything you have done since the beginning of time is suspect . . . I have never done anything I consider wrong but I can't take the pressure."[71]

After the IIA/VOA investigation, McCarthy announced that he would soon be undertaking further extensive investigations of a number of other governmental agencies, including the Army, the Atomic Energy Commission, the Central Intelligence Agency, the Government Printing Office, and the U.S. delegation to the United Nations. In essence, he was serving notice of his intention to take on the Eisenhower administration directly, thereby positioning himself for a run at the presidency in 1956.

During the summer of 1953, McCarthy threw down the gauntlet by denouncing the administration for carrying on trade relations with

Communist countries. Although Eisenhower disliked McCarthy intensely and made a point of maintaining his distance from the senator, McCarthy's usefulness to the Republican Party made the president reluctant to lock horns with him. "I just will not," he told one of his close advisers, "I *refuse*—to get into the gutter with that guy."[72] (Eisenhower's brother Arthur, however, called McCarthy "the most dangerous menace to America" and lamented, "It's too bad we have such a man in public life.")[73]

Throughout the fall, McCarthy's "investigations" became increasingly crazed. One after another, the members of the subcommittee stopped attending hearings, until they became a one-man show. In October, McCarthy began a closed-door probe of the Army, claiming to have discovered a spy ring therein. Thirty-three civilian employees were suspended, but after a monthlong internal investigation Secretary of the Army Robert T. Stevens announced that all thirty-three had been exonerated.

As McCarthy continued his attack on the Army, it became clear to Eisenhower that he was going to have to intervene. In November, he attempted to undercut McCarthy's influence by remarking that he hoped the issue of Communists in the government would be a moot point by the midterm election. McCarthy disputed Eisenhower's contention, changing, as was his wont, what the president had actually said and claiming instead in a nationally broadcast speech that Eisenhower had "expressed the hope that by election time in 1954, the subject of communism would be a dead and forgotten issue. The raw, harsh fact is that communism is an issue and will be an issue in 1954."[74] White House aides interpreted McCarthy's challenge as a declaration of war on the president.

McCarthy continued his investigation of the Army for four more months, accusing, badgering, insulting, demeaning, and terrorizing dozens of innocent civilians and Army personnel, many of whom lost their jobs as a result. In February, while questioning Brigadier General Ralph W. Zwicker, a highly decorated World War II veteran, McCarthy said that Zwicker "lacked the brains of a 5-year-old child" and was "not fit to wear that uniform," and had the effrontery to tell him, "General, you should be removed from any command."[75] He then gave reporters a distorted account of Zwicker's testimony.

The day after McCarthy's impertinent bullying of Zwicker, Secretary of the Army Stevens issued an order prohibiting any more Army officers from testifying at McCarthy's hearings. Furious, McCarthy called Stevens on February 20 and threatened him. Stevens was unmoved. "I am going to try to prevent my officers from going before your committee," said the secretary, "until you and I have an understanding as to the abuse they are going to get."[76]

"Just go ahead and try it, Robert," McCarthy shot back. "I am going to kick the brains out of anyone who protects Communists. If that is [your] policy . . . , you just go ahead and do it. I will guarantee you that you will live to regret it."

Vice President Nixon stepped in, urging a meeting between Stevens and the subcommittee Republicans—McCarthy, Everett Dirksen of Illinois, Karl Mundt of South Dakota, and Charles E. Potter of Michigan. Entering the meeting room, one observer noted, Stevens was like "a goldfish in a tank of barracuda."[77] Invoking party unity, the senators browbeat the secretary into publicly retracting his order.

In a public statement on March 3, 1954, Eisenhower decried the "disregard of standards of fair play" by certain congressional committees. Within the hour, McCarthy issued a defiant response, declaring, "If a stupid, arrogant or witless man in a position of power appears before our committee and is found aiding the Communist party, he will be exposed. The fact that he might be a general places him in no special class so far as I am concerned."[78] The following day, he claimed to have established "beyond any shadow of a doubt by sworn testimony that certain individuals in the Army have been protecting, promoting, covering up and honorably discharging known Communists."[79] In *The New York Times,* James Reston wrote, "President Eisenhower turned the other cheek . . . and Senator Joseph R. McCarthy, always an obliging fellow, struck him about as hard as the position of the President will allow."[80]

With McCarthy's defiance of the president, the press and broadcast media—which to a great extent had remained neutral or supported him in the past—now perceived the genuine threat he represented and began to turn against him. In what was perhaps the turning point in McCarthy's stranglehold on America, the television journalist Edward R. Murrow devoted the entire March 9 installment of his nationwide *See It Now* program to exposing the senator. The show broadcast films of McCarthy humiliating and intimidating witnesses, and Murrow repeatedly refuted McCarthy's "facts" with hard evidence, exposing the deceit and fabrications for what they were.

Murrow's celebrated closing monologue was a powerful indictment of McCarthy's agenda and tactics. "The line between investigating and persecuting is a very fine one," said Murrow,

> and the junior senator from Wisconsin has stepped over it repeatedly. His primary achievement has been in confusing the public mind, as between the internal and the external threats of Communism. We must not confuse dissent with disloyalty. We must remember always that accusation is not proof and that conviction depends upon evidence and due process of law. We will not walk in fear, one of another. We will not be driven by fear into an age of unreason, if we dig deep in our history and our doctrine, and remember that we are not descended from fearful men—not from men who feared to write, to speak, to associate and to defend causes that were, for the moment, unpopular. This is no time for men who oppose Senator McCarthy's methods to keep silent.[81]

The momentum against McCarthy was given a further push when the Army released a report on March 11 accusing him and the subcommittee's chief counsel, Roy Cohn, of attempting to secure preferential treatment for David Schine, another McCarthy aide, who had been drafted the previous November. Two days later, Nixon signaled the White House's stance by criticizing McCarthy in a nationally televised speech, saying, "Men who have in the past done effective work exposing Communists in this country have, by reckless talk and questionable method, made themselves the issue rather than the cause they believe in so deeply."[82]

Stung by "that prick Nixon," as McCarthy privately referred to him, and claiming that the Army was trying to blackmail him into abandoning his investigation, McCarthy announced the next day that he was temporarily relinquishing the chairmanship of the subcommittee so the panel could conduct a public investigation into the Army's charges against Cohn and himself.[83] The inquiry would be directed by Mundt. Before the hearings began, McCarthy was forced to resign from the subcommittee; he was, however, allowed to choose his successor, and selected a strong supporter, the archconservative Henry C. Dworshak of Idaho.

The impending hearings clearly held the key to McCarthy's political future, and as they approached, his support continued to slip away. Newspapers from across the political spectrum lambasted him on their editorial pages. In public opinion polls, McCarthy's approval ratings declined sharply, going from a 50-29-21 percent favorable-unfavorable-no opinion ratio on January 15 to a 38-46-16 percent ratio on April 4.[84]

The subcommittee replaced Cohn with the Tennessee trial lawyer Ray H. Jenkins as its chief counsel, and the Army engaged the prominent sixty-three-year-old Boston attorney Joseph Welch as its representative. The Army-McCarthy hearings began on April 22, and for the next month and a half they became the first such governmental proceedings to be televised from gavel to gavel. The Senate minority leader, Lyndon Johnson, arranged the telecast with the American Broadcasting Company in the belief that showing the entire proceedings "would make people see what the bastard was up to."[85]

Johnson's intuition was correct. Television brought McCarthy's customary arrogance and truculence into the living rooms of America, and his loathsome character and malevolent behavior were fully revealed. As Cohn later wrote, "With his easily erupting temper, his menacing monotone, his unsmiling mien, and his perpetual 5-o'clock shadow, he did seem the perfect stock villain. Central casting could not have come up with a better one."[86]

The climax of the hearings came on June 9, when McCarthy introduced the name of Frederick G. Fisher, an attorney in Welch's firm who had originally been one of the team chosen to assist on the case. When Welch had learned, however, that Fisher had been a member of the left-wing National Lawyers Guild as a Harvard law student, he had sent Fisher back to Boston.

The Fisher matter was supposed to be off-limits. Two days earlier, Cohn and Welch had agreed that in exchange for McCarthy's not bringing it up, there would be no mention of Cohn's having failed the physical exam for admission to West Point. McCarthy had approved the arrangement, so when he went back on the bargain, introducing Fisher's name and charging that he had been a member of "the legal arm of the Communist Party," Cohn and Welch were stunned.[87] The former was visibly upset and hastily wrote a note to McCarthy that said, "This is the subject which I have committed to Welch we would not go into. Please respect our agreement as an agreement, because this is not going to do any good."[88] McCarthy crumpled the note and persisted with his smear of Fisher and Welch.

When, after several minutes, Welch was finally able to get the floor, he delivered a speech that, more than any other single event, spelled the end of McCarthy's career. "Until this moment, Senator, I think I never really gauged your cruelty or your recklessness," Welch began.

Fred Fisher is a young man who went to the Harvard Law School and came into my firm and is starting what looks to be a brilliant career with us . . . Little did I dream you could be so reckless and cruel as to do an injury to that lad . . . I fear he shall always bear a scar needlessly inflicted by you. If it were in my power to forgive you for your reckless cruelty, I will do so. I like to think I am a gentleman, but your forgiveness will have to come from someone other than me . . . Let us not assassinate this lad further, Senator. You have done enough. Have you no sense of decency, sir, at long last? Have you left no sense of decency?[89]

The hearing room erupted with applause, and McCarthy was all but finished. Soon afterward, Senator Ralph Flanders of Vermont, a seventy-four-year-old liberal Republican, defied the party leadership and introduced a resolution calling for McCarthy's censure. On September 27, a bipartisan select committee of six senators submitted a report unanimously supporting censure. Two weeks later, the Senate passed a resolution to "condemn" rather than "censure"—an inconsequential difference—by a vote of 67–22, with every Democrat and half the Republicans present voting for it. Senator after senator, many of whom by their erstwhile silence had facilitated McCarthy's reign of terror, now rose to self-righteously denounce him.

The meteoric rise and fall of Joe McCarthy was complete. He quickly became a pariah, ignored by the press, the public, and his fellow legislators alike. He served out two and a half more years of his term, until his death on May 2, 1957, from cirrhosis of the liver, but he was never again a factor in the Senate or in national affairs, despite his continued harangues and attacks on everybody and anybody he deemed worthy of such attention.

"The damage that Joe McCarthy did is incalculable," wrote Fred Cook in *The Nightmare Decade*. "There are no scales on which to weigh his impact on the soul of the nation, but it is safe to say that he left America less free than he found it."[90]

For all the hundreds of individuals McCarthy accused, he never discovered or exposed a single Communist or any instance of espionage. In no small way, he was a creation of the press; even those reporters who despised McCarthy—and they were by far the majority—lent him credibility by their relentless coverage of his baseless charges and masterful evasions.

To be sure, he had his defenders, most notably William F. Buckley Jr., who with L. Brent Bozell wrote a 1954 defense of the senator titled *McCarthy and His Enemies.* While criticizing his excesses, they supported McCarthy's crusade as "a movement around which men of good will and stern morality can close ranks."[91]

Called by one biographer "the most gifted demagogue ever bred on these shores," McCarthy was, as noted, more than anything else, an opportunist who exploited the political climate of his times, profiting from an environment that was created and cultivated by many others.[92] As another of his biographers has astutely noted, "McCarthy could have been stopped cold at any time by, say, J. Edgar Hoover, Richard Nixon, or Dwight Eisenhower—men with authority, who knew when he was bluffing and lying."[93] The truth, however, is that for all the later condemnation of McCarthy, he served a useful purpose for such "men with authority"—he carried out their dirty work, and it was only when he went too far and careened out of control that they found it expedient to put him out of business.

McCarthy was done, but McCarthyism lived on. The red scare was hardly over, as the "men with authority" carried on.

CHAPTER 13

There Were Many
Wrecked Lives

Eisenhower may have disliked McCarthy's crudeness and renegade approach, and maintained his distance from the senator, but he was in full accord with the Republican Party's support of McCarthy's red-hunting agenda. As the Eisenhower historian Herbert S. Parmet has written, "When Dwight Eisenhower . . . arrived in Washington there was little doubt that . . . the public was more insecure than the nation."[1] Like Truman, Eisenhower almost certainly understood that the security threat from domestic Communism was minuscule. In 1944, when the population of the United States was 150 million, Communist Party membership peaked at eighty thousand and steadily declined thereafter; by 1951, the year before Eisenhower was elected, the CP had fewer than thirty-two thousand members. Like his predecessor, however, Eisenhower recognized the political benefits of the crusade against American Communists and was dedicated to hounding radicals.

In April 1953, barely three months after taking office—with McCarthy and two other congressional Republicans at his side—Eisenhower announced a further tightening of the loyalty program. Under Executive Order 10450, the standards for dismissal were changed from mere "disloyalty" to any behavior that could be construed as inconsistent with "the interests of the national security."[2]

Attorney General Herbert Brownell proclaimed, "Under the new program, an employee or applicant for employment may be loyal in his own mind, but still, because of personal habits of conduct, a background of negligence, or failure to observe reasonable rules of security, he is in fact a security risk and therefore not acceptable as a government employee."[3] The new rules meant that government workers could be fired for alcohol abuse, homosexuality, psychological disorders, associating with radicals, or any "behavior, activities, or associations which tend to show that the individual is not reliable or trustworthy."[4] It was much easier, in other words, to label a person a "security risk" than a "disloyal American." Moreover, all decisions were the responsibility of departmental heads, whose verdicts were final. As a result of the new policy, more than twenty-seven hundred of the ninety-three hundred government employees who had already been investigated and cleared once again found themselves under investigation.

The State Department was particularly vulnerable, terrorized as it was by the former FBI agent and McCarthy confidant Scott McLeod, who was brought in to rid the department of subversives. As head of the department's Bureau of Security and Consular Affairs, McLeod and his staff of about two dozen former FBI agents created what one employee called "a police-state atmosphere," coming into State Department offices after hours and scrutinizing desks, drawers, and file cabinets.[5] State Department personnel quickly came to regard McLeod as a "bogeyman [whose] shadow . . . lurks over every desk and over every conference table" of the department.[6] In the first year of McLeod's tenure, 306 civilian employees and 178 aliens were fired from the department without a single hearing having been held or any concrete proof having been presented that any of those 484 dismissed individuals were security risks. McLeod's influence was so pernicious that the *New York Herald Tribune* columnist Stewart Alsop defined "McLeodism" as "the State Department's dutiful imitation of McCarthyism."[7]

At the same time, with Eisenhower's blessing, the FBI, HUAC, and the Senate Internal Security Subcommittee were ratcheting up the ongoing assault on the teaching profession that had been simmering on a low heat since the inception of the Cold War.

In April 1948, George Parker, a teacher at Evansville College in Indiana, was dismissed because of his "political activities, both on and off campus."[8] These included introducing "political discussion" in his philosophy and religion classes and distributing literature for Henry Wallace's presidential campaign while serving as chairman of the county Citizens for Wallace Committee. Parker had raised the hackles of Evansville conservatives by being photographed with Wallace at a local campaign rally, and the college's president, Lincoln Hale, caved in to community pressure to fire Parker.

In January 1949, the cases of six tenured University of Washington professors were brought before the faculty Committee on Tenure and Academic Freedom. Two of the professors, who were acknowledged Communist Party members, and a third who was not had refused to answer, before the state's Un-American Activities Committee, the question of whether or not they were Communists. The other three, who had long since left the party, admitted past membership but refused to name others who had been members. None of the six had violated any of the five grounds for a tenured faculty member's dismissal: "incompetency, neglect of duty, physical or mental incapacity, dishonesty or immorality, and conviction of a felony involving moral turpitude."[9] The Tenure and Academic Freedom Committee recommended retaining all except the associate psychology professor Ralph Gundlach—the one man among the six, perversely enough, who had never been a Communist. The university's president, Raymond B. Allen, ignored the committee's recommendations, firing Gundlach and the two others who had refused to answer the "are you now or have you ever been?" question and placing the three who declined to name names on two-year probation.

In June—the same month that HUAC sent a letter to eighty-one institutions of higher learning, demanding to see a list of textbooks used in various academic disciplines—Truman and the U.S. commissioner of education, Earl McGrath, both endorsed the National Education Association's policy that "members of the Communist Party shall not be employed in the American schools."[10] This principle had been formulated by the NEA's Educational Policies Commission, whose twenty members included Eisenhower—then president of Columbia University—and Harvard's president, James B. Conant.

At the NEA national convention the following month, the policy barring Communists from teaching was approved by a near-unanimous vote of the three thousand delegates, who at the same time insisted that "the campaign against Communist teachers be conducted in a democratic fashion; that no one should be unjustly accused; that no 'witch hunts' should take place. Only the bona fide dues-paying Communist teacher . . . should be hounded out of the schools."[11]

By this time, twenty-five states required teachers to sign a loyalty oath, as the chill continued to spread. In November 1950, Dr. Willard Goslin, widely recognized as "one of the nation's ablest public school-men," resigned after serving two years as superintendent of schools in Pasadena, California.[12] Goslin had been hounded out of the district by right-wing citizens' groups who labeled him a "Communist subversive" and carried on a two-year campaign against his progressive approach to education, which included rezoning the district to create racially integrated schools, instituting sex-education courses, broadening the reading-writing-arithmetic curriculum, and creating a grading system with only "satisfactory" and "unsatisfactory" as categories. In explaining his "subversive" educational agenda, Goslin said, "The primary purpose of the public school is not to get a bright boy a soft white-collar job but to underwrite and extend democracy in this country."[13]

Early in 1951, the regents of the University of Colorado hired the former FBI agents Dudley Hutchinson and Harold Hafer to ferret out subversives on campus. In a 126-page report, the two identified nine faculty and two staff members who were suspected of being Communists. Two of the faculty members refused to talk to the investigators and were informed that their contracts would not be renewed.

Fear and conformity were fast becoming oppressive presences in American education. As the prominent educator Robert Hutchins observed, "The question is not how many teachers have been fired, but how many think they might be, and for what reasons . . . The entire teaching profession of the U.S. is now intimidated."[14]

In May 1951, *The New York Times* reported the results of a study it had conducted of seventy-two major American colleges and universities. Although the article was titled "College Freedoms Being Stifled by Students' Fear of Red Label," the piece made it clear that the trepidation was by no means limited to students but rather affected the entire academic community. This development, said the article, "struck a body-blow at the American educational process, one of democracy's most potent weapons." The story also reported that FBI agents "were constantly inquiring about students applying for Government jobs" and that "Federal security officers were making careful checks of the memberships of liberal organizations."[15]

In June 1952, twenty-eight California public and private colleges and universities, including the University of California and Stanford, each brought to campus a former FBI agent or military intelligence officer whose job it was to report on subversives to the state's Un-American Activities Committee. By the following March, there had been more than a hundred dismissals or resignations, and over two hundred teaching appointments had been prevented. William Wadman, the agent at UC Berkeley, later acknowledged that he had filed reports about every faculty member on campus.

On February 25, 1953, Eisenhower gave the educational witch hunt a great incentive when he declared, during his second presidential press conference, that he was opposed to any "card-carrying Communist in such a responsible position as teaching our youngsters because it is teaching and preaching as opposed to teaching facts." A clever teacher, said Eisenhower, could even "use mathematics to put across a doctrine."[16]

J. Edgar Hoover also took up the theme, saying there was "no room in America for Communists or Communist sympathies in our educational system. Every Communist uprooted from our educational system is one more assurance that it will not degenerate into a medium of propaganda for Marxism."[17] On March 26, Hoover sent out an order to twenty-four field offices, instructing the agents in charge to prepare reports on "subversives" at fifty-six institutions of higher learning, ranging in prestige and influence from Harvard University to Brooklyn College to Fisk University to Contra Costa Junior College.

Anxious to dissociate themselves from any taint of subversion, liberals rushed to support a policy of keeping Communists out of the teaching ranks. "The right of the Communist to teach should be denied," wrote the Socialist Norman Thomas. "The proven Communist has no place in our schools."[18] *Time* magazine reported, "Most top educators seemed to agree that . . . Communists should be barred from teaching."[19] While Barnard's president, Millicent C. McIntosh, decried the "almost pathological fear of Russia" that had stifled the "free exchange of ideas," she also proclaimed, "If a teacher is a Communist . . . he is not fit to teach."[20] McIntosh even advocated institutions of higher learning conducting their own witch hunts, in order to keep Congress from carrying out such purges.

McIntosh was alluding to the ongoing investigations of the teaching profession by HUAC and SISS, which were holding a series of hearings in various cities that would eventually include Boston, New York, Newark, Philadelphia, and others.

The committees' purpose in taking their shows on the road was spelled out by the Pennsylvania Democrat Francis Walter, who chaired HUAC from 1955 to 1963. "By this means," explained Walter, "active Communists will be exposed before their neighbors and fellow workers, and I have every confidence that the loyal Americans who work with them will do the rest of the job."[21] This was exactly what happened in Flint, Michigan, when HUAC came to town. Automobile workers who had been subpoenaed and appeared before the committee were dragged from their factories and beaten by mobs. Some families were evicted from their homes and forced into hiding, and the office of a lawyer who had represented the subpoenaed workers was smeared with red paint. Michigan's representative Kit Clardy, a HUAC member and outspoken McCarthy supporter whose district included Flint, was delighted. "This is the best kind of reaction there could have been to our hearings," he gloated.[22]

In mid-1953, *The Harvard Crimson* reported that of the more than one hundred college and university professors who had invoked the Fifth Amendment before one of the congressional investigating committees, fifty-four had been fired or suspended, and more than a hundred grade-school teachers had been similarly discharged or suspended for refusing to cooperate.

In California, the Dilworth Act of 1953 required that all teachers take a non-Communist oath or be dismissed. The law also conferred investigative powers on local school boards, and the same year another statute, the Luckel Act, gave the state board of education the same authority. More than a hundred teachers lost their jobs, and an equal number were refused employment.

The most extensive and unremitting educational purge took place in New York City. It started in 1949, with the passage of the Feinberg Law, a state statute aimed at "elimination of subversive persons from the public school system."[23] Under the law, membership in any organization that the state board of regents determined to be "subversive" was considered "prima facie evidence of disqualification" to teach in the state's public schools. Each school district was required to conduct an annual investigation, complete with written reports, of all teachers and other school employees to determine if they had committed "subversive acts" or belonged to "subversive organizations." Those found guilty were to be fired. The legislation painted with such a broad brush that "subversive" activities could be construed to include publishing articles, distributing literature, or endorsing someone else's article or speech—whether these activities occurred during school or not. A teachers' union spokesperson called the act "the most vicious, sweeping heresy hunt ever conjured up . . . [T]he Feinberg Law is not aimed at subversive teaching but is a weapon for terrorizing all teachers . . . into abject, cowardly submission to authority."[24] The Supreme Court justice William O. Douglas wrote, "The law inevitably turns the school system into a spying project."[25]

On May 3, 1950, eight New York City teachers were suspended without pay. At their hearings, although the examiner declared in each case, "I have heard no proof of any conduct unbecoming a teacher . . . in the classroom or in extracurricular activity," he nevertheless recommended their dismissals.[26] The eight teachers were released for insubordination under Section 903 of the city charter, by which a city employee could be fired for refusing to answer official questions concerning official conduct.

In January 1951, the board of education assigned New York City's assistant corporation counsel, Saul Moskoff, to conduct investigations of public school teachers. At board headquarters, Moskoff set up an office that included complete files on suspected teachers and a comprehensive card file titled "Communism in the New York Schools."[27] The office also contained an interrogation room, complete with recording devices and a two-way mirror through which suspected teachers could be secretly observed. They were questioned about "what books they read, what people they knew, what feelings they harbored about Spain, whether they voted for the ALP [American Labor Party] and about the . . . petitions they had signed."[28]

By the time SISS began its fall 1952 hearings in New York City, twenty-four teachers had been dismissed, and forty-nine more had resigned or retired while being investigated. SISS subpoenaed the entire leadership of the left-wing teachers' union, every one of whom was fired for taking the Fifth. In all, the committee called twenty-five New York City teachers; the board of education dismissed thirteen of them without any hearings.

New York City's educational witch hunt continued throughout the rest of the decade. In March 1955, the board of education voted 7–1 to require teachers to inform on their colleagues when so ordered by the superintendent of schools. Five who refused to do so were suspended without pay.

Parallel carnage occurred at the city's five municipal colleges, where by June 1953 there had been fourteen dismissals. In September, the board of higher education created a special committee to interrogate all of the system's nineteen hundred teachers. The next April, three professors at Hunter College were fired, and dozens more dismissals followed.

The casualty figures from the New York City inquisition are stark. On the K–12 level, 38 teachers were discharged, and 283 more either resigned or retired after being investigated and questioned. In all, 321 individuals, the vast majority of them Jewish, lost their jobs. According to a 1971 *New York Times* report, some of the released teachers took positions in private schools—often at greatly reduced salaries—others went into higher education, a few became psychologists, and many worked at nonteaching jobs. In the city colleges, 58 individuals either were fired, resigned, or retired. Hundreds more at both the K–12 and the college levels were interrogated and "absolved."[29]

Reflecting on the effect of the educational purge, one dismissed New York City teacher uttered what could very well be the slogan of the decade: "There were many wrecked lives."[30]

On other fronts, the Eisenhower administration continued to perpetuate the red scare. In October 1953, six months after the president's new loyalty program went into effect, the White House claimed that 1,456 government employees had been dismissed since the introduction of the new regulations. Over the next year, the announced numbers steadily climbed, until several weeks before the 1954 midterm elections, the Civil Service Commission, at Vice President Nixon's urging, disclosed that nearly 7,000 federal workers had been fired or had resigned under the Eisenhower program. On the campaign trail, Nixon triumphantly proclaimed, "We're kicking the Communists and fellow travelers and security risks out of government . . . by the thousands."[31] But after the election, in which the Democrats recaptured Congress, the CSC admitted that of those "thousands" who had left their government positions, over 90 percent did so through ordinary procedures—a mere 342 had been dismissed as a result of the security-review process, and half of those had been hired since Eisenhower took office.

What percentage of those 342 "security risks" represented any real danger to the nation has never been determined, but as the case of Abraham Chasanow indicates, the security-review process was dangerously fallible. Chasanow, a twenty-three-year employee of the Navy's Hydrographic Office, was suspended without pay on July 29, 1953, on the word of "unidentified informants" who accused him of "Left-Wing associations."[32] Chasanow was dismissed the following April, and it was only when his attorney presented additional evidence to Assistant Secretary of the Navy James H. Smith Jr. that the latter established a special hearing board to reconsider the case. When the credibility of Chasanow's accusers crumbled, he was reinstated with back pay on September 1, 1954, after a "thirteen-month nightmare."

In reinstating Chasanow, Smith conceded that the Navy was "probably a little naïve" in not checking the accuracy of the accusations sooner. Chasanow believed that the accusations against him came either from anti-Semites or from opponents of the cooperative housing project he had been instrumental in developing. In a letter about the case to the secretary of the Navy, the chairman of the executive committee of the American Jewish Congress wrote that "under the present loyalty program there is far too much room for action based on suspicion, arbitrary conjecture and secrecy."[33] There were other instances in which falsely accused government employees were dismissed and later reinstated, but how many cases there were in which accused employees were similarly blameless but never returned to their jobs can only be surmised.

The witch-hunters pressed on. Between 1953 and 1956, forty-two more Communist leaders were indicted for violations of the Smith Act. In May 1954, Attorney General Herbert Brownell upheld the long-standing tradition of wanton, extralegal spying on civilians by governmental agencies when he authorized the FBI to use surveillance microphones in uncovering the activities of "espionage agents, possible saboteurs, and subversive persons." Brownell stressed that such surveillance did not have to be limited to developing "evidence for prosecution."[34]

The same year, encouraged by the Eisenhower administration, Congress passed a rash of new antisubversive laws, including statutes revoking the citizenship of individuals convicted of advocating violent overthrow of the government; requiring Communist organizations to register all printing equipment; broadening the definitions of sabotage and espionage; and making peacetime espionage a capital crime.

The most repressive new law was the Communist Control Act of 1954, which extended the Internal Security Act of 1950. The law outlawed the Communist Party, and as an outlawed entity it was not entitled to any of the "rights, privileges, and immunities" that legal organizations enjoyed.[35] The Communist Party was, at last, illegitimate, a step that even the rabidly anti-Communist J. Edgar Hoover had advised against in 1948.[36]

The Communist Control Act constrained labor unions as well. Section 13A(a) established that any union designated as "Communist-infiltrated" by the attorney general and the Subversive Activities Control Board lost all "rights, privileges, and immunities" normally granted to labor organizations under existing law.

The Eisenhower administration also went after left-wing labor leaders. By 1956, it had achieved twenty perjury convictions of individuals who had taken the non-Communist oath required by the draconian Taft-Hartley Act.

While the government was conducting its campaign against Communists, fellow travelers, and other left-wing "subversives," it was also carrying on a parallel scapegoating of another minority group. This effort began in 1947, when a State Department board set up to create departmental security guidelines determined that in addition to Communists and their associates, employees who evidenced "habitual drunkenness, sexual perversion, moral turpitude, financial irresponsibility or criminal record" were to be purged from the agency. Such individuals, it was argued, while perhaps not guilty of disloyalty, were nonetheless considered to possess "such basic weakness of character or lack of judgment" that they might unwittingly be compromised by an association with subversives, who would then employ blackmail to obtain state secrets.[37]

The seemingly inclusive grouping was a smoke screen; the new guidelines were aimed primarily and almost exclusively at gays. By the beginning of 1950, ninety-one homosexuals—eighty-nine men and two women—either were dismissed from the State Department or resigned while under investigation.

On February 28, 1950, not three weeks after McCarthy's Wheeling address and just eight days after his five-hour speech to the Senate, Secretary of State Dean Acheson and Deputy Undersecretary for Administration John Peurifoy appeared before a subcommittee of the Senate Appropriations Committee. Acheson outlined the main categories of security risks, including members of the Communist, Nazi, and Fascist parties, persons engaged in espionage or who had knowingly divulged classified information, and persons who, while not being any of those, had habitually associated with such people. Acheson then indicated another category of security risk: any individual who had, "as a matter of character, any defect . . . which could be preyed upon or which might be used by somebody who was attempting to penetrate into the Department." Senator Styles Bridges of New Hampshire, the committee's ranking Republican, asked Acheson, "Such as homosexuality or a person with a criminal record?" to which the secretary of state responded, "That would be included."[38]

Bridges pressed Acheson for more specifics, wanting to know how many employees had been dismissed under the McCarran rider, by which the secretary of state had absolute discretion to fire any employee for security reasons.[39] When Acheson said there had been only one, Bridges wanted to know how many others had resigned while under investigation.

Peurifoy jumped in and answered, "In this shady category that you referred to earlier, there are 91 cases, sir."

Bridges was not satisfied. "What do you mean by 'shady category'?" he demanded.

Peurifoy responded, "We are talking about people of moral weakness and so forth that we have gotten rid of in the Department."

Pat McCarran insisted, "Now will you make your answer a little clearer, please?"

Having run out of wiggle room, Peurifoy admitted, "Most of these were homosexuals."

Peurifoy's disclosure was a bombshell. All of a sudden the issue of "perverts" in the government became headline news and a rallying point for the Republicans. In a speech to the American Society of Newspaper Editors, McCarthy disdainfully lumped "Communists and queers" together.[40] The chairman of the Republican National Committee, Guy George Gabrielson, informed seven thousand party workers, "Perhaps as dangerous as the actual Communists are the sexual perverts who have infiltrated our Government in recent years."[41] And on the floor of the Senate, the McCarthyite Kenneth Wherry demanded to know, "Who could be more dangerous to the United States of America than a pervert?"[42] Following the logic of his mentor McCarthy, Wherry conflated Communists and homosexuals. "You can't hardly separate homosexuals from subversives," he told the *New York Post*'s Max Lerner. "Mind you, I don't say every homosexual is a subversive, and I don't say every subversive is a homosexual. But a man of low morality is a menace in the government, whatever he is, and they are all tied up together."[43]

In May, a Senate panel was assigned to investigate the issue of homosexuals in the government, headed by Clyde Hoey of North Carolina, chairman of the Committee on Expenditures in Executive Departments. Despite the widely accepted belief that "perverts are . . . poor security risks because of their vulnerability to blackmail," the Hoey Committee found no evidence to support that position.[44] On the contrary, it was unable to establish a single instance in which an American homosexual had been blackmailed into divulging classified information. Nevertheless, the committee's December 1950 report stated unequivocally that "sex perverts in Government constitute security risks" and that "one homosexual can pollute a Government office."[45] It was now official: gays, lesbians, and other sexual "deviates" were fully as dangerous as "subversives."

In March 1951, the State Department security officer Carlisle Humelsine wrote a letter to all mission chiefs in the department, alerting them to the "problem" of homosexual employees and asking them to get rid of "this influence."[46]

In the next two years, 53 more gays were separated from the State Department. By the time Eisenhower took office at the beginning of 1953, there had been 144 dismissals and/or resignations.

Early in the Eisenhower administration, Humelsine testified about "a homosexual as a security risk" before an executive session of the Senate Foreign Relations Committee. He told the committee, "This has been a problem, as you all know, that has plagued the Department of State and Foreign Service."[47] At the time of Humelsine's testimony, 258 more State Department employees had been fired or had resigned, bringing the total number of gays and lesbians who had left the service to 402.

Now Scott McLeod, the new head of the State Department's Bureau of Security and Consular Affairs, took over the purge. McLeod had already overseen the firing of sixteen "moral deviates" and five "security risks" in his first ten days on the job.[48] By the end of March, one department security officer proudly proclaimed, "Our batting average [is] now one a day."[49]

Making the discovery and dismissal of homosexuals a major component of his crusade, McLeod created the "Miscellaneous M Unit" to investigate homosexuality cases. The "queer" hunt now became an integral facet of the larger witch hunt. According to internal State Department memos, 192 employees were dismissed in the first nine months of 1953, for "Security (Exclusive of Homosexuality)," while 114 were let go for "Security (Homosexuals)."[50]

The Miscellaneous M Unit's method was to extract "confessions" from suspects—a refusal to cooperate was considered tantamount to an admission of "guilt"—and then threaten to reveal their secrets unless they cooperated and named others. In the vast majority of cases, there were no hearings. As the State Department security officer Peter Szluk, who referred to himself as "the hatchet man," later boasted, "Hearings . . . what the hell for? That was a waste of time! . . . Szluk says the son of a bitch is a queer, out he goes!"[51]

Any untoward suspicion—of political or sexual deviance—was duly reported, as workers rushed to inform on their colleagues. "Every allegation is now being investigated," pledged McLeod.[52]

In all, close to a thousand State Department employees were dismissed for "sex perversion" during the Cold War years. In *The Lavender Scare*, David K. Johnson estimates that figure to be one-fifth of the total number of homosexuals who lost their government jobs in that time.

Always one to sense which way the wind was blowing, J. Edgar Hoover had jumped on the bandwagon in June 1951, instituting the FBI's own Sex Deviates program, which began by providing government officials with all "information concerning allegations" of homosexuality of both "present and past employees."[53]* By 1954, the FBI was also providing information to other law-enforcement agencies, as well as to institutions of higher learning.

---

*There has been a great deal written by Hoover biographers and FBI historians concerning the matter of Hoover's sexuality. The question of whether or not he was a homosexual has not been conclusively answered.

The scapegoating of gays was carried out despite there having been, as Stewart and Joseph Alsop (the latter himself a homosexual) wrote, "not a single case of actual subversion in all the State Department's security firings—and it is doubtful if there was one such case throughout the Government."[54]

Nativism and xenophobia also came into play during the Cold War. In a systematic rerun of the Depression-era scapegoating of Mexicans and Mexican-Americans, the Eisenhower administration instituted Operation Wetback in July 1954. The program was designed to crack down on the large numbers of illegal immigrants in the southwestern states who formed the cheap-labor backbone of the region's agricultural industry. Under Operation Wetback, police officers and Border Patrol agents made sweeps of Mexican-American barrios, stopping "Mexican-looking" individuals on the street and requiring them to produce identification. The program caused a storm of protest on both sides of the border, and it was abandoned in the fall, but not before more than half a million people, many of them the U.S.-born children of illegal aliens (and therefore American citizens), were either deported or "voluntarily" repatriated. What had taken the better part of a decade in the 1930s was accomplished in less than six months in 1954.

Meanwhile, the surveillance game had a new player. The Central Intelligence Agency—created by the 1947 National Security Act as the successor to the Office of Strategic Services, which had coordinated intelligence activities during World War II—was established to "collect intelligence through human sources and by other appropriate means."[55] The NSA specifically stated that the "Agency shall have no police, subpoena, or law enforcement powers or internal security functions," but all too soon the CIA was deeply into the business of spying on U.S. citizens.

In February 1953, with the knowledge and consent of U.S. postal authorities, the agency began keeping track of all correspondence sent between the United States and the Soviet Union that passed through the New York postal facilities. A 1975 Senate investigation of the CIA found that while the ostensible purpose of this operation was to give U.S. intelligence agencies information about Soviet intelligence activities, it gradually grew to encompass much wider parameters. By the time of the Vietnam War, the program was targeting domestic dissenters and war protesters, and its main purpose had become bolstering the FBI's internal security functions.

When the CIA first approached postal authorities with the proposal for the project, it was presented as being only to examine the outsides of pieces of mail, but early on, agents started secretly opening a small number of letters, reading their contents, and then resealing them. That this was the intent from the start is spelled out by the July 1952 internal memo proposing the program. "Once our unit was in position," says the memo, "its activities and influence could be extended gradually, so as to secure from this source every drop of potential information available. At the outset, however, as far as the Post Office is concerned, our mail target could be the securing of names and addresses for investigation and possible further contact."[56]

By the end of 1955, eight agents were working full-time on mail interception, and several others were participating on a part-time basis. A November memo noted that the opening of mail was being carried on without the knowledge or approval of postal officials. While the memo stated that any disclosure of this activity would be likely to cause "serious public reaction"—perhaps even a congressional inquiry—it also confidently maintained that "any problem arising could be satisfactorily handled."[57]

There is no doubt that the CIA was fully aware of the illegality of the program, as internal memos indicate an ongoing concern with what might follow if the operation were discovered. In February 1962, a memo from the deputy chief of counterintelligence acknowledged that "a flap would put us [the project] out of business immediately and give rise to grave charges of criminal misuse of the mail by government agencies." If the program did come to light, however, "it should be relatively easy to 'hush up' the entire affair, or to explain that it consists of legal mail activities conducted by the Post Office at the request of authorized Federal Agencies . . . [I]t might become necessary, after the matter has cooled off during an extended period of investigation, to find a scapegoat to blame for the unauthorized tampering with the mails."[58]

By 1959, the CIA was opening 13,000 pieces of mail a year. The New York City project continued until 1973, and in its final year alone CIA agents handled 4.35 million pieces of mail, examining the outsides of 2.3 million of them, photographing the exteriors of 33,000, and opening 8,700. Mail interception was also carried out for shorter periods of time in San Francisco, New Orleans, and Hawaii.

In 1975, a Senate investigation of the CIA found that the interceptions were "illegal and improper." Even the simple examination of envelopes as carried out was against the law. As the Senate report noted, "Mail cover operations (examining and copying of envelopes only) are legal when carried out in compliance with postal regulations on a limited and selective basis involving matters of national security. The New York mail intercept did not meet these criteria."[59]

Moreover, such activity was in direct contravention of the CIA's charter. "The nature and degree of assistance given by the CIA to the FBI in the New York mail project," says the Senate report, "indicate that the primary purpose eventually became participation with the FBI in internal security functions. Accordingly, the CIA's participation was prohibited under the National Security Act."[60]

In conclusion, the report leaves no doubt about the legality of the mail-opening operation: "The CIA's domestic mail opening programs were unlawful. United States statutes specifically forbid opening the mail."[61]

All told, the surveillance state underwent an enormous expansion during the Cold War years. In 1958, an independent study estimated that 20 percent of all employed Americans had been subjected to some type of loyalty or security screening.[62] This included about fourteen million people in the federal civil service, the military, the Atomic Energy Commission, the private sector associated with defense contracts, and at seaports. In *The Great Fear*, David Caute estimates that in the federal government alone, approximately twenty-seven hundred employees were dismissed, and twelve thousand more resigned between 1947 and 1956.[63]

The witch-hunt investigations were carried out with the sworn testimony of several dozen former Communists who were paid professional informers. One of the most prominent of the group, Harvey Matusow, later wrote a book titled *False Witness*, in which he detailed his own perjured testimony and that of others.

The second great red scare was the most intense and protracted period of political repression in the history of the United States. The persecution of Communists brought about the demise of the Communist Party, although, as Caute observes, "no plausible evidence ever emerged to prove that the CP drew up contingency plans to sabotage vital industries and lines of communication in the event of war. The government took a sledgehammer to squash a gnat."[64] In so doing, the government was not only eliminating the gnat but also attempting to prevent the spread of the gnat's "subversive" ideas. It was those ideas— that is, a powerful critique of the social inequities of the capitalist system—rather than any tangible political power, that made the Communist Party so threatening to the established order.

Once again, in a time of crisis, the government found it expedient to scapegoat minority groups—in this case political and sexual minorities—manufacturing hysteria over the supposed danger they posed, and then using that hysteria as a justification for a crackdown on civil liberties and a suppression of dissent. And once again, the American people fell in line with the government, as liberals and conservatives, Democrats and Republicans all joined in the scapegoating.

The second great red scare had subsided by the end of the 1950s, but the undemocratic methods used to crush the Communist Party and to hound gays would continue to be used against political minority groups for another decade and a half.

CHAPTER 14

There Are No Rules

In July 1954, President Eisenhower asked the retired Air Force lieutenant general James H. Doolittle to chair a committee that would "undertake a comprehensive study of the covert activities of the Central Intelligence Agency" and make recommendations aimed at improving "the conduct of these operations."[1] The Doolittle Committee's secret report, which was presented to Eisenhower on October 19 and remained classified for more than twenty years, ended with what a 1970s Senate investigative committee called a "chilling" conclusion. "It is now clear," stated the Doolittle Report,

> that we are facing an implacable enemy whose avowed objective is world domination by whatever means and at whatever cost. There are no rules in such a game. Hitherto acceptable norms of human conduct do not apply. If the United States is to survive, longstanding American concepts of "fair play" must be reconsidered. We must develop effective espionage and counterespionage services and must learn to subvert, sabotage and destroy our enemies by more clever, more sophisticated and more effective means than those used against us.[2]

In dealing with American Communists during the 1950s, the FBI and other agencies conducting domestic intelligence readily embraced the mind-set expressed in the Doolittle Report. Eisenhower himself expressed no hesitation about employing such an approach in the battle against domestic Communism—when he once reprimanded the chief justice of the Supreme Court, Earl Warren, for the high court's decisions upholding the constitutional rights of homegrown Communists, and Warren in turn asked him, "What would you do with Communists in America?" Eisenhower matter-of-factly stated, "I would kill the S.O.B.s."[3]

In defending the roundups of 1919–20, Attorney General A. Mitchell Palmer had established the precedent that law-abiding political dissidents were not entitled to the protections of the Constitution when he wrote that the Justice Department "decided that there could be no nice distinctions drawn between the theoretical ideals of the radicals and their actual violations of our national laws."[4] The same principle was also enforced against Communists during the Cold War.

During the 1960s and early 1970s, this approach was applied not only toward Communists but against virtually every other dissident strain in American life, as the Cold War state of mind continued to permeate American public life. Intelligence and law-enforcement agencies came to regard any individual or group that challenged or even merely questioned the status quo as "the enemy" and, as such, deemed them fair game for the most underhanded and unethical sorts of dirty tricks. By this logic, peaceful American citizens were transformed into the equivalent of foreign combat troops or foreign espionage/sabotage agents, thereby justifying the use of whatever legal, illegal, and extralegal methods were necessary to defeat them.

Such procedures were carried out primarily by the FBI, the CIA, the National Security Agency, the Internal Revenue Service, and Army Intelligence, but also to varying degrees by the Secret Service; the Civil Service Commission; the Immigration and Naturalization Service; the Departments of State, Justice, the Treasury, and Health, Education, and Welfare; the Post Office Department; the Office of Economic Opportunity; and Presidents Lyndon Johnson and Richard Nixon.

According to the 1970s Senate committee that investigated these government activities, such methods were "used to disrupt the lawful political activities of individual Americans and groups to discredit them, using dangerous and degrading tactics which are abhorrent in a free and decent society . . . The tactics used against Americans often risked and sometimes caused serious emotional, economic, or physical damage. Actions were taken which were designed to break up marriages, terminate funding or employment, and encourage gang warfare between violent rival groups."[5] Abuses by the FBI alone included committing extortion and mail and wire fraud, inciting violence, and sending obscene materials through the mail.

The new offensive against First Amendment rights was initially proposed on August 28, 1956, when Alan Belmont, head of the FBI's Internal Security Section, sent a memo to the agency official L. V. Boardman, saying that the FBI's already existing efforts to discredit the Communist Party and its leaders were about to become "an all-out disruptive attack on the CP from within."[6]

At the time, party membership had fallen below five thousand, about fifteen hundred of whom were FBI agents and informers, and as a letter from J. Edgar Hoover to the presidential special assistant Dillon Anderson a year earlier clearly indicates, the bureau did not consider actual espionage or sabotage by the CP to be a danger. On the contrary, Hoover maintained, the only threats the party posed were "influence over the masses, ability to create controversy leading to confusion and disunity, penetration of specific channels in American life where public opinion is molded, and espionage and sabotage *potential.*"[7] In other words, when the FBI began its new "counterintelligence" program, it was concerned not with imminent illegal actions by the Communist Party but with any influence the party might have on the ideas and the thinking of Americans.

Belmont's memo lists several disruptive actions the FBI was actively working on and concludes with the assurance: "The Internal Security Section is giving this program continuous thought and attention and we are remaining alert for situations which might afford additional opportunities for further disruption of the CP, USA."[8]

The new plan, called "Counterintelligence Program–Communist Party USA," received Hoover's enthusiastic approval. While various disruptive tactics had been directed at the CP in the past, COINTELPRO-CPUSA was the first structured, methodical course of action in this realm and, as such, ushered in a new and devastating era of covert attacks on political dissidents.

COINTELPRO-CPUSA was undertaken without the knowledge or consent of the attorney general, the president, or Congress and from its inception was governed by Hoover's obsession with secrecy. The attorney general and the White House were not informed until nearly two years later, when Hoover revealed in a May 1958 memo how select informants had been instructed to provoke contentious discussions on hot-button issues within the party, and how the bureau had carried out anonymous mailings to certain CP members who might be swayed by anti-Communist propaganda. These and other disruptive actions stimulated acrimonious debates, fomented suspicions and jealousies, and "increased factionalism at all levels of the organization."[9] The memo boasted that party leaders were unable to decide whether these actions were initiated by the government or by dissidents within the party.

What the memo did not spell out, however, were other commonly employed tactics, which is hardly surprising because many of them were illegal. The FBI used anonymous letters and telephone calls, for example, to spread defamatory information—usually untrue—to spouses and colleagues, including accusations of homosexuality, adultery, and sexually transmitted disease. Another common bureau practice was to feed news stories to "friendly" reporters and columnists, accusing specific party members—without evidence—of a variety of criminal activities, including embezzlement, fraud, and bigamy. The FBI also notified friends, neighbors, employers, co-workers, business associates, and neighborhood shopkeepers that an individual was a Communist, causing frequent losses of employment, income, and social contacts. In many instances, the bureau gave the names and addresses of underground CP members to the Internal Revenue Service, resulting in widespread harassment audits of these individuals. Hoover personally approved all of these actions.

One of the most effective ploys was called "putting the snitch jacket" on somebody. This technique played upon the ubiquitous fears of informers within the ranks, by planting "evidence," or through anonymous letters and phone calls asserting that a certain individual was a stool pigeon. Placing the snitch jacket on someone served multiple purposes, including deflecting suspicion from actual FBI agents and informants, crippling the party's effectiveness by eliminating capable leaders, and exploiting existing rifts by intensifying dissension among rival factions. While not illegal, the gambit was nonetheless morally and ethically questionable, resulting as it often did in denunciation and expulsion from the party, which brought the loss of employment and social ostracism of the victim and the victim's family. In a number of these cases, those accused committed suicide or died of stress-related heart attacks.

One man, William Albertson, a dedicated longtime party member and high-ranking officer, spent the better part of a decade trying to restore his name, to no avail, as his and his family members' lives were effectively ruined. According to an FBI internal report, this "crippled the activities of the New York State communist organization and the turmoil within the party continues to this date."[10]

COINTELPRO-CPUSA gained steam after a series of June 1957 Supreme Court decisions essentially struck down the Smith Act, which had prohibited advocating or belonging to any organization that advocated the overthrow of the government. According to one FBI unit chief, the Court rulings had rendered the Smith Act "technically unenforceable," making it "impossible to prosecute Communist Party members."[11] Deprived of this weapon in the war against "subversion," Hoover stepped up the FBI's extralegal efforts to persecute radicals.

In 1958, using the same convoluted logic applied by the Bureau of Investigation chief William Burns to radicals in the early 1920s and by General John DeWitt and Colonel Karl Bendetsen to the Japanese in the early 1940s, Hoover argued that the very lack of Communist activity and influence was proof positive that the CP was still dangerously powerful. "The Communist Party of the United States," he told HUAC, "is not out of business; it is not dead; it is not even dormant. It is, however, well on its way to achieving its current objective, which is to make you believe that it is shattered, ineffective, and dying."[12]

Fueled by Hoover's paranoia, demagoguery, and megalomania, the FBI had, by the end of the 1950s, as the political scientist Robert Goldstein notes, "achieved a position as a virtually autonomous, unsupervised and untouchable organization only marginally compatible with the requirements of a democratic society." From that invulnerable position, the bureau initiated a rash of new programs modeled on COINTELPRO-CPUSA. Employing actions and methods similar to those undertaken against the CP and its members, these programs were directed at a wide range of individuals, organizations, and movements, until, as Sanford J. Ungar wrote in his comprehensive study of the FBI, "the Bureau was—as if in a wartime crisis—monitoring almost all forms of political dissent." As Hoover's biographer Curt Gentry observed, "The COINTELPROs began slowly and then, like a virus feeding upon itself, grew rapidly and monstrously. Each new perceived threat . . . brought forth a new COINTELPRO."[13] In the process, the FBI forsook its law-enforcement mission and focused instead on intelligence gathering, becoming once again the secret police force that Harlan Fiske Stone had warned against in 1924, when he reined in the bureau's precursor.

A 1970s Senate investigating committee labeled the COINTEL-PROs "a sophisticated vigilante operation aimed squarely at preventing the exercise of First Amendment rights of speech and association [and] the propagation of dangerous ideas . . . Many of the techniques used would be intolerable in a democratic society even if all the targets had been involved in violent activity, but COINTELPRO went far beyond that . . . In essence, the Bureau took the law into its own hands, conducting a sophisticated vigilante operation against domestic enemies."[14]

With the COINTELPRO operations, the FBI's intelligence gathering took on a far wider purpose than simply preventing the commission of crimes. As David Wise points out in *The American Police State*, the bureau, "by infiltrating and spying on selected groups in American society, arrogated to itself the role of a thought police. It decided which groups were legitimate, and which were a danger—by FBI standards—to the Republic . . . In short, the FBI filled the classic role of a secret political police."[15]

Until early 1960, the FBI's counterintelligence program was directed against the CP. In March of that year, however, field offices received instructions to step up COMINFIL—"Communist infiltration"—investigations of other organizations, ranging in scope from the NAACP to the National Committee for a Sane Nuclear Policy to the Boy Scouts of America. By the time the decade was out, the FBI had files on more than 430,000 law-abiding individuals and organizations, as investigations reached into every area of American political activity.

At first, the targets of these operations were individual Communists. The most common action was to inform the leader of a labor union or other organization that a certain member of the group belonged to the CP, with the expectation that the person would then be drummed out.

But the priority quickly shifted. "Although," said the Senate committee's report, "COMINFIL investigations were supposed to focus on the Communist Party's alleged efforts to penetrate domestic groups, in practice the target often became the domestic groups themselves."[16]

This approach was used to perfection against the National Committee for a Sane Nuclear Policy. SANE, as it was commonly known, was at the forefront of the antinuclear peace movement. With twenty-five thousand members in 1958, the organization rapidly gained momentum, and by 1960 it appeared that SANE could become a significant force in American politics.

To undermine the group's growing influence, the FBI supplied a reporter with information about Communists taking part in a SANE demonstration, which succeeded in turning up the media spotlight on the organization. After an enormous rally in New York's Madison Square Garden in May—at which Eleanor Roosevelt, the union leader Walter Reuther, Michigan's governor G. Mennen Williams, and other notables spoke—the chairman of the Senate Internal Security Subcommittee, Thomas J. Dodd of Connecticut, claimed that "the Communists were responsible for a very substantial percentage of the overflow turnout" and called for SANE "to purge their ranks ruthlessly" of CP members.[17]

SANE offered a defiant reply, saying, "As a matter of democratic principle and practice we resent the intrusion of a Congressional Committee into the affairs of an organization which during its entire life has acted only in accordance with its declared principles . . . [SANE] itself is entirely capable of carrying out its principles and guaranteeing that it will not permit their betrayal or subversion under any pressure."[18]

Unfortunately, the group's actions did not meet its lofty words, and SANE undertook a purge of its membership, expelling Communists and fellow travelers. Three members of the national board, including Linus Pauling, resigned in protest. "SANE could have responded," wrote Robert Gilmore of the American Friends Service Committee in his letter of resignation, "with a ringing challenge to the cold war stratagem of discredit and divide, with a clear affirmation of the right of everyone to debate and dissent . . . The fact that SANE turned down this opportunity is, to my mind, a great tragedy."[19] A large number of members across the country also left the organization.

The FBI's release of information to a newsman had its desired effect. SANE was never again as effective or powerful.

A few months after the bureau's COMINFIL action against SANE, Hoover launched a second COINTELPRO operation. The triumph of the Cuban revolution at the beginning of 1959 had radicalized the left throughout much of Latin America, and the possibility of the spread of Communism in the hemisphere alarmed the U.S. government. In August, concerned over the newly invigorated Puerto Rican independence movement, Hoover wrote to the special agent in charge in San Juan to tell him, "The Bureau is considering the feasibility of instituting a program of disruption" aimed at Puerto Rican nationalist groups. Hoover emphasized, "In considering this matter, you should bear in mind the Bureau desires to disrupt the activities of these organizations and is not interested in mere harassment."[20]

It was against the law for the FBI to conduct foreign intelligence operations, but Hoover justified the bureau's involvement in Puerto Rico's internal affairs by arguing that the Caribbean island was unique because of its relationships with both the United States and Latin America. Three months later, Hoover proposed subjecting Puerto Rican nationalists to types of dirty tricks similar to those employed in COINTELPRO-CPUSA, including anonymous mailings and inciting factionalism within the groups.

In addition to those techniques, the San Juan FBI office committed criminal acts. Bureau agents, for example, read and confiscated mail addressed to independence movement leaders, as the former office employee Gloria Teresa Caldas de Blanco testified in a sworn affidavit.[21]

The Puerto Rican operation, which continued for over a decade, was supposedly "directed against organizations which seek independence for Puerto Rico through other than lawful peaceful means," but at least two of the targeted groups—the Puerto Rican Independence Movement and the Federation of Pro-Independence University Students—were avowedly nonviolent.[22] The Puerto Rican Independence Movement leader, Juan Mari Brás, was singled out for intense persecution, which almost unquestionably contributed to the severe heart attack he suffered in August 1964, after the San Juan office sent anonymous letters charging that he was incompetent and had close ties to the Castro government in Cuba. Citing the heart attack as one of the successes of its campaign against him and the movement, the office bragged to Hoover that these "letters did nothing to ease his tensions, and . . . he felt the effects of them deeply." Another activist, Delfin Ramos, spent close to two years in jail after the FBI arrested him for possession of explosives. The charges were finally dropped and he was released when the San Juan office admitted in court that there was no evidence against him and that there never had been. The federal district court judge Juan R. Torruella was so outraged he declared, "In all my years as a judge, I have never seen anything as incredible and scandalous."[23]

A year after the operation in Puerto Rico began, the FBI instituted a third COINTELPRO, this one aimed at the Socialist Workers Party, a splinter group of about five hundred members that espoused Leon Trotsky's program of worldwide revolution (in contrast to the CP, which embraced the Stalinist model of concentrating on strengthening socialism in the Soviet Union). As with COINTELPRO-CPUSA, COINTELPRO-SWP was a formalization of the investigation and harassment the bureau had been carrying out against the SWP for decades.

On October 12, 1961, Hoover sent a memo to the SACs of field offices already participating in COINTELPRO-CPUSA, instructing them to initiate a similar disruption program against the SWP. Hoover was particularly concerned that the SWP was running candidates for public office, as well as supporting Cuba and the budding civil rights movement. Nothing in Hoover's memo indicated that the SWP was engaged in anything remotely illegal—on the contrary, running candidates for public office can only be considered one of the most fundamental forms of participation in the American democratic process.

For the next ten years, the FBI concentrated on sabotaging the SWP's electoral efforts, provoking internal disputes, exacerbating animosity between the SWP and the CP, exposing and hounding individual SWP members through anonymous letters, and undermining the party's active participation in the civil rights and antiwar movements.

In Orange, New Jersey, for just one example, the bureau went after Walter Elliott, an automobile salesman and the scoutmaster of a local Boy Scout troop, for no other reason than that his wife was a member of the SWP. "Individuals who have subversive backgrounds," said an internal FBI memo, "especially those as Elliott who remain in the scouting movement for the expressed purpose of influencing young minds, represent a distinct threat to the goal of the scouting movement and should be removed or neutralized."[24] Unable to locate any derogatory material by which the bureau could anonymously discredit him, an FBI agent finally called the national headquarters of the Boy Scouts and extracted an assurance that Elliott's tenure as a scoutmaster would not be extended past his current term.

COINTELPRO-SWP was a prime example of what one former intelligence expert called "J. Edgar Hoover's obsession with the unimportant," as the bureau overlooked the real danger of espionage posed by actual Soviet spies, in favor of harassing a minuscule, law-abiding organization. Following one Smith Act prosecution in 1941, the FBI did not bring another federal prosecution against the SWP in thirty-five more years of investigation, yet it squandered untold agent hours and agency resources on "a party whose membership, by F.B.I. count, wouldn't fill a high school football stadium," as a 1975 *New York Times* article put it. "In the same decade that crime rates in American cities escalated and organized crime expanded its interests . . . the men of the Newark F.B.I. field office were working at fever pitch to drive a scoutmaster . . . from his job."[25]

One of the most malicious operations undertaken by the FBI in the 1960s was the relentless crusade conducted for years against Martin Luther King Jr. Beginning in October 1962, with a COMINFIL investigation of the Southern Christian Leadership Conference and its head, Dr. King, the program rapidly escalated into an all-out, no-holds-barred attempt to shame and discredit King.

The investigation was originally based on highly dubious allegations that two of King's advisers were Communists, a charge the Senate investigating committee found "inconclusive," reporting that there was nothing to link the two men with the CP and "no evidence that either of those Advisers attempted to exploit the civil rights movement to carry out the plans of the Communist Party." Terming the FBI's scrutiny of King and its efforts to destroy him "a shameful chapter in the nation's history," the committee report stated that despite FBI investigators' conclusions that there was no Communist influence among King and his advisers, the bureau's investigations and attempted discrediting of him continued.[26]

The FBI had maintained a file on Martin Luther King since 1958, and the agency began its infiltration of the SCLC in 1961. In February 1962, Hoover wrote, "King is no good," and despite the Atlanta office's determination, in November 1961, that there was no reason to initiate a national security investigation of the civil rights activist, Hoover informed the Atlanta SAC in May 1962 that King's name "should be placed in Section A of the Reserve Index and tabbed Communist," that is, someone to be arrested and detained in the event of a national emergency.[27]

A month after the FBI's COMINFIL investigation of the SCLC and Dr. King began in October 1962, King criticized the bureau publicly. In agreeing with a report by the Southern Regional Council that censured the FBI for standing by as civil rights demonstrators were beaten in Albany, Georgia, King said, "One of the great problems we face with the FBI in the South is that the agents are white Southerners who have been influenced by the mores of the community. To maintain their status, they have to be friendly with the local police and people who are promoting segregation. Every time I saw FBI men in Albany, they were with the local police force."[28]

The reaction of the FBI brain trust to King's remarks was that they "dovetail with information . . . indicating that King's advisors are Communist Party (CP) members and he is under the domination of the CP."[29] The bureau decided to contact the civil rights leader and "set him straight," but King failed to return a phone call from the director of the FBI's Crime Records Division, Cartha D. DeLoach.[30] Hoover, still enraged over King's criticism of the bureau, took the failure to return DeLoach's call as a declaration of war. In August 1963, with the March on Washington in the planning, Hoover wrote in the *Yale Political Magazine*, "Extremists [who] have gone so far as to accuse the FBI of racism . . . are no less bigoted in their thinking than those who parade around in white sheets."[31]

As the August 28 March on Washington approached, Hoover instructed field offices to be "extremely alert" for indications that the CP was behind the upcoming mass demonstration.[32] After reviewing a mountain of testimony from the field offices, however, the bureau's Domestic Intelligence Division reported six days before the march that there was no evidence of its being initiated or controlled by the CP. The following day, the division submitted a sixty-seven-page paper to Hoover, stating that the Communist Party—whose membership was down to 4,453—had been spectacularly unsuccessful in its attempts to influence African-Americans in general and the civil rights movement and March on Washington in particular.[33]

Hoover went ballistic. "This memo reminds me vividly of those I received when Castro took over Cuba," he wrote furiously on the memo that accompanied the report. "You contended then that Castro & his cohorts were not Communists & not influenced by Communists. Time alone has proved you wrong. I for one can't ignore the memos . . . re King . . . et al. as having only an infinitesimal effect on the efforts to exploit the American Negro by the Communists."[34]

William Sullivan, head of the Domestic Intelligence Division, was now in Hoover's doghouse, and he knew there was only one way out. After King delivered his "I have a dream" speech at the March, Sullivan wrote to Hoover, saying, "The Director is correct. We were completely wrong," and calling King "the most dangerous Negro of the future in this Nation from the standpoint of Communism, the Negro and national security."[35]*

On October 1, Hoover sent out a letter to the SACs, ordering them to enlarge investigations of Communist influence among African-Americans, using all the proven techniques to "neutralize or disrupt the Party's activities in the Negro field."[36] That month, after a number of previously unsuccessful attempts, Hoover was finally able to persuade Attorney General Robert F. Kennedy to approve wiretaps of Dr. King's home telephone and the phones at the SCLC's Atlanta and New York offices.

All the while, as King's standing, influence, and reputation continued to grow, Hoover's loathing for him increased in equal measure. Across the December memo informing him that King had been selected as *Time* magazine's "Man of the Year," Hoover scribbled, "They had to dig deep in the garbage to come up with this one."[37]

That same month, without informing Robert Kennedy, the FBI undertook a concerted campaign aimed at "neutralizing King as an effective Negro leader and developing evidence concerning King's continued dependence on communists for guidance and direction." The planned strategies included investigating SCLC employees, closely monitoring the SCLC's finances, identifying and investigating the organization's contributors, and continuing "to keep close watch on King's personal activities," particularly his use of alcohol and his

---

* Twelve years later, Sullivan told the Senate investigating committee, "I put in this memorandum what Hoover wanted to hear. He was so damn mad at us . . . [W]e had to engage in a lot of nonsense which we ourselves did not believe in . . . or we would be finished" (Church Committee, bk. 3, pp. 107 n. 118, 108).

involvement with women other than his wife. This information was intended to be used "at the proper time when it can be done without embarrassment to the Bureau, [to] expose King as an immoral opportunist who is not a sincere person but is exploiting the racial situation for personal gain."[38]

The FBI also, without approval, began bugging King's hotel rooms, and as early as January 5, 1964, in Washington, D.C., the microphones recorded him engaged in a raucous party with two women and several other SCLC leaders. Three days later, Sullivan submitted a memo stating that King not only represented "a very real security problem to this country" but also was "a disgrace to the Negro people of this country . . . while at the same time purporting to be a minister of the gospel . . . King must, at some propitious point in the future, be revealed to the people of this country and to his Negro followers as being what he actually is—a fraud, demagogue and moral scoundrel."[39]* Across the bottom of the memo, Hoover wrote, "I am glad to see that 'light' has finally, though dismally delayed, come to the Domestic Int. Div. I struggled for months to get over the fact the Communists were taking over the racial movement but our experts here couldn't or wouldn't see it."

The continued hotel room surveillance yielded the desired results. In addition to documenting King's extramarital sexual activity, the microphones recorded him on one occasion telling a string of off-color jokes.

With the tapes of King's after-hours indiscretions as evidence, the bureau now opened a two-pronged attack, aiming at both King's politics and his morals. In early March, a packet of incriminating material was sent to Robert Kennedy. On March 9, Hoover and DeLoach met with President Lyndon Johnson; the three spent the entire afternoon talking about Martin Luther King, and Hoover presented LBJ with a copy of taped highlights recorded in King's hotel rooms.

Also in March, when Hoover learned that Marquette University, the school that had awarded him an honorary degree in 1950, was con-

---

* A measure of how out of touch with reality the FBI brass was can be inferred from Sullivan's suggestion of Samuel R. Pierce Jr. as the successor to King once the latter had been discredited. Pierce, a member of a prominent Park Avenue law firm, was a former judge, assistant district attorney for New York City, assistant U.S. attorney, and a Republican. Hoover gave the plan his approval, though Pierce, presumably, had no idea he was being touted as King's "replacement."

sidering doing the same for King, he brought FBI pressure to bear on Marquette, and no degree was offered.

The following month the feud between Hoover and King became public when the FBI director's comments before an executive session of a House appropriations subcommittee in January were released. "We do know that Communist influence does exist in the Negro movement," Hoover had told the panel, "and it is this influence which is vitally important."[40]

King issued an immediate and stern rebuttal. In a press release the next day, he said:

> It is very unfortunate, that Mr. J. Edgar Hoover, in his claims of alleged communist influence in the civil rights movement, has allowed himself to aid and abet the salacious claims of southern racists and the extreme right-wing elements. We challenge all who raise the "red" issue, whether they be newspaper columnists or the head of the FBI himself—to come forward and provide real evidence . . . We are confident that this cannot be done . . . It is difficult to accept the word of the FBI on communist infiltration in the civil rights movement, when they have been so completely ineffectual in resolving the continued mayhem and brutality inflicted upon the Negro in the deep south. It would be encouraging to us if Mr. Hoover and the FBI would be as diligent in apprehending those responsible for bombing churches and killing little children as they are in seeking out alleged communist infiltration in the civil rights movement.[41]

In early May, Hoover countered, stating publicly, "The existence and importance of the communist influence in the Negro movement should not be ignored or minimized, nor should it be exaggerated . . . It is up to the civil rights organizations themselves to recognize this and face up to it."[42] Again, King fired right back. On May 10, appearing on *Face the Nation*, he said he found it "unfortunate" that "such a great man" as J. Edgar Hoover would make such allegations.[43]

On November 18, Hoover held a rare press conference for women reporters in which he called King "the most notorious liar in the country" and "one of the lowest characters in the country," remarks that catapulted his hatred for King onto the front pages of newspapers.[44] King, who was vacationing in the Bahamas and working on his Nobel acceptance speech, sent a telegram to Hoover offering to meet and discuss their differences, and also issued a press release: "I cannot conceive of Mr. Hoover making a statement like this without being under extreme pressure. He has apparently faltered under the awesome burden, complexities and responsibilities of his office. Therefore, I cannot engage in a public debate with him. I have nothing but sympathy for this man who has served his country so well."[45]

Hoover's response was to have DeLoach offer copies of the hotel room surveillance transcript to select reporters, including Benjamin Bradlee, then the Washington bureau chief for *Newsweek*. Bradlee turned down the proposal and then told a number of colleagues about what had been proffered. Unable to get media coverage or a government leak of the material, the bureau resorted to a variation of one of its tried-and-true COINTELPRO gambits.

FBI technicians compiled a tape from the Washington, D.C., hotel room recording, and on November 21 an agent flew to Florida to mail a package containing the tape to SCLC headquarters in Atlanta. The bureau was aware that King was traveling and that his wife, Coretta, opened his mail when he was on the road.

In his biography of Hoover, Curt Gentry underscores the significance of this ploy. "The head of the nation's police force was protecting the national interest by using intimate tapes to wreak havoc in a man's marriage . . . But this was not only a highly bizarre and obscene initiative; it was plainly illegal."[46] Equally significant, the recordings were made illegally—Hoover had never informed the attorney general about the surveillance of King's hotel rooms or obtained permission to conduct such an operation.

Accompanying the tape was a fraudulent letter, apparently written by Sullivan, suggesting that the tape would be made public unless King committed suicide:

> King, look into your heart. You know you are a complete fraud and a great liability to all of us Negroes. White people in this country have enough frauds of their own but I am sure they don't have one at this time that is anywhere near your equal. You are no clergyman and you know it. I repeat you are a colossal fraud and an evil, vicious one at that. You could not believe in God . . . Clearly you don't believe in any personal principles.
>
> King, like all frauds your end is approaching. You could

have been our greatest leader. You, even at an early age, have turned out to be not a leader but a dissolute, abnormal moral imbecile . . . But you are done. Your "honorary" degrees, your Nobel Prize (what a grim farce) and other awards will not save you. King, I repeat you are done . . .

The American public, the church organizations that have been helping—Protestant, Catholic and Jews will know you for what you are—an evil, abnormal beast. So will others who have backed you. You are done.

King, there is only one thing left for you to do. You know what it is. You have just 34 days . . . You are done. There is but one way out for you. You better take it before your filthy, abnormal fraudulent self is bared to the nation.[47]

The package sat at SCLC headquarters until the beginning of January 1965, when it would be delivered to King's home and opened by Coretta King.

In the meantime, intermediaries arranged a face-to-face meeting between Hoover and King, and on December 1 the two met for an hour in Hoover's office, along with Cartha DeLoach and three of King's close aides, the Reverend Ralph Abernathy, Walter Fauntroy, and Andrew Young. Hoover utterly dominated the encounter. After Abernathy and King began with short complimentary statements about Hoover and the bureau, the director spoke for most of the allotted time, giving a self-aggrandizing account of the FBI's record on civil rights in the South.*

At the end of the meeting, King diplomatically told reporters that it had been "a quite amicable discussion" and said, "I sincerely hope we can forget the confusions of the past and get on with the job that Congress, the Supreme Court and the President have outlined, the job of providing freedom and justice for all citizens of this nation."[48]

If there were any chance that Hoover might have eased up on King, that possibility was killed when an FBI wiretap caught King in a phone conversation, recounting his impressions of the meeting and saying, "The old man talks too much." As William Sullivan later wrote, when Hoover "found out what King had said about him, King was lost."[49]

---

* Years later, Andrew Young described the conference as "a completely nonfunctional meeting" (see "Playboy Interview: Andrew Young," *Playboy*, July 1977, p. 75).

The bureau now sent a monograph from Sullivan's unit titled "Communism and the Negro Movement: A Current Analysis" to LBJ, and obtained White House permission to circulate the paper widely. CIA director John McCone, Acting Attorney General Nicholas Katzenbach, Secretary of Defense Robert McNamara, USIA director Carl Rowan, and Secretary of State Dean Rusk, as well as the military intelligence offices and the National Science Foundation, all received copies.

King was aware that the FBI was disseminating derogatory material about him, and it weighed heavily on his mind, adding to the already immense burden of his position. On December 5, after having shown up a half hour late for a news conference before leaving for Stockholm, where he would receive the Nobel Peace Prize, he told reporters his tardiness was a result of "complete exhaustion" and that he had been advised he needed "a long period of rest."[50] By the end of the year, he was all but debilitated.

Hoover, on the other hand, was going strong. On January 1, 1965, he turned seventy, the mandatory retirement age for federal employees. The previous May, however, LBJ had praised Hoover as a "quiet, humble and magnificent public servant" and signed an executive order exempting him from compulsory retirement for "an indefinite period of time."[51] Johnson's order effectively meant that Hoover would remain in his position for life.

Four days after Hoover's birthday, Coretta King discovered the tape and letter that the FBI had sent in November. She listened to a small part of the recording, then called her husband. King, Abernathy, Young, and the Reverend Joseph Lowery went to the King house and listened to the tape with Mrs. King. There was no doubt about the source of the package, which had no return address; only the FBI would have the resources to carry out hotel room microphone surveillance in Washington, D.C., and have it mailed from Florida.

"They are out to break me," said King in a phone conversation the next day. He told another friend, "They are out to get me, harass me, break my spirit."[52]

Young called DeLoach and asked to meet with him and/or Hoover. DeLoach agreed, and Young and Abernathy hastened to Washington. In their meeting, DeLoach denied that the FBI had any interest in King's personal life and referred them to HUAC for information about Communist influence in SCLC. Young was frustrated by the meeting, finding DeLoach to have "almost a kind of fascist mentality. It really kind of scared me . . . There really wasn't any honest conversation."[53]

The tapes were never made public, no doubt because Hoover knew that doing so would reveal the bureau's illegal actions in the matter. King survived the crisis, but the FBI's harassment of him continued right up to and even after his death. Early in 1965, the agency tried to bring about the cancellation of a dinner to honor King in Atlanta, and Hoover also sought to block an invitation to King from the Baptist World Alliance to speak at its 1965 congress in Miami. The following year, the bureau was instrumental in preventing the Teamsters' union from making a contribution to SCLC, and further attempted to stop a Ford Foundation grant to the organization. When King spoke against the Vietnam War in April 1967, the bureau stepped up its efforts to discredit him. In October, Hoover approved a plan to circulate an editorial to "publicize King as a traitor to his country and his race and thus reduce his income" from fund-raising efforts.[54] The planned Poor People's March on Washington at the end of the year brought forth another virulent attack. In March 1969, almost a year after King was assassinated, Hoover approved DeLoach's suggestion to try to derail the congressional momentum to declare his birthday a national holiday. As late as the end of 1970, Hoover was still fulminating about King, telling *Newsweek* that the civil rights leader "was the last person in the world who should ever have received" the Nobel Prize, and adding, "I held him in complete contempt."[55]

In March 1979, the House Select Committee on Assassinations concluded that the FBI's hounding of King was based on nothing more than Hoover's "personal vendetta against the civil rights leader."[56] FBI agents themselves admitted that despite the "massive surveillance" of King, "there was never a recommendation for prosecution for violation of any Federal or State law. Nor . . . were grounds for any national security concerns ever established."[57]

In addition to the cited counterintelligence programs, there were three other official COINTELPRO operations: "White Hate Groups," "Black Nationalist Hate Groups," and "New Left." The first was a narrow, concentrated operation, while the other two were wide-ranging programs directed against entire movements.

COINTELPRO–White Hate Groups was noteworthy in two ways. To begin with, it was the first COINTELPRO that was not instituted by the FBI itself, but rather was launched as a result of external pressure. Moreover, while the focus of COINTELPRO-WHG was the Ku Klux Klan and several other far-right groups, including the American Nazi Party and the National States Rights Party, the degree of repression on the right never approached the all-encompassing surveillance of and overbearing crackdown on the left. Whereas the tentacles of COINTELPRO-CPUSA and COINTELPRO-SWP (and later COINTELPRO–New Left) reached well beyond those organizations to encompass many other groups and individuals, the White Hate Groups operation confined itself to the targeted groups themselves. The White Citizens' Councils, for example, many of which were Klan fronts, were never investigated or placed under surveillance; nor was the John Birch Society, which stood at the very vanguard of the radical right.

COINTELPRO-WHG began in the summer of 1964, foisted on the FBI by President Johnson and the Justice Department after years of the bureau's stonewalling on civil rights prosecutions and attempts at discrediting civil rights leaders like Martin Luther King. During the spring of 1964, there had been fifty race-related murders, beatings, and bombings in the South, culminating in the killings of the civil rights workers James Chaney, Andrew Goodman, and Michael Schwerner near Philadelphia, Mississippi, in the early morning hours of June 22.

Even before the murders of Chaney, Goodman, and Schwerner, Robert Kennedy had written to LBJ to propose an FBI operation in the Deep South, suggesting that the FBI could employ the techniques used in infiltrating the Communist Party and other groups. After the murders, Johnson sent the former CIA director Allen Dulles to Mississippi to assess the situation, and Dulles recommended that there be a significant increase in FBI agents in the state, in order to control and prosecute terrorist activities. LBJ instructed Hoover to "put people after the Klan and study it from one county to the next. I want the FBI to have the best intelligence system possible to check on the activities of these people."[58] Hoover had no choice but to comply.

On September 2, a directive to seventeen field offices launched a new COINTELPRO against the Klan and other affiliated white hate groups. The field offices increased their infiltration of various Klan organizations, with more than 750 new informers, and by 1965 the bureau had over 2,000 plants—about 20 percent of the organizations' total membership—working throughout the KKK network.

The new operation was at once similar to and different from existing COINTELPROs. The most obvious similarity was that the techniques employed in COINTELPRO-WHG were adapted from those used in other operations—anonymous letters and telephone calls, planted news stories, the snitch jacket, fomenting and exploiting rivalries, and IRS harassment.* The most striking difference was that COINTELPRO-WHG targeted groups and individuals engaged in illegal activities, while the other operations were for the greatest part aimed at law-abiding organizations and citizens.

As with existing COINTELPROs, the FBI did not hesitate to violate the law in order to achieve its goals. KKK informers and infiltrators often took part in violent acts, and the bureau, while not condoning such behavior, did not expressly forbid participation. "You can do anything to get your information," the FBI told the informer Gary Thomas Rowe, who was ultimately indicted for the March 1965 slaying of the civil rights demonstrator Viola Liuzzo. "We don't want you to get involved in *unnecessary* violence, but the point is to get the information."[59] In reality, given the nature of the Klan and other similar groups, any infiltrator who tried to discourage violence was endangering both his credibility and his life.

COINTELPRO-WHG is a clear example of how the FBI's focus had shifted from law enforcement to intelligence gathering—in a number of instances, the bureau went so far as to obstruct justice in order to protect its informants. In the case of Rowe, who was in a car with two Klansmen when they shot Mrs. Liuzzo and who subsequently testified at their 1965 trial and conviction, it was not until thirteen years later that he himself was indicted in the killing. It can be surmised that only his value to the FBI kept him from being charged sooner.

The bureau also impeded justice in the September 1963 Birmingham church bombing in which four black girls were killed. The FBI had enough evidence to proceed with a prosecution, but it made no move in that direction and for years even refused to cooperate with a

---

* In one anonymous mailing, postcards were sent to six thousand Klan members, whose names and addresses had been gained from stolen membership lists, with the message "KLANSMEN, trying to hide your identity behind your sheet? You received this. Someone KNOWS who you are!" In another, a letter from "A God-fearing klanswoman" was sent to the wife of a Grand Dragon to inform her that her husband "has been committing the greatest of sins of our Lord for many years. He has . . . been committing adultery" (both quoted in Donner, *Age of Surveillance*, pp. 208, 210).

state investigation of the crime. Finally, in 1977, with the aid of bureau information, a former Klansman was convicted in the case.

Among the most troubling aspects of COINTELPRO-WHG were the numerous instances in which paid FBI informants, with bureau knowledge, approval, and cooperation, worked to incite violence. A stark example took place in Meridian, Mississippi, shortly after midnight on June 30, 1968.

For almost a year, the Meridian-Jackson area had been plagued by a severe wave of anti-Jewish and antiblack bombings. Despite intensive investigation and the existence of a reward fund in the tens of thousands of dollars raised by the Jewish community, the FBI and local law-enforcement agencies were unable to solve the crimes. In desperation, the FBI paid an intermediary to arrange a meeting with two members of the White Knights of the Ku Klux Klan, a group suspected of committing over three hundred acts of violence, including bombings, burnings, beatings, and nine murders. Bureau agents conspired with Alton Wayne Roberts—who was under a ten-year sentence in the murders of Chaney, Goodman, and Schwerner—and his younger brother Raymond to set up the bombing of a Jewish businessman's home, in order to apprehend two other Klansmen suspected of being behind the Meridian-Jackson bombings. The Roberts brothers were paid $36,500 and promised immunity from prosecution in several church bombings, in exchange for arranging the explosion with the two wanted Klansmen, Thomas Albert Tarrants III and Danny Joe Hawkins. FBI agents staked out the targeted home, but at the appointed time Tarrants showed up instead with Kathy Ainsworth, who had no police record and was completely unknown to the FBI. A gun battle broke out, during which Ainsworth was killed and Tarrants wounded. In the ensuing pursuit of Tarrants, a police officer and a bystander were also wounded.

In an editorial about the case, the *Los Angeles Times* wrote:

> The courts have held that in order to capture a suspect the police may help him commit a crime he could otherwise reasonably be expected to commit, but the police may not entrap an innocent person into a crime. What constitutes impermissible entrapment depends on the facts of the case. The Mississippi case, though, raises a moral question that, we submit, is not ambiguous . . . The authorities stretched beyond acceptable lim-

its the bonds of restraint which the people put upon their government in the interest of the liberty of all citizens.

The *Times* editorial also made another point:

No matter how great the provocation, the police can never take
it on themselves to decide who is guilty, who is innocent; who is
to live, and who to die. For, if they should feel free to make such
decisions in one place about the Ku Klux Klan—an organization
which every liberty-loving person must loathe—might they not
feel free to make such decisions about another group in another
place, say, for instance, the Black Panthers? Now, there are no
doubt many citizens who loathe the Panthers as much as the
Klan is loathed. Yet could one therefore advocate that the police
resort to such methods in order to quash the Panthers? The very
suggestion is repugnant to our concept of liberty.[60]

In fact, the FBI had been using just "such methods" in a COIN-
TELPRO against the Black Panthers for more than a year, and against
other "Black Nationalist Hate Groups" for two and a half years.

CHAPTER 15

We Never Gave It a Thought

The summer of 1967 was one of violent discontent in black communities across America. More than 150 riots broke out in U.S. cities, including Atlanta, Birmingham, Boston, Buffalo, Chicago, Cincinnati, Detroit, Milwaukee, Minneapolis, Newark, New York, Rochester, and Tampa. In August, Hoover created two initiatives in response. The first was the establishment of the "Rabble Rouser Index," a list of the names and background information on "known rabble rousers . . . who have demonstrated a propensity for fomenting racial disorder."[1]* The second was the creation of COINTELPRO–Black Nationalist Hate Groups, announced in a letter from Hoover to twenty-three field offices. The instructions for the program were similar to those of other COINTELPROs, and organizations warranting "intensified attention" included the Congress of Racial Equality, Deacons for Defense and Justice, Nation of Islam, Revolutionary Action Movement, Southern Christian Leadership Conference, and Student Nonviolent Coordinating Committee. In addition, specific individuals were singled out, including H. Rap Brown, Stokely Carmichael, Elijah Muhammad, and Maxwell Stanford.

The methods used in COINTELPRO-BNHG included the by-now-customary ploys: agents provocateurs, anonymous letters, blackmail, bogus news stories, burglary, defamation of character,

---

* In November, the index was broadened to cover anyone whose activities had a bearing on national security, including black nationalists, white supremacists, Puerto Rican nationalists, anti-Vietnam demonstration leaders, and other "extremists." The following March, the list was renamed the "Agitator Index."

derogatory cartoons, disinformation, electronic surveillance, extortion, false identity, forgery, and snitch jackets. FBI agents also encouraged local police to arrest members of targeted groups on little or no evidence, as was the case with the Revolutionary Action Movement in Philadelphia during the summer of 1968. According to an FBI internal memo, Philadelphia police kept RAM leaders in jail for most of the summer by arresting them on every possible charge, until they could no longer afford bail.

A rather more sinister case occurred in Seattle, where in May 1970, at the FBI's behest, the informer Alfie Burnett attempted to recruit a former member of the Black Panthers to blow up a building. The ex-Panther was unavailable, so Burnett turned to Larry Ward, a twice-wounded, thrice-decorated twenty-two-year-old black Vietnam veteran, offering him $75 to carry out the job. When Ward showed up to plant the bomb, he was killed in a police ambush. "The police wanted a bomber and I got one for them," said Burnett. "I didn't know Larry Ward would be killed." In discussing the case, Seattle's police intelligence chief, Captain John Williams, insisted, "As far as I can tell, Ward was a relatively decent kid. Somebody set this whole thing up. It wasn't the police department."[2]

Hoover micromanaged COINTELPRO-BNHG, as he did all the other counterintelligence operations, with every proposed action requiring the approval of FBI headquarters before being put into play. From its inception, COINTELPRO-BNHG was also characterized by an underlying racism and nativism that reflected Hoover's prejudices. Robert Wall, a special agent with the Washington office, later wrote that "the appalling racism of the FBI on every level became glaringly apparent to me." Driven by this endemic racism, COINTELPRO-BNHG was carried out with a ferocity and brutality unmatched in any of the other COINTELPROs. As Hoover bluntly stated in a follow-up to the memo expanding the operation, "The Negro youth and moderate must be made to understand that if they succumb to revolutionary teaching, they will be dead revolutionaries."[3]

Just as he had in his vendetta against Martin Luther King, Hoover disguised his racist bent behind a declared concern for national security. But as Dr. James Turner, president of the African Heritage Studies Association—then the largest organization of scholars in African and African-American studies—stated in 1974, the fundamental motivation behind COINTELPRO-BNHG was a "conscious and concerted" effort "to break the momentum developed in black communities."[4]

While COINTELPRO-BNHG was an across-the-board attack on emerging African-American awareness and black pride, there was one group that bore the brunt of the assault. The Black Panther Party, which was not even mentioned in the FBI's original COINTELPRO-BNHG memo, soon became the main focus of the operation. By destroying the Black Panthers, the FBI effectively managed to undermine the entire movement.

Founded in Oakland in 1966 by the Merritt College students Huey Newton and Bobby Seale, the militant Black Panther Party for Self Defense soon became known for patrolling the high-crime slums of Oakland's inner-city ghetto in their black berets and black leather jackets, openly bearing firearms. They made a practice of following police cars around the neighborhoods, keeping an eye out for arrests, and advising detainees of their rights. For all their violent tendencies, the Panthers—at least early on—also demonstrated a civic-minded spirit, organizing eviction protests, working with welfare recipients, counseling African-American prisoners, and establishing a free breakfast program that fed thousands of ghetto children daily.

Seale, the party's chairman, later recalled formulating the Panthers' platform: "We want power to determine our own destiny in our own black community. We want organized political electoral power. Full employment. Decent housing. Decent education to tell us about our true selves. Not to have to fight in Vietnam. An immediate end to police brutality and murder of black people. The right to have juries of our peers in the courts. We summed it up: We wanted land, bread, housing, education, clothing, justice, and peace."[5]

From the beginning, the Panthers' inflammatory rhetoric and street-theater tactics were aimed at grabbing headlines, and on May 2, 1967, they made the front pages of newspapers across the country when about thirty members, including five women, brazenly marched into the California State Capitol brandishing guns and wearing bandoliers of bullets, to protest proposed legislation to outlaw the carrying of a loaded weapon in public. The bill was a transparent attempt to curtail the Panthers' armed shadowing of police cars in the ghetto. A dozen or more of the group made it into the assembly chamber, where the state legislature was in session. The intruders were ejected by sergeants at arms, but violence was avoided, and the incident thrust the Panthers into the national spotlight.

Six months later, the Black Panthers' minister of defense, Huey Newton, and a woman companion were stopped by two Oakland policemen at 5:00 a.m. for a routine traffic violation. When Newton got out of his car, there was an exchange of gunfire, and after the smoke cleared, one police officer was dead. Newton and the other officer were wounded, and Newton was jailed on a murder charge.

"Free Huey" now became a rallying cry. At an Oakland rally in February 1968, Stokely Carmichael, the confrontational and controversial head of the Student Nonviolent Coordinating Committee, appeared along with Eldridge Cleaver, the Panthers' minister of information, who had been paroled after serving nine years on an assault charge and was widely known for his prison memoir, *Soul on Ice*. In their speeches that day, Carmichael and Cleaver announced the merger of the Black Panther Party and SNCC.

The alliance of the Panthers and SNCC seriously disquieted the FBI, and within weeks the bureau extended COINTELPRO-BNHG to eighteen additional field offices. In the memo announcing the program's expansion, George C. Moore, head of the Racial Intelligence Section, a new division created to coordinate COINTELPRO-BNHG, listed the long-range goals of the operation. The first was "Prevent the *coalition* of militant black nationalist groups [that] might be the first step toward a real 'Mau Mau' in America, the beginning of a true black revolution." The rest were:

> 2. Prevent the *rise of a "messiah"* who could unify, and electrify, the militant black nationalist movement. Malcolm X might have been such a "messiah"; he is the martyr of the movement today. Martin Luther King, Stokely Carmichael and Elijah Muhammad all aspire to this position . . .
>
> 3. Prevent *violence* on the part of black nationalist groups . . . Through counterintelligence it should be possible to pinpoint potential troublemakers and neutralize them before they exercise their potential for violence.
>
> 4. Prevent militant black nationalist groups and leaders from gaining *respectability*, by discrediting them to three separate segments of the community . . . [T]o, first, the responsible Negro community. Second . . . to the white community, both the

responsible community and to "liberals" who have vestiges of sympathy for militant black nationalist groups simply because they are Negroes. Third, these groups must be discredited in the eyes of Negro radicals, the followers of the movement . . .

  5. A final goal should be to prevent the long-range *growth* of black nationalist organizations, especially among youth.[6]

A month after the Free Huey rally, the Panthers announced their affiliation with the predominantly white Peace and Freedom Party, and Cleaver was nominated to be the PFP's candidate for president of the United States. Now the FBI had a new concern, as the Panthers were beginning to attract the support of white radicals and anti–Vietnam War activists.

The rise of the black liberation and anti–Vietnam War movements called forth two repressive laws—the Anti-Riot Act of 1968, passed in April, and the Omnibus Crime Bill of 1968, passed in June. The former, a provision of the landmark 1968 Civil Rights Act, made it a crime to cross state lines with the intent of inciting a riot or of aiding and abetting a riot. The latter statute was the first law in U.S. history that explicitly legalized electronic surveillance by the federal government.

On April 4, a month after COINTELPRO-BNHG was expanded, Martin Luther King was assassinated in Memphis, and riots erupted in black communities across the country. On the night of April 6, under circumstances that have never been clearly defined, there was a fire-fight between Oakland police and more than a dozen Black Panthers. Two policemen and two party members were wounded, as the rest of the Panthers took refuge in a nearby house. Cleaver and the Panthers' treasurer, Bobby Hutton, who had been the party's first recruit and at seventeen was the group's youngest member, holed up in the base-ment. After a ninety-minute gun battle, police fired tear gas into the house, and Cleaver and Hutton threw their guns out onto the street and emerged in their underwear, hands raised high over their heads. They were immediately surrounded, and the unarmed Hutton was slain by a volley of police bullets. According to the coroner, he was shot at close range at least six times.

At once, the Black Panthers became the primary object on the COINTELPRO-BNHG radar screen. The special agent Wayne Davis of the Washington FBI office later remembered that "there was a great deal of fear about the Panthers' philosophy . . . I think that the law enforcement and the government structure saw this as perhaps the beginnings of a breakdown in respect for law enforcement and obedience to the laws—and perhaps the seeds of anarchy."[7]

Eight Black Panthers were arrested in connection with the April 6 shoot-out, including Cleaver, whose parole was then revoked, and Chief of Staff David Hilliard. With Hutton dead, and Newton, Cleaver, and Hilliard in custody, the party leadership was decimated, but the attendant publicity also brought with it a spate of new recruits. Soon there were forty chapters throughout the country, and *The Black Panther*, the party's weekly newspaper, enjoyed a circulation of 150,000.

In June, Cleaver was released on a writ of habeas corpus, and he took up where he had left off. Embarking on a nationwide speaking tour, he threatened, "Free Huey or the sky's the limit."[8]

Hoover now described the Black Panthers as "the greatest threat to the internal security of the country . . . Leaders and representatives of the Black Panther Party travel extensively all over the United States preaching their gospel of hate and violence not only to ghetto residents, but to students in colleges, universities and high schools as well."[9]

To intimidate Stokely Carmichael, the FBI contacted his mother to warn her of a fabricated Black Panther plot to kill her son. Carmichael dissolved his alliance with the Panthers and left the country for Africa.

In September, Newton was sentenced to two to fifteen years for manslaughter. Soon after, Cleaver's release on parole was overturned, and he was ordered to return to jail in sixty days. At the end of November, he too left the United States.

November also marked the beginning of a vicious FBI campaign to provoke a gang-style war between the San Diego chapter of the Panthers and a rival group, the United Slaves, known as US. Learning of tensions between the two groups, the bureau worked vigorously to inflame hostilities that culminated in several killings.

In January 1969, two Panthers were killed by US members in an incident on the UCLA campus, but in March the two groups attempted to forge a peace accord. Reporting on an April 2, 1969, "friendly confrontation between US and the BPP," the San Diego field office told FBI headquarters that neither side showed any weapons and that the two groups tried to negotiate their differences.[10] Refusing to let the peace process proceed, however, the San Diego office mailed the Panthers a series of cartoons, approved by headquarters, that ridiculed them and appeared to come from US. Within days, the fragile truce between the two groups broke down, violence resumed, and in May another Black Panther was killed.

The San Diego office continued to provoke the situation for months, and boasted to headquarters of the success of its efforts: "Shootings, beatings, and a high degree of unrest continue to prevail in the ghetto area of southeast San Diego . . . [I]t is felt that a substantial amount of the unrest is directly attributable to this program."[11]

One of the most unsettling of COINTELPRO tactics, the use of agents provocateurs, also played a significant role in the war against the Black Panthers. In New York, a member who was either an FBI agent or an informer reportedly made an unsolicited gift of sixty sticks of dynamite, resulting in the arrest of thirteen Panthers on charges of conspiring to bomb public places. In other instances involving Panthers in New York and Indiana, agents provocateurs purportedly instigated burglaries and robberies, supplying weapons, maps, and getaway cars.

In Chicago, the FBI played a direct role in the assassination of the Panther leader Fred Hampton, a gifted and charismatic organizer, whose talents and achievements earned him a spot on the FBI's Rabble Rouser Index. As chairman of the Chicago chapter of the party, Hampton had been responsible for initiating a number of successful community programs in Chicago's South Side ghetto, as well as for forging an alliance with the white-dominated Students for a Democratic Society, one of the main groups targeted by a separate FBI operation called COINTELPRO–New Left.

In 1968, the bureau recruited nineteen-year-old William O'Neal, who was under indictment on felony charges, offering to pay him and drop the charges against him if he would infiltrate Hampton's group. O'Neal agreed and rapidly rose to become Hampton's personal bodyguard and the Chicago chapter's chief of security, in charge of members' weapons.

The Chicago police had hounded the local Panthers relentlessly, carrying out repeated raids on Panther offices, and tensions exploded into a couple of shoot-outs in July and October 1969. On November 13, there was a third gun battle in which two policemen died.

At about the same time, O'Neal told the FBI that "if David Hilliard, national BPP chief of staff, goes to jail [in connection with the

April 6, 1968, Oakland shoot-out], Hampton will be appointed to fill Hilliard's position."[12] O'Neal also supplied the bureau with a floor plan of the Panther apartment where the Panthers' arsenal of weapons was stored, and where Fred Hampton often slept. The drawing included the location of Hampton's bed.

The FBI gave the information to local law-enforcement officials, and on December 4 Chicago police carried out a predawn raid on the apartment. The twenty-one-year-old Hampton, who never awoke and had very likely been drugged (phenobarbital was found in the apartment), was shot four times—including twice in the head at point-blank range—and killed, along with another Panther, Mark Clark. Police initially described the ensuing firefight as a "fierce gun battle," but federal ballistics experts established that police officers had fired more than eighty rounds, while only one bullet was fired in return—by Clark, as he was falling after being shot.[13] A federal grand jury brought no indictments against any government officials or police officers, and attempted murder charges against the seven Panthers who survived the raid were later dropped.

With its leadership decimated, the Black Panther Party was on the ropes. The final blow in the systematic destruction of the organization was the FBI-induced rift between Huey Newton and Eldridge Cleaver, engineered through a series of forged letters to both men, beginning in August 1970, that succeeded in driving a permanent wedge between them. While their personal differences may have made such a fracture inevitable, Cleaver believed the bureau was at least partially responsible. "The FBI was very instrumental in the split," he said. "They very skillfully fed our egos and our paranoia."[14]

By the end of 1970, the Black Panthers were all but finished as a force to be reckoned with. In 1968 and 1969, there had been more than thirty police raids on Panther offices in eleven states, and over four hundred confrontations between police and party members. The harassment was constant. Panthers were arrested for a panoply of crimes that included illegal use of a bullhorn, illegal placement of a table outside an office, incorrectly crossing the street, putting up posters, selling newspapers on a highway, spitting on the sidewalk, and using profanity.

As always, Hoover called the shots. When the agents of the bureau's special Black Panther unit in San Francisco informed him that they considered it unlikely that the Panthers would mount a violent revolution, he sent a blistering response, telling them—as he had told William Sullivan when the latter had had the poor judgment to find no Communist influence in the civil rights movement—"Your reasoning is not in line with Bureau objectives."[15] When they offered the opinion that no matter what else was done against the Panthers, the Breakfast for Children program should be left in place, Hoover fired back, "You have obviously missed the point. The BPP is not engaged in the 'Breakfast for Children' program for humanitarian reasons. The program was formed by the BPP for obvious reasons, including their effort to create an image of civility, assume control of Negroes, and to fill adolescent children with their insidious poison."[16]

In the end, the war on the Black Panthers was successful. About thirty Panthers were dead—some, like Fred Hampton, Mark Clark, and Bobby Hutton, at the hands of government agents, others as a result of FBI-assisted internecine warfare with other black militant groups. Imprisonment and exile took care of dozens, perhaps hundreds more. With the Panthers' defeat, the wider militant black power movement, which had been gaining momentum for a decade until the FBI stepped in with COINTELPRO-BNHG, was broken.

In May 1966, Hoover wrote to the special agents in charge of the field offices to say, "We are an intelligence agency, and as such are expected to know what is going on or is likely to happen." As the 1975 report of the Senate investigating committee observed, Hoover's characterization of the bureau summed up the approach that "the FBI could and should know everything that might someday be useful in some undefined manner."[17] Such an approach is, in fact, the mind-set and raison d'être of the secret police force of an authoritarian state—and what Hoover had envisioned for the FBI since his earliest days in the agency.

Nowhere was this approach more discernible than in COINTELPRO–New Left, beginning in May 1968. In the words of Frederick A. O. Schwarz Jr., the Senate committee's chief counsel, FBI surveillance of the New Left movement was tantamount to "a comprehensive listing of everything those people thought or did on any subject you can imagine their having a concern with."[18] Perhaps most alarming of all, this staggeringly broad-based surveillance was conducted without any formal delineation of what the New Left comprised. In his testimony before the Senate committee, the supervisor of the operation said, "I cannot recall any document that was written defining New Left as such . . . It has never been strictly defined, as far as I know . . . It is more or less an attitude, I would think." In other words, anybody who was perceived to have this nebulous "attitude" was a candidate for investigation. Frank Donner called COINTELPRO–New Left "an undisguised assault by the self-appointed defenders of the American way of life against an entire milieu."[19]

The chief catalyst in the rise of the New Left was the Vietnam War. Opposition to the war began slowly, with minimal support, yet in March 1965, Hoover told the House Appropriations Committee that the protests were proof of "how unified, organized and powerful an element the Communist movement is in the United States today."[20]

On April 17, 1965, a march on Washington attracted between fifteen thousand and twenty-five thousand protesters. A week and a half later, LBJ and Hoover met to discuss the protests and Johnson's conviction that they were encouraging America's enemies. Hoover immediately ordered up the preparation of a bureau report emphasizing the "communist influence" in the Students for a Democratic Society, so that Johnson would know "exactly what the picture is."* In Hoover's mind, as Sanford Ungar points out in *FBI*, there were "clear and automatic links running from protest to violence, to anarchist agitation to an actual revolution."[21]

The resulting report, "Communist Activities Relative to United States Policy on Vietnam," indicated just the opposite of what Hoover and Johnson wanted and expected to hear. The report found, for example, that the April 17 demonstration had not been "communist instituted, dominated or controlled," and that while the CP would have liked to influence the New Left and the antiwar movement, its efforts had not been successful.[22] Johnson and Hoover refused to accept such conclusions, and the FBI director instructed the SACs to step up their investigations of student organizations. Johnson, in turn, asked Hoover to run "name checks" on dozens of individuals who had signed telegrams protesting the war.[23]

---

* He also called for the bureau "to penetrate the Students for Democratic Society [*sic*] so that we will have proper informant coverage similar to what we have in the Ku Klux Klan and the Communist Party itself" (see Church Committee, bk. 3, p. 484).

The antiwar movement now began gaining traction. On May 20–21, a thirty-six-hour marathon teach-in on the Vietnam War was held on the campus of the University of California, Berkeley, where the previous December a semester of Free Speech Movement protests had culminated in the arrest of some eight hundred students during the occupation of the campus administration building. The May 1965 teach-in at UC Berkeley attracted more than twenty thousand people.

The following October, a Senate subcommittee reported that the control of the anti-Vietnam movement had been taken over by "Communists and extremist elements" who were anti-American and pro-Vietcong and were planning massive civil disobedience, including "the burning of draft cards and the stopping of troop trains."[24] The same month, Johnson let it be known that he fully endorsed the Justice Department's investigation of possible Communist infiltration of the antiwar movement.

The assault on the character, integrity, and patriotism of antiwar demonstrators increased. On November 1, Hoover publicly quoted a letter he had written to a Vietnam veteran in which he had said, "Anti-Vietnam demonstrators in the U.S. represent a minority for the most part composed of halfway citizens who are neither morally, mentally or emotionally mature."[25] Attorney General Nicholas Katzenbach warned that there were Communists in SDS, and Senator Thomas Dodd's Internal Security Subcommittee issued a 235-page report claiming that the antiwar movement was largely controlled by Communists. On *Meet the Press*, Secretary of State Dean Rusk declared that "the worldwide Communist apparatus is working very hard" in support of antiwar demonstrations, and "the net effect of these demonstrations will be to prolong the war, not shorten it."[26]

As the war escalated, antiwar sentiment at home grew correspondingly. On April 4, 1967, Martin Luther King delivered his landmark address "Beyond Vietnam: A Time to Break Silence," a ringing indictment of the Vietnam War, at New York City's Riverside Church near Columbia University. In the speech, King rebuked "the greatest purveyor of violence in the world today—my own government."[27] On both April 27, 1967, and October 21, 1967, a million people took to the streets all across America to protest the war.

COINTELPRO–New Left was initially a response to the unrest on college campuses, which were strongholds of the antiwar movement. The possibility of such a program was first suggested by Hoover in an April 2, 1968, memo to the SACs. In a typical example of Hoover hyperbole, he wrote, "The emergence of the new left movement as a subversive force dedicated to the complete destruction of the traditional values of our democratic society presents us with an unprecedented challenge in the security field."[28]

On April 4, a year to the day that he delivered "Beyond Vietnam," Martin Luther King was shot to death. Less than three weeks later, on the campus near where he had given the speech, Columbia University students occupied five buildings, including the office of President Grayson Kirk, and held the buildings for six days before university officials called in the police. More than seven hundred students were arrested, and there were over a hundred injuries to police and protesters.

Within days of the Columbia uprising, an internal memo recommended the institution of a new COINTELPRO:

> Our Nation is undergoing an era of disruption and violence caused to a large extent by various individuals generally connected with the New Left. Some of these activists urge revolution in America and call for the defeat of the United States in Vietnam. They continually and falsely allege police brutality and do not hesitate to utilize unlawful acts to further their so-called causes. The New Left has on many occasions viciously and scurrilously attacked the Director and the Bureau in an attempt to hamper our investigation of it and to drive us off the college campuses. With this in mind, it is our recommendation that a new Counterintelligence Program be designed to neutralize the New Left and the Key Activists.[29]

The program was authorized on May 9, and instructions to field offices were issued by the end of the month. Again, the suggested techniques were the customary array employed in the existing COINTELPROs.

Two weeks later, Hoover sent a directive to the SACs, instructing them to document three areas *vis-à-vis* the New Left: (1) false allegations of police brutality, for the purpose of countering widespread student accusations; (2) immorality, in order to demonstrate "the scurrilous and depraved nature of many of the characters, activities, habits, and living conditions representative of New Left adherents"; and (3) actions of college administrators, to illustrate the necessity of "taking a firm stand" and establishing what "aid and encouragement" may have been offered to student protesters by faculty members.[30]

The freewheeling lifestyles of many of the New Left's young adults were particularly galling to the puritanical Hoover. Their "immorality" was confirmed by reports received from the field offices. The Boston office, for example, sent along an account from one informant who related that members of an urban commune changed sexual partners frequently, held antiwar meetings sitting around their apartment "completely in the nude," neglected personal hygiene, and had poor eating habits.[31] The report offered no indication of how these individuals' sexual, hygienic, and eating tendencies made them a threat to national security.

"Immorality" notwithstanding, student unrest and protests continued to spread. In the first six months of 1968, there were over 220 antiwar demonstrations at more than a hundred American colleges and universities. Going into the summer, the National Mobilization Committee to End the War in Vietnam organized a massive protest for the Democratic National Convention in Chicago in August. As thousands of protesters poured into the city, close to twelve thousand Chicago police officers and seventy-five hundred Illinois National Guardsmen were on hand, as well as a thousand FBI agents, many of them undercover.

On the night of August 28, after several days of peaceful, albeit tense, demonstrations, the forces of law and order unleashed a full-scale riot, as Chicago police beat and clubbed protesters mercilessly for more than fifteen minutes in a fearsome abuse of power that was telecast live across the nation, and the American public witnessed what Theodore White called "a scene . . . from the Russian Revolution."[32] More than 660 individuals were arrested, and over a thousand were injured, including sixty-five journalists and close to two hundred police officers.

With the evidence overwhelmingly indicating police brutality and use of unwarranted force, Hoover ordered the Chicago office to collect evidence disproving such charges and to use the news media to convince the public. On September 9, he followed up with a letter to all offices that had sent agents to the convention, instructing them to question those agents for evidence that militants had provoked police and had staged incidents to make it appear that police reacted with undue force.

Despite Hoover's efforts to whitewash events, the Walker Report, written for the National Commission on the Causes and Prevention of Violence and issued three months after the convention, found that "to read dispassionately the hundreds of statements describing at firsthand the events . . . is to become convinced of the presence of what can only be called a police riot."[33]

The events at the Democratic National Convention undoubtedly contributed to Richard Nixon's triumph in the November presidential election. When Nixon assumed office at the beginning of 1969, he inherited the enormously expanded surveillance apparatus developed by the Johnson administration. Nixon would take the structure to new and greater heights, establishing what the political scientist Robert Goldstein in 1978 called "a mind-set more hostile to basic concepts of civil liberty than any administration in American history."[34]

The violence at the Democratic National Convention and the subsequent failure to convict any police officers of assault triggered a split in the already fractured Students for a Democratic Society, which by 1968 had grown to eighty thousand members and was beset with internal strife. The most radical faction split off to form the Weather Underground, spawning a violent fringe element that began carrying out bombings and arson on campuses and against government facilities. In the FBI's infiltration of the Weather Underground and other ultramilitant groups, agents provocateurs were used repeatedly, and they were responsible for inciting and even carrying out many violent incidents.

Examples of FBI agents or informants acting as agents provocateurs in COINTELPRO–New Left include, but are not limited to, the following:

- The FBI informant Larry D. Grathwohl, one of the most radical members of the Weather Underground, taught his companions to build bombs, took part in the bombing of a Cincinnati public school, and planned the bombing of a Detroit police facility while in constant contact with the FBI.[35]
- In May 1970, during demonstrations at the University of Alabama to commemorate the deaths of four Kent State University students killed by National Guardsmen, the Tusca-

loosa police undercover narcotics agent and FBI informant Charles R. Grimm Jr. engaged in arson and threw missiles at police.[36]

• Between September 1971 and May 1972, William W. Lemmer, a regional coordinator of Vietnam Veterans Against the War and an FBI informer, was responsible for a bomb threat, an attempted bombing, and an illegal protest at an Air Force base, all of which led to arrests.[37]

• In New York, the FBI informant George Demerle, a former member of the John Birch Society, helped assemble a duffel bag full of time bombs that were planted on an Army truck.[38]

• In Seattle, the FBI hired the disillusioned SDS member Horace L. Parker to spy on the organization's University of Washington chapter. Instructed by the FBI to "do anything necessary" to protect his credibility, Parker supplied drugs, weapons, and explosives to the group.[39]

• The FBI informer Robert W. Hardy provided "90 percent of the burglary tools and much of the expertise" used when twenty-eight people broke into the Federal Building in Camden, New Jersey, in August 1971 to destroy draft files.[40] "I taught them everything they knew," said Hardy, "how to cut glass and open windows without making any noise . . . how to open file cabinets without a key."[41] The group was acquitted on the grounds that the government had used an informer as an agent provocateur.

• One of the most notorious agents provocateurs, Thomas Tongyai, alias "Tommy the Traveler," was on the payroll of both the FBI and local police departments. Tongyai traveled from campus to campus in New York state, offering students "bombs, guns and instruction in guerilla tactics."[42] In the spring of 1970, he posed as an SDS organizer at Hobart College, a nine-hundred-student liberal arts campus in the Finger Lakes region. "The best cover for an undercover agent who wanted to get on to the campus was portraying the part of a radical extremist, which I did," he explained. According to Hobart students, Tongyai "provided materials for the firebombing of an Air Force Reserve Officer Training Corps office," and two freshmen were arrested after carrying out the project.[43]

In the final analysis, despite FBI investigations of 500,000 "subversives" between 1960 and 1974, not one individual was prosecuted for planning, advocating, or attempting to overthrow the U.S. government—which was the alleged reason for those half-million investigations.

In all, more than 2,350 separate COINTELPRO actions were carried out. When George Moore, head of the FBI's Racial Intelligence Section, appeared before the Senate committee in November 1975, he was asked if anybody in the bureau had ever raised the issue of the constitutionality or legal authority of COINTELPRO programs. "No," Moore replied, "we never gave it a thought." Similarly, Mark Felt, assistant director of the Bureau's Inspection Division, acknowledged to the committee in February 1976 that his job was to "determine whether the program was being pursued effectively as opposed to whether it was proper . . . There was no instruction in the Inspector's manual that the Inspector should be on the alert to see that constitutional values are being protected."[44]*

As noted, the FBI was not the only government agency investigating domestic "subversives" during this period. In all, more than a dozen other federal agencies, including the CIA, Army Intelligence, and the National Security Agency, were engaged in widespread domestic intelligence work under the Johnson and Nixon administrations, and they all shared information.

The CIA had at least four programs going, including the aforementioned mail-opening operation. The largest CIA program was Operation CHAOS, instituted by LBJ in 1967, and later continued by Nixon. The program was aimed at determining the extent of foreign involvement in the antiwar movement, and despite several reports that such influence was negligible, both presidents continued to ask for the operation's expansion. In its assessment of the program, the *Rockefeller Commission Report* concluded that parts of Operation CHAOS were illegal, and the Senate investigating committee found that a major purpose of CHAOS was to support the FBI's internal security work.

Army Intelligence compiled files on some hundred thousand Amer-

---

* Thirty years later, Felt was revealed to be the "Deep Throat" contact who fed the *Washington Post* reporters Carl Bernstein and Bob Woodward the inside material that broke open the Watergate scandal.

icans and virtually every group working for peaceful change in America. The investigations focused on all the usual suspects on the left, but also included right-wing organizations like the John Birch Society and Young Americans for Freedom, as well as such middle-of-the-road groups as the Urban League, the NAACP, the National Organization for Women, the Anti-Defamation League of B'nai B'rith, and Business Executives to End the War in Vietnam. The quality of this intelligence was on a par with the FBI's; in a 1972 report titled *Army Surveillance of Civilians*, the Senate Subcommittee on Constitutional Rights found that the files were notable only for "their utter uselessness . . . [T]he Army . . . was merely wasting time, money and manpower, and infringing on the rights of the citizens it was supposed to be safeguarding."[45]

The NSA's Project MINARET, begun in 1967, compiled "watch lists" of names, ranging "from members of radical political groups, to celebrities, to ordinary citizens involved in protests against their Government."[46]

In March 1970, in order to coordinate all the intelligence efforts and facilitate better surveillance of the dissident movements sweeping the country, the presidential assistant Tom Huston suggested that Nixon order an overarching review of intelligence gathering. The president agreed, and on June 5 he convened a White House meeting of top intelligence officials, where he appointed a committee to improve the quality of intelligence, particularly vis-à-vis the New Left. In less than three weeks, the Interagency Committee on Intelligence (Ad Hoc)—consisting of Hoover; the CIA's director, Richard Helms; the director of the Defense Intelligence Agency, Lieutenant General Donald V. Bennett; and the NSA's director, Vice Admiral Noel Gayler—produced a report dealing with how to close intelligence gaps and enhance coordination among the intelligence agencies. What the report kept secret, however, were what the Senate investigating committee called "the improper domestic activities of the CIA and FBI," including the mail-opening program, Operation CHAOS, and various COINTELPROs that were unknown outside the bureau.[47]

Huston summarized the report and recommended that Nixon implement the recommendations for relaxing the restrictions on domestic intelligence collection. These included giving intelligence and counterintelligence agents the authority to "(1) monitor the international communications of U.S. citizens; (2) intensify the electronic surveillance of domestic dissenters and selected establishments; (3) read the international mail of American citizens; (4) break into specified establishments and into homes of domestic dissenters; and, (5) intensify the surveillance of American college students."[48]

On July 14, Nixon approved the proposals, a decision that later provided the basis for Article II of the House of Representatives' impeachment charges against him. On July 23, Huston wrote to Hoover, Helms, Bennett, and Gayler, giving them the green light to remove the indicated restrictions on intelligence gathering. Four days later, however, Nixon had a change of mind and retracted his approval.

Despite Nixon's rescinding his endorsement of the Huston Plan, as it has come to be known, the intelligence agencies implemented several of its provisions on their own, including the expansion of the NSA's watch lists and the CIA's mail-opening and CHAOS operations. The FBI lowered its minimum age for informers to eighteen, in order to increase its surveillance activities on college campuses. The agencies also formed a permanent interagency committee, as suggested in the Huston Plan.

The Huston Plan was not an aberration. The 1970s Senate investigating committee found that, "placed in perspective, the Huston Plan must be viewed as but a single example of a continuous effort by counterintelligence specialists to expand collection capabilities at home and abroad often without the knowledge or approval of the President or the Attorney General, and certainly without the knowledge of Congress or the people." The committee also discovered that the intelligence agencies hid illegal programs from one another. At its most profound level, "the Huston Plan episode is a story of lawlessness and impropriety at the highest levels of government."[49]

After Nixon resigned the presidency in August 1974, the syndicated Washington columnist Joseph Kraft, who had been the subject of an intense eavesdropping effort beginning in 1969—including occasions when he was out of the country—looked back on the Nixon years and reflected, "We came a hell of a lot closer to a police state than I thought possible."[50]

The series of events that reversed the movement toward such a state began on March 8, 1971. As most of America watched the heavyweight title fight between Joe Frazier and Muhammad Ali that evening, three or four individuals broke into the Media, Pennsylvania, office of the FBI and made off with more than a thousand documents from the office's unlocked file cabinets. The raiders were part of a twenty-person team that called itself the Citizens' Commission to Investigate the FBI.*

After waiting two weeks, during which time the mystery of the break-in deepened, the group began mailing small batches of select documents to legislators and reporters, and also sent some papers to the individual groups that were the subject of them. *The Washington Post* and *The New York Times* began to cover the story and even publish some of the papers, rejecting Attorney General John Mitchell's argument that divulging the documents "could endanger the lives or cause other serious harm to persons engaged in investigative activities on behalf of the United States."[51] The slow release of the purloined papers guaranteed maximum exposure, as the tactic kept the story in the news for months.

Even before the NBC reporter Carl Stern noticed the cryptic word "COINTELPRO" at the top of a relatively unimportant memo on the New Left and began investigating its meaning, the dissemination of the Media documents was a devastating blow to the credibility of the FBI. They revealed the bureau to be a secret police force that had its tentacles around every aspect of American life. As Mark Felt later wrote, the Media break-in was "a watershed event. The selective and sustained publication of the stolen documents changed the FBI's image, possibly forever in the minds of many Americans."[52]

As a result of the disclosures made by the documents stolen in the Media break-in and the subsequent furor, Hoover ordered the end of all existing COINTELPROs on April 28. But the memo to the SACs also left the door open for future COINTELPRO-like operations by saying, "In exceptional instances where counterintelligence action is warranted, it will be considered on a highly selective individual basis with tight procedures to insure absolute security."[53] In fact, as late as July 1976, *The New York Times* reported that FBI agents had been involved in assaults, wiretapping, and the burning of automobiles as they carried out security investigations in the preceding five years. Agents beat up antiwar leaders to intimidate them and kidnapped at least one individual for the same reason. The bureau also conducted

---

* This break-in was the group's only known action, and none of the members has ever been publicly identified.

COINTELPRO-like operations against the women's movement and the American Indian Movement, and any number of agents continued to engage in COINTELPRO-like actions on their own, with or without official bureau approval. "The full extent," observes Nancy Chang in *Silencing Political Dissent*, "to which COINTELPRO shifted the trajectory of political life in the United States will never be known."[54]

With the Media break-in, Hoover and the bureau came under heavy fire. On the floor of the House of Representatives on March 31, Majority Leader Hale Boggs, Democrat of Louisiana, demanded that Hoover resign. At the beginning of April, *Life* featured a cover story suggesting that his forty-seven-year reign as "Emperor of the FBI" should end. Days later, in the Dow Jones weekly, *The National Observer*, a story titled "The Life and Times of a 76-Year-Old Cop" described how, while "pursuing a hot case, Mr. Hoover was seen holding onto the corridor wall for strength." Enraged, Hoover unsuccessfully tried to get the author of the story, Nina Totenberg, fired. In early May, a *Newsweek* cover story, "Hoover's FBI: Time for a Change?" cited a Gallup poll in which 51 percent of people interviewed believed it was time for the director to retire.[55]

At seventy-six, Hoover was six years past the mandatory retirement age for government employees, and clearly in decline. His already tenuous hold on reality was slipping even further. William Sullivan, who was once considered his heir apparent, and whose falling-out with Hoover has been documented in detail, later remarked that Hoover had seemed "stark, raving mad" and "not of sound mind" from 1969 on. "He became extremely erratic," recalled Sullivan. "If you crossed him, he'd go into a rage."[56]

At the beginning of 1972, Sullivan spoke publicly for the first time since having been forced into retirement by Hoover three months earlier, following an exchange of letters in which Sullivan had had the audacity to criticize the director and provide him with an unsolicited assessment of the bureau's shortcomings. Now, on January 10, in accepting a job with an insurance investigative agency, Sullivan said he was pleased to be "associated with a new enterprise which does not suffer from fossilized bureaucratic traditions and obsolete policies."[57]

The following month, *Win* magazine, a publication of the War

Resisters League, printed a nearly complete collection of the documents stolen in the Media break-in.

On May 1, Jack Anderson's syndicated column, which appeared in about a thousand newspapers, contained a scorching attack on Hoover and the FBI. Hoover hated Anderson, having referred to him on various occasions as a "flea ridden dog," an "odious garbage collector," "lower than dog shit," and "lower than the regurgitated filth of vultures."[58]

In the piece, Anderson ripped the director for indulging his prurient interest in innocent people's private lives while neglecting the job of fighting crime. "FBI chief J. Edgar Hoover, the old curmudgeon of law enforcement," wrote Anderson, "fiercely resisted a White House suggestion that he spare a few hundred agents to crack down on drug abuses. But he can spare agents to snoop into the sex habits, business affairs and political pursuits of individuals who aren't even remotely involved in illegal activity." Anderson named Ralph Abernathy, Muhammad Ali, Harry Belafonte, Marlon Brando, Joe Louis, and Joe Namath as being among the "diverse figures" whose files contained "titillating tidbits." "Hoover . . . appears to have a hang-up on sex. His gumshoes go out of their way to find out who's sleeping with whom in Washington and Hollywood." The column also stated that "no American who speaks his mind is altogether safe from the all-seeing FBI" and observed, "The FBI keeps a particularly hostile eye on newsmen who are critical of government policies," citing the "indefatigable muckraker I. F. Stone" as an example. Noting that "it's no secret that the FBI hounded the late Dr. Martin Luther King Jr., the apostle of racial brotherhood and nonviolent protest," Anderson further revealed "Now the FBI is watching his widow, Coretta King."[59] All in all, it was as scathing a public attack as had ever been leveled at Hoover.

The following morning, the director was found dead at his home. The official cause of death was high blood pressure, and some in the bureau said it was Anderson's May Day column that killed him. Hoover was eight days shy of his forty-eighth anniversary as head of the FBI.

The series of events that reversed the drift toward authoritarianism in America gained added momentum during the Watergate scandal, which was triggered by the arrest of five men for breaking and entering

Democratic National Committee headquarters on June 17, 1972. The scandal brought down Nixon's presidency, revealing the methods and tactics used by the administration against the Democratic Party— the same types of methods and tactics employed by the FBI in its COINTELPRO operations—and leading to Nixon's resignation on August 9, 1974.

By then, the NBC reporter Carl Stern had managed, after repeated refusals by the Justice Department, to obtain through the Freedom of Information Act several of the FBI's COINTELPRO documents, including the May 1968 memo authorizing COINTELPRO– New Left and the April 1971 communication canceling all existing COINTELPROs. Additional requests for COINTELPRO documents came pouring in from a number of sources, including other journalists, the Senate committee investigating Watergate, the House Judiciary Committee, and the Senate Judiciary Committee.

The growing furor prompted Attorney General William Saxbe to form an internal Justice Department committee to investigate COINTELPRO operations. The committee's report, issued in November 1974, was essentially a whitewash that attempted to justify the programs by placing them in "the context and climate" in which they had been established. The report disingenuously insisted that while some COINTELPRO activities involved "isolated instances of practices that can only be considered abhorrent in a free society, . . . these improper activities were not the[ir] purpose or indeed even the[ir] major characteristic."[60]

The following month, *The New York Times* published a front-page story by Seymour Hersh that blew open the CIA's extensive, illegal involvement in domestic surveillance of the antiwar movement and other dissident groups, going back to the 1950s. Hersh's piece listed dozens of illegal actions, including break-ins, wiretapping, and the interception of mail.

On January 27, 1975, the Senate voted to establish the Senate Select Committee to Study Governmental Operations with Respect to Intelligence Activities, chaired by the Idaho Democrat Frank Church. Assisted by a 150-member support staff, the panel of six Democrats and five Republicans met for nine months, issuing fourteen reports in 1975 and 1976 that consisted of over fifty thousand pages, the bulk of which has been made public. The reports documented the full story of the COINTELPRO operations, as well as offering a wide-ranging account of the activities of the CIA and other civilian and military intelligence agencies going back decades, all of which pointed to the propensity of intelligence operatives to regard themselves as above the law.

The Church Committee summarized its findings as follows:

> Too many people have been spied upon by too many Government agencies and too much information has been collected. The Government has often undertaken the secret surveillance of citizens on the basis of their political beliefs, even when those beliefs posed no threat of violence or illegal acts on behalf of a hostile foreign power. The Government, operating primarily through secret informants, but also using other intrusive techniques such as wiretaps, microphone "bugs," surreptitious mail opening, and break-ins, has swept in vast amounts of information about the personal lives, views, and associations of American citizens. Investigations of groups deemed potentially dangerous—and even of groups suspected of associating with potentially dangerous organizations—have continued for decades, despite the fact that those groups did not engage in unlawful activity. Groups and individuals have been harassed and disrupted because of their political views and their lifestyles. Investigations have been based upon vague standards whose breadth made excessive collection inevitable. Unsavory and vicious tactics have been employed—including anonymous attempts to break up marriages, disrupt meetings, ostracize persons from their professions, and provoke target groups into rivalries that might result in deaths . . .
>
> Government officials—including those whose principal duty is to enforce the law—have violated or ignored the law over long periods of time and have advocated and defended their right to break the law.[61]

In light of the committee's revelations, President Gerald Ford instructed Attorney General Edward Levi to formulate new guidelines that would limit governmental surveillance. Levi took his cue from Harlan Fiske Stone's 1924 curbs on the FBI's forerunner, stressing that the new "domestic security guidelines proceed from the proposition that Government monitoring of individuals or groups because they hold unpopular or controversial political views is intolerable in our society."[62] Echoing Stone's restraints, the 1976 guidelines placed strict limitations on the FBI, restricting the bureau's investigative authority to criminal activity, forbidding the investigation of individuals and groups not advocating violence, and prohibiting the disruption of groups or the discrediting of individuals legally exercising their First Amendment rights. "All investigations undertaken through these guidelines shall be designed and conducted so as not to limit the full exercise of rights protected by the Constitution and laws of the United States."[63] Equally important, the Levi guidelines provided a structure to safeguard these limits on the bureau's power.

In keeping with the new rules, the FBI ended its thirty-eight-year-long investigation of the Socialist Workers Party, which, despite some eight million file entries, had resulted in just one prosecution—thirty-five years earlier, under the Smith Act, in a case that Attorney General Francis Biddle later called a mistake.

The new strictures imposed on the FBI by the Levi guidelines were complemented by similar restraints on the CIA, the NSA, and the other intelligence agencies. The days of manufactured hysteria, governmental scapegoating, rampant surveillance, and secret rule were supposedly at an end.

Epilogue: An Aggressive Assault on Civil Liberties

Significant step forward though they were, the Levi guidelines suffered from the same limitation as Harlan Fiske Stone's 1924 directives—they were not law. Although the Church Committee recommended legislation, the National Intelligence Reorganization and Reform Act of 1978—which would have established statutory charters for all intelligence agencies, as well as created a director of national intelligence—never made it out of committee in either house of Congress. Accordingly, subsequent administrations were free to modify the Levi guidelines as they pleased.

In fact, not even a decade passed before another attorney general began chipping away at Levi's standards. In 1983, President Ronald Reagan's attorney general, William French Smith, broadened the guidelines in several areas. Under Smith's rules, the FBI was allowed to (1) take notes and photographs of people at public demonstrations without any indication of illegal activity, (2) use informants and infiltrate organizations during preliminary investigations without any reasonable suspicion of illegal activity, and (3) investigate individuals and organizations who advocated illegal activity without any likelihood of such conduct actually occurring. Nevertheless, despite these modifications, the core of the Levi guidelines remained intact.

In a direct breach of the new guidelines, however, the FBI, during Reagan's presidency, resumed its practice of spying on American citizens engaged in legal political activity. With orders to collect "information on the locations, leadership, and activities of CISPES," the bureau infiltrated the Committee in Solidarity with the People of El

Salvador, an organization opposed to U.S. foreign policy in Central America.[1] Although the FBI found no evidence of illegal action, the scrutiny continued for four years, during which time the bureau compiled files on 2,375 individuals and 1,330 additional groups other than CISPES. In the course of these investigations, agents photographed peaceful demonstrations, watched rallies on college campuses, conducted surveillance of churches and church groups, infiltrated countless meetings, inspected trash, collected mailing lists and phone numbers, recorded license plates, and obtained records of long-distance telephone calls. Despite the massive effort, there was not a single criminal charge filed—as had been the case so many times over the years.

A General Accounting Office study of the FBI during the Reagan years reported that between January 1982 and June 1988, the bureau carried out approximately 19,500 terrorism investigations, but in only 12 percent of those cases had the agency actually received any reliable information to indicate that the subject of the investigation was directly involved in terrorist activity.

During President Bill Clinton's early days in office, nativism underwent a reawakening after a group of radical Muslims detonated a car bomb in the underground parking lot of the World Trade Center in lower Manhattan in February 1993, killing six people and injuring more than a thousand. The FBI quickly established the identities of ten Muslim fundamentalists who were involved in the crime—which was intended to be merely the first in a series of bombings in and around New York City.

Arabs and Muslims had actually been in the FBI's crosshairs as early as November 1986, when a secret interagency task force known as the Alien Border Control Committee sent the Justice Department a report called "Alien Terrorists and Undesirables: A Contingency Plan."[2] The report accurately listed a number of Arab countries as being likely sources of terrorists, but in a disquieting echo of the scapegoating that occurred during the two world wars, it also proposed the construction of a remote detention camp in Louisiana to hold "alien undesirables" while they awaited deportation.

After the 1993 World Trade Center attack, the FBI zeroed in on alien Arabs and Arab-Americans. Writing in the *Georgetown Immigra-*

tion Law Journal in 1999, Susan Akram reported that FBI and INS agents had conducted widespread investigations of Arab and Arab-American communities in many U.S. cities, including Detroit, Los Angeles, New York, San Francisco, and Tampa. Seeking information that would inform the government about terrorist activities, agents threatened individuals with deportation proceedings against them or their relatives unless they informed on friends, relations, or neighbors.[3]

When the Alfred P. Murrah Federal Building in Oklahoma City was destroyed by a forty-eight-hundred-pound car bomb on April 19, 1995, in a manner reminiscent of the World Trade Center explosion, suspicion fell first on Middle Eastern terrorists, but law-enforcement agencies quickly determined that the attack had been carried out by homegrown American extremists. Within weeks, the FBI's director, Louis J. Freeh, told Congress that the Justice Department had agreed to allow the bureau to "reinterpret" the Smith guidelines and initiate an investigation of "a domestic terrorism group if that group advocated violence or force with respect to achieving any political or social objectives," even without any evidence of an actual or imminent violation of the law.[4]

It was a slippery slope. Ira Glasser, director of the ACLU, called the new approach a dangerous step backward. "Any time you abandon the idea of a criminal predicate for an investigation, you have to find something else," he warned. "What would that be? Maybe it's national origin, maybe race, maybe political beliefs, maybe militant rhetoric. That's been the history of the F.B.I. which we have come to deplore. When you don't use a criminal predicate, you must find some other proxy that inevitably tramples on constitutional principles."[5]

The Oklahoma and New York attacks also led to the passage of the Antiterrorism and Effective Death Penalty Act of 1996.[6] Among other provisions, the law further eroded the Levi/Smith guidelines, granting the FBI greater investigative powers, making it illegal to contribute to a group designated a "foreign terrorist organization," and creating a distinct deportation process for aliens accused of being terrorists. In *Terrorism and the Constitution*, the Georgetown University law professor David Cole and the director of the Center for Democracy and Technology, James X. Dempsey, labeled the statute "one of the worst assaults on the Constitution in decades," noting, "It resurrected guilt by association as a principle of criminal and immigration law. It created a special court to use secret evidence to deport foreigners labeled as 'terrorists.' It made support for the peaceful humanitarian and political activities of selected foreign groups a crime."[7]

Ethnic and religious communities were not the only targeted groups. After the 1999 protests against the World Trade Organization in Seattle, the FBI went after the antiglobalization movement, using many of the same techniques that had been employed in the COINTELPRO operations. "We want to be proactive and keep these things from happening," the FBI spokesman Gordon Compton told the press.[8]

Nothing in the premillennial era, however, could have prepared Americans for the far-reaching effects brought about by the events of September 11, 2001.

In the days and weeks following the strikes on the Twin Towers and the Pentagon, there were hundreds of attacks on Arab and Arab-American Muslims and Christians. Several people were murdered, and a number of mosques were attacked. Sikhs, Baha'is, and Hispanics were also targeted.

While President George W. Bush commendably denounced such behavior, saying it represented "the worst of humankind,"[9] his administration was at the same time misusing immigration law to round up more than 750 alien Arabs and Muslims and hold them without charges for months, until they could be cleared of any involvement in terrorism before being deported—procedures that Attorney General John Ashcroft defended as "aggressive arrest and detention tactics in the war on terror."[10] A June 2003 report on the arrests by the Justice Department's inspector general, however, found that many of the detainees were incarcerated on nothing more than suspicion, with no shred of evidence against them.

More than six months after 9/11, Arab and Muslim communities in the United States were still suffering the psychological effects of the aftermath. "Our people are still terrorized," said Randall Hamud, a Lebanese-American lawyer who defended Arab immigrants arrested after 9/11. "Even those who are naturalized US citizens feel the fear."[11] In a situation that harked back to the plight of German aliens and German-Americans during World War I, of Mexican aliens and

Mexican-Americans during the Great Depression and Operation Wetback, and of Japanese aliens and Japanese-Americans after Pearl Harbor, Arab immigrants and Arab-Americans faced political profiling, as their patriotism was now perceived to be inherently suspect and in need of proving. And just as liberals and leftists suffered from self-censorship during the Cold War, the Arab-American community experienced a chilling effect after 9/11. Michel Shehadeh, western regional director of the American-Arab Anti-Discrimination Committee, observed, "Throughout our community people have started to not attend group activities. Membership in organizations has dropped. Subscriptions to publications have dropped. More and more people are changing their names. Lots of students have left the country . . . It's very, very sad."[12]

Following the example of earlier administrations, but far exceeding those earlier models, the Bush government exploited fears engendered by 9/11 in order to carry out blatant crackdowns on civil liberties and dissent, and usher in a new era of broad-based government spying. The full history of George W. Bush's presidency will be written in the decades to come, but a quick sketch of those years reveals a White House and Congress bent on repression as the means to achieving an authoritarian agenda.

In October 2001, Congress passed the USA PATRIOT Act, authorizing law-enforcement agencies to share information obtained in criminal investigations with intelligence agencies, including the CIA and NSA, as well as with other federal departments, including the INS, Department of Defense, and Secret Service. The legislation also allows law-enforcement agencies to share—without a court order and with no significant restrictions on subsequent use—intercepted telephone conversations and e-mail communications.

By February 2002, less than six months after 9/11, the ACLU of Northern California reported that "the Bush administration has already launched an aggressive assault on civil liberties in the name of national security: detaining hundreds of foreign-born suspects with little regard for due process, eroding client-attorney privilege, announcing proposals for military tribunals, and rounding up young men based on their national origin."[13]

In April, in a misguided effort to reinforce public security, Bush unveiled the Terrorism Information and Prevention System, a program reminiscent of World War I's American Protective League. Under TIPS, cable technicians, letter carriers, meter readers, ship captains, truck drivers, and other workers were to be responsible for reporting "suspicious" activity to law-enforcement officials. The subsequent outcry over the prospect of Americans spying on one another led Congress to deny funding for the program.*

On May 30, Ashcroft announced that he was scrapping the Levi/Smith guidelines, saying they "have hampered our ability to fight terrorism."[14] The FBI was now authorized to monitor libraries, political groups, religious organizations—including houses of worship—and the Internet.

By then, the National Security Agency was secretly scrutinizing—under a presidential order and without court-approved warrants—the international phone calls and e-mails of hundreds, perhaps thousands, of individuals within the United States. When *The New York Times* brought the program to light in December 2005, a former senior official in the area of national security law said, "This is really a sea change. It's almost a mainstay of this country that the N.S.A. only does foreign searches."[15] In April 2010, a federal judge ruled that the program was illegal.

The Bush administration was also conducting—similarly without court-approved warrants or subpoenas—a secret operation that examined the banking transactions of thousands of Americans and others in this country. The program was once again revealed by the *Times*, which called it another of the administration's "attempts to break down longstanding legal or institutional barriers to the government's access to private information about Americans and others inside the United States."[16] The program was instituted as an emergency response to 9/11, but when the *Times* broke the story in June 2006, what had begun as an "urgent, temporary measure had become permanent

---

* The TIPS idea was later picked up by the Department of Homeland Security and put into practice as the School Bus Watch program, with the intent of training 600,000 school bus drivers to report on "suspicious" behavior. At least one former Homeland Security intelligence official, John Rollins, found the prospect alarming. "Today, it's bus drivers, tomorrow it could be postal officials," he cautioned, "and the next day, it could be, 'Why don't we have this program in place for the people who deliver the newspaper to the door?' We could quickly get into a society where we're all spying on each other. It may be well intentioned, but there is a concern of going a bit too far" (*Fredericksburg* [Va.] *Free Lance-Star*, Feb. 18, 2006).

nearly five years later without specific Congressional approval or formal authorization."*

In a throwback to the Vietnam War era, the FBI made a practice of scrutinizing demonstrations against the U.S. occupation of Iraq. A statement by a bureau spokesman sounded a disheartening reprise of past justifications for monitoring peaceful and legal protest: "We're not concerned with individuals who are exercising their constitutional rights. But it's obvious that there are individuals capable of violence at these events. We know that there are anarchists that are actively involved in trying to sabotage and commit acts of violence at these events, and we also know that these large gatherings would be a prime target for terrorist groups."[17] Yet a month before this rationalization was offered, an FBI memo stated that the bureau "possesses no information indicating that violent or terrorist activities are being planned as part of these protests."[18] The bureau also spied on other "dissident" groups, including Greenpeace, the People for the Ethical Treatment of Animals, and the ACLU.

The Pentagon also kept track of peace groups and political organizations judged to be hostile to the Bush administration. Beginning in May 2003, a secret program called Threat and Local Observation Notice—initiated by Deputy Secretary of Defense Paul Wolfowitz—was used to gather information on war protesters. TALON, which was intended to collect unconfirmed "threat information and security anomalies" that might indicate planned terrorist attacks,[19] also yielded reports on dozens of peaceful organizations and events, including Truth Project, a small Florida group that set up antimilitary informational tables alongside military recruiters at high schools; a street-theater presentation outside the headquarters of Halliburton in Texas; a Students Against War protest at the University of California, Santa Cruz; and a Veterans for Peace demonstration at New Mexico State

---

* One of the hallmarks of the Bush government was its obsession with secrecy, and the administration asked the *Times* not to publish both the wiretapping and the banking stories. The paper delayed publication of the first for a year in order to do additional research, and agreed to omit some information that administration officials claimed could be "useful to terrorists." In the case of the second story, the newspaper decided that it was "a matter of public interest" and went ahead with publication. The administration was not pleased in either case: in the second piece, the White House deputy press secretary, Dana Perino, was quoted as saying, "The President is concerned that once again The New York Times has chosen to expose a classified program that is working to protect our citizens."

University in Las Cruces. All together, the database contained 263 reports on 180 antiwar groups and events

In the 2005 NBC News story that made TALON public, the former Army Intelligence officer Christopher Pyle—whose January 1970 article in *The Washington Monthly* had blown the whistle on the military's spying on antiwar and civil rights groups during the Vietnam War era—said, "The documents tell me that military intelligence is back conducting investigations and maintaining records on civilian political activity. The military made promises that it would not do this again."[20] TALON was cut back after the NBC News story was published, and two years later it was terminated.

But TALON was merely one component of a much larger operation called Counterintelligence Field Activity, created by executive order in February 2002 to establish a database that contains information concerning potential terrorist threats against the Department of Defense. The "terrorists" who were monitored under CIFA included gay, lesbian, and bisexual groups at New York University and at the Berkeley and Santa Cruz campuses of the University of California.

Between 2002 and 2006, FBI agents illegally searched more than two thousand telephone records, under the false pretext of nonexistent terrorism "emergencies." The phone records collected included those of *Washington Post* and *New York Times* reporters. The FBI lawyer Patrice Kopistansky tried to alert her superiors, e-mailing them, "We have to make sure we are not taking advantage of this system, and that we are following the letter of the law without jeopardizing national security," but the illegalities continued for another two years after her warning.[21]

In *It Can Happen Here*, Joe Conason summed up the Bush government's cavalier attitude toward constitutional guarantees when he wrote that "the mind-set of the administration . . . [is] reflected in all of the illegal or dubious surveillance programs that the . . . regime has instigated. They are all important because they demonstrate the unilateral will of the president to use any means at his disposal, whether approved by Congress and the courts or not, and his utter determination to create a surveillance society that no longer vests any meaning in traditional ideas of freedom and privacy."[22] This attitude was unfortunately supported by a large majority in Congress, as well as by a large segment of the American public.

. . .

While the election of President Barack Obama may have stemmed the all-out assault on civil liberties that had been mounted during Bush's two terms in office, it would be a mistake to conclude that the threat is past. The Alien Enemies Act and the USA PATRIOT Act are still on the books; nativism, Islamophobia, and homophobia are vigorously on the march; and minorities and dissidents remain vulnerable.

In the summer of 2009, it came to light that in the cities of Olympia and Tacoma, Washington, the Army had infiltrated and was spying on both the antiwar group Port Militarization Resistance and a local chapter of SDS.

In Arizona, a controversial statute enacted in 2010 requires immigrants to carry their papers at all times and empowers police to stop and check the immigration status of anybody suspected of being in the country illegally. Polls taken shortly after the passage of the law indicated that a majority of Americans supported it.

In New York City, police have compiled a database of nearly 2.8 million people who were stopped on the street between 2005 and 2009, and although close to 90 percent were utterly innocent of any offense, their names remain in the computer.[23] "Information contained in the stop, question and frisk database remains there indefinitely, for use in future investigations," NYC's police commissioner, Ray Kelly, informed the city council in 2009. "Therefore, there are no existing Police Department guidelines that mandate the removal of information once it has been entered in the database."[24] Fifty-two percent of the people stopped were African-Americans, 30 percent were Latinos, and 10 percent were whites, and the rest were members of other racial or ethnic groups.

In 1975, while chairing the Senate committee investigating abuses conducted by intelligence agencies in this country, Frank Church spoke of the "very extensive capability of intercepting messages" and warned that this capacity "at any time could be turned around on the American people, and no American would have any privacy left, such is the capability to monitor everything, telephone conversations, telegrams. It doesn't matter. There would be no place to hide."[25]

More than three and a half decades on, technology has advanced the government's surveillance power a quantum leap beyond what it was when Church issued his alert. But while the surveillance apparatus that has played such a key role in the scapegoating of one or another minority group since World War I is more pervasive and invasive than ever, it is not necessarily more efficient. As a July 2010 investigative series in *The Washington Post* reported, the staggering number of organizations—1,271 government agencies and 1,931 private companies—working on intelligence programs in the United States creates significant "redundancy and waste," as "many security and intelligence agencies do the same work." Moreover, the *Post* found, the sheer volume of intelligence reports—fifty thousand published every year—guarantees that many are "routinely ignored."[26]

As of this writing, there have been two thwarted suicide bombings on U.S.-bound airplanes, an unsuccessful car bombing of Times Square, and assorted other attempted terrorist attacks on U.S. targets. Clearly, rigorous security measures are required, but as we "reposition the line between law enforcement and individual rights," as Stephen J. Schulhofer has written in *The Enemy Within*, we will be well-advised to keep in mind that such an adjustment does not imply the need to "suspend the mechanism of accountability and control that traditionally frame governmental power. If anything, there may be *more* need as government investigative power expands."[27]

Democracy requires vigilance. It is fragile and can be undermined. In his introduction to Louis Post's *Deportations Delirium of Nineteen-Twenty*, the lawyer and civil rights activist Moorfield Storey warned of the danger of taking democracy for granted. "We read with pride the Declaration of Independence," cautioned Storey,

> and we boast of our wonderful Constitution with the security it affords to the meanest citizen. We pride ourselves on our freedom of speech, our protection against unwarrantable searches and seizures, the bulwark against oppression afforded by our right to due process of law, and we comfortably assume that in practice the provisions of the Constitution are respected . . . As an abstract proposition it does not seem possible to us that the officers of the United States should under pretense of enforcing the laws trample on the Constitution, and we drift on compla-

cently assured of our safety, in the confident belief that all is going well under the best of all possible governments.[28]

One of the most insidious degradations of democracy is the scapegoating of minorities—be they ethnic, racial, religious, political, or sexual—because to deny the civil liberties of any specific group, even in the name of national security, is to take the first step toward curtailing the civil liberties of all. It is a testament to the resiliency of the American political system that despite the recurring persecutions of minorities since World War I—and the ensuing manufactured hysteria, clandestine violations of the Constitution, illegal surveillance of civilians, and concomitant threats to civil liberties—we have thus far managed to right the ship of state each time such a challenge to democracy has presented itself.

It would be imprudent, however, to assume that it will always be so. Each such trial has been more perilous than the previous one, and persisting in such behavior is manifestly reckless. One of these times, we could reach a point of no return.

Notes

Abbreviations

AG	Attorney General
Church Committee	Senate Select Committee to Study Governmental Operations with Respect to Intelligence Activities (see www.aarc library.org/publib/contents/church/contents_church_reports.htm)
CR	*Congressional Record*
CWRIC Papers	Commission on Wartime Relocation and Internment of Civilians
DOJ	Department of Justice
LAT	*Los Angeles Times*
LOC	Library of Congress
NARA	National Archive and Records Administration
NYT	*The New York Times*
U.S. Stat.	*United States Statutes at Large*
WP	*The Washington Post*

Prologue: Against the Wall

1. For more on the Prager affair, see Weinberg, *Labor, Loyalty, & Rebellion;* Schwartz, "Lynching of Robert Prager"; Hickey, "Prager Affair"; Luebke, *Bonds of Loyalty;* and Ott, "Anti-German Hysteria."

2. *St. Louis Labor,* April 13, 1918.

3. Creel, "Public Opinion in War Time," pp. 185–86; Creel, *How We Advertised America,* p. 5.

4. Frank Cobb, "The Press and Public Opinion," *New Republic,* Dec. 31, 1919, p. 144.

5. *Evening Sun,* Oct. 22, 1918, quoted in *Viereck's: The American Monthly,* Nov. 1918, p. 88. Another New York paper published a complete list of the names and addresses of all German and Austro-Hungarian alien enemies living in the city, and later published the list in a book edition (*New York Herald,* Dec. 3–28, 1917).

6. *El Paso Herald,* Dec. 24, 1917; *El Paso Morning Times,* Dec. 24, 1917.

7. National Civil Liberties Bureau, *War-Time Prosecutions and Mob Violence,* p. 6.

8. Ibid.

9. *Chicago Tribune,* March 2, 1918.

10. *Denver Post*, March 4, 1918.

11. *NYT*, March 4, 1918.

12. National Civil Liberties Bureau, *War-Time Prosecutions and Mob Violence*, p. 7. Others sources spell the name Schopke.

13. Quoted in Weinberg, *Labor, Loyalty, & Rebellion*, pp. 119–20.

14. *Collinsville Herald*, May 31, 1918.

15. *Collinsville Herald*, May 28, 1918.

16. *Collinsville Herald*, April 12, 1918.

17. *Collinsville Herald*, May 28, 1918.

18. Luebke, *Bonds of Loyalty*, p. 9.

19. *NYT*, April 11, 1918.

20. Translation by the author. The original German read: "Liebe Eltern, Ich muss heute den 4-4-18 sterben. Bitte betet fur mich, meine lieben Eltern. Das ist mein letze Brief oder Lebenzeugen von mir. Euer lieber Sohn und Bruder, Robt. Paul" (*St. Louis Post-Dispatch*, April 6, 1918). Prager's state of mind can be seen in his various misspellings (*fur* for *für, letze* for *letzte, Lebenzeugen* for *Lebenzeugen*). In this condition, it is possible he wrote *Lebenszeugen* (literally, "life witness") when he actually meant *Lebenszeichen*, "sign of life." The author is grateful to Gerhard Bock for his speculations on this matter, and for his assistance with the translation.

21. *NYT*, April 11, 1918.

22. Dunphy, "Lynching of Robert Prager," p. 37.

23. Truman, *Memoirs*, vol. 2, p. 272.

24. Wendell Phillips, *Speeches Before the Massachusetts Anti-Slavery Society*, p. 13. The quotation is often mistakenly attributed to Thomas Jefferson. The source of Phillips's remark may have been John Philpot Curran's July 10, 1790, "Speech on the Right of Election of Lord Mayor of Dublin," in which he said, "The condition upon which God hath given liberty to man is eternal vigilance."

Chapter 1: The Fine Gold of Untainted Americanism

1. Baker, Dodd, and Leach, *Public Papers of Woodrow Wilson*, vol. 3, p. 379.

2. Shaw, *Messages and Papers of Woodrow Wilson*, p. 150.

3. Ibid., pp. 150–51.

4. Creel, "Hopes of the Hyphenated," p. 350.

5. *Cincinnati Volksblatt*, Dec. 9, 1915, quoted in Wittke, *German-Americans and the World War*, p. 43.

6. La Follette, "Neutrality," p. 1.

7. *NYT*, Feb. 1, 1915.

8. "The decent Americans who are of German birth or descent ought to and in the majority of cases ultimately will stand for what I represent, just as other citizens do and will stand," wrote Roosevelt. "But the professional hyphenated German-Americans I shall smite with the sword of the Lord and of Gideon when ever I get the chance" (Roosevelt to William Franklin Knox, Dec. 21, 1915, in *Letters of Theodore Roosevelt*, vol. 8, p. 998).

9. *NYT*, May 15, 1915.

10. *Literary Digest*, Oct. 30, 1915, p. 943.

11. Editorial in *New York Evening Sun*, quoted in ibid., Aug. 28, 1915, p. 388; "The German Campaign Against American Neutrality," *Outlook*, Aug. 25, 1915, p. 934.

12. *NYT*, May 14, 1916.

13. Torelle, Barton, and Holmes, *Political Philosophy of Robert M. La Follette*, p. 194.

14. Villard to Wilson, Oct. 30, 1915, Villard Papers, Houghton Library, Harvard University.

15. Address of May 20, 1916, in Link, *Papers of Woodrow Wilson*, vol. 37, p. 81.

16. June 14, 1916, in Baker, Dodd, and Leach, *Public Papers of Woodrow Wilson*, vol. 4, pp. 209–10.

17. Roosevelt, *America for Americans*, pp. 3–4.

18. On July 22, the San Francisco Chamber of Commerce sponsored a parade that attracted over fifty thousand marchers, but a half hour after the start of the pageant a bomb exploded near the Ferry Building at Steuart and Market streets, killing ten people and injuring forty. Within days, two high-profile Socialist labor leaders, Tom Mooney and Warren Billings, were arrested and charged with murder. The trials that followed were a travesty of justice, complete with perjured testimony, false evidence, and prosecutorial conspiracy. Mooney and Billings were convicted and received death and life sentences, respectively, but in the outcry that followed, Mooney's sentence was reduced to life. Despite revelations, within the year after their convictions, that both men had been framed, Mooney and Billings spent more than twenty years in San Quentin before being pardoned by California's governor Culbert Olson in 1939.

19. Democratic National Committee, *Democratic Text Book 1916*, p. 9.

20. Villard to G. F. Peabody, Sept. 19, 1916, Villard Papers.

21. 39 *U.S. Stat.* 919.

22. Chafee, "Sedition," p. 638.

23. *Annual Report of the Attorney General of the United States for the Year 1918*, p. 56.

24. *NYT*, March 1, 1917.

25. *NYT*, March 2, 1917.

26. *NYT*, March 24, 1917.

27. *LAT*, April 2, 1917.

28. Jordan, *Days of a Man*, p. 728.

29. *NYT*, April 3, 1917.

30. Ibid. Also see "An Address to a Joint Session of Congress," April 2, 1917, in Link, *Papers of Woodrow Wilson*, vol. 41, pp. 519–27.

31. *Cincinnati Times-Star*, March 5, 1917.

32. Roosevelt to Henry Cabot Lodge, Feb. 20, 1917, in *Letters of Theodore Roosevelt*, vol. 8, p. 1157.

33. See *CR* 55, 65th Cong., 1st sess., pp. 224–34.

34. Pinchot, *History of the Progressive Party*, p. 128.

35. *CR* 55, 65th Cong., 1st sess., p. 209.

36. Ibid., pp. 212–14.

37. *NYT*, April 6, 1917.

38. *CR* 55, 65th Cong., 1st sess., p. 337.

39. Ibid., p. 332.

40. Kennedy, *Over Here*, p. 20.

Chapter 2: A Democracy Gone Mad

1. Other signs read, "A Liberty Bond Is a First Mortgage on Labor," "War Is Hell, Jingo Capitalists Should Go to War," "Down with Secret Diplomacy. Capitalism Must Go," "We Are Not Pacifists, We Believe in War upon Our Enemy—Capitalism," and "Democratize Germany, What About Frisco and the Danbury Hatters?" The account

of the parade is based on articles in *Boston Globe*, *NYT*, *New York Call*, *Boston Evening Record*, *Boston Journal* (all July 2, 1917), and *Milwaukee Leader* (July 9, 1917).

2. See *Chicago Tribune* and *NYT*, May 28, 1917.

3. Wilson to Cleveland H. Dodge, April 4, 1917, Woodrow Wilson Papers, Manuscripts Division, LOC.

4. *Report of the Attorney General for 1917*, pp. 57–59.

5. Ibid., p. 56.

6. Warren to Gregory, March 30, 1917, DOJ file 9-4-94½, NARA.

7. Shaw, *Messages and Papers of Woodrow Wilson*, p. 150.

8. *Report of the Attorney General for 1918*, pp. 16–17.

9. Quoted in Mock and Larson, *Words That Won the War*, p. 23.

10. See Chapter 1, above.

11. AUAM to Wilson, April 17, 1917, ACLU files, vol. 26, reel 3, Mudd Library, Princeton University.

12. Scheiber, *Wilson Administration and Civil Liberties*, p. 16.

13. O'Brian, "Civil Liberty in War Time," pp. 280–81.

14. Daniels, *Cabinet Diaries*, p. 173.

15. *NYT*, Sept. 1, 1915.

16. Creel, *Rebel at Large*, p. 196.

17. For the most complete history of the American Protective League, see Jensen, *Price of Vigilance*. Also see Hough, *Web*.

18. A. Bruce Bielaski to Special Agents, March 22, 1917, Daniel Frey Papers, UCLA.

19. *Official Bulletin*, May 12, 1917.

20. O'Brian, "Civil Liberty in War Time," p. 279.

21. Roche, *Quest for the Dream*, p. 43.

22. Hough, *Web*, p. 163.

23. "Suggestions of Attorney-General Gregory to Executive Committee in Relation to the Department of Justice," p. 309.

24. Cummings and McFarland, *Federal Justice*, p. 420.

25. Jensen, *Army Surveillance in America*, p. 137.

26. Koons to Postmasters, April 25, 1917, reprinted in *Official Bulletin*, May 10, 1917.

27. Nagler, "Victims of the Home Front," p. 204.

28. *Report of the Attorney General for 1918*, p. 15.

29. *Literary Digest*, June 9, 1917; *NYT*, June 6, 1917.

30. Young, *Fifteen Patriotic Editorials from "The Des Moines Capital,"* pp. 1–2, italics added.

31. Hulet M. Wells Papers, Special Collections, University of Washington Libraries.

32. *NYT*, May 19, 1917.

33. Murphy, *World War I and the Origin of Civil Liberties in the United States*, p. 211.

34. See ublib.buffalo.edu/libraries/exhibits/panam/law/images/tragedyatbuff.html.

35. Goldman, "Promoters of the War Mania," pp. 5–11.

36. Quoted in Drinnon, *Rebel in Paradise*, p. 21.

37. *NYT*, June 6, 1917.

38. *NYT*, June 12, 1917.

39. *NYT*, June 16, 1917.

40. *Wall Street Journal*, July 11, 1917.

41. *CR* 55, 65th Cong., 1st sess., p. 1695.

42. Ibid., p. 2062.

43. *LAT*, April 21, 1917; *NYT*, June 4, 1917.

44. *NYT*, May 23, 1917.

45. *CR* 55, 65th Cong., 1st sess., p. 1779.

46. Ibid., p. 2062.

47. Ibid., pp. 1695, 1696.

48. Ibid., p. 1780.

49. 40 *U.S. Stat.* 217–19.

50. Borah to E. A. Burrell, quoted in Claudius O. Johnson, *Borah of Idaho*, p. 214.

Chapter 3: The Heel of the Government

1. *American Socialist*, April 21, 1917.

2. Blum, "A. S. Burleson," pp. 74–75.

3. See Chapter 2, above.

4. Sinclair to Wilson, Oct. 22, 1917, Woodrow Wilson Papers, Manuscripts Division, LOC.

5. Burleson to Postmasters of the First, Second, and Third Classes, June 16, 1917, quoted in Murphy, *World War I and the Origins of Civil Liberties in the United States*, p. 98.

6. *American Socialist*, May 5, 1917.

7. *NYT*, Oct. 10, 1917.

8. Gerald Gunther, *Learned Hand*, p. 153, quoted in Stone, *Perilous Times*, p. 164.

9. William L. O'Neill, *The Last Romantic*, p. 40, quoted in Stone, *Perilous Times*, p. 164.

10. *Report of the Attorney General for 1918*, p. 52.

11. Pinchot, Eastman, and Reed to Wilson, July 12, 1917, Wilson Papers.

12. Eastman, "Post Office Censorship," p. 24.

13. Eastman, Pinchot, and Reed to Wilson, July 12, 1917, Wilson Papers.

14. Wilson to Burleson, July 13, 1917, Wilson Papers.

15. *Masses Publishing Company v. Patten*, 244 Fed. 535 (SD NY, 1917). Zechariah Chafee discusses the decision at length in *Freedom of Speech*, pp. 46–56. *Freedom of Speech* is dedicated to Learned Hand.

16. Eastman, *Love and Revolution*, p. 61. The judge began his decision by saying, "No other instance of application to a Judge of the Appellate Court to stay an appealed order of this nature is known to me."

17. Sinclair to Wilson, Oct. 22, 1917, Wilson Papers.

18. Baker, *Woodrow Wilson*, vol. 7, pp. 178–79.

19. Wilson to Burleson, Oct. 11 and 18, 1917, Wilson Papers.

20. Wilson to Burleson, Sept. 4, 1917, Wilson Papers. Only twice did Wilson direct Burleson to lift a mailing ban, and both were personal favors. The first involved Norman Thomas's *World Tomorrow*, the second Villard's *Nation*. See Johnson, "Wilson, Burleson, and Censorship in the First World War," pp. 54–56.

21. Wilson to Herbert Croly, Oct. 22, 1917, Wilson Papers.

22. Dubofsky, *We Shall Be All*, p. 147.

23. Quoted in National Civil Liberties Bureau, *The Truth About the I.W.W.*, pp. 17–18.

24. Quoted in ibid., p. 9.

25. Quoted in Preston, *Aliens and Dissenters*, p. 41.

26. *Solidarity*, May 14, 1914.

27. F. W. Estabrook to Charles D. Hilles, Sept. 5, 1912, DOJ file 150139, NARA.

28. Taft to George W. Wickersham, Sept. 7, 1912, DOJ file 150139-28, NARA.

29. *Industrial Worker*, Feb. 10, 1917.

30. *Solidarity*, Feb. 17, 1917.

31. "Confidential Report on California, Oregon, and Washington," quoted in Hyman, *Soldiers and Spruce*, p. 45.

32. National Civil Liberties Bureau, *Truth About the I.W.W.*, p. 3.

33. Bruère, *Following the Trail of the I.W.W.*, p. 5.

34. Gannett, "I.W.W.," p. 448.

35. G. W. Anderson to Gregory, DOJ file 186701-22-1, NARA.

36. National Civil Liberties Bureau, *Truth About the I.W.W.*, p. 37.

37. Parks to Gregory, Aug. 29, 1917, DOJ file 186701-27-17, NARA. A devastating indictment of the labor practices and unconstitutional procedures of the Butte mine owners can be found in Lowndes Maury (law partner of the U.S. attorney for Montana, Burton K. Wheeler) to Wilson, Sept. 25, 1917, Wilson Papers.

38. Dubofsky, *We Shall Be All*, p. 373.

39. *Independent*, July 21, 1917; *Wall Street Journal*, July 13, 1917; *NYT*, July 12, 1917.

40. *NYT*, June 29, 1917.

41. *NYT*, July 13, 1917.

42. Rader, "Montana Lumber Strike of 1917," p. 189.

43. Quoted in Dubofsky, *We Shall Be All*, p. 385.

44. Wheeler to Gregory, Aug. 21, 1917, DOJ file 186701-27-15, NARA.

45. Report of E. W. Byrn, Aug. 7, 1917, DOJ file 186701-27-15, NARA.

46. Quoted in Bruère, *Following the Trail of the I.W.W.*, p. 13.

47. Baker, *Woodrow Wilson*, vol. 7, pp. 208, 209.

48. Link, *Papers of Woodrow Wilson*, vol. 43, p. 128.

49. Quoted in Dubofsky, *We Shall Be All*, p. 386. In fact, an Army census taken at Columbus showed that on August 6 of the men still held, 468 were citizens (199 native-born, 269 naturalized), 472 had registered for the draft, and 433 were married. Among the foreign-born, twenty nationalities were represented, including 141 Britons and 268 Mexicans, but only 20 Germans. Of the 530 aliens, 181 had taken first papers, and 86 claimed second papers (AG file 370.6, NARA; and *Report on the Bisbee Deportations*, p. 5).

50. *NYT*, July 14, 1917; *LAT*, July 15, 1917.

51. "All Women and Children Keep off Streets Today," *Bisbee Daily Review*, July 12, 1917.

52. *CR* 55, 71st Cong., 2nd sess., p. 8717.

53. *Report on the Bisbee Deportations*, p. 6.

54. *NYT*, Aug. 2, 1917. For a fuller account of the Little murder, see Gutfeld, "Murder of Frank Little," pp. 177–92.

55. "Break the I.W.W. Now," *Independent*, July 21, 1917, p. 87.

56. *Solidarity*, Oct. 20, 1917.

57. Fitts to Fall, Aug. 30, 1917, DOJ file 186701-27-16, NARA.

58. Reed, "One Solid Month of Liberty," p. 1.

Chapter 4: A Peculiar Sort of Mental Hysteria

1. Francis Garrecht to Gregory, July 14, 1917, DOJ file 186701-49-10, NARA.

2. McConnell to Caminetti, July 21, 1917, INS file 53531/192, NARA.

3. 39 *U.S. Stat.* 875–76.

4. Caminetti to Post, July 25, 1917, INS file 53531/192, NARA.

5. Caminetti to Post, Aug. 28, 1917, INS file 53531/192, NARA.

6. Quoted in Dubofsky, *We Shall Be All*, pp. 405–6.

7. Ibid., p. 350.

8. See Chapter 3, above.

9. Gregory to Wilson, Aug. 21, 1917, Woodrow Wilson Papers, Manuscripts Division, LOC.

10. *NYT*, Sept. 6, 1917.

11. Kane to Gregory, Sept. 7, 1917, DOJ file 186701-39-4, NARA.

12. *NYT*, Oct. 10, 1917.

13. *Report of the Attorney General for 1917*, pp. 62–63.

14. Cunningham, *Prisoners at Fort Douglas*, p. vi.

15. William Barnes Glidden, "Casualties of Caution" (unpublished MS), p. 61; Scheiber, *Wilson Administration and Civil Liberties*, p. 45.

16. Glidden, "Casualties of Caution," p. 61, from Glidden's 1969 interview with John Lord O'Brian.

17. Palmer to Wilson, Nov. 8, 1917, Wilson Papers.

18. *NYT*, Nov. 21, 1917.

19. National Civil Liberties Bureau, *Outrage on Rev. Herbert S. Bigelow of Cincinnati, Ohio*, pp. 9, 10.

20. *NYT*, July 3, 1917.

21. *NYT*, Dec. 2, 1917.

22. *NYT*, Jan. 20, 1918.

23. See Prologue, above.

24. *NYT*, April 4, 1918.

25. *Collinsville Herald*, April 6, 1918.

26. *Chicago Daily Tribune*, April 6, 1918.

27. Kennedy, *Over Here*, p. 79.

28. *WP*, April 12, 1918.

29. *Report of the Attorney General for 1918*, p. 18.

30. 40 *U.S. Stat.* 553–54.

31. *CR* 55, 65th Cong., 2nd sess., p. 4638.

32. "Citizens or Subject?" *Kansas City Star*, April 6, 1918, reprinted in *Roosevelt in "The Kansas City Star,"* pp. 131–32.

33. *CR* 55, 65th Cong., 2nd sess., p. 6036.

34. Ibid., p. 4562.

35. Ibid., p. 4636.

36. Ibid., App., p. 335.

37. Ibid., pp. 6050, 5541.

38. *NYT*, April 25, 1918.

39. "Espionage Cases," pp. 417–20.

40. See National Civil Liberties Bureau, *Conviction of Mrs. Kate Richards O'Hare and North Dakota Politics*.

41. Quoted in Peterson and Fite, *Opponents of War*, p. 185.

42. *Writings and Speeches of Eugene V. Debs*, pp. 417–33.

43. Quoted in Ginger, *Bending Cross*, p. 365.

44. Jensen, *Price of Vigilance*, p. 193.

45. *NYT*, Sept. 8, 1918.

46. Gregory to Wilson, Sept. 9, 1918, Gregory Papers, LOC.

47. *CR* 55, 65th Cong., 2nd sess., p. 9976.

48. "Civil Liberties Dead," p. 282.

49. *NYT*, Sept. 6, 1918.

50. Ibid.

51. *CR* 55, 65th Cong., 2nd sess., p. 10063.

52. *NYT*, Sept. 6, 1918.

53. Gregory to Wilson, Sept. 9, 1918, Gregory Papers.

54. *Report of the Attorney General for 1918*, p. 26.

55. Powers, *Secrecy and Power*, p. 55.

56. Cushman, "Civil Liberty After the War," p. 6.

Chapter 5: The Gravest Menace to the Country

1. *NYT*, Dec. 20, 1919.

2. Murray in *Red Scare*, p. 196, gives the lower number; Post in *Deportations Delirium*, p. 22, cites the higher figure.

3. *NYT*, Dec. 22, 1919.

4. *NYT*, Dec. 23, 1919.

5. *New York Tribune*, Dec. 22, 1919.

6. *NYT*, Dec. 22, 1919.

7. Sisson, *German-Bolshevik Conspiracy*, p. 3.

8. Donner, *Age of Surveillance*, p. 33.

9. On November 12, the day after the armistice was signed, Stevenson had submitted a report to MID claiming that "without a question, there is an organized conspiracy to overthrow the present form of the American government" (see Hagedorn, *Savage Peace*, p. 32). As for his claim to be a BI agent, Regin Schmidt notes that this is impossible to validate, as the bureau files on Stevenson are missing from NARA (see *Red Scare*, p. 139).

10. U.S. Senate Committee on the Judiciary, *Brewing and Liquor Interests*, vol. 3, pp. 14–16, 36.

11. Ibid., p. 35.

12. *NYT*, Jan. 25, 1919.

13. Hagedorn, *Savage Peace*, p. 57.

14. *NYT*, Feb. 1, 1919.

15. U.S. Senate Committee on the Judiciary, *Brewing and Liquor Interests*, vol. 2, p. 2717.

16. Ibid., p. 2780.

17. Ibid., vol. 3, p. 893.

18. Howe, *Confessions of a Reformer*, pp. 273–74.

19. Quoted in Schmidt, *Red Scare*, pp. 128–29.

20. *CR* 55, 65th Cong., 3rd sess., p. 3637.

21. *NYT*, Feb. 8, 1919.

22. *Seattle Union Record*, Feb. 4, 1919.

23. *Seattle Star*, Feb. 4, 1919, quoted in Murray, *Red Scare*, p. 61.

24. *LAT,* Feb. 8, 1919.

25. Ibid.

26. *WP,* Feb. 10, 1919. The editorial called the strike "a revolutionary movement aimed at existing government."

27. Thirteen men were arrested in a "riot" several days before the strike began. Pointing out that more than half were Russians, the Washington congressman Albert Johnson referred to them as "a great array of Slovinskys and Ivan Kerenskys and names of that sort" (*NYT,* Feb. 8, 1919; the *Times* story misidentifies Johnson as "Representative Royal Johnston." Royal Johnson [no *t*] was a congressman from South Dakota).

28. *NYT,* Feb. 8, 1919.

29. *NYT,* Feb. 9, 1919.

30. *Proceedings of the Conference with the President of the United States and the Secretary of Labor of the Governors of the States and Mayors of Cities in the East Room of the White House,* p. 33.

31. *Christian Science Monitor,* March 12, 1919.

32. *NYT,* March 11, 1919; *LAT,* March 11, 1919.

33. *NYT,* March 21, 1919. The committee's official name was the Joint Legislative Committee Investigating Seditious Activities.

34. His name is alternately spelled "Kaplan" in both contemporary and later reports.

35. *NYT,* May 1, 1919.

36. *NYT,* May 2, 1919.

37. *Nation,* May 10, 1919.

38. *NYT,* May 4, 1919.

39. Ibid.

40. Quoted in Post, *Deportations Delirium,* p. 39.

41. *NYT,* May 21, 1919.

42. Post, *Deportations Delirium,* p. 39.

43. *WP,* July 3, 1919.

44. *NYT,* June 4, 1919. In the same editorial, the *Times* also resurrected the nativist scare, saying "the old German propaganda, pretty effectually silenced while we were in the war, is again heard in the land."

45. *Literary Digest,* June 14, 1919, p. 9.

46. Ibid.

47. Post, *Deportations Delirium,* p. 44.

48. Quoted in Schmidt, *Red Scare,* p. 150.

49. *Sundry Civil Appropriation Bill, 1920,* p. 306.

50. Post, *Deportations Delirium,* p. 49.

51. *Sundry Civil Appropriation Bill, 1920,* p. 304.

52. Flynn subsequently denied that he had pinpointed July 4 as the day.

53. See Chapter 1, n. 18, above.

54. *NYT,* June 13, 1919.

55. *New York Tribune,* June 22, 1919.

Chapter 6: A Skimming of the Great American Melting-Pot

1. *NYT,* June 19, 1919; *LAT,* July 4, 1919.

2. *LAT,* July 4, 1919.

3. "News of the Week," *Christian Register,* July 10, 1919.

4. Quoted in Schmidt, *Red Scare*, p. 182.

5. *New York Tribune*, July 29, 1919; *NYT*, July 28, 1919.

6. AG, *Investigation Activities of the Department of Justice*, p. 162.

7. *NYT*, July 31, 1919.

8. *NYT*, Aug. 27, 1919.

9. AG, *Investigation Activities of the Department of Justice*, p. 13.

10. *Baltimore Sun*, quoted in Post, *Deportations Delirium*, p. 49.

11. *Annual Report of the Attorney General for 1920*, pp. 173–74.

12. See *Annual Report of the Attorney General for 1921*, p. 129.

13. *Sundry Civil Appropriation Bill*, 1922, pt. 2, p. 1150.

14. Benjamin Gitlow, one of the founders of the Communist Labor Party, estimated that the total number of members and sympathizers in 1919 was no more than a million, slightly less than 1 percent of the population (*Whole of Their Lives*, p. 53).

15. Higham, *Strangers in the Land*, p. 227.

16. According to the immigration commissioner general, Anthony Caminetti, the deportations were not related to the general strike, and "orders for the deportations had been signed before the Seattle situation had developed" (*NYT*, Feb. 11, 1919).

17. *Chicago Tribune*, Feb. 10, 1919, reprinted the same day in *NYT*.

18. *Chicago Tribune*, Feb. 10, 1919.

19. *Literary Digest*, March 1, 1919, p. 16. The newspaper quotations that follow are all from this source.

20. Howe, *Confessions of a Reformer*, p. 275.

21. Daniels, *Cabinet Diaries*, p. 418.

22. Memorandum upon the Work of the Radical Division, Aug. 1, 1919, to March 15, 1920, quoted in Schmidt, *Red Scare*, p. 254.

23. AG, *Investigation Activities of the Department of Justice*, p. 30.

24. See Schmidt, *Red Scare*, p. 256.

25. The information on strikes comes from *Monthly Labor Review*, June 1920, p. 200.

26. Quoted in Fuess, *Calvin Coolidge*, p. 206.

27. *Boston Herald*, Sept. 10, 1919; *Boston News Bureau*, quoted in *Literary Digest*, Sept. 20, 1919, p. 3; *Boston Evening Transcript*, Sept. 10, 1919.

28. *Boston Evening Transcript*, Sept. 10, 1919.

29. *NYT*, Sept. 12, 1919.

30. *Wall Street Journal*, Sept. 12, 1919; *Evening Public Ledger*, quoted in *Literary Digest*, Sept. 27, 1919, p. 8.

31. Quoted in *Literary Digest*, Sept. 27, 1919, p. 7.

32. Quoted in ibid.

33. *Autobiography of Calvin Coolidge*, p. 134.

34. Burke to George Kelleher, Sept. 12, 1919, quoted in Schmidt, *Red Scare*, p. 217.

35. *NYT*, Sept. 15, 1919; *Boston News Bureau*, quoted in *Literary Digest*, Sept. 20, 1919, p. 3.

36. Quoted in Senate Report No. 289, *Investigating Strike in Steel Industries*, 66th Cong., 1st sess., p. 4.

37. *NYT*, Sept. 1, 1919.

38. *NYT*, Sept. 11, 1919.

39. *New York Tribune*, *New York World*, and *Chicago Tribune* quotations are all from *Literary Digest*, Oct. 4, 1919, pp. 12–13; *Wall Street Journal*, Oct. 23, 1919.

40. Interchurch World Movement, *Public Opinion and the Steel Strike*, pp. 94–95.
41. *NYT,* Oct. 14, 1919.
42. Murray, *Red Scare*, p. 139; *NYT,* Sept. 23, 1919.
43. Foster, *From Bryan to Stalin*, pp. 48–49.
44. National Association of Manufacturers, *Onward March of the Open Shop*, p. 7.
45. Ford and Foster, *Syndicalism*, p. 28.
46. See Chapter 4, above.
47. *CR* 58, 66th Cong., 1st sess., pp. 6479, 5854.
48. Brody, *Labor in Crisis*, pp. 143–44.
49. *Attorney General A. Mitchell Palmer on Charges*, p. 171.
50. Quoted in Schmidt, *Red Scare*, p. 227.
51. Interchurch World Movement, *Public Opinion and the Steel Strike*, p. 58.
52. Wood to George W. Perkins, quoted in Brody, *Labor in Crisis*, p. 135.
53. Uncited newspaper article quoted in ibid.
54. *NYT,* Oct. 14, 1919.
55. Senate Report No. 289, *Investigating Strike in Steel Industries*, p. 21.
56. Interchurch World Movement, *Report on the Steel Strike of 1919*, p. 15.
57. Quoted in Brody, *Labor in Crisis*, p. 158.
58. *Portland Oregonian*, Oct. 6, 1919.
59. Quoted in Coben, "Study in Nativism," p. 72.
60. Quoted in Brody, *Labor in Crisis*, p. 117. Also see Murray, *Red Scare*, p. 309, n. 34.
61. *NYT,* Oct. 15, 1919.
62. Ibid.
63. *NYT,* Oct. 17, 1919.
64. *United Mine Workers Journal*, Nov. 1, 1919.
65. Ibid.
66. See Murray, *Red Scare*, p. 155.
67. *Seattle Times*, quoted in *Literary Digest*, Nov. 8, 1919, p. 13.
68. *New York Tribune*, quoted in ibid.
69. *New York World*, Nov. 7, 1919.
70. See Schmidt, *Red Scare*, pp. 231–32.

Chapter 7: A Lawless Government

1. *Atlanta Constitution*, Nov. 9, 1919.
2. AG, *Investigation Activities of the Department of Justice*, p. 161. The second quotation is an amalgam of three translations, none of which is satisfying in itself. See the two versions published in the *New York Times* on Nov. 8 and 9, 1919, and the Justice Department version quoted in AG, *Investigation Activities of the Department of Justice*.
3. See Chapter 5, n. 2, above.
4. Claghorn, *Immigrant's Day in Court*, p. 373.
5. John W. Abercrombie to all Commissioners of Immigration and Inspectors in Charge, March 14, 1919, quoted in Schmidt, *Red Scare*, p. 266.
6. Memo for Chief of Bureau, July 16, 1919, quoted in ibid.
7. Memorandum for Mr. Burke, Sept. 15, 1919, quoted in ibid., pp. 264–65.
8. *NYT,* Nov. 8, 1919.
9. See Schmidt, *Red Scare*, p. 268, n. 117.
10. See National Popular Government League, *To the American People*, pp. 11–16.

11. These figures are from Schmidt, *Red Scare*, p. 268, based on Justice Department figures as given in "List, Union of Russian Workers (Raid of Nov. 7, 1919)," an attachment to Hoover's Jan. 22, 1920, memo to Burke. Murray's *Red Scare* offers numbers of "about 200 men and women" arrested (the same figure the Nov. 8 *NYT* story gives) and 39 held, for which no source is cited (see Murray, p. 197). Given the sourcing, Schmidt's figures would appear to be the more reliable.

12. *NYT*, Nov. 8, 1919.

13. Ibid; *New York World*, Nov. 8, 1919; *NYT*, Nov. 9, 1919. For individual testimony, see National Popular Government League, *To the American People*, pp. 16–20.

14. *NYT*, Nov. 8, 1919.

15. *NYT*, Nov. 9, 1919.

16. *NYT*, Nov. 11, 1919.

17. *NYT*, Nov. 9, 1919.

18. *Ohio State Journal*, Nov. 12, 1919; *Atlanta Constitution*, Nov. 10, 1919; *Pittsburgh Post*, Nov. 13, 1919.

19. See AG, *Investigation Activities of the Department of Justice*.

20. Pencak, *For God and Country*, p. 320.

21. Chaplin, *Centralia Conspiracy*, p. 120. One witness testified that the ex-mayor's rope was "possibly twelve feet or more."

22. Quoted in "American Soldiers in Parade Killed by Reds," p. 8.

23. *CR* 59, 66th Cong., 2nd sess., p. 448.

24. *Pittsburgh Press*, Nov. 13, 1919; *Boston Evening Transcript*, Nov. 12, 1919; "American Soldiers in Parade Killed by Reds," p. 8.

25. F. W. McIntosh, report, Nov. 20, 1919, quoted in Schmidt, *Red Scare*, p. 106.

26. Simmons to Burke, telegram, Nov. 15, 1919.

27. *Attorney General A. Mitchell Palmer on Charges*, p. 108.

28. Quoted in Hays, *Trial by Prejudice*, p. 267.

29. Howe, *Confessions of a Reformer*, pp. 274–75.

30. *NYT*, Nov. 27, 1919.

31. Howe, *Confessions of a Reformer*, p. 327.

32. *NYT*, Nov. 27, 1919.

33. Post, *Deportations Delirium*, p. 26.

34. Hoover to Caminetti, Dec. 22, 1919, quoted in Schmidt, *Red Scare*, p. 281.

35. Quoted in Coben, *A. Mitchell Palmer*, p. 224.

36. *Colyer et al. v. Skeffington, Commissioner of Immigration*, reprinted in Senate Committee on the Judiciary, *Charges of Illegal Practices of the Department of Justice*, p. 53.

37. Quoted in Preston, *Aliens and Dissenters*, p. 210.

38. Post, *Deportations Delirium*, pp. 56–57.

39. Quoted in Preston, *Aliens and Dissenters*, p. 218.

40. Senate Committee on the Judiciary, *Charges of Illegal Practices of the Department of Justice*, pp. 398–99.

41. *NYT*, Jan. 1, 1920.

42. Post, *Deportations Delirium*, p. 90.

43. *NYT*, Jan. 4, 1920.

44. Post, *Deportations Delirium*, p. 92.

45. *NYT*, Jan. 4, 1920.

46. *Annual Report of the Attorney General of the United States for the Year 1920*, p. 176.

47. Post, *Deportations Delirium*, p. 95.

48. *Colyer et al. v. Skeffington, Commissioner of Immigration,* in Senate Committee on the Judiciary, *Charges of Illegal Practices of the Department of Justice,* p. 58.

49. Post, *Deportations Delirium,* p. 97.

50. National Popular Government League, *To the American People,* p. 11.

51. Quoted in Post, *Deportations Delirium,* pp. 139–40.

52. Quoted in ibid., p. 143.

53. Quoted in Senate Committee on the Judiciary, *Charges of Illegal Practices of the Department of Justice,* p. 346.

54. *NYT,* Jan. 21, 1920.

55. Post, *Deportations Delirium,* p. 159.

56. Ibid., p. 187.

57. *Investigation of Administration of Louis F. Post,* pp. 78–79. Post also intervened in the case of the unofficial Soviet ambassador Ludwig C. A. K. Martens, whom Palmer was planning to arrest in a spectacular manner and then have deported. Post arranged for Martens to surrender quietly at the Labor Department office and allowed him to leave the country on his own. When Martens arrived in Russia, Post canceled the deportation order so that Martens would not be banned from reentering the United States at a later time.

58. *NYT,* May 2, 1920.

59. Quoted in Post, *Deportations Delirium,* p. 233.

60. *Investigation of Administration of Louis F. Post,* pp. 61–62.

61. Quoted in Post, *Deportations Delirium,* p. 246.

62. *Investigation of Administration of Louis F. Post,* p. 248.

63. National Popular Government League, *To the American People,* p. 4.

64. *Attorney General A. Mitchell Palmer on Charges,* pp. 6, 73–74.

65. *Indianapolis News,* June 2, 1920; *Christian Science Monitor,* June 25, 1920.

66. *NYT,* Nov. 12, 1919.

67. *NYT,* Sept. 18, 1920.

68. *Rocky Mountain News,* Sept. 18, 1920.

69. See Avrich, *Sacco and Vanzetti,* pp. 204–7.

70. Post, *Deportations Delirium,* p. 158.

71. Murray, "Outer World and Inner Light," p. 265.

72. Murray, *Red Scare,* p. 17.

73. See Chapter 6, above.

74. Quoted in Post, *Deportations Delirium,* p. 327.

75. Ibid., p. 326.

Chapter 8: Grave Abuses and Unnecessary Hardships

1. *CR* 64, 67th Cong., 4th sess., p. 3027.

2. See ibid., pp. 3051–73.

3. *Hearing Before Subcommittee of House Committee on Appropriations, Department of Justice Appropriation Bill, 1923,* pt. 2, pp. 131, 145.

4. *Hearing Before Subcommittee of House Committee on Appropriations, Department of Justice Appropriation Bill, 1925,* p. 93.

5. See Lowenthal, *Federal Bureau of Investigation,* p. 293; and Crawford, "J. Edgar Hoover," p. 232.

6. *Investigation of Hon. Harry M. Daugherty,* vol. 1, p. 88.

7. Ibid., p. 90.

8. Ibid., p. 89.

9. Quoted in American Civil Liberties Union, *The Nation-Wide Spy System Centering in the Department of Justice*, p. 3.

10. See Powers, *Secrecy and Power*, pp. 138–39.

11. See Senate Committee on the Judiciary, *Charges of Illegal Practices of the Department of Justice*, p. 19.

12. Quoted in Cummings and McFarland, *Federal Justice*, pp. 430–31.

13. Quoted in *NYT*, March 30, 2007.

14. See Hoffman, *Unwanted Mexican Americans*, p. 7.

15. Ibid., p. 9.

16. See Divine, *American Immigration Policy*, p. 53.

17. See Hoffman, *Unwanted Mexican Americans*, p. 7.

18. "Immigration from Countries of the Western Hemisphere," p. 782.

19. Ibid., p. 739.

20. Quoted in Chinea, "Ethnic Prejudice and Anti-immigrant Policies in Times of Economic Stress," p. 10. Also see www.houstonculture.org/hispanic/conquest5.html.

21. "Immigration from Countries of the Western Hemisphere," p. 43; "Western Hemisphere Immigration," p. 75.

22. Divine, *American Immigration Policy*, p. 57.

23. McKay, "Federal Deportation Campaign in Texas," p. 109; newspaper quoted in ibid., p. 108.

24. Hoffman, *Unwanted Mexican Americans*, p. 40.

25. Quoted in ibid., p. 43.

26. Quoted in Guerin-Gonzales, *Mexican Workers and American Dreams*, p. 81.

27. Both quoted in Hoffman, *Unwanted Mexican Americans*, p. 43.

28. Quoted in Guerin-Gonzales, *Mexican Workers and American Dreams*, p. 81.

29. *LAT*, Jan. 13, 1931.

30. Quoted in Hoffman, *Unwanted Mexican Americans*, p. 44.

31. *LAT*, Jan. 31, 1931.

32. *LAT*, Feb. 10, 1931.

33. *NYT*, Feb. 16, 1931.

34. Jackson, "Doak the Deportation Chief," pp. 295–96; *Annual Report of the Commissioner General of Immigration, 1931*, p. 35.

35. *Report on the Enforcement of the Deportation Laws of the United States*, p. 177.

36. Oppenheimer, "Deportation Terror," pp. 231–32.

37. *LAT*, Feb. 15, 1931.

38. Quoted in Hoffman, *Unwanted Mexican Americans*, p. 57.

39. *La Opinión*, Feb. 27, 1931. In *Unwanted Mexican Americans*, Hoffman points out inconsistencies in the reporting (see p. 62). Unfortunately, this was the only newspaper account published.

40. Quoted in Hoffman, *Unwanted Mexican Americans*, p. 65.

41. "Editorial Paragraphs."

42. *LAT*, June 8, 1931.

43. McWilliams, *North from Mexico*, p. 193. McWilliams mistakenly dated the departure as having taken place in February, which was when it was originally scheduled, but it was delayed until March 23.

44. See Balderrama, *In Defense of La Raza*, p. 28.

45. *NYT*, April 12, 1931.

46. Quoted in McKay, "Federal Deportation Campaign in Texas," p. 108.

47. See Bogardus, "Mexican Repatriates," p. 174.
48. McWilliams, "Getting Rid of the Mexican," p. 323.
49. *NYT*, Dec. 8, 1931.
50. *NYT*, July 9, 1932.
51. See Hoffman, *Unwanted Mexican Americans*, pp. 124–25.
52. Ibid., p. 126; Balderrama, *Decade of Betrayal*, pp. 149–51.
53. Clark, *Deportation of Aliens from the United States to Europe*, p. 488.

Chapter 9: The Utmost Degree of Secrecy

1. *NYT*, May 25, 1923.
2. See Chapter 8, above.
3. "The ACLU and the FBI," p. 25.
4. See Gentry, *J. Edgar Hoover*, pp. 208–9.
5. Church Committee, vol. 6, p. 554.
6. Ibid., p. 556.
7. Ibid.
8. Ibid., p. 555.
9. Dern to Cummings, Jan. 6, 1936, quoted in Church Committee, bk. 3, p. 393.
10. Stone to Hoover, May 13, 1924, quoted in Gentry, *J. Edgar Hoover*, p. 127.
11. Church Committee, vol. 6, p. 559.
12. J. Edgar Hoover, confidential memo, Aug. 24, 1936, in Theoharis, *From the Secret Files of J. Edgar Hoover*, p. 180.
13. Ibid., p. 181.
14. J. Edgar Hoover, confidential memo, Aug. 25, 1936, in ibid., p. 182.
15. See Donner, *Age of Surveillance*, pp. 53–55. Unfortunately, Hoover's memos are the only surviving accounts of these two meetings. Although one of the memos states that Roosevelt said "he would . . . put a handwritten memorandum of his own in his safe in the White House, stating that he had instructed the Secretary of State to request this information," no such document has ever been found among FDR's papers (see Theoharis, *From the Secret Files of J. Edgar Hoover*, p. 181).
16. Quoted in Church Committee, bk. 3, p. 396.
17. See ibid.
18. Theoharis, *Spying on Americans*, p. 40.
19. Edward Tamm (FBI assistant director) to Hoover, August 28, 1936, quoted in Church Committee, bk. 3, p. 397.
20. Ibid., p. 564.
21. Ibid., p. 565.
22. Ibid., p. 566.
23. FDR cut Hoover's requested funding in half, to $150,000, and granted the two military intelligence agencies $50,000 apiece, an increase of $15,000 from the requested amount.
24. See Theoharis and Cox, *Boss*, p. 172.
25. Quoted in Church Committee, bk. 3, p. 413.
26. Theoharis and Cox, *Boss*, p. 172.
27. Hoover to All Law Enforcement Officials, press release, Sept. 6, 1939, in Theoharis, *From the Secret Files of J. Edgar Hoover*, p. 184.
28. *NYT*, Sept. 15, 1939.
29. Quoted in Church Committee, bk. 3, p. 413.

30. Hoover to SACs [Special Agents in Charge], June 15, 1940, www.foitimes .com/internment/chrono.htm.

31. See Chapter 2, above.

32. Roosevelt to Jackson, Stephen Spingarn Papers, National Defense—Internal Security Folder 2, Harry S. Truman Library, quoted in Theoharis, *Spying on Americans*, pp. 98–99.

33. Hoover to McGuire, memo, Aug. 21, 1940, DOJ file 66-6200-100-13, NARA.

34. Address at Graduation Exercises, 15th sess., National Police Academy, Oct. 5, 1940, quoted in Lowenthal, *Federal Bureau of Investigation*, p. 360.

35. Jackson to All Departmental and Agency Heads, memo, n.d., in Theoharis, *From the Secret Files of J. Edgar Hoover*, pp. 185–86.

36. Hoover to Jackson, memo, April 1, 1941, in ibid., p. 190.

37. Hoover to SACs, DOJ file 66-6200-100-33X, NARA.

38. See www.internmentarchives.com/specialreports/smithsonian/smithsonian10 .php.

39. Biddle, *In Brief Authority*, p. 206.

40. www.foitimes.com/internment/chrono.htm.

41. Morton Grodzins, interview with Ennis, Sept. 17, 1942, quoted in Grodzins, *Americans Betrayed*, p. 232.

42. See Commission on Wartime Relocation and Internment of Civilians, *Personal Justice Denied*, p. 55.

43. Mangione, *An Ethnic at Large*, p. 284.

44. *Public Hearings of the Commission on Wartime Relocation and Internment of Civilians*, July 14, 1980, reel 1, p. 52.

45. Biddle, *In Brief Authority*, p. 208.

46. Ibid.

47. *Public Hearings of the Commission on Wartime Relocation and Internment of Civilians*, July 14, 1980, reel 1, p. 47.

48. *Hearings on the Sixth Supplemental National Defense Appropriation Bill for 1942*, pt. 1, pp. 393, 395.

49. Both cases are discussed in Harris, "Alien Enemy Hearing Board."

50. Buchanan, *United States and World War II*, vol. 2, p. 326.

Chapter 10: A Jap Is a Jap

1. DeWitt, *Final Report*, p. 3.

2. See Schmidt, *Red Scare*, p. 203, n. 150, for the sources of all the quotations in this paragraph.

3. *Japanese Immigration Legislation*, p. 22.

4. Ibid., pp. 48, 41.

5. Division of Far Eastern Affairs to State Department, memo, Aug. 24, 1934, State Department file 894.20211-131, NARA, quoted in Kumamoto, "Search for Spies," p. 49.

6. Quoted in Robinson, *By Order of the President*, p. 56.

7. Roosevelt to Chief of Naval Operations, memo, quoted in ibid.

8. See Kumamoto, "Search for Spies," pp. 50–51, 54–55.

9. Knox to Roosevelt, Oct. 9, 1940, CWRIC Papers, reel 3, frame 3603.

10. *Pacific Citizen*, Oct. 18, 1942.

11. *Rafu Shimpo*, Nov. 12, 1941.

12. See CWRIC Papers, reel 17, frames 19456–61.

13. Curtis Munson, "Japanese on the West Coast," pp. 13–6, CWRIC Papers, reel 3, frames 3685–88.

14. An Intelligence Officer, "Japanese in America," p. 497.

15. *San Francisco Chronicle*, Dec. 16, 1941.

16. Biddle, *In Brief Authority*, p. 214.

17. *LAT*, April 14, 1943.

18. Henry L. Stimson, diary, Feb. 3, 1942, CWRIC Papers, reel 17, frame 19632.

19. Quoted in Hersey, "Mistake of Terrifically Horrible Proportions," p. 16.

20. Transcript of meeting with Assistant Attorney General Rowe, Jan. 4, 1942, CWRIC Papers, reel 2, frame 1260.

21. DeWitt and Gullion, telephone conversation, Dec. 26, 1941, quoted in Conn, "Decision to Evacuate the Japanese from the Pacific Coast," p. 128.

22. MID on Counter Fifth Column, July 29, 1940, MID file 9794-186, NARA, quoted in Kumamoto, "Search for Spies," p. 53.

23. Quoted in Hersey, "Mistake of Terrifically Horrible Proportions," p. 20.

24. See Barkley, "Attack on Pearl Harbor by Japanese Armed Forces," pt. 39, pp. 1–21, also available at www.ibiblio.org/pha/pha/roberts/roberts.html.

25. Ibid., p. 12.

26. *LAT*, Jan. 22, 1942. See also Commission on Wartime Relocation and Internment of Civilians, *Personal Justice Denied*, p. 70.

27. *San Francisco Examiner*, Jan. 29, 1942.

28. *LAT*, Feb. 2, 1942.

29. F. W. McNabb to Warren, Jan. 3, 1942, quoted in Grodzins, *Americans Betrayed*, p. 24.

30. Quoted in Taylor, "People Nobody Wants," p. 66.

31. Grodzins, *Americans Betrayed*, pp. 97, 95.

32. See Fox, *Unknown Internment*, pp. 1–2.

33. Memo for the Provost Marshal General, Jan. 31, 1942, quoted in Conn, "Decision to Evacuate the Japanese from the Pacific Coast," p. 134.

34. Grodzins, *Americans Betrayed*, p. 87.

35. Memorandum for the Provost Marshal General, Feb. 4, 1942, RG 389, box 1217, file 014.311, Provost Marshal General's Office, NARA.

36. Quoted in Hersey, "Mistake of Terrifically Horrible Proportions," p. 31.

37. *Pacific Citizen*, Sept. 24, 1949.

38. See www.nps.gov/archive/manz/hrs/hrs2c.htm.

39. *WP*, Feb. 12 and 15, 1942.

40. Memo, "Luncheon Conversation with the President," Feb. 7, 1942, CWRIC Papers, reel 5, frame 5750.

41. Biddle to Stimson, Feb. 9, 1942, CWRIC Papers, reel 12, frame 13414.

42. Stimson, diary, Feb. 10, 1942, quoted in Irons, *Justice at War*, p. 55.

43. In "The Decision to Evacuate the Japanese from the Pacific Coast," Stetson Conn says that an afternoon White House conference took place between Stimson and Roosevelt (p. 143), whereas in "Japanese Evacuation from the West Coast," Conn states that their communication was in a telephone call (p. 131).

44. Conn, "Decision to Evacuate the Japanese from the Pacific Coast," p. 142.

45. Stimson, diary, Feb. 11, 1942, quoted in Irons, *Justice at War*, p. 58.

46. McCloy and Bendetsen, telephone conversation, quoted in Conn, "Japanese Evacuation from the West Coast," p. 132.

47. See Chapter 8, above.
48. DeWitt, *Final Report*, p. 34.
49. See CWRIC Papers, reel 5, frames 5754–55.
50. Morton Grodzins, interview with Rowe, Oct. 15, 1942, Japanese American Evacuation and Resettlement Records, Bancroft Library, University of California, Berkeley, frame :0208, folder A 7.02.
51. DeWitt, *Final Report*, p. 26.
52. Biddle, *In Brief Authority*, p. 207.
53. See Conn, "Japanese Evacuation from the West Coast," pp. 136–37.
54. Biddle, *In Brief Authority*, p. 207; Conn, "Japanese Evacuation from the West Coast," p. 137.
55. Biddle, *In Brief Authority*, p. 213.
56. Commission on Wartime Relocation and Internment of Civilians, *Personal Justice Denied*, p. 18.
57. Grodzins, *Americans Betrayed*, pp. 174–75, 172.
58. See Fox, *Unknown Internment*, p. 51; also p. 55.
59. Biddle to Stimson, Feb. 9, 1942, CWRIC Papers, reel 12, frame 13414.
60. Quoted in Fox, "Relocation of Italian Americans in California During World War II," p. 41.
61. Fox, *Unknown Internment*, p. 55.
62. Grodzins, *Americans Betrayed*, p. 175.
63. Quoted in Greiff, *Handbook of Reparations*, p. 261.
64. See Robinson, *By Order of the President*, p. 41.
65. *Brooklyn Daily Eagle*, July 18, 1920.
66. See Howard, *Concentration Camps on the Home Front*, pp. 152, 172, 223–24.
67. Biddle, *In Brief Authority*, pp. 235, 219.
68. Donner, *Age of Surveillance*, p. 54n.
69. See Israel, "Military Justice in Hawaii," pp. 236–49.
70. "Memorandum Regarding Activities of the United States Government in Removing from the Other American Republics Dangerous Subversive Aliens," Nov. 3, 1942, Subject Files, box 180, Special War Problems Division, RG 59, NARA, quoted in Donald, *We Were Not the Enemy*, p. 96. See also Friedman, *Nazis and Good Neighbors*, p. 199.

Chapter 11: Scare Hell Out of the Country

1. See *Department of State Bulletin*, May 27, 1945, pp. 951–52.
2. See Cantril and Strunk, *Public Opinion*, p. 962.
3. Ladd to Hoover, Feb. 27, 1946, quoted in Church Committee, bk. 3, p. 429.
4. Ibid., p. 430.
5. Quoted in *Attorney General A. Mitchell Palmer on Charges*, p. 244.
6. See Chapter 9, above.
7. Hoover to Clark, March 8, 1946, quoted in Church Committee, bk. 3, p. 430.
8. *NYT*, Oct. 4, 1939.
9. Quoted in Truman, *Memoirs*, vol. 2, *Years of Trial and Hope*, p. 275.
10. *NYT*, Oct. 4, 1939.
11. See Emerson and Helfeld, "Loyalty Among Government Employees," pp. 10, 12.
12. Griffith, *Politics of Fear*, p. 32.

13. *CR* 87, 77th Cong., 1st sess., p. 887.

14. *CR* 88, 77th Cong., 2nd sess., p. 1420.

15. *CR* 94, 79th Cong., 2nd sess., p. 5217.

16. *Washington Star,* April 28, 1957; *Hearings Regarding Communist Espionage in the United States Government,* 80th Cong., 2nd sess., p. 561.

17. Carr, *House Committee on Un-American Activities,* p. 269; Goodman, *Committee,* p. 200.

18. *WP,* March 11, 1946.

19. Ibid.

20. See Bontecou, *Federal Loyalty-Security Program,* p. 290.

21. *NYT,* June 2, 1946.

22. Mazo and Hess, *Nixon,* pp. 39–40; *Milwaukee Journal,* Oct. 23, 1946.

23. *Boston Herald,* Nov. 1, 1946.

24. Quoted in Steinke and Weinstein, "McCarthy and the Liberals."

25. *NYT,* Jan. 23, 1947.

26. *Report of the President's Temporary Commission on Employee Loyalty,* pp. 21, 23.

27. Quoted in Redding, *Inside the Democratic Party,* p. 41.

28. Truman to George H. Earle, Feb. 28, 1947, quoted in Donovan, *Conflict and Crisis,* p. 293.

29. Executive Order 9835, reprinted in Bontecou, *Federal Loyalty-Security Program,* p. 275.

30. See Cook, *Nightmare Decade,* p. 64.

31. *NYT,* March 23, 1947.

32. Executive Order 9835, reprinted in Bontecou, *Federal Loyalty-Security Program,* p. 280.

33. *NYT,* April 13, 1947; Commager, *Freedom and Order,* pp. 73–74.

34. Barth, *Loyalty of Free Men,* p. 125.

35. Ibid., pp. 129–30.

36. Quoted in Goldman, *Crucial Decade,* p. 59.

37. avalon.law.yale.edu/20th_century/trudoc.asp.

38. *Public Papers of Harry S. Truman, 1947,* p. 239.

39. *NYT,* March 27, 1947.

40. *Hearings Regarding Communist Espionage in the United States Government,* p. 1347.

41. *CR* 120, 93rd Cong., 2nd sess., p. 8936.

42. Hoover to Tolson, Tamm, Ladd, and Nichols, June 24, 1947, in Leab and Lester, *Communist Activity in the Entertainment Industry,* reel 2, frames 641–42.

43. O'Reilly, *Hoover and the Un-Americans,* p. 171.

44. Cook, *Nightmare Decade,* p. 570.

45. American Civil Liberties Union, *In Times of Challenge,* p. 4.

46. *CR* 96, 81st Cong., 2nd sess., p. 10806.

47. Barth, *Loyalty of Free Men,* pp. 107, 106.

48. Freeland, *Truman Doctrine,* p. 210.

49. Scandrett to Phyllis Auty, Oct. 25, 1948, quoted in Paterson, *Cold War Critics,* p. 14; American Civil Liberties Union, *Our Uncertain Liberties,* p. 4.

50. *Hearings Before the Committee on Un-American Activities on H.R. 1884 and H.R. 2122,* pt. 2, p. 49.

51. Chambers, *Witness,* p. 472.

52. Cooke, *Generation on Trial,* p. 10.

53. *Deseret News*, Feb. 10, 1950.

54. See Church Committee, bk. 3, p. 438.

55. Ladd to Hoover, Jan. 12, 1948, quoted in ibid.

56. Church Committee, vol. 6, p. 418.

57. Ibid., pp. 416–26. The references that follow are from the memo.

58. Wilkinson, "Era of Libertarian Repression," p. 286.

59. Clifford to Truman, Nov. 19, 1947, quoted in Paterson, *Cold War Critics*, p. 13, and in O'Reilly, *Hoover and the Un-Americans*, p. 176.

60. Quoted in O'Reilly, *Hoover and the Un-Americans*, p. 176.

61. Macdonald, quoted in Wittner, *Rebels Against War*, p. 196; Thompson, Reuther, and Foster, quoted in MacDougall, *Gideon's Army*, pp. 249, 262.

62. *NYT*, Jan. 12, 1950.

63. See McGrath, "Democracy's Road to Freedom," p. 427.

64. Quoted in Theoharis, "Rhetoric of Politics," p. 215.

65. American Civil Liberties Union, *In the Shadow of Fear*, p. 3.

Chapter 12: A Neurotic Nightmare

1. *NYT*, Jan. 26, 1950.

2. *NYT*, April 16, 1949.

3. *NYT*, Jan. 26, 1950.

4. *Time*, Feb. 6, 1950.

5. *CR* 96, 81st Cong., 2nd sess., p. 1007.

6. Ibid.

7. *NYT*, Jan. 26, 1950.

8. *NYT*, Feb. 1, 1950.

9. *Wheeling Intelligencer*, Feb. 10, 1950.

10. *CR* 92, 79th Cong., 2nd sess., p. A4892.

11. See Reeves, *Life and Times of Joe McCarthy*, pp. 228–29.

12. *NYT*, Feb. 12, 1950.

13. *Denver Post*, Feb. 11, 1950.

14. Griffith, *Politics of Fear*, p. 55.

15. *Denver Post*, Feb. 11, 1950.

16. *NYT*, Feb. 12, 1950.

17. The entire proceedings can be found at *CR* 96, 81st Cong., 2nd sess., pp. 1952–81.

18. Quoted in Rovere, *Senator Joe McCarthy*, p. 135.

19. Quoted in Demaris, *Director*, p. 167.

20. See Reeves, *Life and Times of Joe McCarthy*, p. 245.

21. Quoted in Rovere, *Senator Joe McCarthy*, p. 136.

22. *State Department Employee Loyalty Investigation*, p. 38.

23. Ibid., p. 42.

24. *NYT*, March 9, 1950.

25. *State Department Employee Loyalty Investigation*, pp. 176, 187.

26. *NYT*, March 9, 1950.

27. *NYT*, March 21, 1950.

28. *Madison Capital Times*, March 21, 1950.

29. *State Department Employee Loyalty Investigation*, p. 278.

30. Ibid., p. 92.

31. Ibid., pp. 279–80.

32. Ibid., p. 284.

33. *NYT*, March 27, 1950.

34. *Madison Capital Times*, March 27, 1950.

35. *State Department Employee Loyalty Investigation*, p. 484.

36. Ibid., pp. 397, 409.

37. Ibid., p. 411.

38. Ibid., p. 418.

39. Ibid., p. 441.

40. *NYT*, April 21, 1950.

41. *NYT*, May 7, 1950.

42. *St. Petersburg Evening Independent*, May 1, 1950.

43. *Milwaukee Journal*, May 4, 1950.

44. *State Department Employee Loyalty Investigation*, p. 329.

45. *CR* 96, 81st Cong., 2nd sess., pp. 7894–95.

46. Quoted in Cabell Phillips, *Truman Presidency*, p. 374.

47. *NYT*, July 18, 1950.

48. Ibid.

49. Goldstein, *Political Repression in Modern America*, p. 323.

50. tucnak.fsv.cuni.cz/~calda/Documents/1950s/Inter_Security_50.html.

51. Langer, quoted in Griffith, *Politics of Fear*, p. 121; *NYT*, Aug. 31, 1950; *WP*, Aug. 31, 1950.

52. *NYT*, Jan. 7, 1951.

53. *WP*, Dec. 24, 1950.

54. McWilliams, *Witch Hunt*, p. 16; McWilliams, "Witch Hunt's New Phase," p. 454.

55. See Chapter 11, above.

56. *Public Papers of Harry S. Truman*, 1950, pp. 271–72.

57. See Chapter 11, above, italics added.

58. *NYT*, April 29, 1951, italics added.

59. Theoharis, "Escalation of the Loyalty Program," pp. 257, 264.

60. *NYT*, Aug. 15, 1951.

61. *Maryland Senatorial Election of 1950*, pp. 8, 37.

62. *NYT*, Aug. 7, 1951.

63. *NYT*, July 4, 1952.

64. Quoted in Herman, *Joseph McCarthy*, p. 199.

65. Benton to A. M. Gilbert, Aug. 8, 1952, quoted in Griffith, *Politics of Fear*, p. 176.

66. "Who Will Stand Up to McCarthy."

67. *NYT*, Jan. 18, 1953.

68. Quoted in Theoharis, *FBI and American Democracy*, pp. 93, 94.

69. Sullivan, *Bureau*, p. 35.

70. *NYT*, Feb. 20, 1953.

71. *NYT*, March 7, 1953.

72. Hughes, *Ordeal of Power*, p. 81.

73. *NYT*, July 25, 1953.

74. *NYT*, Nov. 26, 1953.

75. *Communist Infiltration in the Army*, p. 153.

76. *NYT*, June 6, 1954.

77. "Investigations."

78. *NYT*, March 4, 1954.

79. *NYT*, March 5, 1954.

80. *NYT*, March 4, 1954.

81. See en.wikiquote.org/wiki/Edward_R._Murrow.

82. *NYT*, March 14, 1954.

83. Quoted in Reeves, *Life and Times of Joe McCarthy*, p. 578.

84. See Gallup, *Gallup Poll*, pp. 1203, 1225.

85. Quoted in Dallek, *Lone Star Rising*, p. 454.

86. Cohn, *McCarthy*, p. 208.

87. *Special Senate Investigation on Charges and Countercharges Involving: Secretary of the Army Robert T. Stevens, John G. Adams, H. Struve Hensel and Senator Joe McCarthy, Roy M. Cohn, and Francis P. Carr* (hereafter *Army-McCarthy Hearings*), p. 2427.

88. Cohn, *McCarthy*, p. 203.

89. *Army-McCarthy Hearings*, pp. 2428–29.

90. Cook, *Nightmare Decade*, p. 543.

91. Buckley and Bozell, *McCarthy and His Enemies*, p. 335.

92. Rovere, *Senator Joe McCarthy*, p. 3.

93. Reeves, *Life and Times of Joe McCarthy*, p. 675.

Chapter 13: There Were Many Wrecked Lives

1. Parmet, *Eisenhower and the American Crusades*, pp. 238–39.

2. Executive Order 10450, www.archives.gov/federal-register/codification/executive-order/10450.html.

3. *NYT*, March 18, 1953.

4. Executive Order 10450.

5. Parmet, *Eisenhower and the American Crusades*, p. 240.

6. *WP*, Jan. 24, 1954.

7. *International Herald Tribune*, Aug. 7, 1953.

8. See "Academic Freedom and Tenure: Evansville College," p. 76.

9. McWilliams, *Witch Hunt*, p. 162.

10. See Chapter 11, above.

11. *NYT*, July 10, 1949.

12. *Time*, Nov. 27, 1950.

13. *NYT*, March 8, 1969.

14. Quoted in Caute, *Great Fear*, p. 429.

15. *NYT*, May 10, 1951.

16. *NYT*, Feb. 26, 1953.

17. *NYT*, April 4, 1953.

18. *NYT*, Feb. 8, 1953.

19. "Education: The Danger Signs."

20. *NYT*, March 20, 1953.

21. Quoted in Donner, *Un-Americans*, p. 64.

22. Quoted in ibid., p. 41.

23. *NYT*, Sept. 13, 1949.

24. *NYT*, July 16, 1949.

25. www.law.cornell.edu/supct/html/historics/USSC_CR_0342_0485_ZD2.html.

26. Quoted in Caute, *Great Fear*, p. 435.

27. Matusow, *False Witness*, p. 90.

28. Caute, *Great Fear*, p. 438.

29. *NYT*, Dec. 1, 1971.

30. Ibid.

31. *Congress and the Nation*, vol. 1, p. 21.

32. *NYT*, Sept. 2, 1954.

33. Ibid.

34. Brownell to Hoover, May 20, 1954, quoted in Ungar, *FBI*, p. 445.

35. 68 *U.S. Stat.* 775–80, Public Law 637, chap. 886, pp. 775–80; see tucnak.fsv .cuni.cz/~calda/Documents/1950s/Communist_54.html.

36. See Chapter 11, above.

37. Quoted in Johnson, *Lavender Scare*, p. 21.

38. *Departments of State, Justice, Commerce and the Judiciary Appropriations for 1951*, p. 598.

39. See Chapter 11, above.

40. See Chapter 12, above.

41. Quoted in *NYT*, April 19, 1950.

42. *CR* 96, 81st Cong., 2nd sess., p. 5699.

43. Lerner, *Unfinished Country*, p. 313.

44. Ibid.

45. *Employment of Homosexuals and Other Sex Perverts in Government*, pp. 5, 4.

46. *Executive Sessions of the Senate Foreign Relations Committee (Historical Series)*, vol. 5, p. 72.

47. Ibid., p. 70.

48. *WP*, March 13, 1953.

49. Quoted in Johnson, *Lavender Scare*, p. 130.

50. See ibid.

51. Quoted in Fariello, *Red Scare*, p. 124.

52. Quoted in Johnson, *Lavender Scare*, p. 131.

53. See Theoharis, *FBI and American Democracy*, p. 96.

54. *WP*, Jan. 20, 1954.

55. See www.law.cornell.edu/uscode/50/usc_sec_50_00000403----004a.html.

56. Quoted in *Rockefeller Commission Report*, p. 102.

57. Quoted in ibid., p. 105.

58. Quoted in ibid., p. 107.

59. Ibid., pp. 102, 115.

60. Ibid., p. 115.

61. Ibid.

62. See Johnson, *Lavender Scare*, p. 137.

63. Caute, *Great Fear*, p. 275.

64. Ibid., p. 187.

Chapter 14: There Are No Rules

1. Eisenhower to Doolittle, July 26, 1954, in *Papers of Dwight David Eisenhower*, vol. 15, doc. 993.

2. Church Committee, bk. 4, pp. 52–53, n. 9.

3. *Memoirs of Earl Warren*, pp. 5–6.

4. Palmer, "Case Against the Reds," p. 174.

5. Church Committee, bk. 2, pp. 211–16.

6. Quoted in Church Committee, vol. 6, p. 372.

7. Hoover to Anderson, July 29, 1955, quoted in Church Committee, bk. 2, p. 66 n. 271, italics added.

8. Quoted in Church Committee, vol. 6, p. 376.

9. Hoover to AG, in ibid., pp. 819–20.

10. Quoted in Donner, *Age of Surveillance*, p. 192.

11. Quoted in Church Committee, bk. 3, p. 17.

12. Quoted in *Communist Infiltration and Activities in the South*, p. 2754.

13. Goldstein, *Political Repression in Modern America*, p. 410; Ungar, *FBI*, p. 140; Gentry, *J. Edgar Hoover*, p. 444.

14. Church Committee, bk. 3, pp. 3–27.

15. Wise, *American Police State*, pp. 310–11.

16. Church Committee, bk. 2, p. 175.

17. Quoted in Wittner, *Rebels Against War*, p. 258.

18. Quoted in Glazer, "Peace Movement in America," p. 293.

19. Quoted in ibid., p. 260.

20. Hoover to SAC, San Juan, Aug. 4, 1960, in Churchill and Vander Wall, *COINTELPRO Papers*, p. 68.

21. See Lichtenstein and Wimhurst, "Red Alert in Puerto Rico," p. 782.

22. Hoover to SAC, San Juan, Aug. 4, 1960, in Churchill and Vander Wall, *COINTELPRO Papers*, p. 68.

23. Quoted in Lichtenstein and Wimhurst, "Red Alert in Puerto Rico," pp. 781, 782.

24. Quoted in Donner, *Age of Surveillance*, p. 200.

25. Quoted in *NYT*, March 23, 1975.

26. Church Committee, bk. 3, pp. 84, 85, 86.

27. Quoted in ibid., p. 82.

28. *NYT*, Nov. 19, 1962.

29. Alex Rosen to Alan Belmont, Nov. 20, 1962, quoted in Church Committee, bk. 3, pp. 90–91.

30. Alan Belmont to Clyde Tolson, Nov. 26, 1963, quoted in ibid., p. 91.

31. Quoted in Gentry, *J. Edgar Hoover*, p. 527.

32. Hoover to SACs, July 18, 1963, quoted in Church Committee, bk. 3, p. 105.

33. See Garrow, *FBI and Martin Luther King, Jr.*, p. 68.

34. Quoted in ibid.

35. Sullivan to Belmont, quoted in Church Committee, bk. 3, pp. 107–8.

36. Quoted in ibid., pp. 110–11.

37. Quoted in Gentry, *J. Edgar Hoover*, p. 568.

38. Sullivan (by Baumgardner) to Belmont, Dec. 24, 1963, quoted in Garrow, *FBI and Martin Luther King, Jr.*, pp. 102–3. The memo is also reproduced with deletions in the House Select Committee on Assassinations Hearings, *Investigation of the Assassination of Martin Luther King, Jr.*, vol. 6, pp. 156–58.

39. Sullivan to Belmont, reproduced in *Nation*, June 17, 1978, p. 717.

40. *NYT*, April 22, 1964.

41. Quoted in Church Committee, bk. 3, p. 155.

42. Quoted in ibid., p. 156.

43. Quoted in ibid.

44. *NYT*, Nov. 19, 1964; DeLoach to Mohr, memo, Nov. 18, 1964, quoted in Church Committee, bk. 3, p. 157.

45. *NYT*, Nov. 20, 1964.

46. Gentry, *J. Edgar Hoover*, pp. 572–73.

47. Quoted in Garrow, *FBI and Martin Luther King, Jr.*, pp. 125–26.

48. *NYT*, Dec. 2, 1964.

49. Quoted in Sullivan, *Bureau*, p. 140.

50. *NYT*, Dec. 5, 1964.

51. *NYT*, May 9, 1964.

52. Quoted in Garrow, *FBI and Martin Luther King, Jr.*, p. 134.

53. Quoted in ibid., p. 135.

54. Quoted in Donner, *Age of Surveillance*, p. 218.

55. *Newsweek*, Dec. 14, 1970.

56. *Final Report of the House Select Committee on Assassinations*, p. 434.

57. *NYT*, March 9, 1975.

58. Quoted in Whitehead, *Attack on Terror*, p. 91.

59. Quoted in Donner, *Age of Surveillance*, pp. 207–8, italics added.

60. *LAT*, Feb. 13, 1970.

Chapter 15: We Never Gave It a Thought

1. C. D. Brennan to Sullivan, Aug. 3, 1967, quoted in Church Committee, bk. 3, p. 511.

2. Quoted in Donner, "Hoover's Legacy," p. 693.

3. Wall, "Special Agent for the FBI," p. 16; Hoover to SACs, April 3, 1968, quoted in Davis, *Spying on America*, p. 103.

4. *NYT*, April 6, 1974. The article mistakenly identifies COINTELPRO-BNHG as beginning with the directive of October 12, 1961, which was actually the letter that initiated COINTELPRO-SWP.

5. Quoted in Hampton and Fayer, *Voices of Freedom*, p. 353.

6. Moore to Sullivan, Feb. 29, 1968, in Church Committee, vol. 6, pp. 389–90.

7. Quoted in Hampton and Fayer, *Voices of Freedom*, p. 513.

8. Bergman and Weir, "Revolution on Ice," p. 46.

9. Quoted in Church Committee, bk. 3, pp. 187–88.

10. San Diego Field Office to FBI Headquarters, April 10, 1969, quoted in ibid., p. 191.

11. San Diego Field Office to FBI Headquarters, Sept. 18, 1969, quoted in ibid., pp. 192–93.

12. Quoted in Bergman and Weir, "Casualties of a Secret War," p. 47.

13. *NYT*, May 25, 1974.

14. Quoted in Bergman and Weir, "Revolution on Ice," p. 48.

15. Quoted in ibid., p. 46.

16. Hoover to SAC, San Francisco, June 30, 1968, quoted in Gentry, *J. Edgar Hoover*, pp. 622–23.

17. Hoover to SACs, May 3, 1966, quoted in Church Committee, bk. 2, p. 70.

18. Quoted in Church Committee, vol. 6, p. 15.

19. Church Committee, bk. 3, p. 23 n. 99; Donner, *Age of Surveillance*, p. 232.

20. "From J. Edgar Hoover: A Report on Campus Reds," p. 84.

21. Hoover memo, April 28, 1965, quoted in Church Committee, bk. 3, p. 484; Ungar, *FBI*, p. 140.

22. Quoted in Church Committee, bk. 3, p. 485.

23. Hoover to Marvin Watson (special assistant to the president), June 4, 1965, quoted in ibid., p. 489.

24. *Anti-Vietnam Agitation and the Teach-In Movement*, pp. xiv–xv.

25. Quoted in Stout, *People*, p. 45.

26. *NYT*, April 17, 1967.

27. Martin Luther King Jr., "Beyond Vietnam: A Time to Break Silence," www.hartford-hwp.com/archives/45a/058.html.

28. Hoover to SACs, April 2, 1968, in Church Committee, vol. 6, p. 667.

29. Charles D. Brennan to Sullivan, May 9, 1968, in ibid., p. 393.

30. Hoover to SACs, May 23, 1968, quoted in Church Committee, bk. 3, p. 24.

31. Boston Field Office to FBI Headquarters, memo, June 13, 1968, quoted in ibid., pp. 24–25, n. 105.

32. White, *Making of the President, 1968*, p. 373.

33. Walker, *Rights in Conflict*, p. 5.

34. Goldstein, *Political Repression in Modern America*, p. 462.

35. *NYT*, May 20, 1973. Also see Davis, *Spying on America*, p. 152.

36. See www.bhamweekly.com/birmingham/article-1593-when-the-world-itself-seemed-afire.html.

37. See Nicosia, *Home to War*, pp. 249–51; also *Time*, Aug. 20, 1973.

38. See Rapoport, *Terrorism*, p. 198.

39. *NYT*, Dec. 6, 1970.

40. *NYT*, May 21, 1973.

41. Quoted in Wise, *American Police State*, p. 311.

42. *NYT*, June 7, 1970.

43. *NYT*, June 19, 1970.

44. Church Committee, bk. 3, pp. 11 n. 48, 64.

45. Senate Subcommittee on Constitutional Rights, *Army Surveillance of Civilians*, p. 97.

46. Church Committee, bk. 3, pp. 749–50.

47. Ibid., p. 980.

48. Ibid., p. 926.

49. Ibid., pp. 927, 980.

50. Quoted in Wise, *American Police State*, p. 30.

51. Quoted in Ungar, *FBI*, p. 485.

52. Felt, *FBI Pyramid from the Inside*, pp. 98–99.

53. Quoted in Gentry, *J. Edgar Hoover*, p. 682.

54. Chang, *Silencing Political Dissent*, p 32.

55. *Life*, April 9, 1971; *National Observer*, quoted in Gentry, *J. Edgar Hoover*, p. 681; *Newsweek*, May 10, 1971.

56. *Boston Evening Globe*, May 16, 1973.

57. *LAT*, Jan. 10, 1972.

58. Quoted in Gentry, *J. Edgar Hoover*, p. 720.

59. *St. Petersburg Times*, May 1, 1972.

60. *FBI COINTELPRO Activities*, pp. 3, 4.

61. Church Committee, bk. 2, p. 5.

62. *FBI Oversight*, serial no. 2, pt. 3, 94th Cong., 1st and 2nd sess., p. 257.

63. *FBI Oversight*, serial no. 33, pt. 1, 95th Cong., 1st sess., p. 50. The entire "Attorney General's Guidelines on Domestic Security Investigations" are reprinted on pp. 50–53.

Epilogue: An Aggressive Assault on Civil Liberties

1. Quoted in Theoharis, *FBI: A Comprehensive Reference Guide*, p. 134.
2. See Cole and Dempsey, *Terrorism and the Constitution*, p. 37.
3. Akram, "Scheherazade Meets Kafka," p. 70.
4. *NYT*, May 4, 1995.
5. Ibid.
6. See thomas.loc.gov/cgi-bin/query/z?c104:S.735.ENR:.
7. Cole and Dempsey, *Terrorism and the Constitution*, pp. 2–3.
8. Quoted in Scher, "Crackdown on Dissent," p. 24.
9. *NYT*, Sept. 18, 2001.
10. *NYT*, June 8, 2003.
11. Quoted in "Big Chill," p. 17.
12. Quoted in ibid., pp. 17–19.
13. Ehrlich, "Taking Liberties."
14. *NYT*, May 31, 2002.
15. *NYT*, Dec. 16, 2005.
16. *NYT*, June 23, 2006.
17. *NYT*, Nov. 23, 2003.
18. Quoted in ibid.
19. Quoted in Conason, *It Can Happen Here*, p. 192.
20. "Is the Pentagon Spying on Americans?" MSNBC, Dec. 14, 2005, www.msnbc.msn.com/id/10454316/.
21. Quoted in *WP*, Jan. 19, 2010.
22. Conason, *It Can Happen Here*, p. 195.
23. See Bob Herbert's columns "Watching Certain People" and "Big Brother in Blue."
24. Quoted in Herbert, "Watching Certain People."
25. Quoted in *LAT*, Aug. 18, 1975.
26. *WP*, July 19, 2010.
27. Schulhofer, *Enemy Within*, p. 4.
28. Moorfield Storey, introduction to *Deportations Delirium*, by Post, p. ix.

Bibliography

The following are the essential works, the starting points, if you will. Other sources cited can be found in Works Cited and Other Essential Works (see below).

Overview

Three especially helpful books are Frank J. Donner's *Age of Surveillance*, Robert Justin Goldstein's *Political Repression in Modern America*, and Geoffrey R. Stone's *Perilous Times*.

There are any number of books on J. Edgar Hoover and the FBI. I drew mainly on Curt Gentry's *J. Edgar Hoover*, Max Lowenthal's *Federal Bureau of Investigation*, Athan Theoharis's *FBI and American Democracy*, and Sanford J. Ungar's *FBI*. Theoharis's many studies of Hoover and the bureau are invaluable.

The reports of the Church Committee provide a comprehensive narrative and contain quotations from and reproductions of many primary documents; of particular value are *Book 2, Intelligence Activities and the Rights of Americans; Book 3, Supplementary Detailed Staff Reports on Intelligence Activities and the Rights of Americans;* and *Volume 6, Hearings on the Federal Bureau of Investigation.*

World War I

The four indispensable works are Paul L. Murphy's *World War I and the Origin of Civil Liberties in the United States*, H. C. Peterson and Gilbert C. Fite's *Opponents of War, 1917–1918*, Harry N. Scheiber's *Wilson Administration and Civil Liberties, 1917–1921*, and William Preston Jr.'s *Aliens and Dissenters*. The last book also covers the red scare.

Red Scare

The basic works are Robert K. Murray's *Red Scare* and Regin Schmidt's *Red Scare*. The most authoritative account of the Palmer raids is Louis F. Post's *Deportations Delirium of Nineteen-Twenty*.

Mexican Deportations and Repatriations

The main sources are Francisco Balderrama's *Decade of Betrayal*, Camille Guerin-Gonzales's *Mexican Workers and American Dreams*, and Abraham Hoffman's *Unwanted Mexican Americans in the Great Depression*.

World War II

On the German-American internment, see Arnold Krammer's *Undue Process;* on the Italian-American internment, see Lawrence DiStasi's *Una storia segreta* and Stephen Fox's *Unknown Internment.* The story of interned German Latin Americans is told in Max Paul Friedman's *Nazis and Good Neighbors,* and that of interned Japanese Latin Americans is told in Thomas Connell's *America's Japanese Hostages* and C. Harvey Gardiner's *Pawns in a Triangle of Hate.*

The literature on the Japanese-American relocation and internment is vast. Morton Grodzins's *Americans Betrayed* is the foundation of all subsequent research. Also essential are the Commission on Wartime Relocation and Internment of Civilians report *Personal Justice Denied;* the Army report *Command Decisions,* edited by Kent Roberts Greenfield; and John L. DeWitt's *Final Report: Japanese Evacuation from the West Coast, 1942.*

Cold War

Three good accounts of the period are Fred J. Cook's *Nightmare Decade,* David Caute's *Great Fear,* and Robert Griffith's *Politics of Fear.* Eleanor Bontecou's *Federal Loyalty-Security Program* covers the loyalty program. For the relationship between the FBI and HUAC, see Kenneth O'Reilly's *Hoover and the Un-Americans.* On Joe McCarthy, Thomas C. Reeves's *Life and Times of Joe McCarthy* and Richard H. Rovere's *Senator Joe McCarthy* provide complementary perspectives. David K. Johnson's *Lavender Scare* deals with the scapegoating of homosexuals in the federal government.

COINTELPRO

Noam Chomsky's introduction to Nelson Blackstock's *COINTELPRO* is very informative. Ward Churchill and Jim Vander Wall's *COINTELPRO Papers* contains reproductions of many documents. For the FBI's war on Martin Luther King, see David J. Garrow's *FBI and Martin Luther King, Jr.*

Works Cited and Other Essential Works

Collections

American Civil Liberties Union files. Mudd Library, Princeton University.

Attorney General files. National Archives and Records Administration, Washington, D.C.

Commission on Wartime Relocation and Internment of Civilians Papers. Frederick, Md.: University Publications of America, 1983.

Department of Justice files. National Archives and Records Administration, Washington, D.C.

Frey, Daniel, Papers. University of California, Los Angeles.

Gregory, Thomas W., Papers. Manuscripts Division, Library of Congress.

Japanese American Evacuation and Resettlement Records. Bancroft Library, University of California, Berkeley.

Provost Marshal General's Office files, National Archives and Records Administration.

Villard, Oswald Garrison, Papers. Houghton Library, Harvard University.

Wells, Hulet M., Papers. Special Collections, University of Washington.

Wilson, Woodrow, Papers. Manuscripts Division, Library of Congress, Washington, D.C.

Web Sites

Antiterrorism and Effective Death Penalty Act of 1996. thomas.loc.gov/cgi-bin/query/z?c104:S.735.ENR:.

"Attack on Pearl Harbor by Japanese Armed Forces." www.ibiblio.org/pha/pha/roberts/roberts.html.

Communist Control Act of 1954. tucnak.fsv.cuni.cz/~calda/Documents/1950s/Communist_54.html.

Douglas, William O. Dissenting opinion in *Adler v. Board of Education of City of New York*. At www.law.cornell.edu/supct/html/historics/USSC_CR_0342_0485_ZD2.html.

Executive Order 10450. www.archives.gov/federal-register/codification/executive-order/10450.html

Goldman, Emma. "The Tragedy at Buffalo." ublib.buffalo.edu/libraries/exhibits/panam/law/images/tragedyatbuff.html.

Hoover, J. Edgar. "Memo to SACs." June 15, 1940. www.foitimes.com/internment/chrono.htm.

———. "Memo to SACs." Dec. 8, 1941. www.foitimes.com/internment/chrono.htm.

Internal Security Act of 1950. tucnak.fsv.cuni.cz/~calda/Documents/1950s/Inter_Security_50.html.

King, Martin Luther, Jr. "Beyond Vietnam: A Time to Break Silence." www.hartford-hwp.com/archives/45a/058.html.

"Mass Evacuation of Japanese in Perspective." www.nps.gov/archive/manz/hrs/hrs2c.htm.

Murrow, Edward R. en.wikiquote.org/wiki/Edward_R._Murrow.

Myers, Lisa, Douglas Pasternak, Rich Gardella, and the NBC Investigative Unit. "Is the Pentagon Spying on Americans?" MSNBC, Dec. 14, 2005. www.msnbc.msn.com/id/10454316/

National Security Act of 1947. www.law.cornell.edu/uscode/50/usc_sec_50_00000403----004a.html.

"Presidential Proclamation 2525." www.internmentarchives.com/specialreports/smithsonian/smithsonian10.php.

Rockefeller Commission Report. www.aarclibrary.org/publib/contents/church/contents_church_reports_rockcomm.htm.

Senate Select Committee to Study Governmental Operations with Respect to Intelligence Activities. www.aarclibrary.org/publib/contents/church/contents_church_reports.htm.

Truman Doctrine. avalon.law.yale.edu/20th_century/trudoc.asp.

Vogel, Richard D. "Stolen Birthright: The U.S. Conquest and Exploitation of the Mexican People." www.houstonculture.org/hispanic/conquest5.html.

"When the World Itself Seemed Afire." www.bhamweekly.com/birmingham/article-1593-when-the-world-itself-seemed-afire.html.

Government Reports and Publications

Annual Report of the Attorney-General of the United States for the Year 1917; 1918; 1920; 1921. Washington, D.C.: U.S. Department of Justice, Office of the Attorney General, 1918; 1919; 1921; 1922.

Annual Report of the Commissioner General of Immigration, 1931. Washington, D.C.: U.S. Government Printing Office, 1931.

The Anti-Vietnam Agitation and the Teach-In Movement. Washington, D.C.: U.S. Government Printing Office, 1965.

Attorney General. *Investigation Activities of the Department of Justice.* Washington, D.C.: U.S. Government Printing Office, 1919.

Attorney General A. Mitchell Palmer on Charges Made Against Department of Justice by Louis F. Post and Others. Washington, D.C.: U.S. States Government Printing Office, 1920.

"Attorney General's Guidelines on Domestic Security Investigations." *FBI Oversight.* Washington, D.C.: U.S. Government Printing Office, 1975.

Barkley, Alben William. "Attack on Pearl Harbor by Japanese Armed Forces." In *Hearings Before the Joint Committee on the Investigation of the Pearl Harbor Attack,* pt. 39, pp. 1–21. Washington, D.C.: U.S. Government Printing Office, 1946.

Commission on Wartime Relocation and Internment of Civilians. *Personal Justice Denied.* Washington, D.C.: U.S. Government Printing Office, 1983.

Committee on Public Information. *The Official Bulletin.* Washington, D.C.: Committee on Public Information, 1917–18.

Communist Control Act of 1954. Public Law 83-637. 68 *United States Statutes at Large* 775–80. Washington, D.C.: United States Government Printing Office, 1955.

Communist Infiltration and Activities in the South. Washington, D.C.: U.S. Government Printing Office, 1958.

Communist Infiltration in the Army. Washington, D.C.: U.S. Government Printing Office, 1954.

Congress and the Nation, 1945–1964: A Review of Government and Politics in the Postwar Years. Washington, D.C.: Congressional Quarterly Service, 1965.

Congressional Record. Washington, D.C.: U.S. Government Printing Office, 1917–76.

Department of State Bulletin. Washington, D.C.: U.S. Department of State, Bureau of Public Affairs, 1945.

Departments of State, Justice, Commerce and the Judiciary Appropriations for 1951. Washington, D.C.: U.S. Government Printing Office, 1950.

DeWitt, John L. *Final Report: Japanese Evacuation from the West Coast, 1942.* Washington, D.C.: U.S. Government Printing Office, 1943.

Employment of Homosexuals and Other Sex Perverts in Government. Washington, D.C.: U.S. Government Printing Office, 1950.

Espionage Act of 1917. Public Law 65-24. 40 *United States Statutes at Large* 217–19. Washington, D.C.: United States Government Printing Office, 1919.

Executive Sessions of the Senate Foreign Relations Committee (Historical Series). Washington, D.C.: U.S. Government Printing Office, 1951.

FBI COINTELPRO Activities. Washington, D.C.: Department of Justice, 1974.

Final Report of the House Select Committee on Assassinations. Washington, D.C.: U.S. Government Printing Office, 1979.

Hearing Before Subcommittee of House Committee on Appropriations, Department of Justice Appropriation Bill, 1923; 1925. Washington, D.C.: U.S. Government Printing Office, 1922; 1924.

Hearings Before the Committee on Un-American Activities on H.R. 1884 and H.R. 2122. Washington, D.C.: U.S. Government Printing Office, 1947.

Hearings on the Sixth Supplemental National Defense Appropriation Bill for 1942. Washington, D.C.: U.S. Government Printing Office, 1942.

Hearings Regarding Communist Espionage in the United States Government. Washington, D.C.: U.S. Government Printing Office, 1948.

House Select Committee on Assassinations Hearings. *Investigation of the Assassination of Martin Luther King, Jr.* Washington, D.C.: U.S. Government Printing Office, 1979.

Immigration Act of 1917. Public Law 64-301. 39 *United States Statutes at Large* 874–98. Washington, D.C.: United States Government Printing Office, 1917.

"Immigration from Countries of the Western Hemisphere." In *Hearings Before the House Committee on Immigration and Naturalization, 1928.* Washington, D.C.: U.S. Government Printing Office, 1928.

Investigation of Administration of Louis F. Post, Assistant Secretary of Labor, in the Matter of Deportation of Aliens. Washington, D.C.: U.S. Government Printing Office, 1920.

Investigation of Hon. Harry M. Daugherty. Washington, D.C.: U.S. Government Printing Office, 1924.

Japanese Immigration Legislation, Hearings Before the Committee on Immigration, United States Senate. Washington, D.C.: U.S. Government Printing Office, 1924.

Maryland Senatorial Election of 1950: Report of the Subcommittee on Privileges and Elections. Washington, D.C.: U.S. Government Printing Office, 1951.

Munson, C. B. "Japanese on the West Coast." In Commission on Wartime Relocation and Internment of Civilians Papers. Frederick, Md.: University Publications of America, 1983.

Proceedings of the Conference with the President of the United States and the Secretary of Labor of the Governors of the States and Mayors of Cities in the East Room of the White House. Washington, D.C.: U.S. Government Printing Office, 1919.

Public Hearings of the Commission on Wartime Relocation and Internment of Civilians. Washington, D.C.: National Archives, National Archives and Records Service, General Services Administration, 1983.

Report of the President's Temporary Commission on Employee Loyalty. Washington, D.C.: Department of Justice, 1947.

Report on the Bisbee Deportations Made by the President's Mediation Commission to the President of the United States, November 6, 1917. Washington, D.C.: U.S. Government Printing Office, 1918.

Report on the Enforcement of the Deportation Laws of the United States. Washington, D.C.: U.S. Government Printing Office, 1931.

Sedition Act of 1918. Public Law 65-150. 40 *United States Statutes at Large* 553–54. Washington, D.C.: United States Government Printing Office, 1919.

Senate Committee on the Judiciary. *Charges of Illegal Practices of the Department of Justice.* Washington, D.C.: U.S. Government Printing Office, 1921.

Senate Report No. 289, *Investigating Strike in Steel Industries.* Washington, D.C.: U.S. Government Printing Office, 1919.

Senate Select Committee to Study Governmental Operations with Respect to Intelligence Activities. *Book 2, Intelligence Activities and the Rights of Americans.* Washington, D.C.: U.S. Government Printing Office, 1976.

———. *Book 3, Supplementary Detailed Staff Reports on Intelligence Activities and the Rights of Americans.* Washington, D.C.: U.S. Government Printing Office, 1976.

———. *Volume 6, Hearings on the Federal Bureau of Investigation.* Washington, D.C.: U.S. Government Printing Office, 1976.

Sisson, Edgar Grant. *The German-Bolshevik Conspiracy.* Washington, D.C.: Committee on Public Information, 1918.

Special Senate Investigation on Charges and Countercharges Involving: Secretary of the Army Robert T. Stevens, John G. Adams, H. Struve Hensel and Senator Joe McCarthy, Roy M. Cohn, and Francis P. Carr. Washington, D.C.: U.S. Government Printing Office, 1954.

State Department Employee Loyalty Investigation. Washington, D.C.: U.S. Government Printing Office, 1950.

Sundry Civil Appropriation Bill, 1920; 1922. Washington, D.C.: U.S. Government Printing Office, 1919; 1921.

Threats Against the President Act of 1917. Public Law 64-319. 39 *United States Statutes at Large* 919. Washington, D.C.: United States Government Printing Office, 1917.

U.S. Senate Committee on the Judiciary. *Brewing and Liquor Interests and German and Bolshevik Propaganda.* Washington, D.C.: U.S. Government Printing Office, 1919.

Walker, Daniel. *Rights in Conflict.* New York: Dutton, 1968.

"Western Hemisphere Immigration." In *Hearings Before the House Committee on Immigration and Naturalization, 1930.* Washington, D.C.: U.S. Government Printing Office, 1930.

Articles

"Academic Freedom and Tenure: Evansville College." *Bulletin of the American Association of University Professors* 35, no. 1 (Spring 1949): 74–111.

"The ACLU and the FBI." *Civil Liberties Review,* Nov./Dec. 1977.

Akram, Susan. "Scheherezade Meets Kafka." *Georgetown Immigration Law Journal* 14 (Fall 1999): 51–113.

"American Soldiers in Parade Killed by Reds." *United Presbyterian,* Nov. 20, 1919.

Bergman, Lowell, and David Weir. "Casualties of a Secret War." *Rolling Stone,* Sept. 9, 1976, p. 47.

———. "Revolution on Ice." *Rolling Stone,* Sept. 9, 1976, pp. 41–49.

Bogardus, Emory S. "Mexican Repatriates." *Sociology and Social Research* (Nov.–Dec. 1933).

Chafee, Zechariah. "Sedition." In *Encyclopedia of the Social Sciences.*

Chinea, Jorge. "Ethnic Prejudice and Anti-immigrant Policies in Times of Economic Stress." *East Wind, West Wind* (Winter 1996): 9–13.

"Civil Liberties Dead." *Nation,* Sept. 14, 1918.

Coben, Stanley. "A Study in Nativism: The American Red Scare of 1919–20." *Political Science Quarterly* 79, no. 1 (March 1964): 52–75.

Cooper, Marc. "The Big Chill." *Nation,* June 3, 2002, pp. 17–20.

Crawford, Kenneth G. "J. Edgar Hoover." *Nation,* Feb. 27, 1937.

Creel, George. "The Hopes of the Hyphenated." *Century,* Jan. 1916.

———. "Public Opinion in War Time." *Annals of the American Academy of Political and Social Science* 78 (July 1918): 185–94.

Cushman, Peter E. "Civil Liberty After the War." *American Political Science Review* 38, no. 1 (Feb. 1944): 1–20.

Donner, Frank J. "Hoover's Legacy." *Nation,* June 1, 1974.

Dunphy, John J. "The Lynching of Robert Prager." *Illinois Magazine,* May–June 1984.

Eastman, Max. "The Post Office Censorship." *Masses,* Sept. 1917.

"Editorial Paragraphs." *Nation,* Aug. 19, 1931.

"Education: The Danger Signs." *Time,* April 13, 1953.

Ehrlich, Dorothy. "Taking Liberties." [ACLU of Northern California] *Daily Journal*, Feb. 26, 2002.

Emerson, Thomas I., and David M. Helfeld. "Loyalty Among Government Employees." *Yale Law Journal* 58 (Dec. 1948): 1–143.

"The Espionage Cases." *Harvard Law Review* 32, no. 4 (Feb. 1919): 417–20.

"From J. Edgar Hoover: A Report on Campus Reds." *U.S. News & World Report*, May 31, 1965.

Gannett, Lewis S. "The I.W.W." *Nation*, Oct. 20, 1920.

"The German Campaign Against American Neutrality." *Outlook*, Aug. 25, 1915, p. 934.

Glazer, Nathan. "The Peace Movement in America—1961." *Commentary* 31, no.4 (April 1961): 288–96.

Goldman, Emma. "The Promoters of the War Mania." *Mother Earth*, March 1917.

Gutfeld, Arnon. "The Murder of Frank Little." *Labor History* 10, no. 2 (Spring 1969): 177–92.

Harris, Charles W. "The Alien Enemy Hearing Board as a Judicial Device in the United States During World War II." *International and Comparative Law Journal* 14, no. 4 (Oct. 1965): 1360–70.

Herbert, Bob. "Big Brother in Blue." *New York Times*, March 13, 2010.

———. "Watching Certain People." *New York Times*, March 2, 2010.

Hickey, Donald R. "The Prager Affair: A Study in Wartime Hysteria." *Journal of the Illinois State Historical Society* 62, no. 2 (Summer 1969): 117–34.

Intelligence Officer. "The Japanese in America." *Harper's Magazine* 185, no. 1189 (Oct. 1942): 489–97.

"Investigations." *Time*, March 8, 1954.

Jackson, Gardner. "Doak the Deportation Chief." *Nation*, March 18, 1931, pp. 295–96.

Johnson, Donald. "Wilson, Burleson, and Censorship in the First World War." *Journal of Southern History* 28, no. 1 (Feb. 1962): 46–58.

Kumamoto, Bob. "The Search for Spies." *Amerasia Journal* 6, no. 2 (Fall 1979): 45–75.

La Follette, Robert. "Neutrality." *La Follette's Magazine* 7, no. 9 (Sept. 1915).

Lichtenstein, William, and David Wimhurst. "Red Alert in Puerto Rico." *Nation*, June 30, 1979.

McGrath, Earl James. "Democracy's Road to Freedom." *NEA Journal*, Sept. 1949.

McKay, R. Reynolds. "The Federal Deportation Campaign in Texas." *Borderlands Journal* (Fall 1981).

McWilliams, Carey. "Getting Rid of the Mexican." *American Mercury*, Jan. 1933.

———. "The Witch Hunt's New Phase." *New Statesman and Nation*, Oct. 27, 1951.

Monthly Labor Review, June 1920.

Murray, Robert K. "The Outer World and the Inner Light." *Pennsylvania History* 36, no. 3 (July 1969): 265–89.

O'Brian, John Lord. "Civil Liberty in War Time." *Proceedings of the Forty-second Annual Meeting of the New York Bar Association*, pp. 275–313.

Oppenheimer, Reuben. "The Deportation Terror." *New Republic*, Jan. 13, 1932, pp. 231–32.

Palmer, A. Mitchell. "The Case Against the Reds." *Forum* 53 (Feb. 1920): 173–85.

"The Press and Public Opinion." *New Republic*, Dec. 31, 1919.

Rader, Benjamin G. "The Montana Lumber Strike of 1917." *Pacific Historical Review* 36, no. 2 (May 1967): 189–207.

Reed, John. "One Solid Month of Liberty." *Masses*, Sept. 1917.

Scher, Abby. "The Crackdown on Dissent." *Nation*, Feb. 5, 2001.

Schwartz, E. A. "The Lynching of Robert Prager, the United Mine Workers, and the Problems of Patriotism in 1918." *Journal of the Illinois State Historical Society* 95, no. 4 (Winter 2002/2003): 414–37.

Steinke, John, and James Weinstein. "McCarthy and the Liberals." *Studies on the Left* 2, no. 3 (1962).

"Suggestions of Attorney-General Gregory to Executive Committee in Relation to the Department of Justice." *American Bar Association Journal* 4 (1918).

Taylor, Frank. "The People Nobody Wants." *Saturday Evening Post*, May 9, 1942, pp. 24–25, 64, 66–67.

"TRIALS: I Do Not Intend to Turn My Back." *Time*, Feb. 6, 1950.

Wall, Robert. "Special Agent for the FBI." *New York Review of Books*, Jan. 27, 1972.

"Who Will Stand Up to McCarthy." *New Republic*, Jan. 12, 1953.

Wilkinson, Frank. "The Era of Libertarian Repression—1948 to 1973." *University of Akron Law Review* 7 (Winter 1974): 280–309.

Books and Pamphlets

American Civil Liberties Union. *In the Shadow of Fear: American Liberties, 1948–49.* New York: American Civil Liberties Union, 1949.

———. *In Times of Challenge: U.S. Liberties, 1946–47.* New York: American Civil Liberties Union, 1947.

———. *The Nation-Wide Spy System Centering in the Department of Justice.* New York: American Civil Liberties Union, 1924.

———. *Our Uncertain Liberties: U.S. Liberties, 1947–48.* New York: American Civil Liberties Union, 1948.

Avrich, Paul. *Sacco and Vanzetti: The Anarchist Background.* Princeton, N.J.: Princeton University Press, 1991.

Baker, Ray Stannard. *Woodrow Wilson: Life and Letters.* Garden City, N.Y.: Doubleday, Page, 1927–39.

Baker, Ray Stannard, William E. Dodd, and Howard S. Leach, eds. *The Public Papers of Woodrow Wilson.* New York: Harper & Brothers, 1925–27.

Balderrama, Francisco. *In Defense of La Raza: The Los Angeles Mexican Consulate and the Mexican Community, 1929 to 1936.* Tucson: University of Arizona Press, 1982.

Balderrama, Francisco, and Raymond Rodríguez. *Decade of Betrayal: Mexican Repatriation in the 1930s.* Rev. ed. Albuquerque: University of New Mexico Press, 2006.

Barth, Alan. *The Loyalty of Free Men.* New York: Viking Press, 1951.

Biddle, Francis. *In Brief Authority.* Garden City, N.Y.: Doubleday, 1962.

Blum, John Morton. "A. S. Burleson." In *Dictionary of American Biography.* Vol. 11, supp. 2. Edited by John A. Garraty. New York: Charles Scribner's Sons, 1995.

Bontecou, Eleanor. *The Federal Loyalty-Security Program.* Ithaca, N.Y.: Cornell University Press, 1953.

Brody, David. *Labor in Crisis: The Steel Strike of 1919.* Philadelphia: Lippincott, 1965.

Bruère, Robert W. *Following the Trail of the I.W.W.: A First-Hand Investigation into Labor Troubles in the West, a Trip into the Copper and Lumber Camps of the Inland Empire with the Views of the Men on the Job.* New York: New York Evening Post, 1918.

Buchanan, A. Russell. *The United States and World War II: Military and Diplomatic Documents.* Columbia: University of South Carolina Press, 1972.

Buckley, William F., Jr., and Brent Bozell. *McCarthy and His Enemies.* Chicago: H. Regnery, 1954.

Cantril, Hadley, and Mildred Strunk. *Public Opinion, 1935–1946.* Princeton, N.J.: Princeton University Press, 1951.

Carr, Robert K. *The House Committee on Un-American Activities, 1945–1950.* Ithaca, N.Y.: Cornell University Press, 1952.

Caute, David. *The Great Fear: The Anti-Communist Purge Under Truman and Eisenhower.* New York: Simon & Schuster, 1978.

Chafee, Zechariah. *Freedom of Speech.* New York: Harcourt, Brace, and Howe, 1920.

Chambers, Whittaker. *Witness.* New York: Random House, 1952.

Chang, Nancy. *Silencing Political Dissent.* New York: Seven Stories Press, 2002.

Chaplin, Ralph. *The Centralia Conspiracy: The Truth About the Armistice Day Tragedy.* Chicago: General Defense Committee, 1924.

Chomsky, Noam. Introduction to *COINTELPRO: The FBI's Secret War on Political Freedom,* by Nelson Blackstock. New York: Monad Press, 1975.

Churchill, Ward, and Jim Vander Wall. *The COINTELPRO Papers: Documents from the FBI's Secret Wars Against Domestic Dissent.* Boston: South End Press, 1990.

Claghorn, Kate Holladay. *The Immigrant's Day in Court.* New York: Arno Press, 1969.

Clark, Jane Perry. *Deportation of Aliens from the United States to Europe.* New York: Columbia University Press, 1931.

Coben, Stanley. *A. Mitchell Palmer: Politician.* New York: Columbia University Press, 1963.

Cohn, Roy. *McCarthy.* New York: New American Library, 1968.

Cole, David, and James X. Dempsey. *Terrorism and the Constitution: Sacrificing Civil Liberties in the Name of National Security.* New York: New Press, 2002.

Commager, Henry Steele. *Freedom and Order: A Commentary on the American Political Scene.* New York: G. Braziller, 1966.

Conason, Joe. *It Can Happen Here: Authoritarian Peril in the Age of Bush.* New York: St. Martin's Press, 2007.

Conn, Stetson. "The Decision to Evacuate the Japanese from the Pacific Coast." In *Command Decisions.* Edited by Kent Roberts Greenfield. Washington, D.C.: Office of the Chief of Military History, United States Army, 1960.

———. "Japanese Evacuation from the West Coast." In *Guarding the United States and Its Outposts.* Washington, D.C.: Office of the Chief of Military History, United States Army, 1964.

Connell, Thomas. *America's Japanese Hostages: The World War II Plan for a Japanese Free Latin America.* Westport, Conn.: Praeger, 2002.

Cook, Fred J. *The Nightmare Decade: The Life and Times of Senator Joe McCarthy.* New York: Random House, 1971.

Cooke, Alistair. *A Generation on Trial: U.S.A. v. Alger Hiss.* New York: Knopf, 1950.

Coolidge, Calvin. *The Autobiography of Calvin Coolidge.* New York: Cosmopolitan Book Corp., 1929.

Creel, George. *How We Advertised America.* New York: Harper & Brothers, 1920.

———. *Rebel at Large: Recollections of Fifty Crowded Years.* New York: G. P. Putnam's Sons, 1947.

Cummings, Homer S., and Carl McFarland. *Federal Justice: Chapters in the History of Justice and the Federal Executive.* New York: Macmillan, 1937.

Cunningham, Raymond K. *Prisoners at Fort Douglas: War Prison Barracks Three and the Alien Enemies, 1917–1920*. Salt Lake City: Fort Douglas Military Museum, 1983.

Curran, John Philpot. "Speech on the Right of Election of Lord Mayor of Dublin." In *Speeches of Phillips, Curran, and Grattan, the Celebrated Irish Orators*. Philadelphia: Key and Mielke, 1831.

Dallek, Robert. *Lone Star Rising: Lyndon Johnson and His Times, 1908–1960*. New York: Oxford University Press, 1991.

Daniels, Josephus. *The Cabinet Diaries of Josephus Daniels, 1913–1921*. Edited by E. David Cronon. Lincoln: University of Nebraska Press, 1963.

Davis, James Kirkpatrick. *Spying on America: The FBI's Domestic Counterintelligence Program*. New York: Praeger, 1992.

Debs, Eugene V. *Writings and Speeches of Eugene V. Debs*. New York: Hermitage Press, 1948.

Demaris, Ovid. *The Director*. New York: Harper's Magazine Press, 1975.

Democratic National Committee. *The Democratic Text Book 1916*. New York: Democratic National Committee, 1916.

DiStasi, Lawrence, ed. *Una storia segreta*. Berkeley, Calif.: Heyday Books, 2001.

Divine, Robert A. *American Immigration Policy, 1924–1952*. New Haven, Conn.: Yale University Press, 1957.

Donald, Heidi Gurcke. *We Were Not the Enemy*. New York: iUniverse, 2006.

Donner, Frank J. *The Age of Surveillance: The Aims and Methods of America's Political Intelligence System*. New York: Knopf, 1980.

———. *The Un-Americans*. New York: Ballantine, 1961.

Donovan, Robert J. *Conflict and Crisis: The Presidency of Harry S. Truman, 1945–1948*. New York: Norton, 1977.

Drinnon, Richard. *Rebel in Paradise: A Biography of Emma Goldman*. Chicago: University of Chicago Press, 1961.

Dubofsky, Melvyn. *We Shall Be All: A History of the Industrial Workers of the World*. New York: Quadrangle/New York Times Book Co., 1969.

Eastman, Max. *Love and Revolution*. New York: Random House, 1964.

Eisenhower, Dwight D. *The Papers of Dwight David Eisenhower*. Edited by Louis Galambos, Alfred D. Chandler, and Daun Van Ee. Baltimore: Johns Hopkins Press, 2001.

Fariello, Griffin. *Red Scare: Memories of the American Inquisition*. New York: Norton, 1995.

Felt, Mark. *The FBI Pyramid from the Inside*. New York: Putnam, 1979.

Ford, Earl C., and William Z. Foster. *Syndicalism*. Chicago: W. Z. Foster, 1913.

Foster, William Z. *From Bryan to Stalin*. New York: International Publishers, 1937.

Fox, Stephen. "The Relocation of Italian Americans in California During World War II." In DiStasi, *Una storia segreta*.

———. *The Unknown Internment: An Oral History of the Relocation of Italian Americans During World War II*. Boston: Twayne Publishers, 1990.

Friedman, Max Paul. *Nazis and Good Neighbors: The United States Campaign Against the Germans of Latin America in World War II*. New York: Cambridge University Press, 2003.

Fuess, Claude M. *Calvin Coolidge: The Man from Vermont*. Boston: Little, Brown, 1940.

Gallup, George Horace. *The Gallup Poll: Public Opinion, 1935–1971*. New York: Random House, 1972.

Gardiner, C. Harvey. *Pawns in a Triangle of Hate: The Peruvian Japanese and the United States*. Seattle: University of Washington Press, 1981.

Garrow, David J. *The FBI and Martin Luther King, Jr.: From "Solo" to Memphis.* New York: Norton, 1981.

Gentry, Curt. *J. Edgar Hoover: The Man and the Secrets.* New York: Norton, 1991.

Ginger, Ray. *The Bending Cross: A Biography of Eugene Victor Debs.* New Brunswick, N.J.: Rutgers University Press, 1949.

Gitlow, Benjamin. *The Whole of Their Lives: Communism in America—a Personal History and Intimate Portrayal of Its Leaders.* New York: Charles Scribner's Sons, 1948.

Goldman, Eric F. *The Crucial Decade: America, 1945–1955.* New York: Knopf, 1956.

Goldstein, Robert Justin. *Political Repression in Modern America: From 1870 to 1976.* Rev. ed. Urbana: University of Illinois Press, 2001.

Goodman, Walter. *The Committee: The Extraordinary Career of the House Committee on Un-American Activities.* New York: Farrar, Straus and Giroux, 1968.

Greenfield, Kent Roberts, ed. *Command Decisions.* Washington, D.C.: Office of the Chief of Military History, United States Army, 1960.

Greiff, Pablo de, ed. *The Handbook of Reparations.* New York: Oxford University Press, 2006.

Griffith, Robert. *The Politics of Fear: Joseph R. McCarthy and the Senate.* Lexington: University Press of Kentucky, 1970.

Grodzins, Morton. *Americans Betrayed: Politics and the Japanese Evacuation.* Chicago: University of Chicago Press, 1949.

Guerin-Gonzales, Camille. *Mexican Workers and American Dreams: Immigration, Repatriation, and California Farm Labor, 1900–1939.* New Brunswick, N.J.: Rutgers University Press, 1994.

Hagedorn, Ann. *Savage Peace: Hope and Fear in America, 1919.* New York: Simon & Schuster, 2007.

Hampton, Henry, and Steve Fayer. *Voices of Freedom: An Oral History of the Civil Rights Movement from the 1950s Through the 1980s.* With Sarah Flynn. New York: Bantam Books, 1991.

Hays, Arthur Garfield. *Trial by Prejudice.* New York: Covici, Friede, 1933.

Herman, Arthur. *Joseph McCarthy: Reexamining the Life and Legacy of America's Most Hated Senator.* New York: Free Press, 2000.

Hersey, John. "A Mistake of Terrifically Horrible Proportions." In *Manzanar,* by John Armor and Peter Wright. New York: Times Books, 1988.

Higham, John. *Strangers in the Land.* New Brunswick, N.J.: Rutgers University Press, 1955.

Hoffman, Abraham. *Unwanted Mexican Americans in the Great Depression: Repatriation Pressures, 1929–1939.* Tucson: University of Arizona Press, 1974.

Hough, Emerson. *The Web.* Chicago: Reilly & Lee, 1919.

Howard, John. *Concentration Camps on the Home Front: Japanese Americans in the House of Jim Crow.* Chicago: University of Chicago Press, 2008.

Howe, Frederic C. *The Confessions of a Reformer.* New York: Charles Scribner's Sons, 1925.

Hughes, Emmet John. *The Ordeal of Power: A Political Memoir of the Eisenhower Years.* New York: Atheneum, 1963.

Hyman, Harold M. *Soldiers and Spruce: Origins of the Loyal Legion of Loggers and Lumbermen.* Los Angeles: Institute of Industrial Relations, University of California, 1963.

Interchurch World Movement. *Public Opinion and the Steel Strike: Supplementary Reports of the Investigators to the Commission of Inquiry, the Interchurch World Movement.* New York: Harcourt, Brace, 1921.

————. *Report on the Steel Strike of 1919.* Harcourt, Brace, and Howe, 1920.

Irons, Peter H. *Justice at War: The Inside Story of the Japanese American Internment.* New York: Oxford University Press, 1983.

Israel, Fred I. "Military Justice in Hawaii, 1941–1944." In *The Diversity of Modern America: Essays in History Since World War One.* Edited by David Bruner. New York: Appleton-Century-Crofts, 1970.

Jensen, Joan M. *Army Surveillance in America, 1775–1980.* New Haven, Conn.: Yale University Press, 1991.

————. *The Price of Vigilance.* Chicago: Rand McNally, 1968.

Johnson, Claudius O. *Borah of Idaho.* New York: Longmans, Green, 1936.

Johnson, David K. *The Lavender Scare: The Cold War Persecution of Gays and Lesbians in the Federal Government.* Chicago: University of Chicago Press, 2004.

Jordan, David Starr. *The Days of a Man: Being Memories of a Naturalist, Teacher, and Minor Prophet of Democracy.* Yonkers on Hudson, N.Y.: World Book Company, 1922.

Kennedy, David M. *Over Here: The First World War and American Society.* New York: Oxford University Press, 1980.

Krammer, Arnold. *Undue Process: The Untold Story of America's German Alien Internees.* London: Rowman & Littlefield, 1997.

Leab, Daniel, and Robert Lester, eds. *Communist Activity in the Entertainment Industry.* Bethesda, Md.: University Publications of America, 1991.

Lerner, Max. *The Unfinished Country: A Book of American Symbols.* New York: Simon & Schuster, 1959.

Link, Arthur Stanley, ed. *The Papers of Woodrow Wilson.* Princeton, N.J.: Princeton University Press, 1966–94.

————. *Woodrow Wilson and the Progressive Era, 1910–1917.* New York: Harper, 1954.

Lowenthal, Max. *The Federal Bureau of Investigation.* New York: Sloane, 1950.

Luebke, Frederick C. *Bonds of Loyalty.* DeKalb: Northern Illinois University Press, 1974.

MacDougall, Curtis D. *Gideon's Army.* New York: Marzani & Munsell, 1965.

Mangione, Jerre. *An Ethnic at Large: A Memoir of America in the Thirties and Forties.* New York: Putnam, 1978.

Matusow, Harvey. *False Witness.* New York: Cameron & Kahn, 1955.

Mazo, Earl, and Stephen Hess. *Nixon: A Political Portrait.* New York: Harper & Row, 1967.

McWilliams, Carey. *North from Mexico: The Spanish-Speaking People of the United States.* New York: Greenwood Press, 1948.

————. *Witch Hunt: The Revival of Heresy.* Boston: Little, Brown, 1950.

Mock, James R. *Censorship 1917.* Princeton, N.J.: Princeton University Press, 1941.

Mock, James R., and Cedric Larson. *Words That Won the War: The Story of the Committee on Public Information, 1917–1919.* Princeton, N.J.: Princeton University Press, 1939.

Murphy, Paul L. *World War I and the Origin of Civil Liberties in the United States.* New York: Norton, 1979.

Murray, Robert K. *Red Scare: A Study in National Hysteria, 1919–1920.* Minneapolis: University of Minnesota Press, 1955.

Nagler, Jörg. "Victims of the Home Front." In *Minorities in Wartime.* Edited by Panikos Panayi. Oxford, UK: Berg, 1993.

National Association of Manufacturers. *Onward March of the Open Shop*. New York, 1921.

National Civil Liberties Bureau. *The Conviction of Mrs. Kate Richards O'Hare and North Dakota Politics*. New York: National Civil Liberties Bureau, 1918.

———. *The Outrage on Rev. Herbert S. Bigelow of Cincinnati, Ohio*. New York: National Civil Liberties Bureau, 1918.

———. *The Truth About the I.W.W.: Facts in Relation to the Trial at Chicago by Competent Industrial Investigators and Noted Economists*. New York: National Civil Liberties Bureau, 1918.

———. *War-Time Prosecutions and Mob Violence: Involving the Rights of Free Speech, Free Press, and Peaceful Assemblage*. New York: National Civil Liberties Bureau, 1919.

National Popular Government League. *To the American People: Report upon the Illegal Practices of the United States Department of Justice*. Chicago: American Freedom Foundation, 1920.

Nicosia, Gerald. *Home to War*. New York: Crown, 2001.

O'Reilly, Kenneth. *Hoover and the Un-Americans: The FBI, HUAC, and the Red Menace*. Philadelphia: Temple University Press, 1983.

Ott, Franziska, ed. "The Anti-German Hysteria: The Case of Robert Paul Prager, Selected Documents." In *The Anti-German Hysteria of World War One*. Edited by Don H. Tolzmann. Munich: K. G. Saur, 1995.

Parmet, Herbert S. *Eisenhower and the American Crusades*. New York: Macmillan, 1972.

Paterson, Thomas G. *Cold War Critics: Alternatives to American Foreign Policy in the Truman Years*. Chicago: Quadrangle Books, 1971.

Pencak, William. *For God and Country: The American Legion, 1919–1941*. Boston: Northeastern University Press, 1989.

Peterson, H. C., and Gilbert C. Fite. *Opponents of War, 1917–1918*. Madison: University of Wisconsin Press, 1957.

Phillips, Cabell. *The Truman Presidency: The History of a Triumphant Succession*. New York: Macmillan, 1966.

Phillips, Wendell. *Speeches Before the Massachusetts Anti-Slavery Society, January, 1852*. Boston: R. F. Wallcut, 1852.

Pinchot, Amos. *History of the Progressive Party, 1912–1916*. New York: New York University Press, 1958.

Post, Louis F. *The Deportations Delirium of Nineteen-Twenty*. Chicago: C. H. Kerr, 1923.

Powers, Richard Gid. *Secrecy and Power: The Life of J. Edgar Hoover*. New York: Free Press, 1987.

Preston, William, Jr. *Aliens and Dissenters: Federal Suppression of Radicals, 1903–1933*. New York: Harper & Row, 1963.

Rapoport, David C. *Terrorism*. London: Routledge, 2005.

Redding, Jack. *Inside the Democratic Party*. Indianapolis: Bobbs-Merrill, 1958.

Reeves, Thomas C. *The Life and Times of Joe McCarthy: A Biography*. New York: Stein and Day, 1982.

Robinson, Greg. *By Order of the President: FDR and the Internment of Japanese Americans*. Cambridge, Mass.: Harvard University Press, 2001.

Roche, John P. *The Quest for the Dream: The Development of Civil Rights and Human Relations in Modern America*. New York: Macmillan, 1963.

Roosevelt, Theodore. *America for Americans: Speech at St. Louis, Missouri, May 31st, 1916*. N.p., n.d.

————. *The Letters of Theodore Roosevelt.* Edited by Elting Elmore Morison. Cambridge, Mass.: Harvard University Press, 1951–54.

————. *Roosevelt in "The Kansas City Star": War-Time Editorials.* Boston: Houghton Mifflin, 1921.

Rovere, Richard H. *Senator Joe McCarthy.* New York: Harcourt, Brace, 1959.

Scheiber, Harry N. *The Wilson Administration and Civil Liberties, 1917–1921.* Ithaca, N.Y.: Cornell University Press, 1960.

Schmidt, Regin. *Red Scare: FBI and the Origins of Anticommunism in the United States, 1919–1943.* Copenhagen: Museum Tusculanum Press, University of Copenhagen, 2000.

Schulhofer, Stephen J. *The Enemy Within.* New York: Century Foundation Press, 2002.

Shaw, Albert, ed. *The Messages and Papers of Woodrow Wilson.* New York: Review of Reviews, 1924.

Stone, Geoffrey R. *Perilous Times: Free Speech in Wartime from the Sedition Act of 1798 to the War on Terrorism.* New York: Norton, 2004.

Stout, Richard T. *People.* New York: Harper & Row, 1970.

Sullivan, William. *The Bureau: My Thirty Years in Hoover's FBI.* With Bill Brown. New York: Norton, 1979.

Theoharis, Athan. "The Escalation of the Loyalty Program." In *Politics and Policies of the Truman Administration.* Edited by Barton J. Bernstein. Chicago: Quadrangle Books, 1970.

————. *The FBI: A Comprehensive Reference Guide.* Phoenix: Oryx Press, 1999.

————. *The FBI and American Democracy: A Brief Critical History.* Lawrence: University Press of Kansas, 2004.

————. *From the Secret Files of J. Edgar Hoover.* Chicago: Ivan R. Dee, 1991.

————. "The Rhetoric of Politics." In *Politics and Policies of the Truman Administration.* Edited by Barton J. Bernstein. Chicago: Quadrangle Books, 1970.

————. *Spying on Americans: Political Surveillance from Hoover to the Huston Plan.* Philadelphia: Temple University Press, 1978.

Theoharis, Athan, and John Stuart Cox. *The Boss: J. Edgar Hoover and the Great American Inquisition.* Philadelphia: Temple University Press, 1988.

Torelle, Ellen, Albert O. Barton, and Fred L. Holmes, comps. *The Political Philosophy of Robert M. La Follette: As Revealed in His Speeches and Writings.* Madison, Wis.: Robert M. La Follette Co., 1920.

Truman, Harry S. *Memoirs.* Garden City, N.Y.: Doubleday, 1955–56.

————. *Public Papers of the Presidents of the United States: Harry S. Truman.* Washington, D.C.: U.S. Government Printing Office, 1961–66.

Ungar, Sanford J. *FBI.* Boston: Little, Brown, 1976.

Van Riper, Paul. *History of the United States Civil Service.* Evanston, Il.: Row, Peterson, 1958.

Warren, Earl. *The Memoirs of Earl Warren.* Garden City, N.Y.: Doubleday, 1977.

Weinberg, Carl R. *Labor, Loyalty, & Rebellion.* Carbondale: Southern Illinois University Press, 2005.

White, Theodore. *The Making of the President, 1968.* New York: Atheneum, 1969.

Whitehead, Don. *Attack on Terror: The FBI Against the Ku Klux Klan in Mississippi.* New York: Funk & Wagnalls, 1970.

Wise, David. *The American Police State: The Government Against the People.* New York: Random House, 1976.

Wittke, Carl Frederick. *German-Americans and the World War.* Columbus: Ohio State Archaeological and Historical Society, 1936.

Wittner, Lawrence S. *Rebels Against War: The American Peace Movement, 1941–1960.* New York: Columbia University Press, 1969.

Young, Lafayette. *Fifteen Patriotic Editorials from "The Des Moines Capital."* Des Moines, Iowa: Des Moines Capital, 1917.

Acknowledgments

As is always the case, many people helped me in the making of this book. If I have inadvertently forgotten to recognize any of them, I sincerely apologize.

To begin with, I must thank my dear friend Ellen Gunther, who first called my attention to the plight of the Latin American Japanese deported to the United States and interned in this country during World War II. That was the spark that kindled my interest in the more encompassing tale presented here.

The idea for the book as it exists grew out of discussions with Andrew Miller and Dan Frank of Pantheon. Andrew has been unfailingly supportive, patient, and astute throughout the process. If the narrative moves along smoothly and avoids stridency, the credit goes to his discerning perspective.

Raymond Cunningham shared his research on the subject of German aliens and German-Americans during World War I. Regin Schmidt kindly read the chapters on the first red scare and offered suggestions. Francisco Balderrama did the same for the chapter on the Mexican deportations and repatriations during the Great Depression.

On the subject of alien enemies during World War II, I had assistance from John Christgau, Karen Ebel, Lothar Eiserloh, Costanza Foran, Isao Fujimoto, and Arthur Jacobs. Heidi Donald and Grace Shimizu provided help with the story of Latin American deportees.

On a number of occasions, the government documents specialist Patricia Inouye of Shields Library at the University of California, Davis, guided me through the often bewildering maze of government publications.

I am greatly indebted to my cousin Jody Stecher, who read the entire manuscript and made countless helpful suggestions.

I thank copy editor Ingrid Sterner for her meticulous attention to detail and Linda Huang for her stunning cover design.

My agent, Steve Wasserman, is a thoroughgoing professional and a friend.

I am grateful to my parents, Ben and Edna, for having raised me to understand the minority point of view, without which I could never even have conceived of this project.

And more than anybody, I thank my wife, Marti, who endured a planned two-year project's stretching into three and a half years. I could never have done it without her support. She is the most generous person I know, and I am immeasurably fortunate to be married to her.

Index

AMERICAN DREAMERS
How the Left Changed a Nation
by Michael Kazin

American Dreamers is the definitive history of the reformers, radicals, and idealists who have fought for a different America, from the abolitionists to Noam Chomsky and Michael Moore. While the history of the left is a long story of idealism and determination, it has also been a story of movements that failed to gain support from mainstream America. In *American Dreamers*, Michael Kazin tells a new history of the movements that, while not fully succeeding on their own terms, nonetheless made lasting contributions to American society. Among these culture-shaping events are the fight for equal opportunity for women, racial minorities, and homosexuals; the inclusion of multiculturalism in the media and school curricula; and the creation of books and films with altruistic and anti-authoritarian messages. Deeply informed, judicious and impassioned, and superbly written, this is an essential book for our times and for anyone seeking to understand our political history and the people who made it.

History/Politics

AGE OF GREED
The Triumph of Finance and the Decline of America, 1970 to the Present
by Jeff Madrick

Age of Greed shows how the single-minded and selfish pursuit of immense personal wealth has been on the rise in the United States over the last forty years. Economic journalist Jeff Madrick tells this story through incisive profiles of the individuals responsible for this dramatic shift in our country's fortunes, from the architects of the free-market economic philosophy (such as Milton Friedman and Alan Greenspan) to the politicians and businessmen (including Nixon, Reagan, Boesky, and Soros) who put it into practice. Their stories detail how a movement initially conceived as a moral battle for freedom instead brought about some of our nation's most pressing economic problems, including the intense economic inequity and instability America suffers from today.

Current Affairs/Finance

BEYOND OUTRAGE: EXPANDED EDITION
*What Has Gone Wrong with Our Economy and
Our Democracy, and How to Fix It*
by Robert B. Reich

America's economy and democracy are working for the benefit of ever-fewer privileged and powerful people. But rather than just complain about it or give up on the system, we must join together and make it work for all of us. In this timely book, Robert B. Reich argues that nothing good happens in Washington unless citizens are energized and organized to make sure Washington acts in the public good. The first step is to see the big picture. *Beyond Outrage* connects the dots, showing why the increasing share of income and wealth going to the top has hobbled jobs and growth for everyone else, undermining our democracy; caused Americans to become increasingly cynical about public life; and turned many of us against one another. He also explains why the proposals of the "regressive right" are dead wrong and provides a clear roadmap of what must be done instead.

Current Affairs/Economy

THE MYTH OF THE MUSLIM TIDE
Do Immigrants Threaten the West?
by Doug Saunders

Since September 11, 2001, a growing chorus has warned that Western society and values are at risk of being overrun by a tide of Islamic immigrants; these sentiments reached their most extreme expression with Anders Breivik's infamous shooting spree in Norway. In *The Myth of the Muslim Tide*, Doug Saunders offers a brave challenge to these ideas, debunking popular misconceptions about Muslims and their effect on the communities in which they live. He demonstrates how modern Islamophobia echoes historical responses to earlier immigrant groups, especially Jews and Catholics. Above all, he provides a set of concrete proposals to help absorb these newcomers and make immigration work.

Current Affairs

VINTAGE BOOKS AND ANCHOR BOOKS
Available wherever books are sold.
www.randomhouse.com